Ronald W. Reagan and his Family

"As you look toward the future, always remember the treasures of our past. Every generation stands on the shoulders of the generation that came before. Jealously guard the values and principles of our heritage. They did not come easy."

— Ronald W. Reagan
May 1984 commencement address at the United States Air Force Academy in Colorado Springs, Colorado

The Family of
RONALD W. REAGAN
Second Edition

by
Curt J. Gronner, DDS

CLEARFIELD

Copyright © 2004 by Curt J. Gronner
All Rights Reserved.

First Edition, 2000

Second Edition printed for
Clearfield Company, Inc. by
Genealogical Publishing Co., Inc.
Baltimore, Maryland
2004

International Standard Book Number: 0-8063-5224-8

Made in the United States of America

Cover photograph of Ronald W. Reagan used by permission of Mrs. E. M. (Phyllis) Cole.

Table of Contents

Register Report of Thomas Reagan 5
Kinship Report of Thomas Reagan 10
Register Report of John Baker 11
Kinship Report of John Baker 38
Register Report of Benjamin R Bechtel 45
Kinship Report of Benjamin R Bechtel 51
Register Report of Johnnie Blue 53
Kinship Report of Johnnie Blue 100
Register Report of George Bristle 111
Kinship Report of George Bristle 114
Register Report of Henry E. Gerdes 115
Kinship Report of Henry E. Gerdes 118
Register Report of Eilt Habben 119
Kinship Report of Eilt Habben 125
Register Report of Samuel Luckett 127
Kinship Report of Samuel Luckett 129
Register Report of William McFarlane 131
Kinship Report of William McFarlane 179
Register Report of Nathaniel Pierce 191
Kinship Report of Nathaniel Pierce 201
Register Report of Jacob Smith 205
Kinship Report of Jacob Smith 211
Register Report of Andrew Wilson 213
Kinship Report of Andrew Wilson 255
Register Report of Claudio Wilson 265
Kinship Report of Claudio Wilson 270
Index 271

ACKNOWLEDGEMENTS

I received considerable Reagan material from the Tampico, ILL, Historical Society which had been contributed by Wm. Adaams Reitwiesner, Gary Boyd Roberts, Michael Pollock, David Williamson, Nancy Gubb Frederick and Arlene Onken. Also furnishing material were Mrs. Dwight (Janice) Wilson, Mrs. Ronald (Vickie) Wiebenga, Mrs. Elsey Pierce Walters, and Mrs. Verna Janvrin-Muschal, who kindly also proofread the manuscript and offered added material with that. The many records of Whiteside County which were available in the Genealogy Room of the Odell Public Library, in Morrison, the County seat, were much used and appreciated.

"The Genealogy of Ronald Wilson Reagan" by Michael F. Pollock which was published in the May/June 1991 issue of Heritage Quest was also used.

Also used:

"History of Whiteside County, Ils" by Bent/Wilson, 1877, gave biographies of various of the early settlers, ancestors of Reagan and related families.

"History of Whiteside County, Illinois" by William W. Davis, V. 1 & 2, published by The Pioneer Publishing Co., 1908.

"Portrait and Biographical Album of Whiteside County, Illinois" published by Chapman Brothers, Chicago, 1885

To settle the estate of Donald Hunt a genealogical search was made for heirs by International Probate Research, Malibu, CA, Edward C. Azarian, President. This provided extensive material of interest. Donald Hunt was a cousin of Pres. Reagan.

To those others who are not named, but did help, my thanks.

My hope is that this will be of interest to all you readers. Enjoy.

              Curt J. Gronner, BS, DDS
              200 Wyndemere Circle, E300
              Wheaton, IL 60187-2429

Introduction

This compilation of the Family of Ronald Wilson Reagan, fortieth President of the United States, was brought together with the help of many people.

I lived in Morrison, Illinois, during my childhood and college days. After WW II, I bought a practice there. My wife, Bernice, son Bruce [who now practices dentistry in Chicago, Illinois], and I lived there until 2001 when Bernice and I moved to Wheaton, Illinois. Many Reagan relatives lived in or near Morrison and in Whiteside County, of which Morrison is the county seat. A high school and scouting friend was Dwight Wilson, a great nephew of Ronald Reagan. This was no great deal at that time except that Reagan was in the movies. He became a representative of General Electric and came to the Morrison GE plant to "visit." I never met him but his relatives and friends were happy to see him, and the press loved it.

I was interested in the area history and deeply involved with the Morrison Historical Society. It owns large photos of Dwight's grandparents and, being interested in genealogy, I printed up two pages of the Wilson family, courtesy of Dwight's wife. On the occasion of a visit to Reagan's birthplace in Tampico, Whiteside County, I found much more material on his family and was kindly permitted to copy it. This led to speaking to and visiting other local relatives who also helped me by sharing their findings. The material with the photos was enlarged.

In the course of this, I was told of and permitted to borrow the California Court proceedings of the Donald Hunt estate. He had died intestate, no wife or child, with a sizeable sum of money for the court to dispense. A genealogical firm was hired to find all the relatives, and their records covered many, many people. While Reagan received a large part of the estate as a full cousin, no one else was that closely related. Some of the shares were a 1/169th part of the remainder! No one ever told me how much that was.

With all this accumulated material and with the help of some friendly Reagan relatives, a first edition, 260 pages, spiral-bound book was put together. This volume has been sold through some publicity, most of it local, and through the society. Neither my wife nor myself are related to President Reagan.

I have been in touch, mail and email, with sources in Scotland in an endeavor to find out more about the Renfrewshire origin of the Wilson family. John Wilson, born 1812, first left Paisley, Renfrewshire, Scotland, in 1832 for Canada. While there, he fought on the "wrong" side of the Patriot's War and came to Clyde township, Whiteside County, in 1832, after having been married in Canada. A township is usually six by six miles in size.

Claudio Wilson is the mystery man in this compilation. Born in Paisley in 1787, one of triplets according to his obituary, he became a weaver and inventor. His first marriage to Peggy Downey in 1807 and his early life is well documented by writings there. Just when she died is unknown to me. He made a Canadian trip early and returned to Paisley. In 1823 he came to Lowell, Massachusetts, and worked there for some time. Then he went to Mexico, date and place unknown. In 1852 he came to Clyde Township and settled near John Wilson and other Reagan kin. He died there in 1870 at the age of 83.

His second marriage as well as his death occurred in Whiteside County and were noted in county records. I have found no mention of his relationship to anyone in the area. I have checked the local Sentinel of the time of his coming to Clyde and at the time of his death with no success. He rated an obituary both in the Sentinel and the Sterling Gazette of Sterling, Illinois, nearby. It mentions the triple birth and his wife and children but gives no other relationship No mention of other family connections are found in his probate proceedings.

The Wressell/Still families' connection to Reagan was seemingly unknown to the local Whiteside families. It was called to my attenion by Mrs. Delories Still. The Still Bible certainly ties in to the Wilson family. The family also has the "oral tradition" that "we connect to Reagan." So I have included them. Early newspaper material also verifies this connection.

I owe thanks to many, many people who helped bring this material together, thank you.

Records available in the Court House and the material available in the Odell Public Library, Morrison, were invaluable in this work. Thanks are also due to the helpful folk there.

I have listed twelve families, two Wilson actually makes thirteen. I have started with the Reagan family and placed the others alphabetically. The Reagan relationship is noted in the "notes" of most of those so found. Each family is indexed and a kinship report is provided for THAT   family. An index at the end locates everyone.

Enjoy, folks!

                    Curt J. Gronner, BS, DDS
                    cgronner@ameritech.net

Descendants of ---

Generation No. 1

1. ---[1] was born in Galty, Knockweaddown, Irelland.

Notes for ---:
Birthplace from Reagan/Davis Ancestry, Ronald V. Jackson

Child of --- is:
2.   i. MICHAEL[2] REAGAN, b. 1822, Tippperary, Ireland; d. March 02, 1864, Fair Haven, Carroll Co., IL.

Generation No. 2

2. MICHAEL[2] REAGAN (---[1]) was born 1822 in Tippperary, Ireland, and died March 02, 1864 in Fair Haven, Carroll Co., IL. He married CATHERINE MULCAHY October 31, 1852 in Southwark, London, England, daughter of PATRICK MULCAHY. She was born August 1829 in Ireland, and died Aft. 1905 in Fulton, Whiteside Co., IL.

Notes for MICHAEL REAGAN:
Sources: Gen of Ronald Wilson Reagan, Fortieth President of the US, Michael F. Pollock, from Heritage Quest, May/June 1991.
    Genealogy from the Tampico Historical Society, Tampico, IL.
    `Reagan family markers cleaned' gives birth/death dates, Clinton Herald, Clinton, IA article undated in my copy.
After their marriage they lived briefly in Peckham, England, In 1858 they emigrated to Carroll Co., ILL. They bought a farm in Fair Haven, ILL. Two children died in infancy between the births of William and Mary.
    Michael, in 1870, had real estate valued at $3,000.
    Appears first in the 1860 census of Carroll Co., IL
Genealogy, some 15 pages, obtained from the Tampico Historical Society, compiled by Wm Addams Reitwiesner, 2201 Salisbury Rd., Silver Spring, MD 20910, aided by Gary B. Roberts, Michael Pollock, and David Williamson. dated 26 Nov 1980. This was added to by Nancy Gubb Frederick, and Arlene T. Onken (of Morrison) Feb. 16, 1981.
    Ronald V. Jackson, 'Reagan/Davis Ancestry', gives birth 1829, death 1884
    From an article 'Roots' in NOW, Jan. 9, 1981.
    'Michael O'Reagan, youngest of six children, left Ireland, ... probably because his wife-to-be was pregnant. He settled in Peckham, in London, worked as a soapmaker, and in 1852,.........., married Catherine Mulcahy nearly six months after the birth of a son.'
    '......John Reagan was the second of Catherine's five children. He was born in Peckham in 1854, four years before the family emigrated to America ..... .
Marriage record of St. George the Martyr, Southwark, Surrey, England gives 'Thirty first October 1852/Michael Reagan, 26 years, Bachelor, Bendey street, (father) Thomas Reagan, laborer// Catherine Mulcahy, 22 years, --,Lekley street, (father) Patrick Mulcahy, laborer. // Married in the St. Georges Catholic Church according to the rites and ceremonies of the Roman Catholics by me/ Michael Regan/ Catharine Mulcahy (marks for each).

Notes for CATHERINE MULCAHY:
In 1885 she moved her family to Fulton, ILL. After the deaths of John & Jennie Reagan, she and her daughter Margaret took care of the four orphaned children.
    Ronald V. Jackson, 'Reagan/Davis Ancestry', gives birthplace as Tipperary, Ireland.
1900 Fulton twp., Whiteside co., IL census: Catherine Reagan, widow, Aug 1829 Ireland Ir Ir,

5 ch, 2 living, to US 1858, Mary Chapman gdau May 1865 IL, Willaim Chapman grson, ...
1891 IL Margaret Reagan gdau .... 1895 IL.
GREAT GRANDMOTHER OF RONALD REAGAN

Children of MICHAEL REAGAN and CATHERINE MULCAHY are:

    i. THOMAS[3] REAGAN, b. May 15, 1852, London, England; d. July 04, 1889, Fair Haven twp, Carroll Co., IL; m. BRIDGET.

    Notes for THOMAS REAGAN:
    Drowned at a 4th of July picnic. Birth date from Clinton Herald article. Burlied at the Catholic cemetery, Fulton.

3.   ii. JOHN MICHAEL REAGAN, b. May 29, 1854, England; d. January 10, 1889, Fulton, Whiteside Co., IL.
    iii. MARGARET REAGAN, b. 1856, Peckham, England; d. Aft. 1900; m. ORSON G. BALDWIN, 1894; b. 1845.

    Notes for MARGARET REAGAN:
    After marriage, they moved to Buchanan, Iowa.

    Notes for ORSON G. BALDWIN:
    He probably had been married before, per Janvrin-Muschal
    This marriage does not show in Wside marriage records, bride's index. Material from Tampico genealogy.
    1900 running a department store in Bennett, cedar co., Iowa. Shortly after they went to Fulton, ILL. also ran a store there. John Reagan had lived with them in Bennett, Iowa and had also worked for them. Nellie Wilson probably clerked in Fulton store, and met her husband there.

    iv. WILLIAM REAGAN, b. December 23, 1858, Fair Haven, Carroll Co., IL; d. October 08, 1883, Fulton, Whiteside Co., IL.

    Notes for WILLIAM REAGAN:
    Birth and death dates from undated Clinton Herald article `Reagan family markers cleaned' by Tom Jargo.

4.   v. MARY REAGAN, b. March 1867, Fair Haven, Carroll Co., IL.

Generation No. 3

3. JOHN MICHAEL[3] REAGAN *(MICHAEL[2], --[1])* was born May 29, 1854 in England, and died January 10, 1889 in Fulton, Whiteside Co., IL. He married JENNIE CUSICK February 28, 1878 in Fulton, Whiteside Co., IL, daughter of PATRICK CUSICK and SARAH HIGGINS. She was born Abt. 1854 in Dixon, IL, and died Abt. July 1889 in Fulton, Whiteside Co., IL.

Notes for JOHN MICHAEL REAGAN:
John and Jennie died of tuberculosis
Death date from Guardianship papers of `Maggie' Reagan for William, son of John/Jennie. His property was Lot 3, Block 8, Range 9, City of Fulton, ILL. Value $50.
1880 WsidecoIL cen311/322 age 25, works on railroad, Eng IR IR
Declaration of intent to become a citizen filed 7 Dec. 1877. Sworn in as a citizen 17 Dec. 1879 by Judge William Brown, in Whiteside county court.
GRANDFATHER OF RONALD REAGAN

Notes for JENNIE CUSICK:
1880 WsidecoFultonIL cen322, age 24, Canada IR NY
GRANDMOTHER OF RONALD REAGAN

Children of JOHN REAGAN and JENNIE CUSICK are:
    i. CATHERINE[4] REAGAN, b. July 14, 1879, Fulton, Whiteside Co., IL.

    Notes for CATHERINE REAGAN:
    1880 WsideFultonIL cen322, age 10 mos.
    AUNT OF RONALD REAGAN

ii. WILLIAM REAGAN, b. January 10, 1881, Fulton, Whiteside Co., IL; d. September 19, 1923, Lee Co., ILL.

Notes for WILLIAM REAGAN:
By 1914 his brother John (Jack) asked the Whiteside county Court to assume custody of William, since he was unable to handle his own affairs. Five years later William was committed to Watertown Hospital, suffering from paranoid delusion, a consequence of his alcoholism. He was transferred, 12 August 1921, to the Dixon State Hospital. He died there.
Guardianship petition of 'Maggie' Reagan gives his birth date as July 10, 1881.
The petition was granted. William owned 'Lot 3, Block 81, R 9, in the city of Fulton etc.. Valued at Fifty dollars. It is improved, not encumbered. Title held in fee by Warranty Deed from Patrick Cusick. William Reagan has the whole interest. No rent. Have supported said William Reagan since his father's death, January 10, 1889. Said William Reagan has no personal property or effects.'
UNCLE OF RONALD REAGAN

5. iii. JOHN EDWARD REAGAN, b. July 13, 1883, Fulton, Whiteside Co., IL; d. 1941.
    iv. ANNA REAGAN, b. May 14, 1885, Fulton, Whiteside Co., IL.

Notes for ANNA REAGAN:
AUNT OF RONALD REAGAN

4. MARY[3] REAGAN *(MICHAEL[2], ---[1])* was born March 1867 in Fair Haven, Carroll Co., IL. She married EDWARD D CHAPMAN June 28, 1890 in Whiteside co., IL.

Notes for MARY REAGAN:
WsidecoIL mar rcd #7937
1870-80 Fairhaven, WsidecoIL censuses show her born1865
1900 FultontwpWSidecoIL cen. with mother, shows dau. Katherine Chapman b. July 1879 in ILL. Too early for the program to accept.
GREAT AUNT OF RONALD REAGAN

Notes for EDWARD D CHAPMAN:
First name, initial from marriage rcd Whiteside co., IL marriage record #7937.

Children of MARY REAGAN and EDWARD CHAPMAN are:
i. WILLIAM[4] CHAPMAN, b. May 1891, Whiteside co., IL.

Notes for WILLIAM CHAPMAN:
1800 census identified as 'Reagan'. 1900 Fulton twp, Whiteside co., IL census: with Catherine Reagan, widow Aug 1829 Ireland, Wm. gson Jan 18181 IL, and Catherian Chapman fdau Jul1879 IL , Ann Reagan gdau ...1885, William Reagan gson ...1891 IL, Margaret Reagan fdau ... 1895 IL

ii. MARGUERITE CHAPMAN, b. February 1895, Whiteside Co., IL.

Notes for MARGUERITE CHAPMAN:
1800 census, Fulton, WsidecoIL, identified as 'Reagan'

Generation No. 4

5. JOHN EDWARD[4] REAGAN *(JOHN MICHAEL[3], MICHAEL[2], ---[1])* was born July 13, 1883 in Fulton, Whiteside Co., IL, and died 1941. He married NELLIE CLYDE WILSON November 18, 1904 in Fulton, Whiteside Co., IL, daughter of THOMAS WILSON and MARY ELSEY. She was born July 24, 1883 in Fulton, Whiteside co., IL, and died July 25, 1962 in Santa Monica, Los Angeles co., CA.

Notes for JOHN EDWARD REAGAN:
Lived with his aunt Margaret Reagan Baldwin after her marriage in 1895 at Buchanan, Iowa. Later Marguerite Chapman also came there after the death of her parents.

Married in St. Emanuel's Catholic Church, Fulton. Marriage application says 'Jack', marriage certificate says 'John'.
    1910 Tampico twp., Whiteside co., IL census: John E. Reagan 26 IL En IL clerk in store, Nellie C. sife 26 IL IL En md 5 yrs. 1 ch living, Neal son 1 IL.

Notes for NELLIE CLYDE WILSON:
Marriage date from WsidecoIL marriage rcd #11878

More About NELLIE CLYDE WILSON:
Burial: Calvary cemetery, Santa Monica, CA

Children of JOHN REAGAN and NELLIE WILSON are:
    i. JOHN NEIL[5] REAGAN, b. September 16, 1908, Tampico, Wside Co., IL; d. California; m. RUTH HOFFMAN, August 31, 1935, Adel, Dallas Co., IA; b. February 23, 1908, Des Moines, Polk Co., Iowa.

    Notes for JOHN NEIL REAGAN:
    They have no children.

6.   ii. RONALD WILSON REAGAN, b. February 06, 1911, Tampico, Wside Co., IL.

Generation No. 5

6. RONALD WILSON[5] REAGAN (*JOHN EDWARD[4], JOHN MICHAEL[3], MICHAEL[2], ---[1]*) was born February 06, 1911 in Tampico, Wside Co., IL. He married (1) SARA JANE FULKS January 16, 1940 in Glendale, CA. She was born January 04, 1914 in St. Joseph, MO. He married (2) ANNE FRANCES ROBBINS March 04, 1952 in North Hollywood, CA, daughter of KENNETH ROBBINS and EDITH LUCKETT. She was born July 06, 1923 in New York, NY.

Notes for RONALD WILSON REAGAN:
    They were divorced June 28, 1948. Michael was adopted. A daughter died in infancy.
    During his 1981 visit to Scotland, Reagan became an Honorary Keeper of the Keepers of the Quaich, a society of connoisseurs of Scotch whiskey. He was unaware of his relationship to Johnnie Blue, the last moonshine distiller on the Scottish peninsula of Kintyre. From the Chicago Tribune of Oct 21, 1981. This article also gives Claudio Wilson, a weaver [whom see] and Peggy Downey [Downie] whom he married in 1807 as the parents of John Wilson, grandparents of Thomas. Claudio married a second time. [see Claudio 1787]

Notes for SARA JANE FULKS:
Also known as Jane Durrell and Jane Wyman

Notes for ANNE FRANCES ROBBINS:
Her legal name was 'Nancy Davis' through adoption.

Children of RONALD REAGAN and SARA FULKS are:
    i. MAUREEN ELIZABETH[6] REAGAN, b. January 04, 1941, Los Angeles, CA.
7.   ii. MICHAEL REAGAN, b. March 18, 1945.

Children of RONALD REAGAN and ANNE ROBBINS are:
    iii. PATRICIA[6] REAGAN, b. October 21, 1952.
    iv. RONALD PRESCOTT REAGAN, b. May 20, 1958; m. DORIA PALMIER, November 24, 1980.

Generation No. 6

7. MICHAEL[6] REAGAN (*RONALD WILSON[5], JOHN EDWARD[4], JOHN MICHAEL[3], MICHAEL[2], ---[1]*) was born March 18, 1945. He married COLLEEN STEARNS.

Notes for COLLEEN STEARNS:
Information from Mrs. Vickie Wiebenga

Child of MICHAEL REAGAN and COLLEEN STEARNS is:
    i. CAMERON MICHAEL^7 REAGAN, b. May 30, 1978.

Kinship of ---

Name	Relationship with ---	Civil	Canon
---	Self		0
Baldwin, Orson G.	Husband of the granddaughter		
Bridget	Wife of the grandson		
Chapman, Edward D	Husband of the granddaughter		
Chapman, Marguerite	Great-granddaughter	III	3
Chapman, William	Great-grandson	III	3
Cusick, Jennie	Wife of the grandson		
Davis, Nancy	Wife of the 2nd great-grandson		
Dutch	2nd great-grandson	IV	4
Fulks, Sara Jane	Wife of the 2nd great-grandson		
Hoffman, Ruth	Wife of the 2nd great-grandson		
Jack	Great-grandson	III	3
Jane	Wife of the grandson		
Moon	2nd great-grandson	IV	4
Mulcahy, Catherine	Daughter-in-law		
O'Regan	Son	I	1
Palmier, Doria	Wife of the 3rd great-grandson		
Patti	3rd great-granddaughter	V	5
Reagan, Anna	Great-granddaughter	III	3
Reagan, Cameron Michael	4th great-grandson	VI	6
Reagan, Catherine	Great-granddaughter	III	3
Reagan, John Edward	Great-grandson	III	3
Reagan, John Michael	Grandson	II	2
Reagan, John Neil	2nd great-grandson	IV	4
Reagan, Margaret	Granddaughter	II	2
Reagan, Mary	Granddaughter	II	2
Reagan, Maureen Elizabeth	3rd great-granddaughter	V	5
Reagan, Michael	Son	I	1
Reagan, Michael	3rd great-grandson	V	5
Reagan, Patricia	3rd great-granddaughter	V	5
Reagan, Ronald Prescott	3rd great-grandson	V	5
Reagan, Ronald Wilson	2nd great-grandson	IV	4
Reagan, Thomas	Grandson	II	2
Reagan, William	Grandson	II	2
Reagan, William	Great-grandson	III	3
Robbins, Anne Frances	Wife of the 2nd great-grandson		
Stearns, Colleen	Wife of the 3rd great-grandson		
Wilson, Nellie Clyde	Wife of the great-grandson		

Descendants of John Baker

Generation No. 1

1. JOHN[1] BAKER was born Abt. 1797 in England, and died May 23, 1858 in Epsom, England. He married ANN. She was born 1803 in England, and died January 17, 1869 in Epsom, England.

Notes for JOHN BAKER:
Bricklayer.
Birth and death dates from Mrs. Verna Janvrin-Muschal
Buried Epsom, England with wife and 3 infants, he 61, she 66.

Children of JOHN BAKER and ANN are:
2.   i.   MARY[2] BAKER, b. Abt. 1819, England; d. Aft. 1860.
       ii.   JESSIE BAKER, b. 1839, England.

Generation No. 2

2. MARY[2] BAKER *(JOHN[1])* was born Abt. 1819 in England, and died Aft. 1860. She married (1) ROBERT ELSEY December 25, 1838 in Kennington, co. Surrey, England, son of HENRY ELSEY and SUSANNAH. He was born January 19, 1817 in Epson, Surrey, England, and died Abt. 1853 in US?.

Notes for MARY BAKER:
R. V. Jackson, 'Reagan/Davis Ancestry', gives birth date as abt. 1820
Married at Faith Churchh, Kennington, Surrey, England.
     The 1860 Whiteside co., Clyde twp., IL census487/476: Mary Wesley 40 F Eng. The 4 Elsey children, Ellen Wesley, and Jessie Baker M 21 Eng, Edwin 16 M Eng are listed with her. This seems to be a misread in the printed copy I worked with, or my misread. I believe it should be Mary Elsey, all else confirms this.

Wesley, Mary 40 F Eng, Elsey, George 21 M Farm lab. Eng, Mary 16 F Eng, Sara 14 F Eng, Emily 11 F Eng, Wesley, Ellen 4 F IL, Chas. 2 M IL, Baker, Jessie 21 M F lab Eng, Edwin 16 M F lab Eng.

Notes for ROBERT ELSEY:
19 Jan. 1817 is baptismal date.
To US about 1850
Painter

Children of MARY BAKER and ROBERT ELSEY are:
3.   i.   GEORGE[3] ELSEY, b. May 1839, England; d. 1919, Wside co., Clydetwp, IL.
       ii.   PETER ELSEY, b. May 16, 1841, Whiteside co, Clyde twp., IL; d. August 18, 1859, Whiteside co, Clyde twp., IL.

         Notes for PETER ELSEY:
         Tombstone gives age 18, son of R & M Elsey
         Fell into a well and drowned.

         More About PETER ELSEY:
         Burial: Round Grove Cemetery

4.   iii.   MARY ANN ELSEY, b. December 28, 1843, Epsom, County Surrey, England; d. October 06, 1900, Fulton, Whiteside Co., IL.
     iv.   SARAH ELSEY, b. 1846, Epsom, co. Surrey, England; d. Aft. 1860; m. FRANK BEACH, December 29, 1864, Whiteside co., IL.

           Notes for SARAH ELSEY:
           WsidecoIL marriage record # 1207

     v.   EMILY ELSEY, b. 1849, Epsom, co. Surrey, England; d. Aft. 1860.

           Notes for EMILY ELSEY:
           Born between Sept. & Nov. 1849.
           WsidecoIL marriage record #3243 gives Emma Elsey md. Richard Lewis, Dec. 22, 1872.

5.   vi.   HENRY ELSEY, d. 1920.

Children of MARY BAKER are:
     vii. ELLEN³ WESLEY, b. Abt. 1855, ILL.; d. Aft. 1870.

           Notes for ELLEN WESLEY:
           1870 WsidecoIL Mt Pleasant census 44/45, with George Elsey, age 15

     viii. CHARLES WESLEY, b. Abt. 1858, ILL.; d. Aft. 1860.

Generation No. 3

3. GEORGE³ ELSEY *(MARY² BAKER, JOHN¹)* was born May 1839 in England, and died 1919 in Wside co., Clydetwp, IL. He married MARIA S. HEACOCK September 26, 1861. She was born July 1846 in Canada, and died 1937 in Wside co., Clydetwp, IL.

Notes for GEORGE ELSEY:
Baptised 9 June 1839, at Epsom, co. Surrey, England
Bd. Center Clyde cemetery, 1840-1919
He was the town clerk of Ustick in 1865.
1860 WsidecoClytwpIL cen 487/476, 21 M Farm laborer, Eng., Mary 16 F Eng, Sara 14 F Eng, Emily 11 F Eng, with Wesley, Mary 40 Eng as head of family.
1870 WsidecoIL Mt. Pleasant, census 44/45, age 30 Clerk, Mona 25 F Canada, Harry 8 M IL, Nellie 3 F IL, Wesley, Ella 15 F IL
Tombstone gives 1840-1919

More About GEORGE ELSEY:
Burial: South Clyde cemetery

Notes for MARIA S. HEACOCK:
South Clyde cem, 1845-1937.
1870 WsidecoMtptwp cen44/45. Mona

Children of GEORGE ELSEY and MARIA HEACOCK are:
     i.   HARRY⁴ ELSEY, b. 1862, Morrison, IL.
     ii.   FRANKIE ELSEY, b. May 1864; d. August 28, 1864, Wside co., Clydetwp, IL.

           Notes for FRANKIE ELSEY:
           Bd. Center Clyde cem. with parents, siblings, age 3 mo..

     iii. GERTRUDE ELSEY, b. 1866.
     iv.   NELLIE ELSEY, b. 1867.

4. MARY ANN[3] ELSEY *(MARY[2] BAKER, JOHN[1])* was born December 28, 1843 in Epsom, County Surrey, England, and died October 06, 1900 in Fulton, Whiteside Co., IL. She married THOMAS WILSON January 25, 1866 in Whiteside co., IL, son of JOHN WILSON and JANE BLUE. He was born April 28, 1844 in Wside co., Clydetwp, IL, and died December 10, 1909 in WSide co., Clydetwp, IL.

Notes for MARY ANN ELSEY:
Bd. Fulton Cem.
Married by Rev. George T. Crissman, per Sentinel 1Feb1860, Whiteside co. marriage record #1454.
1900 Fulton twp., Whiteside co., IL census: Mary Wilson, Dec 1843, En En En, Alexander son Mar 1874, IL, factory worker, Vina dau Apr 18l l80 IL, Nellie dau 16 July 1883 IL
GRANDMOTHER OF RONALD REAGAN

More About MARY ANN ELSEY:
Burial: Fulton Catholic cemetery

Notes for THOMAS WILSON:
Thomas was a prosperous farmer in Whiteside County.
Bd. N. Clyde cem., Wside co.. Place of death uncertain.
WsidecoIL mar rcd #1454
1850 WsidecoIL census484, age 6.
1880 Clyde twp. Whiteside co., IL census: Thomas Wilson 36 farmer IL En En, Mary A. 36 En En En, Emily dau 13 IL, John son 10 IL Jennie dau 8 IL, Alexande 7 IL, George son 4 IL, Mary dau 2 IL.
Not in 1900 census. Absent from home for periods of time, perhaps at this time.
Farmed near White Pigeon, Whiteside co., IL
GRANDFATHER OF RONALD REAGAN

More About THOMAS WILSON:
Burial: North Clyde cemetery

Children of MARY ELSEY and THOMAS WILSON are:

    i. EMILY G.[4] WILSON, b. November 12, 1867, Fulton, Whiteside Co., IL; d. February 21, 1947, O'Fallon, St. Clair, IL; m. STEPHEN A. RUSH, June 03, 1884, Morrison, Whiteside co., IL; b. April 1865, Fulton, Whiteside Co., IL; d. April 05, 1936, O'Fallon, IL.

    Notes for EMILY G. WILSON:
    1900 Wsideco Fulton ILL cen 165, age 31 IL IL En
    They had no children.
    AUNT OF RONALD REAGAN

    More About EMILY G. WILSON:
    Burial: February 25, 1947, Shilo cemetery

    Notes for STEPHEN A. RUSH:
    They had no children.
    Wside co IL marriage record #6376
    1900 Wsideco., Fulton, IL census 165/165, age 35, IL PA PA, boarding house, next door is a long listing of of occupants, probably his boarding house. Also lists: Pannell, Lawra F 20 S IL IL IL servant, domestic.
    1870 WsidecoAlbanyIL census 92/92. Stephen is 8, IL, in family of Henry W. Rush, age. 40, PA wife Marybea, age 37, NY, 8 children.
    Tavern owner, death date from wife's obituary.

6.   ii. JOHN CHARLES WILSON, b. October 09, 1870, Wsideco, Clyde twp, IL; d. June 21, 1942, Clinton, IA.
7.   iii. SARA JANE WILSON, b. June 16, 1871, Clyde twp, Whiteside co., IL; d. March 08, 1920, White Pigeon, Clyde twp, Whiteside Co., IL.
    iv. ALEXANDER THOMAS WILSON, b. March 30, 1874, Whiteside Co., Clyde twp., IL; d. April 26, 1962, Quincy, Adams co., IL; m. (1) MAYME AITKEN; m. (2) MAYME HELMS, June 12, 1912.

Notes for ALEXANDER THOMAS WILSON:
They had no children. Obituary in (unnamed) newspaper gives birth as March 30, 1876. Employed 44 years at Monroe Chemical Co., foreman of the mill rooom. Member First Christian Church and Quincy Lodge of Masons.
UNCLE OF RONALD REAGAN

More About ALEXANDER THOMAS WILSON:
Burial: Greenmount cemetery, Quincy, IL

8.	v.	GEORGE ORVILLE WILSON, b. March 02, 1876, Cordova, Whiteside co., IL; d. April 03, 1951, Clinton, IA.
9.	vi.	MARY LAVINA WILSON, b. April 06, 1879, Wside co., Clydetwp, IL; d. September 06, 1951, Minneapolis, Hennepin co., MN.
10.	vii.	NELLIE CLYDE WILSON, b. July 24, 1883, Fulton, Whiteside co., IL; d. July 25, 1962, Santa Monica, Los Angeles co., CA.

5. HENRY[3] ELSEY *(MARY[2] BAKER, JOHN[1])* died 1920. He married CLARINDA SPENCER 1870.

Notes for HENRY ELSEY:
Served with 15th ILL Vol., shot at Goldwater, TN.

Children of HENRY ELSEY and CLARINDA SPENCER are:
    i. DAUGHTER[4] ELSEY, m. BEN DUFFY.
    ii. ALLEN ELSEY.
    iii. PHILA ELSEY, m. 'MALE' BOOTH.

Generation No. 4

6. JOHN CHARLES[4] WILSON *(MARY ANN[3] ELSEY, MARY[2] BAKER, JOHN[1])* was born October 09, 1870 in Wsideco, Clyde twp, IL, and died June 21, 1942 in Clinton, IA. He married (1) THELMA LILLIAN KEITH, daughter of HERBERT KEITH and JULIA KRAMER. She was born 1911 in Freeport, Stephenson co., IL. He married (2) CATHERINE STARCK January 16, 1893 in Fulton, Whiteside co., IL, daughter of MATHEW STARCK and ELIZABETH BONZLET. She was born November 1873 in Fulton, Whiteside Co., IL.

Notes for JOHN CHARLES WILSON:
WsidecolL mar records #8634 for middle name, Katie Stark
Mrs. D Wilson gives death date as 21 June 1942
Death certificate, Hunt/Wiebenga material, night watchman, Mfg. plant
UNCLE OF RONALD REAGAN

Notes for CATHERINE STARCK:
Katie on marriage record, Katherine and Kate on birth records
4 sons, 5 girls, lived in Clinton, Iowa

Children of JOHN WILSON and CATHERINE STARCK are:
    i. CHARLES LEROY[5] WILSON, b. August 10, 1894, Whiteside co., IL.

    Notes for CHARLES LEROY WILSON:
    WsidecoIL birth rcd #8,050
    COUSIN OF RONALD REAGAN

11.	ii.	ELIZABETH MARY WILSON, b. December 15, 1895, Fulton, Whiteside co., IL; d. August 18, 1984, Estes Park, Larimer co., CO.
12.	iii.	MARY MARGARET WILSON, b. December 19, 1897, Whiteside co., IL; d. February 17, 1985, Clinton, Iowa.
13.	iv.	EARL CLYDE WILSON, b. November 16, 1902, Muscatine, IA; d. December 20, 1971, Rockford, Winnebago co., IL.
14.	v.	LEO VERNON WILSON, SR., b. September 16, 1908, Chadwick, Whiteside co., IL; d. February 16, 1975, Key West, FL.

15.	vi.	JOHN JAMES WILSON, b. May 25, 1905, Iowa; d. March 30, 1970, Freeport, Stephenson co., IL.
	vii.	JEANETTE WILSON, b. April 22, 1910, Chadwick, Whiteside co., IL; d. August 20, 1925, Sterling, Whiteside co., IL.

Notes for JEANETTE WILSON:
'Explosion started fire with kerosene. Accidently burned to death. Home not destroyed' on death certificate.
COUSIN OF RONALD REAGAN

7. SARA JANE[4] WILSON *(MARY ANN[3] ELSEY, MARY[2] BAKER, JOHN[1])* was born June 16, 1871 in Clyde twp, Whiteside co., IL, and died March 08, 1920 in White Pigeon, Clyde twp, Whiteside Co., IL. She married (1) HORACE C. SMITH October 30, 1889 in Fulton, Whiteside co., IL, son of JACOB SMITH and MARTHA SIMONDS. He was born 1866 in Maquoketa, Iowa. She married (2) WALTER S. PIERCE January 20, 1904 in Morrison, Whiteside co., IL, son of NATHANIEL PIERCE and ESTHER HUGGETT. He was born January 03, 1865 in Wateska, WI, and died January 04, 1932 in Morrison, IL.

Notes for SARA JANE WILSON:
Place of death not known, but buried in Fulton.
Divorced 31 May 1897. Death certificate says birthdate is June 16, 1871, age at death 48 yrs., 8 mos. 22 days. Cause of death: cerebral hemorrhage.
AUNT OF RONALD REAGAN

More About SARA JANE WILSON:
Burial: Fulton cemetery. Fulton, IL

Notes for HORACE C. SMITH:
Wside co IL marriage record #7748
Divorced May 31, 1897. Holley is used in all legal documents.
Teamster at time of marriage to Sarah Jane. Marriage license gives Maquoketa.
Perhaps 'Horace'?
UNCLE OF RONALD REAGAN

Notes for WALTER S. PIERCE:
1900 Clyde twp., Whiteside co., IL census: William Pierce, farmer, Jan. 1865 WI IL En, Eliza wife Dec 1871, md , IL Can VT, Walter S. Pierce, twin brother, farmer Jan 1865 WI
1910 Clyde twp., Whiteside co., IL census: Walter Pierce, retail grocer, 44 WI En En, Jennie wf 3l8 IL md 6yrs., 5 children living, IL EN, Elsey dau. 5 IL, Vera dau 2 NE

More About WALTER S. PIERCE:
Burial: West Genesee cem, Coleta, IL

Children of SARA WILSON and HORACE SMITH are:

16.	i.	CHARLES ALFRED[5] SMITH, b. August 22, 1890, Fulton, Whiteside Co., IL; d. December 30, 1968, Sterling, Whiteside co., IL.
17.	ii.	HORACE VERNON SMITH, b. August 18, 1892, Fulton, Whiteside Co., IL; d. October 19, 1968, Walden, CO.
18.	iii.	HARRY WILSON SMITH, b. January 11, 1895, Fulton, Whiteside Co., IL; d. December 12, 1967, Morrison, IL.

Children of SARA WILSON and WALTER PIERCE are:

19.	iv.	ELSEY MAE[5] PIERCE, b. September 17, 1904, White Pigeon, Whiteside co., IL; d. November 30, 1993, Whiteside co, Clyde twp., IL.
20.	v.	VERA MARIE PIERCE, b. February 16, 1908, Tekamah, Burt, Nebraska; d. January 30, 1986, White Pigeon, Whiteside co., IL.
	vi.	MARIE MUNDT, b. November 04, 1911; d. September 27, 1978; Foster child; m. GEORGE ERNST.

Notes for MARIE MUNDT:
Foster daughter

8. GEORGE ORVILLE[4] WILSON *(MARY ANN[3] ELSEY, MARY[2] BAKER, JOHN[1])* was born March 02, 1876 in Cordova, Whiteside co., IL, and died April 03, 1951 in Clinton, IA. He married NORA KLOSTERMAN August 03, 1904 in Lyons, Clinton co., IA. She was born 1882.

Notes for GEORGE ORVILLE WILSON:
UNCLE OF RONALD REAGAN

Notes for NORA KLOSTERMAN:
Age 22 at marriage, per certificate

Child of GEORGE WILSON and NORA KLOSTERMAN is:
    i. GERTRUDE[5] WILSON, Adopted child; m. FRANCIS BURMEISTER, Clinton, Iowa.

        Notes for GERTRUDE WILSON:
        Adopted
        COUSIN OF RONALD REAGAN

9. MARY LAVINA[4] WILSON *(MARY ANN[3] ELSEY, MARY[2] BAKER, JOHN[1])* was born April 06, 1879 in Wside co., Clydetwp, IL, and died September 06, 1951 in Minneapolis, Hennepin co., MN. She married LOUIS HERMAN HUNT September 23, 1903 in Fulton, Whiteside co., IL, son of HERMAN HUNT and MINNIE SCHAUB. He was born October 1879 in Aurora, Adams co., IL.

Notes for MARY LAVINA WILSON:
WsidecoIL marriage record #11586 as Mary Lavina. Also on Social Security application of Donald.
AUNT OF RONALD REAGAN

More About MARY LAVINA WILSON:
Burial: Fulton, IL

Notes for LOUIS HERMAN HUNT:
Wside co., IL marriage record #11588
Name from Social Security application of Donald
1880 census shows him 8/12, taken June 1880
AUNT OF RONALD REAGAN

Child of MARY WILSON and LOUIS HUNT is:
    i. DONALD WILSON[5] HUNT, b. March 30, 1909, Quincy, Adams co., IL; d. April 15, 1991, Los Angeles, CA; m. PAULINE CATHERINE BROOKS, June 18, 1944, Los Angeles, CA; b. 1911, New York, NY.

        Notes for DONALD WILSON HUNT:
        Final decree of divorce July 30, 1946.
        He died intestate, widower, no children so the court ordered a genealogical search for heirs. The result:
        A lengthy document to the Superior Court of the State of California, undated in this file, details the
        relationships of Donald Hunt and the shares to be alloted to the relatives. A genealogy chart is also appended.
        From this and related material I have entered the various people listed, supplementing genealogy previously
        shared with me by members of the families and research by me in various county records. Curt J. Gronner,
        DDS
        Birth certificate, Adams co., IL. Ronald Reagan witnessed the wedding.
        COUSIN OF RONALD REAGAN

        More About DONALD WILSON HUNT:
        Burial: Rosedale cemetery, Los Angeles, CA

        Notes for PAULINE CATHERINE BROOKS:
        Decree of divorce granted her 25 July 1945.

10. NELLIE CLYDE[4] WILSON *(MARY ANN[3] ELSEY, MARY[2] BAKER, JOHN[1])* was born July 24, 1883 in Fulton, Whiteside co., IL, and died July 25, 1962 in Santa Monica, Los Angeles co., CA. She married JOHN EDWARD REAGAN November 18, 1904 in Fulton, Whiteside Co., IL, son of JOHN REAGAN and JENNIE CUSICK. He was born July 13, 1883 in Fulton, Whiteside Co., IL, and died 1941.

Notes for NELLIE CLYDE WILSON:
Marriage date from WsidecoIL marriage rcd #11878

More About NELLIE CLYDE WILSON:
Burial: Calvary cemetery, Santa Monica, CA

Notes for JOHN EDWARD REAGAN:
   Lived with his aunt Margaret Reagan Baldwin after her marriage in 1895 at Buchanan, Iowa. Later Marguerite Chapman also came there after the death of her parents.
   Married in St. Emanuel's Catholic Church, Fulton. Marriage application says 'Jack', marriage certificate says 'John'.
   1910 Tampico twp., Whiteside co., IL census: John E. Reagan 26 IL En IL clerk in store, Nellie C. sife 26 IL IL En md 5 yrs. 1 ch living, Neal son 1 IL.

Children of NELLIE WILSON and JOHN REAGAN are:
   i. JOHN NEIL[5] REAGAN, b. September 16, 1908, Tampico, Wside Co., IL; d. California; m. RUTH HOFFMAN, August 31, 1935, Adel, Dallas Co., IA; b. February 23, 1908, Des Moines, Polk Co., Iowa.

      Notes for JOHN NEIL REAGAN:
      They have no children.

21. ii. RONALD WILSON REAGAN, b. February 06, 1911, Tampico, Wside Co., IL.

Generation No. 5

11. ELIZABETH MARY[5] WILSON *(JOHN CHARLES[4], MARY ANN[3] ELSEY, MARY[2] BAKER, JOHN[1])* was born December 15, 1895 in Fulton, Whiteside co., IL, and died August 18, 1984 in Estes Park, Larimer co., CO. She married RAYMOND JAMES DILLON August 24, 1918 in Chicago, Cook co., ILL. He was born 1898 in Iowa, and died in Chicago, Cook co., IL.

Notes for ELIZABETH MARY WILSON:
Whiteside co., IL birth certificate #101765, #8,416
Death certificate, Hunt material, Wiebenga
COUSIN OF RONALD REAGAN

Notes for RAYMOND JAMES DILLON:
Birth date from birth certificate of child, Katherine
Brakeman , birth cert. 2nd child.
Raymond W. on marriage certificate
COUSIN OF RONALD REAGAN

Children of ELIZABETH WILSON and RAYMOND DILLON are:
   i. MARGARET ELIZA[6] DILLON, b. December 28, 1918, Chicago, Cook co., IL; m. CONANT.

      Notes for MARGARET ELIZA DILLON:
      Twin of Raymond
      COUSIN ONCE REMOVED OF RONALD REAGAN

   ii. RAYMOND JAMES DILLON, b. December 26, 1918, Chicago, Cook co., IL; d. May 15, 1942, Denmark.

      Notes for RAYMOND JAMES DILLON:
      Twin of Margaret, killed in action18 May 1942 while serving on overseas air operations with 408 (RCAF)

Squadron. Buried in Vaerlose Churchyard,, Vaerlose, Denmark. From Wiebenga material, Hunt descendants.
COUSIN ONCE REMOVED OF RONALD REAGAN

More About RAYMOND JAMES DILLON:
Burial: Vearlose Churchyard, Vearlose, Denmark

iii. KATHERINE ANNABELLE DILLON, b. July 03, 1924, Chicago, Cook co., IL.

Notes for KATHERINE ANNABELLE DILLON:
COUSIN ONCE REMOVED OF RONALD REAGAN

22. iv. JOHN CHARLES DILLON, b. October 14, 1921, Clinton, ILL; d. December 21, 1963, Rockford, Winnebago co., IL.

12. MARY MARGARET[5] WILSON *(JOHN CHARLES[4], MARY ANN[3] ELSEY, MARY[2] BAKER, JOHN[1])* was born December 19, 1897 in Whiteside co., IL, and died February 17, 1985 in Clinton, Iowa. She married HARRY JOHN HICKS. He was born 1892 in Morrison, IL, and died Bef. 1985.

Notes for MARY MARGARET WILSON:
WsidecoIL birth rcd #8,769
Death certificate, Clinton co., Iowa, bk 3-7-85, p. 3.
Widowed at time of death
COUSIN OF RONALD REAGAN

More About MARY MARGARET WILSON:
Burial: Grove Hill cemetery, Morrison

Notes for HARRY JOHN HICKS:
Birth certificate shows him as salesman

Children of MARY WILSON and HARRY HICKS are:
i. EARL CLYDE[6] HICKS, b. September 15, 1929, Freeport, Stephenson co., IL.

Notes for EARL CLYDE HICKS:
COUSIN, ONCE REMOVED, OF RONALD REAGAN

23. ii. KATHERINE JANE HICKS, b. January 09, 1917, Garden Plain Twp., Whiteside co., IL; d. November 05, 1986, Garden Plain Twp., Whiteside co., IL.
iii. HARRIET HICKS.

Notes for HARRIET HICKS:
COUSIN ONCE REMOVED OF REAGAN REAGAN

13. EARL CLYDE[5] WILSON *(JOHN CHARLES[4], MARY ANN[3] ELSEY, MARY[2] BAKER, JOHN[1])* was born November 16, 1902 in Muscatine, IA, and died December 20, 1971 in Rockford, Winnebago co., IL. He married HELEN MARIE NELSON November 03, 1923 in Crown Point, Lake co., IN, daughter of ELMER NELSON and EDITH JOHANNSEN. She was born December 26, 1904 in Clinton, Clinton co., IA.

Notes for EARL CLYDE WILSON:
Birth certificate gives birth 1902, marriage certificate gives 1901.
Widowed
COUSIN OF RONALD REAGAN

More About EARL CLYDE WILSON:
Burial: Dakota cemetery, Dakota, IL

Children of EARL WILSON and HELEN NELSON are:

i. EARL CHARLES[6] WILSON, b. February 10, 1925, Chicago, Cook co., IL.

   Notes for EARL CHARLES WILSON:
   COUSIN ONCE REMOVED OF RONALD REAGAN

ii. JANET MAE WILSON, b. September 29, 1931, Chicago, Cook co., IL; m. (1) 'MALE' WITZ, Bef. 1969; m. (2) DONALD LEROY JOHNSON, July 25, 1970, Rockford, Winnebago co., IL; b. 1937.

   Notes for JANET MAE WILSON:
   Name correction of birth certificate dated 21 April 1976 by Janet.
   Janet md. previous to Johnson marriage, a Witz.
   COUSIN ONCE REMOVED OF RONALD REAGAN

iii. VAUGHN FAE WILSON, b. November 24, 1936, Freeport, Stephenson co., IL; m. EUGENE UFKEN, November 19, 1955, Dubuque, Dubuque co., IA; b. August 05, 1921, Huron, SD.

   Notes for VAUGHN FAE WILSON:
   COUSIN ONCE REMOVED OF RONALD REAGAN

iv. RONALD STANLEY WILSON, b. March 30, 1942, Freeport, Stephenson co., IL.

   Notes for RONALD STANLEY WILSON:
   COUSIN ONCE REMOVED OF RONALD REAGAN

14. LEO VERNON[5] WILSON, SR. *(JOHN CHARLES[4], MARY ANN[3] ELSEY, MARY[2] BAKER, JOHN[1])* was born September 16, 1908 in Chadwick, Whiteside co., IL, and died February 16, 1975 in Key West, FL. He married (1) THELMA LILLIAN KEITH, daughter of HERBERT KEITH and JULIA KRAMER. She was born 1911 in Freeport, Stephenson co., IL. He married (2) IONA MAE HOWARD. She was born 1916 in Sheldon Grove, IL. He married (3) IONA JEAN THOMAS February 08, 1957 in Quincy, Adams co., ILL, daughter of CHARLES THOMAS and EMMA MELVIN. She was born 1934 in Kellysville, WV.

Notes for LEO VERNON WILSON, SR.:
His first marriage to Iona Howard??
Business man, Sterling, ILL at time of marriage to Norma jean, age 49, his 3rd marriage. He owned 'Recreation Vehicles Agency' at time of death.
Owned 'Lunch Room' Sterling when Marc was born.
At the time of Marilyn's birth, 1931, he lived at Marion, OH, Thelma at Freeport.
1930 lived at Freeport, ILL
Chadwick birth place from Linda Kay birth certificate
COUSIN OF RONALD REAGAN

More About LEO VERNON WILSON, SR.:
Burial: Oak Knoll cemetery, Sterling, IL

Notes for IONA JEAN THOMAS:
Marriage to Wilson, her first

Children of LEO WILSON and THELMA KEITH are:
   i. JAMES KEITH[6] WILSON, b. January 30, 1938, Galesburg, ILL.

   Notes for JAMES KEITH WILSON:
   Birth certificate #29769, V. 1938, Knox co., IL

   ii. MARILYN JOAN WILSON, b. September 24, 1941, Freeport, Stephenson co., IL; d. December 17, 1951, Beloit, Rock co., IL.

   Notes for MARILYN JOAN WILSON:

Died in an auto accident

    iii. NAOMI JEAN WILSON, b. February 12, 1930, Freeport, Stephenson co., IL; m. JAMES A CAPONE, September 19, 1954, Freeport, Stephenson co., IL; b. 1921.

Children of LEO WILSON and IONA HOWARD are:

    iv. JEANNETTE LYNN[6] WILSON, b. August 03, 1938, Galesburg, Knox co., ILL; m. JAMES H. PIERCE, October 05, 1956, Rock Falls, Whiteside co., IL; b. 1935, Sterling, Whiteside co., IL.

Notes for JEANNETTE LYNN WILSON:
Age 19 at marriage to James Pierce
Birth certificate, Knox co., IL #40686, V. 1944

Notes for JAMES H. PIERCE:
Laborer, Prince Castle Manufactury

    v. TRUDY JEAN WILSON, b. May 18, 1945, Sterling, Whiteside co., IL; m. (1) RANDY GALE GALLENTINE; b. September 06, 1947, Morrison, IL; m. (2) 'MALE' STEVENS.

    vi. LINDA KAY WILSON, b. June 20, 1947, Sterling, Whiteside co., IL; m. (1) 'MALE' TUCKER; m. (2) JAMES JERRY VAN HORN, October 04, 1974, Sterling, Whiteside co., IL; b. 1946, Sterling, Whiteside co., IL; m. (3) DANIEL JOSEPH RYAN, December 18, 1982, Sterling, Whiteside co., IL; b. 1944.

Notes for LINDA KAY WILSON:
COUSIN ONCE REMOVED OF RONALD REAGAN

Notes for DANIEL JOSEPH RYAN:
Lived at Erie, IL at time of marriage to Linda Kay

    vii. KATHY ELIZABETH WILSON, b. February 24, 1949, Sterling, Whiteside co., IL; m. GAIL A. JELLERICHS, March 28, 1970, Sterling, Whiteside co., IL; b. February 18, 1949, Sterling, Whiteside co., IL.

Notes for KATHY ELIZABETH WILSON:
COUSIN ONCE REMOVED OF RONALD REAGAN

Notes for GAIL A. JELLERICHS:
In military service when married to Kathy

    viii. GLENDA JOYCE WILSON, b. September 23, 1957, Sterling, Whiteside co., IL; m. MICHAEL GRANT GIBSON, August 28, 1978, Sterling, Whiteside co., IL; b. September 17, 1957, Sterling, Whiteside co., IL.

Notes for GLENDA JOYCE WILSON:
Married at First Christian Church, Sterling, IL
COUSIN ONCE REMOVED OF RONALD REAGAN

Children of LEO WILSON and IONA THOMAS are:

    ix. MARC LEE[6] WILSON, b. October 12, 1940, Sterling, Whiteside co., IL.

Notes for MARC LEE WILSON:
COUSIN ONCE REMOVED OF RONALD REAGAN

    x. KIMBERLY ANN WILSON, b. April 03, 1960, Sterling, Whiteside co., IL; m. MATHEW LEE SMITH, August 04, 1979, Rock Falls, Whiteside co., IL; b. February 03, 1960, ILL.

    xi. JODY ALLEN WILSON, b. January 24, 1967, Sterling, Whiteside co., IL.

15. JOHN JAMES[5] WILSON (*JOHN CHARLES[4], MARY ANN[3] ELSEY, MARY[2] BAKER, JOHN[1]*) was born May 25, 1905 in Iowa, and died March 30, 1970 in Freeport, Stephenson co., IL. He married MARGIE HOMERDING February 04, 1928 in Chicago, Cook co., ILL.

Notes for JOHN JAMES WILSON:
COUSIN OF RONALD REAGAN

More About JOHN JAMES WILSON:
Burial: Calvary cemetery, Freeport, IL

Children of JOHN WILSON and MARGIE HOMERDING are:
    i. MARIE[6] WILSON.

    Notes for MARIE WILSON:
    Signed Father's death certificate, more of signature is unreadable.
    COUSIN ONCE REMOVED OF RONALD REAGAN

24.   ii. JOHN CHARLES WILSON, JR, b. December 14, 1928, IL; d. October 30, 1983, Mesa, Maricopa co., AZ.

16. CHARLES ALFRED[5] SMITH *(SARA JANE[4] WILSON, MARY ANN[3] ELSEY, MARY[2] BAKER, JOHN[1])* was born August 22, 1890 in Fulton, Whiteside Co., IL, and died December 30, 1968 in Sterling, Whiteside co., IL. He married MABEL MAY SWEIGERT June 26, 1912 in Sterling, Whiteside co., IL, daughter of MILTON SWEIGERT and EVELYN REES. She was born September 18, 1888 in Elroy, Stephenson co., IL, and died February 17, 1972 in Rock Falls, Whiteside co., IL.

Notes for CHARLES ALFRED SMITH:
Retired in 1959 as Manager of Johnston Lumber co., Rock Falls after 50 years of service.
COUSIN OF RONALD REAGAN

More About CHARLES ALFRED SMITH:
Burial: January 02, 1969, Oak Knoll cemetery, Sterling, IL

Notes for MABEL MAY SWEIGERT:
WsidecolL marriage record # 139760.0

More About MABEL MAY SWEIGERT:
Burial: Oak Knoll cemetery, Sterling, IL

Children of CHARLES SMITH and MABEL SWEIGERT are:
25.   i. MILFORD L.[6] SMITH, b. February 21, 1916, Rock Falls, Whiteside co., IL; d. October 29, 1980, Sterling, Whiteside co., IL.
26.   ii. RAYMOND SMITH, b. February 07, 1918, Sterling, Whiteside co., IL; d. March 07, 1997.

17. HORACE VERNON[5] SMITH *(SARA JANE[4] WILSON, MARY ANN[3] ELSEY, MARY[2] BAKER, JOHN[1])* was born August 18, 1892 in Fulton, Whiteside Co., IL, and died October 19, 1968 in Walden, CO. He married DOSSIE MAY MEAKINS February 20, 1915 in Morrison, IL. She was born July 17, 1890 in Coleta, Whiteside co., IL, and died December 03, 1972.

Notes for HORACE VERNON SMITH:
WsidecolL birth record #7,422,   Supt. of Public Aid Department, Whiteside co..
COUSIN OF RONALD REAGAN

More About HORACE VERNON SMITH:
Burial: Grove Hill cemetery, Morrison

Notes for DOSSIE MAY MEAKINS:
School teacher

More About DOSSIE MAY MEAKINS:
Burial: Grove Hill cemetery, Morrison

Children of HORACE SMITH and DOSSIE MEAKINS are:
27.   i. ROBERT CLARE[6] SMITH, b. November 05, 1917, Sterling, Whiteside co., IL.
28.   ii. GENE MEAKIN SMITH, b. March 27, 1922, Sterling, Whiteside co., IL; d. July 09, 1995.

18. HARRY WILSON[5] SMITH *(SARA JANE[4] WILSON, MARY ANN[3] ELSEY, MARY[2] BAKER, JOHN[1])* was born January 11, 1895 in Fulton, Whiteside Co., IL, and died December 12, 1967 in Morrison, IL. He married HULDA PHILENA GOFF January 26, 1916 in Fulton, Whiteside co., IL, daughter of LYMAN GOFF and DELLA BULL. She was born April 20, 1893, and died December 14, 1974.

Notes for HARRY WILSON SMITH:
Owned auto body and paint shop
At time of marriage, lived at Ashton, IL, railroad employee. In 1922 he lived at Elmhurst, Il and was a signal maintainer, C&NW Ry..
COUSIN OF RONALD REAGAN

More About HARRY WILSON SMITH:
Burial: Grove Hill cemetery, Morrison

More About HULDA PHILENA GOFF:
Burial: Grove Hill cemetery, Morrison

Child of HARRY SMITH and HULDA GOFF is:
29.   i. HARRY WILSON[6] SMITH, JR, b. January 20, 1922, Oak Park, Cook co., IL.

19. ELSEY MAE[5] PIERCE *(SARA JANE[4] WILSON, MARY ANN[3] ELSEY, MARY[2] BAKER, JOHN[1])* was born September 17, 1904 in White Pigeon, Whiteside co., IL, and died November 30, 1993 in Whiteside co, Clyde twp., IL. She married CARL B. WALTERS May 20, 1925 in Jordan, Whiteside co., IL. He was born October 22, 1901 in White Pigeon, Whiteside co., IL, and died August 07, 1987.

Notes for ELSEY MAE PIERCE:
Birth certificate says '4th child of this mother'. Vicky Wiebenga / Hunt material, 3 half brothers from Mother's Smith marriage.
She provided much of the information to the Heritage Quest author, Michael F. Pollock.

More About ELSEY MAE PIERCE:
Burial: West Genesee cem., Whiteside co.

More About CARL B. WALTERS:
Burial: West Genesee cem, Coleta, IL

Child of ELSEY PIERCE and CARL WALTERS is:
30.   i. HAROLD EDWARD[6] WALTERS, b. December 02, 1925, White Pigeon, Whiteside co., IL; d. February 19, 1988, Morrison, IL.

20. VERA MARIE[5] PIERCE *(SARA JANE[4] WILSON, MARY ANN[3] ELSEY, MARY[2] BAKER, JOHN[1])* was born February 16, 1908 in Tekamah, Burt, Nebraska, and died January 30, 1986 in White Pigeon, Whiteside co., IL. She married REINHARD F. HABBEN April 03, 1933 in Somonauk, DeKalb co., IL, son of EILT HABBEN and MARIE HOLMRICK. He was born April 30, 1902 in Frisia, nr. Bremerhaven, Germany, and died March 22, 1980 in Morrison, IL.

Notes for VERA MARIE PIERCE:
Married at St. Johns Lutheran Church, Somonauk, IL.
COUSIN OF RONALD REAGAN

More About VERA MARIE PIERCE:
Burial: West Genesee cem, Coleta, IL

Notes for REINHARD F. HABBEN:
Became a US citizen 9 Oct. 1931, Chicago, IL.

More About REINHARD F. HABBEN:
Burial: West Genesee cem, Coleta, IL

Children of VERA PIERCE and REINHARD HABBEN are:
- 31. i. MERNA JOY[6] HABBEN, b. October 12, 1933, Coleta, Whiteside co., IL.
- 32. ii. NORMAN WALTER HABBEN, b. September 10, 1935, Coleta, Whiteside co., IL.
- 33. iii. RONALD LEE HABBEN, b. July 17, 1938, Coleta, Whiteside co., IL.
- 34. iv. MILFORD GENE HABBEN, b. July 04, 1940, Coleta, Whiteside co., IL.
- 35. v. VELMA JANE HABBEN, b. April 10, 1943, Morrison, IL.
- 36. vi. JUDITH MAY HABBEN, b. April 28, 1946, Morrison, IL.
- 37. vii. CAROL ANN HABBEN, b. June 04, 1948, Morrison, IL.
- 38. viii. BEVERLY JOAN HABBEN, b. July 10, 1952, Morrison, IL.
- 39. ix. DONNA ELAINE HABBEN, b. August 04, 1954, Morrison, IL.

21. RONALD WILSON[5] REAGAN *(NELLIE CLYDE[4] WILSON, MARY ANN[3] ELSEY, MARY[2] BAKER, JOHN[1])* was born February 06, 1911 in Tampico, Wside Co., IL. He married (1) SARA JANE FULKS January 16, 1940 in Glendale, CA. She was born January 04, 1914 in St. Joseph, MO. He married (2) ANNE FRANCES ROBBINS March 04, 1952 in North Hollywood, CA, daughter of KENNETH ROBBINS and EDITH LUCKETT. She was born July 06, 1923 in New York, NY.

Notes for RONALD WILSON REAGAN:
They were divorced June 28, 1948. Michael was adopted. A daughter died in infancy.
During his 1981 visit to Scotland, Reagan became an Honorary Keeper of the Keepers of the Quaich, a society of connoisseurs of Scotch whiskey. He was unaware of his relationship to Johnnie Blue, the last moonshine distiller on the Scottish peninsula of Kintyre. From the Chicago Tribune of Oct 21, 1981. This article also gives Claudio Wilson, a weaver [whom see] and Peggy Downey [Downie] whom he married in 1807 as the parents of John Wilson, grandparents of Thomas. Claudio married a second time. [see Claudio 1787]

Notes for SARA JANE FULKS:
Also known as Jane Durrell and Jane Wyman

Notes for ANNE FRANCES ROBBINS:
Her legal name was 'Nancy Davis' through adoption.

Children of RONALD REAGAN and SARA FULKS are:
- i. MAUREEN ELIZABETH[6] REAGAN, b. January 04, 1941, Los Angeles, CA.
- 40. ii. MICHAEL REAGAN, b. March 18, 1945.

Children of RONALD REAGAN and ANNE ROBBINS are:
- iii. PATRICIA[6] REAGAN, b. October 21, 1952.
- iv. RONALD PRESCOTT REAGAN, b. May 20, 1958; m. DORIA PALMIER, November 24, 1980.

Generation No. 6

22. JOHN CHARLES[6] DILLON *(ELIZABETH MARY[5] WILSON, JOHN CHARLES[4], MARY ANN[3] ELSEY, MARY[2] BAKER, JOHN[1])* was born October 14, 1921 in Clinton, ILL, and died December 21, 1963 in Rockford, Winnebago co., IL. He married AMY ADELE ANDERSON July 11, 1942 in Peoria, Peoria co., ILL, daughter of ALEX ANDERSON and EDNA CLARK. She was born 1924 in Freeport, Stephenson co., IL.

Notes for JOHN CHARLES DILLON:
Died in Highway accident.
COUSIN ONCE REMOVED OF RONALD REAGAN

Child of JOHN DILLON and AMY ANDERSON is:
    i. JACKLYN ANN[7] DILLON, b. August 27, 1943, Freeport, Stephenson co., IL; m. DAVID ROBERT SPRINGMAN, October 13, 1978, Freeport, Stephenson co., IL; b. June 20, 1944, Freeport, Stephenson co., IL.

    Notes for JACKLYN ANN DILLON:
    COUSIN, ONCE REMOVED, OF RONALD REAGAN

23. KATHERINE JANE[6] HICKS *(MARY MARGARET[5] WILSON, JOHN CHARLES[4], MARY ANN[3] ELSEY, MARY[2] BAKER, JOHN[1])* was born January 09, 1917 in Garden Plain Twp., Whiteside co., IL, and died November 05, 1986 in Garden Plain Twp., Whiteside co., IL. She married (1) ADOLPH G. KUNAVICH. She married (2) THEODORE DINGMAN Aft. 1946.

Notes for KATHERINE JANE HICKS:
Divorced from Kunavich 1946.
Divorced from Dingman 1960 and resumed her maiden name, Kay J. Hicks, per Ronald G. Kunavich affidavit.
COUSIN, ONCE REMOVED, OF RONALD REAGAN

Notes for ADOLPH G. KUNAVICH:
Divorce 1946 per affidavit of Ronald G. Kunavich

Children of KATHERINE HICKS and ADOLPH KUNAVICH are:
    i. RONALD GEORGE[7] KUNAVICH, b. April 25, 1942, Clinton, Clinton co., IA.

    Notes for RONALD GEORGE KUNAVICH:
    Was 'DPCM Ronald G. Kunavich CM/C' aboard the USS O'Brien DD-975' in Oct. 1987.
    COUSIN TWICE REMOVED FROM RONALD REAGAN

41.   ii. JAMES JOSEPH KUNAVICH, b. October 22, 1943, Clinton, Clinton co., IA; d. April 24, 1971, Oaklawn, Cook co., IL.

24. JOHN CHARLES[6] WILSON, JR *(JOHN JAMES[5], JOHN CHARLES[4], MARY ANN[3] ELSEY, MARY[2] BAKER, JOHN[1])* was born December 14, 1928 in IL, and died October 30, 1983 in Mesa, Maricopa co., AZ. He married (1) O. DARLENE RAINS. He married (2) SHIRLEY GIBSON February 21, 1948 in Freeport, Stephenson co., IL. She was born 1930 in Freeport, Stephenson co., IL. He married (3) GLENDA REITER January 20, 1958 in Alcorn co, MS, daughter of RODNEY REITER and ZELDA. She was born 1937.

Notes for JOHN CHARLES WILSON, JR:
Cremated.
COUSIN ONCE REMOVED OF RONALD REAGAN

Notes for O. DARLENE RAINS:
She gave the information on the death certificate of John, Jr.

Notes for GLENDA REITER:
Noeske marriage assumed from marriage application with John Wilson. Marriage certificate, Alcorn co., MS.

Child of JOHN WILSON and O. RAINS is:
    i. JOHN CHARLES[7] WILSON III, b. June 09, 1948, Freeport, Stephenson co., IL.

Notes for JOHN CHARLES WILSON III:
Listed as 'Jr.' on his birth certificate.
COUSIN TWICE REMOVED OF RONALD REAGAN

25. MILFORD L.[6] SMITH (*CHARLES ALFRED[5], SARA JANE[4] WILSON, MARY ANN[3] ELSEY, MARY[2] BAKER, JOHN[1]*) was born February 21, 1916 in Rock Falls, Whiteside co., IL, and died October 29, 1980 in Sterling, Whiteside co., IL. He married MARIAN D. SCHNEIDER June 01, 1938 in Sterling, Whiteside co., IL, daughter of JOSEPH SCHNEIDER and DELLA MACQUAY. She was born 1916 in Coleta, Whiteside co., IL.

Notes for MILFORD L SMITH:
Served in the military WW II. Cashier, International Harvester.
COUSIN ONCE REMOVED OF RONALD REAGAN

More About MILFORD L. SMITH:
Burial: Oak Knoll cemetery, Sterling, IL

More About MARIAN D. SCHNEIDER:
Burial: Oak Knoll cemetery, Sterling, IL

Children of MILFORD SMITH and MARIAN SCHNEIDER are:
  i. GORDON M.[7] SMITH, b. October 31, 1940, Rock Falls, Whiteside co., IL; d. September 10, 1971, Rock Falls, Whiteside co., IL.

     Notes for GORDON M. SMITH:
     Not married
     COUSIN TWICE REMOVED OF RONALD REAGAN

     More About GORDON M. SMITH:
     Burial: Oak Knoll cemetery, Sterling, IL

  ii. DENNIS SMITH, b. September 14, 1943, Rock Falls, Whiteside co., IL; d. January 28, 1983, Morrison, Whiteside co., IL.

     Notes for DENNIS SMITH:
     Not married
     COUSIN TWICE REMOVED OF RONALD REAGAN

     More About DENNIS SMITH:
     Burial: Oak Knoll cem.

26. RAYMOND[6] SMITH (*CHARLES ALFRED[5], SARA JANE[4] WILSON, MARY ANN[3] ELSEY, MARY[2] BAKER, JOHN[1]*) was born February 07, 1918 in Sterling, Whiteside co., IL, and died March 07, 1997. He married MADELINE WEYRAUCH August 27, 1942.

Notes for RAYMOND SMITH:
FIRST COUSIN ONCE REMOVED OF RONALD REAGAN

More About RAYMOND SMITH:
Burial: Oak Knoll cemetery, Sterling, IL

Children of RAYMOND SMITH and MADELINE WEYRAUCH are:
  i. HUDSON B.[7] SMITH, b. March 12, 1944.

     Notes for HUDSON B. SMITH:
     COUSIN TWICE REMOVED OF RONALD REAGAN

  ii. KAREN SMITH, b. April 1947.

Notes for KAREN SMITH:
COUSIN TWICE REMOVED OF RONALD REAGAN

    iii.   SALLY SMITH, b. May 1950.

Notes for SALLY SMITH:
COUSIN TWICE REMOVED OF RONALD REAGAN

27. ROBERT CLARE[6] SMITH *(HORACE VERNON[5], SARA JANE[4] WILSON, MARY ANN[3] ELSEY, MARY[2] BAKER, JOHN[1])* was born November 05, 1917 in Sterling, Whiteside co., IL. He married (1) DOROTHY BRICKLEY. She was born June 20, 1920, and died May 17, 1984. He married (2) JEANNE WEBB January 11, 1935.

Notes for ROBERT CLARE SMITH:
COUSIN ONCE REMOVED OF RONALD REAGAN

Children of ROBERT SMITH and DOROTHY BRICKLEY are:
42.   i.   TERRY[7] SMITH, b. November 20, 1946.
43.   ii.   VICKI SMITH, b. March 01, 1952.

28. GENE MEAKIN[6] SMITH *(HORACE VERNON[5], SARA JANE[4] WILSON, MARY ANN[3] ELSEY, MARY[2] BAKER, JOHN[1])* was born March 27, 1922 in Sterling, Whiteside co., IL, and died July 09, 1995. He married JANET JANKE February 09, 1946 in Morrison, IL, daughter of HERBERT JANKE and EMMA KLEIST. She was born September 20, 1919 in Weyauwega, WI, and died October 24, 1989 in Sterling, Whiteside co., IL.

Notes for GENE MEAKIN SMITH:
COUSIN ONCE REMOVED OF RONALD REAGAN

Children of GENE SMITH and JANET JANKE are:
44.   i.   DAVID[7] SMITH, b. May 21, 1948.
45.   ii.   THOMAS SMITH, b. February 25, 1952.
46.   iii.   NANCY SMITH, b. October 12, 1955.

29. HARRY WILSON[6] SMITH, JR *(HARRY WILSON[5], SARA JANE[4] WILSON, MARY ANN[3] ELSEY, MARY[2] BAKER, JOHN[1])* was born January 20, 1922 in Oak Park, Cook co., IL. He married JEAN.

Notes for HARRY WILSON SMITH, JR:
Living in TN, 2000.
COUSIN ONCE REMOVED OF RONALD REAGAN

Children of HARRY SMITH and JEAN are:
    i.   DALE[7] SMITH, m. NANCY LEE SPRAGUE, July 02, 1960.

Notes for DALE SMITH:
COUSIN TWICE REMOVED OF RONALD REAGAN

    ii.   BARBARA SMITH.

Notes for BARBARA SMITH:
COUSIN TWICE REMOVED OF RONALD REAGAN

    iii.   DEAN SMITH.

Notes for DEAN SMITH:
COUSIN TWICE REMOVED OF RONALD REAGAN

30. HAROLD EDWARD[6] WALTERS *(ELSEY MAE[5] PIERCE, SARA JANE[4] WILSON, MARY ANN[3] ELSEY, MARY[2] BAKER, JOHN[1])* was born December 02, 1925 in White Pigeon, Whiteside co., IL, and died February 19, 1988 in Morrison, IL. He married RUTH JANE STUART October 22, 1945 in Morrison, IL. She was born July 07, 1924 in Morrison, IL.

More About HAROLD EDWARD WALTERS:
Burial: West Genesee cem., Whiteside co.

Children of HAROLD WALTERS and RUTH STUART are:
- 47. i. PAUL EDWARD[7] WALTERS, b. May 03, 1946, Morrison, IL.
- 48. ii. HARLAN GENE WALTERS, b. February 05, 1948, Morrison, IL.
- 49. iii. JANE KAYE WALTERS, b. April 16, 1950, Morrison, IL.
-     iv. RHONDA RUTH WALTERS, b. September 15, 1952, Morrison, IL; m. DANNY KENNEDY, December 02, 1977, Morrison, IL; b. August 27, 1946.

    Notes for RHONDA RUTH WALTERS:
    Divorced Aug. 30, 1978

    Notes for DANNY KENNEDY:
    Divorced Aug. 30, 1978

- 50. v. DAWN GAIL WALTERS, b. March 19, 1962, Morrison, IL.
- 51. vi. PHILIP DALE WALTERS, b. July 15, 1968, Morrison, IL.

31. MERNA JOY[6] HABBEN *(VERA MARIE[5] PIERCE, SARA JANE[4] WILSON, MARY ANN[3] ELSEY, MARY[2] BAKER, JOHN[1])* was born October 12, 1933 in Coleta, Whiteside co., IL. She married (1) CLYDE ELMER JANVRIN September 02, 1956 in Sterling, Whiteside co., IL. He was born August 24, 1925 in Morrison, IL, and died May 20, 1970 in Morrison, IL. She married (2) ROBERT MICHAEL MUSCHAL Aft. 1971, son of NICHOLAS MUSCHAL and KATHERINE MARX. He was born June 20, 1940 in Chicago, IL.

Notes for MERNA JOY HABBEN:
Md. in St. Johns Lutheran Church, Sterling
Dairy farmer.
Mrs. Merna Habben-Muschal has been of tremendous help in furnishing material and in proofreading my pages. If there are errors, blame me. CJG
COUSIN ONCE REMOVED OF RONALD REAGAN

Notes for CLYDE ELMER JANVRIN:
Dairy farmer, served in the Army.

More About CLYDE ELMER JANVRIN:
Burial: South Clyde cemetery

Notes for ROBERT MICHAEL MUSCHAL:
Painter. Marriage to Merna was his second marriage, also her 2nd.
Auditor and Inspector. Married in United Methodist Church, Morrison, IL.

Children of MERNA HABBEN and CLYDE JANVRIN are:
-     i. ERIC PAUL[7] JANVRIN, b. August 31, 1958, Morrison, IL; m. CAROL TRIMBLE, October 10, 1986, Fulton, Whiteside co., IL; b. November 06, 1956, Fulton, IL.
- 52. ii. KURT REINHARD JANVRIN, b. August 04, 1960, Morrison, IL.
- 53. iii. BRUCE CLYDE JANVRIN, b. December 22, 1961, Morrison, IL.
- 54. iv. ARON KYLE JANVRIN, b. November 13, 1964, Morrison, IL.

32. NORMAN WALTER[6] HABBEN *(VERA MARIE[5] PIERCE, SARA JANE[4] WILSON, MARY ANN[3] ELSEY, MARY[2] BAKER, JOHN[1])* was born September 10, 1935 in Coleta, Whiteside co., IL. He married NORMA JEAN COOK June 02, 1956 in Rock Falls, Whiteside co., IL. She was born June 02, 1937 in Rock Falls, Whiteside co., IL.

Notes for NORMAN WALTER HABBEN:
COUSIN ONCE REMOVED OF RONALD REAGAN

Children of NORMAN HABBEN and NORMA COOK are:
- 55.   i.   RHONDA JANE[7] HABBEN, b. June 24, 1957.
-       ii. ROBERT ALLEN HABBEN, b. August 02, 1958, Morrison, IL.
- 56.   iii. GENE LEROY HABBEN, b. July 07, 1960, Morrison, IL.
- 57.   iv. SARA LEANNE HABBEN, b. March 09, 1967, Morrison, IL.

33. RONALD LEE[6] HABBEN *(VERA MARIE[5] PIERCE, SARA JANE[4] WILSON, MARY ANN[3] ELSEY, MARY[2] BAKER, JOHN[1])* was born July 17, 1938 in Coleta, Whiteside co., IL. He married NANCY JOAN BIELEMA September 02, 1961 in Fulton, Whiteside co., IL. She was born November 15, 1940 in Fulton, IL.

Notes for RONALD LEE HABBEN:
COUSIN ONCE REMOVED OF RONALD REAGAN

Children of RONALD HABBEN and NANCY BIELEMA are:
- 58.   i.   DANIEL LEE[7] HABBEN, b. June 26, 1962, Morrison, IL.
- 59.   ii. DEBRA LOU HABBEN, b. September 17, 1964, Morrison, IL.
-       iii. DAVID ALLEN HABBEN, b. November 08, 1978, Morrison, IL.

34. MILFORD GENE[6] HABBEN *(VERA MARIE[5] PIERCE, SARA JANE[4] WILSON, MARY ANN[3] ELSEY, MARY[2] BAKER, JOHN[1])* was born July 04, 1940 in Coleta, Whiteside co., IL. He married JOANNE PATRICK July 06, 1964 in San Jose, Santa Clara co., CA. She was born May 23, 1943 in Santa Clara, CA.

Notes for MILFORD GENE HABBEN:
COUSIN ONCE REMOVED OF RONALD REAGAN

Children of MILFORD HABBEN and JOANNE PATRICK are:
- 60.   i.   CATHERINE JEAN[7] HABBEN, b. May 08, 1966, Morrison, IL.
-       ii. DONALD PATRICK HABBEN, b. April 08, 1969, Morrison, IL; m. LISA FREDRICK, November 10, 1990, Dixon, Lee co., IL.

    Notes for DONALD PATRICK HABBEN:
    Divorced, no children.

35. VELMA JANE[6] HABBEN *(VERA MARIE[5] PIERCE, SARA JANE[4] WILSON, MARY ANN[3] ELSEY, MARY[2] BAKER, JOHN[1])* was born April 10, 1943 in Morrison, IL. She married WILLIAM RICHARD NORTON, JR December 07, 1963 in Freeport, Stephenson co., IL, son of WILLIAM NORTON and EDNA LOTT. He was born October 20, 1938 in Rockford, ILL.

Notes for VELMA JANE HABBEN:
COUSIN ONCE REMOVED OF RONALD REAGAN

Notes for WILLIAM RICHARD NORTON, JR:
Railroad telegrapher at time of marriage, later truck driver.

Children of VELMA HABBEN and WILLIAM NORTON are:
-       i.   JAMES RICHARD[7] NORTON, b. June 30, 1967, Freport, Stephenson co., IL.

61. ii. JEFFERY MICHAEL NORTON, b. December 23, 1971, Freport, Stephenson co., IL.

36. JUDITH MAY[6] HABBEN *(VERA MARIE[5] PIERCE, SARA JANE[4] WILSON, MARY ANN[3] ELSEY, MARY[2] BAKER, JOHN[1])* was born April 28, 1946 in Morrison, IL. She married DONALD RAY BURMEISTER August 28, 1976 in Dewitt, Clinton co., Iowa. He was born January 23, 1939 in Dewitt, Clinton co., IA.

Notes for JUDITH MAY HABBEN:
COUSIN ONCE REMOVED OF RONALD REAGAN

Notes for DONALD RAY BURMEISTER:
His second marriage.

Children of JUDITH HABBEN and DONALD BURMEISTER are:
  i. JOHN BRANDON[7] BURMEISTER, b. August 25, 1977, Dewitt, Clinton co., IA.
  ii. BRIAN DOUGLAS BURMEISTER, b. October 09, 1980, Dewitt, Clinton co., IA.

37. CAROL ANN[6] HABBEN *(VERA MARIE[5] PIERCE, SARA JANE[4] WILSON, MARY ANN[3] ELSEY, MARY[2] BAKER, JOHN[1])* was born June 04, 1948 in Morrison, IL. She met CHARLES ROBERT ALBRECHT March 01, 1969 in Belvidere, Boone co., IL, son of FRANK ALBRECHT and IRENE HOWE. He was born November 28, 1937.

Notes for CAROL ANN HABBEN:
Born at Morrison Community Hospital
COUSIN ONCE REMOVED OF RONALD REAGAN

Notes for CHARLES ROBERT ALBRECHT:
Married by Robert A. Blodgett, Magistrate, at Belvidere, Boone co., IL
He was an 'assembler' when married.
This was his second marriage. Data from marriage license/Wiebenga material

Children of CAROL HABBEN and CHARLES ALBRECHT are:
62. i. CALE RICHARD[7] ALBRECHT, b. June 06, 1973, Freport, Stephenson co., IL.
  ii. CALEB WILLAIM ALBRECHT, b. May 17, 1975, Freport, Stephenson co., IL.

   Notes for CALEB WILLAIM ALBRECHT:
   Married 1999, one child b. April 2000

38. BEVERLY JOAN[6] HABBEN *(VERA MARIE[5] PIERCE, SARA JANE[4] WILSON, MARY ANN[3] ELSEY, MARY[2] BAKER, JOHN[1])* was born July 10, 1952 in Morrison, IL. She married KENNETH ALDEN ETHRIDGE November 25, 1972 in Pearl City, Jo Davies co., IL. He was born 1939 in Freport, Stephenson co., IL.

Notes for BEVERLY JOAN HABBEN:
COUSIN ONCE REMOVED OF RONALD REAGAN

Children of BEVERLY HABBEN and KENNETH ETHRIDGE are:
  i. JEREMY M.[7] ETHRIDGE, b. July 08, 1978, Freport, Stephenson co., IL.
  ii. KEVIN MARSHALL ETHRIDGE, b. June 29, 1980, Freport, Stephenson co., IL.
  iii. LAURA MARIE ETHRIDGE, b. May 29, 1983, Freport, Stephenson co., IL.

   Notes for LAURA MARIE ETHRIDGE:

  iv. BRADLEY ETHRIDGE, b. March 18, 1988, Freport, Stephenson co., IL.

39. DONNA ELAINE[6] HABBEN *(VERA MARIE[5] PIERCE, SARA JANE[4] WILSON, MARY ANN[3] ELSEY, MARY[2] BAKER, JOHN[1])* was born August 04, 1954 in Morrison, IL. She married THOMAS MICHAEL ARDWIN November 02, 1982 in North Glenn, Adams co., CO, son of DETER ARDWIN and ANNA GAFKA. He was born January 15, 1942 in Detroit, MI.

Notes for DONNA ELAINE HABBEN:
Divorced Jan. 29, 1971, per marriage application, Detroit, MI
COUSIN ONCE REMOVED OF RONALD REAGAN

Notes for THOMAS MICHAEL ARDWIN:
Divorced: Jan. 29, 1971, per marriage application, Detroit, MI

Children of DONNA HABBEN and THOMAS ARDWIN are:
    i. DONNA MARIE[7] ARDWIN, b. March 28, 1987, Denver, Adams co., CO.
    ii. MICHAEL THOMAS ARDWIN, b. January 19, 1989, Denver, Adams co., CO.
    iii. LISA ARDWIN.

40. MICHAEL[6] REAGAN *(RONALD WILSON[5], NELLIE CLYDE[4] WILSON, MARY ANN[3] ELSEY, MARY[2] BAKER, JOHN[1])* was born March 18, 1945. He married COLLEEN STEARNS.

Notes for COLLEEN STEARNS:
Information from Mrs. Vickie Wiebenga

Child of MICHAEL REAGAN and COLLEEN STEARNS is:
    i. CAMERON MICHAEL[7] REAGAN, b. May 30, 1978.

Generation No. 7

41. JAMES JOSEPH[7] KUNAVICH *(KATHERINE JANE[6] HICKS, MARY MARGARET[5] WILSON, JOHN CHARLES[4], MARY ANN[3] ELSEY, MARY[2] BAKER, JOHN[1])* was born October 22, 1943 in Clinton, Clinton co., IA, and died April 24, 1971 in Oaklawn, Cook co., IL. He married ALBERTA LYNN YONKERS January 10, 1963 in Chicago, Cook co., ILL. She was born 1945 in Chicago, Cook co., IL.

Notes for JAMES JOSEPH KUNAVICH:
Divorced before death. Accidental injury, car, Palos Hill, Cook co, IL.
COUSIN TWICE REMOVED OF RONALD REAGAN

More About JAMES JOSEPH KUNAVICH:
Burial: Grove Hill, Morrison, IL

Notes for ALBERTA LYNN YONKERS:
Divorce from Kunavich September, 1969. Married Curtis

Child of JAMES KUNAVICH and ALBERTA YONKERS is:
    i. JAMES JOSEPH[8] KUNAVICH, JR., b. March 29, 1963, Chicago, Cook co., IL.

    Notes for JAMES JOSEPH KUNAVICH, JR.:
    Because his Mother divorced Kunavich and married Curtis, John Kunavich, Jr. assumed the surname 'Curtis' to carry the same name as his Mother, affidavit of 20 Aug. 1992, Fulton, IL in the Donald Hunt estate case.
    COUSIN 3 TIMES REMOVED FROM RONALD REAGAN

42. TERRY[7] SMITH *(ROBERT CLARE[6], HORACE VERNON[5], SARA JANE[4] WILSON, MARY ANN[3] ELSEY, MARY[2] BAKER, JOHN[1])* was born November 20, 1946. He married (1) DONNA ANN RURY January 13, 1967. He married (2) MARIA MARTINEZ August 14, 1983. He married (3) MARGARITA MARISEAL August 17, 1996.

Notes for TERRY SMITH:
Divorced 1981, from Donna, divorced from Maria.
COUSIN TWICE REMOVED OF RONALD REAGAN

Notes for DONNA ANN RURY:
Divorced 1981

Children of TERRY SMITH and DONNA RURY are:
    i. CHRISTOPHER SCOTT^8 SMITH, b. January 29, 1968.

        Notes for CHRISTOPHER SCOTT SMITH:
        COUSIN 3 TIMES REMOVED FROM RONALD REAGAN

    ii. JAMIE SMITH, b. January 23, 1973.

        Notes for JAMIE SMITH:
        Twin of Corie
        COUSIN 3 TIMES REMOVED OF RONALD REAGAN

    iii. CORY SMITH, b. January 23, 1973.

        Notes for CORY SMITH:
        Twin of Jamie
        COUSIN 3 TIMES REMOVED OF RONALD REAGAN

    iv. JENIFER ERIN SMITH, b. January 24, 1978.

        Notes for JENIFER ERIN SMITH:
        COUSIN 3 TIMES REMOVED OF RONALD REAGAN

43. VICKI^7 SMITH *(ROBERT CLARE^6, HORACE VERNON^5, SARA JANE^4 WILSON, MARY ANN^3 ELSEY, MARY^2 BAKER, JOHN^1)* was born March 01, 1952. She married (1) BRUCE UNGER August 07, 1971 in Morrison, IL. He died March 17, 1974. She married (2) RON WIEBENGA October 24, 1975.

Notes for VICKI SMITH:
COUSIN TWICE REMOVED OF RONALD REAGAN

Notes for BRUCE UNGER:
Deceased

More About BRUCE UNGER:
Burial: Grove Hill cemetery, Morrison

Child of VICKI SMITH and BRUCE UNGER is:
    i. BRUCE EDWIN^8 UNGER, JR., b. July 04, 1974; m. KAREN GEORGE, November 06, 1999, Peoria, IL.

        Notes for BRUCE EDWIN UNGER, JR.:
        COUSIN 3 TIMES REMOVED OF RONALD REAGAN

Child of VICKI SMITH and RON WIEBENGA is:
    ii. LESLEY DAWN^8 WIEBENGA, b. April 24, 1977, Morrison, IL; m. CHAD PAUL DEVER, June 06, 1998, Morrison, IL.

        Notes for LESLEY DAWN WIEBENGA:
        COUSIN 3 TIMES REMOVED OF RONALD REAGAN

44. DAVID^7 SMITH *(GENE MEAKIN^6, HORACE VERNON^5, SARA JANE^4 WILSON, MARY ANN^3 ELSEY, MARY^2*

BAKER, JOHN[1]) was born May 21, 1948. He married DEE ANN BILDSTEIN August 09, 1975.

Notes for DAVID SMITH:
Lives in Iowa, divorced.
COUSIN TWICE REMOVED OF RONALD REAGAN

Child of DAVID SMITH and DEE BILDSTEIN is:
  i. CHELSEY[8] SMITH, b. May 20, 1982.

45. THOMAS[7] SMITH (GENE MEAKIN[6], HORACE VERNON[5], SARA JANE[4] WILSON, MARY ANN[3] ELSEY, MARY[2] BAKER, JOHN[1]) was born February 25, 1952. He married (1) CHRISTINE PYRON July 07, 1973. He married (2) DAWN SCHRYVER March 31, 1978. He married (3) CINDY OSTEMA March 09, 1984.

Notes for THOMAS SMITH:
Divorced Feb. 1975 - Christine
Divorced - Dawn - Dec. 1979
COUSIN TWICE REMOVED OF RONALD REAGAN

Notes for CHRISTINE PYRON:
Divorced Feb. 1975

Child of THOMAS SMITH and DAWN SCHRYVER is:
  i. THOMAS S.[8] SMITH, m. CINDY.

Children of THOMAS SMITH and CINDY OSTEMA are:
  ii. MARSHALL[8] SMITH, b. August 22, 1984.
  iii. TAYLOR SMITH, b. December 17, 1996.

46. NANCY[7] SMITH (GENE MEAKIN[6], HORACE VERNON[5], SARA JANE[4] WILSON, MARY ANN[3] ELSEY, MARY[2] BAKER, JOHN[1]) was born October 12, 1955. She married (1) MITCHELL FOREMAN January 04, 1975. She married (2) STEVE MERRILL Aft. January 1980.

Notes for NANCY SMITH:
Divorced Steve Jan. 5, 1980
COUSIN TWICE REMOVED OF RONALD REAGAN

Child of NANCY SMITH and MITCHELL FOREMAN is:
  i. CAMERON RYAN[8] FOREMAN, b. July 14, 1978.

  Notes for CAMERON RYAN FOREMAN:
  COUSIN 3 TIMES REMOVED OF RONALD REAGAN

Child of NANCY SMITH and STEVE MERRILL is:
  ii. DUSTIN[8] MERRILL, b. May 05, 1982.

47. PAUL EDWARD[7] WALTERS (HAROLD EDWARD[6], ELSEY MAE[5] PIERCE, SARA JANE[4] WILSON, MARY ANN[3] ELSEY, MARY[2] BAKER, JOHN[1]) was born May 03, 1946 in Morrison, IL. He married (1) PATRICIA BARTZ February 26, 1965 in Morrison, IL. She was born May 11, 1949 in Morrison, IL. He married (2) SHARON TIESMAN March 19, 1970 in Lyndon, Whiteside co., IL. She was born April 27, 1945.

Notes for PAUL EDWARD WALTERS:
Divorce 1970

Notes for PATRICIA BARTZ:
Divorced 1970

Child of PAUL WALTERS and PATRICIA BARTZ is:
    i. WENDY LEE^8 WALTERS, b. August 21, 1965, Morrison, IL; m. WILLIAM CHARLES HUTCHINSON; b. September 08, 1964, Carroll co., IL.

    Notes for WILLIAM CHARLES HUTCHINSON:
    Divorced

Children of PAUL WALTERS and SHARON TIESMAN are:
    ii. BABY^8 WALTERS, b. March 19, 1973; d. March 19, 1973.

    Notes for BABY WALTERS:
    Stillborn

    More About BABY WALTERS:
    Burial: Fulton cemetery. Fulton, IL

    iii. TORI CHERYL WALTERS, b. April 25, 1974, Morrison, IL; m. JUSTIN EADS, January 13, 1996.
    iv. TROY J. WALTERS, b. November 05, 1975, Morrison, IL; m. CHRISTINA.

    Notes for TROY J. WALTERS:
    Divorced 2002

    Notes for CHRISTINA:
    Divorced 2002

48. HARLAN GENE^7 WALTERS (HAROLD EDWARD^6, ELSEY MAE^5 PIERCE, SARA JANE^4 WILSON, MARY ANN^3 ELSEY, MARY^2 BAKER, JOHN^1) was born February 05, 1948 in Morrison, IL. He married (1) MARIE SHARER February 24, 1967 in Fulton, Whiteside co., IL. She was born May 25, 1947. He married (2) BETH RICK August 31, 1974 in Morrison, IL. She was born January 27, 1945. He married (3) LINDA ROBINSON December 02, 1983 in TX.

Notes for HARLAN GENE WALTERS:
Divorced from Marie 1974
Divorced from Beth Rick
Divorced from Linda 2002

Notes for MARIE SHARER:
Divorce 1974

Notes for BETH RICK:
Divorced

Notes for LINDA ROBINSON:
She has two children, Carolyn and Rebecca. They are children of her previous marriage.

Children of HARLAN WALTERS and MARIE SHARER are:
    i. TERRY HARLAN^8 WALTERS, b. June 06, 1968, Morrison, IL.
    ii. MARK DOUGLAS WALTERS, b. June 16, 1969, Morrison, IL.
    iii. DAVID GENE WALTERS, b. August 26, 1971, Morrison, IL.

Children of HARLAN WALTERS and LINDA ROBINSON are:
    iv. CAROLYN^8.

Notes for CAROLYN:
Child of Mother's previous marriage.

v. REBECCA.

Notes for REBECCA:
Child of Mother's previous marriage.

49. JANE KAYE[7] WALTERS *(HAROLD EDWARD[6], ELSEY MAE[5] PIERCE, SARA JANE[4] WILSON, MARY ANN[3] ELSEY, MARY[2] BAKER, JOHN[1])* was born April 16, 1950 in Morrison, IL. She married (1) LEONARD PRITCHARD March 07, 1969 in Morrison, IL. He was born November 16, 1946. She married (2) FRANK MATCHIE October 07, 1972 in Morrison, IL. He was born June 07, 1947. She married (3) WALTER G. HEATH October 22, 1990 in Morrison, IL.

Notes for JANE KAYE WALTERS:
Divorced 3 Aug 1970 from Pritchard
Divorced from Matchie

Notes for LEONARD PRITCHARD:
Divorced from Jane Kaye 3 Aug. 1970

Notes for FRANK MATCHIE:
Divorced

Child of JANE WALTERS and LEONARD PRITCHARD is:
    i. TIMOTHY ALLEN[8] PRITCHARD, b. September 22, 1969, Morrison, IL; m. ANGELA KAY MACHIE, May 1987, Morrison, IL; b. December 22, 1974, Morrison, IL.

Child of JANE WALTERS and FRANK MATCHIE is:
    ii. ANGELA[8] MATCHIE, b. December 22, 1974; m. SHANE FERGUSON, August 31, 1996.

50. DAWN GAIL[7] WALTERS *(HAROLD EDWARD[6], ELSEY MAE[5] PIERCE, SARA JANE[4] WILSON, MARY ANN[3] ELSEY, MARY[2] BAKER, JOHN[1])* was born March 19, 1962 in Morrison, IL. She married ROBERT JAMES BAUER May 02, 1981 in Morrison, IL. He was born August 06, 1960 in Morrison, IL.

Children of DAWN WALTERS and ROBERT BAUER are:
    i. AMANDA GAIL[8] BAUER, b. July 31, 1991, Clinton, Clinton Co., IA.
    ii. LAYLA MARIE BAUER, b. August 27, 1994, Clinton, Clinton Co., IA.

51. PHILIP DALE[7] WALTERS *(HAROLD EDWARD[6], ELSEY MAE[5] PIERCE, SARA JANE[4] WILSON, MARY ANN[3] ELSEY, MARY[2] BAKER, JOHN[1])* was born July 15, 1968 in Morrison, IL. He married CHRISTINE KRAUSE May 30, 1989 in Dixon, Lee co., IL.

Notes for CHRISTINE KRAUSE:
Adopted by Baughman

Children of PHILIP WALTERS and CHRISTINE KRAUSE are:
    i. STEPHANIE ANNE[8] WALTERS, b. February 11, 1988, Dixon, Lee co., IL.
    ii. TIFFANY MARIE WALTERS, b. May 22, 1990, Dallas, TX.
    iii. MATTHEW WALTERS, b. September 15, 1992.

52. KURT REINHARD[7] JANVRIN *(MERNA JOY[6] HABBEN, VERA MARIE[5] PIERCE, SARA JANE[4] WILSON, MARY ANN[3] ELSEY, MARY[2] BAKER, JOHN[1])* was born August 04, 1960 in Morrison, IL. He married YVONNE

AMMON June 16, 1984 in Long Grove, Lake co., IL. She was born December 19, 1961 in Decatur, Macon co., IL.

Children of KURT JANVRIN and YVONNE AMMON are:
    i. REBECCA LINDSEY[8] JANVRIN, b. May 23, 1988, Trenton, Mercer co., NJ.
    ii. HANNAH KATE JANVRIN, b. October 07, 1990, Trenton, Mercer co., NJ.
    iii. GENEVIEVE JANVRIN, b. 1993.
    iv. MABELINE JANVRIN, b. 1997.

53. BRUCE CLYDE[7] JANVRIN *(MERNA JOY[6] HABBEN, VERA MARIE[5] PIERCE, SARA JANE[4] WILSON, MARY ANN[3] ELSEY, MARY[2] BAKER, JOHN[1])* was born December 22, 1961 in Morrison, IL. He married DIANE MEHLHAUS August 11, 1990 in Dysart, Benton co., IA. She was born February 20, 1961 in Dysart, Benton co., Iowa.

Children of BRUCE JANVRIN and DIANE MEHLHAUS are:
    i. BRICE[8] JANVRIN, b. 1993.
    ii. BRYLEIGH JANVRIN, b. 1998.

54. ARON KYLE[7] JANVRIN *(MERNA JOY[6] HABBEN, VERA MARIE[5] PIERCE, SARA JANE[4] WILSON, MARY ANN[3] ELSEY, MARY[2] BAKER, JOHN[1])* was born November 13, 1964 in Morrison, IL. He married CAROLYN BROWN June 28, 1998.

Child of ARON JANVRIN and CAROLYN BROWN is:
    i. TYLER[8] JANVRIN, b. February 29, 2000.

55. RHONDA JANE[7] HABBEN *(NORMAN WALTER[6], VERA MARIE[5] PIERCE, SARA JANE[4] WILSON, MARY ANN[3] ELSEY, MARY[2] BAKER, JOHN[1])* was born June 24, 1957. She married (1) ALLEN GREELEY June 10, 1978 in Morrison, IL. He was born August 05, 1951 in Morrison, IL. She married (2) ALLEN RAY GREELEY June 10, 1978 in Morrison, IL. He was born August 05, 1951 in Morrison, IL.

Children of RHONDA HABBEN and ALLEN GREELEY are:
    i. MELLISSA JEAN[8] GREELEY, b. December 08, 1980, Morrison, IL.
    ii. WILLIAM NORMAN GREELEY, b. June 19, 1983, Morrison, IL.
    iii. MARLA JANE GREELEY, b. September 04, 1984, Morrison, IL.

56. GENE LEROY[7] HABBEN *(NORMAN WALTER[6], VERA MARIE[5] PIERCE, SARA JANE[4] WILSON, MARY ANN[3] ELSEY, MARY[2] BAKER, JOHN[1])* was born July 07, 1960 in Morrison, IL. He married KAREN ROENIKE February 25, 1989 in Clinton, Iowa.

Children of GENE HABBEN and KAREN ROENIKE are:
    i. TRAVIS[8] HABBEN, b. 1993.
    ii. RYAN HABBEN, b. 1996.
    iii. KRISTIN, b. 1999.

57. SARA LEANNE[7] HABBEN *(NORMAN WALTER[6], VERA MARIE[5] PIERCE, SARA JANE[4] WILSON, MARY ANN[3] ELSEY, MARY[2] BAKER, JOHN[1])* was born March 09, 1967 in Morrison, IL. She married (1) COONAN DICKMAN March 29, 1986 in Morrison, IL. He was born March 24, 1967. She married (2) RANDY FAUST September 1990 in Mo-.

Notes for SARA LEANNE HABBEN:
Divorced Dickman 1990, no children with him.

Notes for COONAN DICKMAN:
Divorced 1990, no children.

Children of SARA HABBEN and RANDY FAUST are:
  i. ADAM CHARLES⁸ FAUST, b. March 23, 1991, Virginia Beach, VA.
  ii. ASHLEY FAUST, b. 1994.

58. DANIEL LEE⁷ HABBEN *(RONALD LEE⁶, VERA MARIE⁵ PIERCE, SARA JANE⁴ WILSON, MARY ANN³ ELSEY, MARY² BAKER, JOHN¹)* was born June 26, 1962 in Morrison, IL. He married BETH HACKER June 20, 1987 in Morrison, IL. She was born January 10, 1962.

Children of DANIEL HABBEN and BETH HACKER are:
  i. LOGAN DANIEL⁸ HABBEN, b. May 14, 1989, Sterling, Whiteside co., IL.
  ii. ABBEY HABBEN, b. 1994.

59. DEBRA LOU⁷ HABBEN *(RONALD LEE⁶, VERA MARIE⁵ PIERCE, SARA JANE⁴ WILSON, MARY ANN³ ELSEY, MARY² BAKER, JOHN¹)* was born September 17, 1964 in Morrison, IL. She married JAMES LEE SNYDER June 11, 1983 in Morrison, IL. He was born October 30, 1963 in Morrison, IL.

Notes for DEBRA LOU HABBEN:
Divorced 1988

Notes for JAMES LEE SNYDER:
Divorced 1988

Children of DEBRA HABBEN and JAMES SNYDER are:
  i. BRANDON⁸ SNYDER, b. October 31, 1985, Germany.
  ii. TIMOTHY SNYDER, b. February 12, 1987, Sterling, Whiteside co., IL.

60. CATHERINE JEAN⁷ HABBEN *(MILFORD GENE⁶, VERA MARIE⁵ PIERCE, SARA JANE⁴ WILSON, MARY ANN³ ELSEY, MARY² BAKER, JOHN¹)* was born May 08, 1966 in Morrison, IL. She married MARK BENNET June 27, 1987 in Dixon, Lee co., IL.

Notes for CATHERINE JEAN HABBEN:
Divorced

Children of CATHERINE HABBEN and MARK BENNET are:
  i. JENNIFER ANN⁸ BENNET, b. October 06, 1990, Sterling, Whiteside co., IL.
  ii. AMANDA BENNET, b. 1994.

61. JEFFERY MICHAEL⁷ NORTON *(VELMA JANE⁶ HABBEN, VERA MARIE⁵ PIERCE, SARA JANE⁴ WILSON, MARY ANN³ ELSEY, MARY² BAKER, JOHN¹)* was born December 23, 1971 in Freport, Stephenson co., IL. He married ANGIE.

Child of JEFFERY NORTON and ANGIE is:
  i. GRACE⁸ NORTON, b. 1999.

62. CALE RICHARD⁷ ALBRECHT *(CAROL ANN⁶ HABBEN, VERA MARIE⁵ PIERCE, SARA JANE⁴ WILSON, MARY ANN³ ELSEY, MARY² BAKER, JOHN¹)* was born June 06, 1973 in Freport, Stephenson co., IL. He married CHRIS.

Notes for CALE RICHARD ALBRECHT:
3rd Great-grandson of John Wilson.
Divorced, 2000

Child of CALE ALBRECHT and CHRIS is:

i. CARRIE⁸ ALBRECHT, b. 1995.

Kinship of John Baker

Name	Relationship with John Baker	Civil	Canon
Aitken, Mayme	Wife of the great-grandson		
Alex	Great-grandson	III	3
Ammon, Yvonne	Wife of the 4th great-grandson		
Anderson, Amy Adele	Wife of the 3rd great-grandson		
Ann	Wife		
Baker, Jessie	Son	I	1
Baker, John	Self		0
Baker, Mary	Daughter	I	1
Bartz, Patricia	Wife of the 4th great-grandson		
Bauer, Amanda Gail	5th great-granddaughter	VII	7
Bauer, Robert James	Husband of the 4th great-granddaughter		
Beach, Frank	Husband of the granddaughter		
Bennet, Amanda	5th great-granddaughter	VII	7
Bennet, Jennifer Ann	5th great-granddaughter	VII	7
Bennet, Mark	Husband of the 4th great-granddaughter		
Bessie	2nd great-granddaughter	IV	4
Bildstein, Dee Ann	Wife of the 4th great-grandson		
Booth, 'Male'	Husband of the great-granddaughter		
Brickley, Dorothy	Wife of the 3rd great-grandson		
Brooks, Pauline Catherine	Wife of the 2nd great-grandson		
Brown, Carolyn	Wife of the 4th great-grandson		
Capone, James A	Husband of the 3rd great-granddaughter		
Carolyn	5th great-granddaughter	VII	7
Christina	Wife of the 5th great-grandson		
Cindy	Wife of the 5th great-grandson		
Conant	Husband of the 3rd great-granddaughter		
Cook, Norma Jean	Wife of the 3rd great-grandson		
Curtis, James J.	5th great-grandson	VII	7
Davis, Nancy	Wife of the 2nd great-grandson		
Dever, Chad Paul	Husband of the 5th great-granddaughter		
Dickman, Coonan	Husband of the 4th great-granddaughter		
Dillon, Jacklyn Ann	4th great-granddaughter	VI	6
Dillon, John Charles	3rd great-grandson	V	5
Dillon, Katherine Annabelle	3rd great-granddaughter	V	5
Dillon, Margaret Eliza	3rd great-granddaughter	V	5
Dillon, Raymond James	Husband of the 2nd great-granddaughter		
Dillon, Raymond James	3rd great-grandson	V	5
Dingman, Theodore	Husband of the 3rd great-granddaughter		
Duffy, Ben	Husband of the great-granddaughter		
Dutch	2nd great-grandson	IV	4
Eads, Chelsea Cheryl	6th great-granddaughter	VIII	8
Eads, Joseph James	6th great-grandson	VIII	8
Eads, Justin	Husband of the 5th great-granddaughter		
Eads, Zachary Philip	6th great-grandson	VIII	8
Elsey, Allen	Great-grandson	III	3
Elsey, Daughter	Great-granddaughter	III	3
Elsey, Emily	Granddaughter	II	2
Elsey, George	Grandson	II	2
Elsey, Gertrude	Great-granddaughter	III	3
Elsey, Harry	Great-grandson	III	3
Elsey, Henry	Grandson	II	2

Name	Relationship with John Baker	Civil	Canon
Elsey, Mary Ann	Granddaughter	II	2
Elsey, Nellie	Great-granddaughter	III	3
Elsey, Peter	Grandson	II	2
Elsey, Phila	Great-granddaughter	III	3
Elsey, Robert	Son-in-law		
Elsey, Sarah	Granddaughter	II	2
Faust, Adam Charles	5th great-grandson	VII	7
Faust, Ashley	5th great-granddaughter	VII	7
Faust, Randy	Husband of the 4th great-granddaughter		
Ferguson, Hunter Michael	6th great-grandson	VIII	8
Ferguson, Shane	Husband of the 5th great-granddaughter		
Foreman, Cameron Ryan	5th great-grandson	VII	7
Foreman, Mitchell	Husband of the 4th great-granddaughter		
Fredrick, Lisa	Wife of the 4th great-grandson		
Fulks, Sara Jane	Wife of the 2nd great-grandson		
Gallentine, Randy Gale	Husband of the 3rd great-granddaughter		
George, Karen	Wife of the 5th great-grandson		
Gibson, Shirley	Wife of the 3rd great-grandson		
Goff, Hulda Philena	Wife of the 2nd great-grandson		
Greeley, Allen	Husband of the 4th great-granddaughter		
Greeley, Allen Ray	Husband of the 4th great-granddaughter		
Greeley, Marla Jane	5th great-granddaughter	VII	7
Greeley, Mellissa Jean	5th great-granddaughter	VII	7
Greeley, William Norman	5th great-grandson	VII	7
Habben, Catherine Jean	4th great-granddaughter	VI	6
Habben, Donald Patrick	4th great-grandson	VI	6
Habben, Gene LeRoy	4th great-grandson	VI	6
Habben, Merna Joy	3rd great-granddaughter	V	5
Habben, Milford Gene	3rd great-grandson	V	5
Habben, Norman Walter	3rd great-grandson	V	5
Habben, Reinhard F.	Husband of the 2nd great-granddaughter		
Habben, Rhonda Jane	4th great-granddaughter	VI	6
Habben, Robert Allen	4th great-grandson	VI	6
Habben, Ryan	5th great-grandson	VII	7
Habben, Sara Leanne	4th great-granddaughter	VI	6
Habben, Travis	5th great-grandson	VII	7
Heacock, Maria S.	Wife of the grandson		
Heath, Walter G.	Husband of the 4th great-granddaughter		
Helms, Mayme	Wife of the great-grandson		
Hicks, Earl Clyde	3rd great-grandson	V	5
Hicks, Harriet	3rd great-granddaughter	V	5
Hicks, Harry John	Husband of the 2nd great-granddaughter		
Hicks, Katherine Jane	3rd great-granddaughter	V	5
Hoffman, Ruth	Wife of the 2nd great-grandson		
Holly	Husband of the great-granddaughter		
Homerding, Margie	Wife of the 2nd great-grandson		
Howard, Iona Mae	Wife of the 2nd great-grandson		
Hulda	Wife of the 2nd great-grandson		
Hunt, Donald Wilson	2nd great-grandson	IV	4
Hunt, Louis Herman	Husband of the great-granddaughter		
Hutchinson, William Charles	Husband of the 5th great-granddaughter		
Jack	Husband of the great-granddaughter		
Janke, Janet	Wife of the 3rd great-grandson		

Name	Relationship with John Baker	Civil	Canon
Janvrin, Aron Kyle	4th great-grandson	VI	6
Janvrin, Brice	5th great-grandson	VII	7
Janvrin, Bruce Clyde	4th great-grandson	VI	6
Janvrin, Bryleigh	5th great-granddaughter	VII	7
Janvrin, Clyde Elmer	Husband of the 3rd great-granddaughter		
Janvrin, Eric Paul	4th great-grandson	VI	6
Janvrin, Genevieve	5th great-granddaughter	VII	7
Janvrin, Hannah Kate	5th great-granddaughter	VII	7
Janvrin, Kurt Reinhard	4th great-grandson	VI	6
Janvrin, Mabeline	5th great-granddaughter	VII	7
Janvrin, Rebecca Lindsey	5th great-granddaughter	VII	7
Janvrin, Tyler	5th great-grandson	VII	7
Jean	Wife of the 3rd great-grandson		
Jellerichs, Gail A.	Husband of the 3rd great-granddaughter		
Jennie	Great-granddaughter	III	3
Johnson, Donald LeRoy	Husband of the 3rd great-granddaughter		
Jr.	3rd great-grandson	V	5
Keith, Thelma Lillian	Wife of the great-grandson		
	Wife of the 2nd great-grandson		
Kennedy, Danny	Husband of the 4th great-granddaughter		
Klosterman, Nora	Wife of the great-grandson		
Krause, Christine	Wife of the 4th great-grandson		
Kristin	5th great-granddaughter	VII	7
Kunavich, Adolph G.	Husband of the 3rd great-granddaughter		
Kunavich, James Joseph	4th great-grandson	VI	6
Kunavich, James Joseph, Jr.	5th great-grandson	VII	7
Kunavich, Ronald George	4th great-grandson	VI	6
Layla Marie Bauer	5th great-granddaughter	VII	7
Lewis	Husband of the great-granddaughter		
Machie, Angela Kay	Wife of the 5th great-grandson		
Mariseal, Margarita	Wife of the 4th great-grandson		
Martinez, Maria	Wife of the 4th great-grandson		
Matchie, Angela	5th great-granddaughter	VII	7
Matchie, Frank	Husband of the 4th great-granddaughter		
May, Denzie	Wife of the 2nd great-grandson		
Mayme	2nd great-granddaughter	IV	4
Meakins, Dossie May	Wife of the 2nd great-grandson		
Mehlhaus, Diane	Wife of the 4th great-grandson		
Merrill, Dustin	5th great-grandson	VII	7
Merrill, Steve	Husband of the 4th great-granddaughter		
Mirissa Jane	6th great-granddaughter	VIII	8
Mona	Wife of the grandson		
Moon	2nd great-grandson	IV	4
Muschal, Robert Michael	Husband of the 3rd great-granddaughter		
Nelson, Helen Marie	Wife of the 2nd great-grandson		
Ostema, Cindy	Wife of the 4th great-grandson		
Palmier, Doria	Wife of the 3rd great-grandson		
Patrick, JoAnne	Wife of the 3rd great-grandson		
Patti	3rd great-granddaughter	V	5
Pierce, Elsey Mae	2nd great-granddaughter	IV	4
Pierce, James H.	Husband of the 3rd great-granddaughter		
Pierce, Vera Marie	2nd great-granddaughter	IV	4
Pierce, Walter S.	Husband of the great-granddaughter		

Name	Relationship with John Baker	Civil	Canon
Pritchard, Leonard	Husband of the 4th great-granddaughter		
Pritchard, Timothy Allen	5th great-grandson	VII	7
Pyron, Christine	Wife of the 4th great-grandson		
Rains, O. Darlene	Wife of the 3rd great-grandson		
Reagan, Cameron Michael	4th great-grandson	VI	6
Reagan, John Edward	Husband of the great-granddaughter		
Reagan, John Neil	2nd great-grandson	IV	4
Reagan, Maureen Elizabeth	3rd great-granddaughter	V	5
Reagan, Michael	3rd great-grandson	V	5
Reagan, Patricia	3rd great-granddaughter	V	5
Reagan, Ronald Prescott	3rd great-grandson	V	5
Reagan, Ronald Wilson	2nd great-grandson	IV	4
Rebecca	5th great-granddaughter	VII	7
Reinhardt	Husband of the 2nd great-granddaughter		
Reiter, Glenda	Wife of the 3rd great-grandson		
Rick, Beth	Wife of the 4th great-grandson		
Robbins, Anne Frances	Wife of the 2nd great-grandson		
Robinson, Linda	Wife of the 4th great-grandson		
Roenike, Karen	Wife of the 4th great-grandson		
Rury, Donna Ann	Wife of the 4th great-grandson		
Rush, Stephen A.	Husband of the great-granddaughter		
Ryan, Daniel Joseph	Husband of the 3rd great-granddaughter		
Schneider, Marian D.	Wife of the 3rd great-grandson		
Schryver, Dawn	Wife of the 4th great-grandson		
Sharer, Marie	Wife of the 4th great-grandson		
Smith, Barbara	4th great-granddaughter	VI	6
Smith, Charles Alfred	2nd great-grandson	IV	4
Smith, Chelsey	5th great-granddaughter	VII	7
Smith, Christopher Scott	5th great-grandson	VII	7
Smith, Cory	5th great-granddaughter	VII	7
Smith, Dale	4th great-grandson	VI	6
Smith, David	4th great-grandson	VI	6
Smith, Dean	4th great-grandson	VI	6
Smith, Dennis	4th great-grandson	VI	6
Smith, Gene Meakin	3rd great-grandson	V	5
Smith, Gordon M.	4th great-grandson	VI	6
Smith, Harry Wilson	2nd great-grandson	IV	4
Smith, Harry Wilson, Jr	3rd great-grandson	V	5
Smith, Horace C.	Husband of the great-granddaughter		
Smith, Horace Vernon	2nd great-grandson	IV	4
Smith, Hudson B.	4th great-grandson	VI	6
Smith, Jamie	5th great-grandson	VII	7
Smith, Jenifer Erin	5th great-granddaughter	VII	7
Smith, Karen	4th great-granddaughter	VI	6
Smith, Marshall	5th great-grandson	VII	7
Smith, Mathew Lee	Husband of the 3rd great-granddaughter		
Smith, Milford L.	3rd great-grandson	V	5
Smith, Nancy	4th great-granddaughter	VI	6
Smith, Raymond	3rd great-grandson	V	5
Smith, Robert Clare	3rd great-grandson	V	5
Smith, Sally	4th great-granddaughter	VI	6
Smith, Taylor	5th great-grandson	VII	7
Smith, Terry	4th great-grandson	VI	6

Name	Relationship with John Baker	Civil	Canon
Smith, Thomas	4th great-grandson	VI	6
Smith, Thomas S.	5th great-grandson	VII	7
Smith, Vicki	4th great-granddaughter	VI	6
Spencer, Clarinda	Wife of the grandson		
Sprague, Nancy Lee	Wife of the 4th great-grandson		
Springman, David Robert	Husband of the 4th great-granddaughter		
Starck, Catherine	Wife of the great-grandson		
Stark, Katie	Wife of the great-grandson		
Stearns, Colleen	Wife of the 3rd great-grandson		
Steven	Husband of the great-granddaughter		
Stevens, 'Male'	Husband of the 3rd great-granddaughter		
Stuart, Ruth Jane	Wife of the 3rd great-grandson		
Sweigert, Mabel May	Wife of the 2nd great-grandson		
Thomas, Iona Jean	Wife of the 2nd great-grandson		
Tiesman, Sharon	Wife of the 4th great-grandson		
Trimble, Carol	Wife of the 4th great-grandson		
Tucker, 'Male'	Husband of the 3rd great-granddaughter		
Tug	Great-grandson	III	3
Ufken, Eugene	Husband of the 3rd great-granddaughter		
Unger, Bruce	Husband of the 4th great-granddaughter		
Unger, Bruce Edwin, Jr.	5th great-grandson	VII	7
Van Horn, James Jerry	Husband of the 3rd great-granddaughter		
Vina	Great-granddaughter	III	3
Walters, Baby	5th great-granddaughter	VII	7
Walters, Carl B.	Husband of the 2nd great-granddaughter		
Walters, David Gene	5th great-grandson	VII	7
Walters, Dawn Gail	4th great-granddaughter	VI	6
Walters, Drew Philip	6th great-grandson	VIII	8
Walters, Harlan Gene	4th great-grandson	VI	6
Walters, Harold Edward	3rd great-grandson	V	5
Walters, Jane Kaye	4th great-granddaughter	VI	6
Walters, Julia Anna	6th great-granddaughter	VIII	8
Walters, Mark Douglas	5th great-grandson	VII	7
Walters, Matthew	5th great-grandson	VII	7
Walters, Paul Edward	4th great-grandson	VI	6
Walters, Philip Dale	4th great-grandson	VI	6
Walters, Rhonda Ruth	4th great-granddaughter	VI	6
Walters, Stephanie Anne	5th great-granddaughter	VII	7
Walters, Terry Harlan	5th great-grandson	VII	7
Walters, Tiffany Marie	5th great-granddaughter	VII	7
Walters, Tori Cheryl	5th great-granddaughter	VII	7
Walters, Troy J.	5th great-grandson	VII	7
Walters, Wendy Lee	5th great-granddaughter	VII	7
Webb, Jeanne	Wife of the 3rd great-grandson		
Wesley, Charles	Grandson	II	2
Wesley, Ellen	Granddaughter	II	2
Weyrauch, Madeline	Wife of the 3rd great-grandson		
Wiebenga, Lesley Dawn	5th great-granddaughter	VII	7
Wiebenga, Ron	Husband of the 4th great-granddaughter		
Wilson, Alexander Thomas	Great-grandson	III	3
Wilson, Charles LeRoy	2nd great-grandson	IV	4
Wilson, Earl Charles	3rd great-grandson	V	5
Wilson, Earl Clyde	2nd great-grandson	IV	4

Name	Relationship with John Baker	Civil	Canon
Wilson, Elizabeth Mary	2nd great-granddaughter	IV	4
Wilson, Emily G.	Great-granddaughter	III	3
Wilson, George Orville	Great-grandson	III	3
Wilson, Janet Mae	3rd great-granddaughter	V	5
Wilson, Jeanette	2nd great-granddaughter	IV	4
Wilson, Jeannette Lynn	3rd great-granddaughter	V	5
Wilson, Jody Allen	3rd great-grandson	V	5
Wilson, John Charles	Great-grandson	III	3
Wilson, John Charles III	4th great-grandson	VI	6
Wilson, John Charles, Jr	3rd great-grandson	V	5
Wilson, John James	2nd great-grandson	IV	4
Wilson, Kathy Elizabeth	3rd great-granddaughter	V	5
Wilson, Kimberly Ann	3rd great-granddaughter	V	5
Wilson, Leo Vernon, Sr.	2nd great-grandson	IV	4
Wilson, Linda Kay	3rd great-granddaughter	V	5
Wilson, Marc Lee	3rd great-grandson	V	5
Wilson, Marie	3rd great-granddaughter	V	5
Wilson, Marilyn Joan	3rd great-granddaughter	V	5
Wilson, Mary LaVina	Great-granddaughter	III	3
Wilson, Mary Margaret	2nd great-granddaughter	IV	4
Wilson, Naomi Jean	3rd great-granddaughter	V	5
Wilson, Nellie Clyde	Great-granddaughter	III	3
Wilson, Ronald Stanley	3rd great-grandson	V	5
Wilson, Sara Jane	Great-granddaughter	III	3
Wilson, Thomas	Husband of the granddaughter		
Wilson, Trudy Jean	3rd great-granddaughter	V	5
Wilson, Vaughn Fae	3rd great-granddaughter	V	5
Witz, 'Male'	Husband of the 3rd great-granddaughter		
Yonkers, Alberta Lynn	Wife of the 4th great-grandson		

Descendants of Benjamin R Bechtel

Generation No. 1

1. BENJAMIN R[1] BECHTEL He married REBECCA MYERS.

Child of BENJAMIN BECHTEL and REBECCA MYERS is:
2.   i. EPHRAIM MYERS[2] BECHTEL, b. March 23, 1833, Columbiana Co., OH; d. January 16, 1928, Wside co., Clydetwp, IL.

Generation No. 2

2. EPHRAIM MYERS[2] BECHTEL *(BENJAMIN R[1])* was born March 23, 1833 in Columbiana Co., OH, and died January 16, 1928 in Wside co., Clydetwp, IL. He married SARA WILSON February 22, 1861 in Whiteside co., IL, daughter of JOHN WILSON and JANE BLUE. She was born March 29, 1841 in Wside co., Clydetwp, IL, and died November 17, 1920 in Wside co., Clydetwp, IL.

Notes for EPHRAIM MYERS BECHTEL:
He came to Clyde Twp. at 19 with his parents.
1870 WsideUsttwpIL census 95/95, age 32, farmer, OH, Sarah 36 F IL, John 8 M IL, Rebecca 6 F IL, Ella 4 F IL. [Only Bechtel in census]
1880 WsideClydetwpIL census 119/121 with son in law David E. Gerdes, dau. Ella (Ellen)
1910 WsideClytwpIL census 56/58, age77, own income, IL Gr PA, Sarah F 68 wf IL Sc Sc
Whiteside marriage record #563. Ephraim N. on marriage record.
Bd. Malvern cemetery.
He died at the home of his daughter, Mrs. David (Ellen) Gerdes. He had been blind for a number of years. He was the last of 11 children to die.
COUSIN OF RONALD REAGAN

More About EPHRAIM MYERS BECHTEL:
Burial: Malvern cemetery

Notes for SARA WILSON:
1850 WsidecoIL census484, age 8, IL
1870 WsidecoIL census95, age 36, I
1910 WsideClytwpIL census, age 68, IL Sc Sc
1920 WsideClytwpcoIL census with David E Gerdes, age 78, with husband Ephraim Bechtel, 86
Bd. Malvern cemetery next to husband
Married by Rev. J. W. White, in Ustick twp., in her parent's home., Wside Sentinel 26 Feb1861
GREAT AUNT OF RONALD WILSON

More About SARA WILSON:
Burial: Malvern cemetery

Children of EPHRAIM BECHTEL and SARA WILSON are:
3.   i. JOHN WILSON[3] BECHTEL, b. February 17, 1862, Wside co., Clydetwp, IL; d. February 22, 1933, Wside co., Clydetwp, IL.
    ii. REBECCA JANE BECHTEL, b. 1864; d. March 11, 1878, WSide co., Clydetwp, IL.

    Notes for REBECCA JANE BECHTEL:
    Bd. Malvern cemetery with parents, died at 14 years. 'Buried from the Franklin School House' from the Sentinel of May 11, 1878. Whiteside co. death certificate #88.
    1870 WsidecoIL cen95, age 6, IL
    COUSIN ONCE REMOVED OF RONALD REAGAN

	iii.	ELLEN W. BECHTEL, b. July 01, 1866, Wside co., Clydetwp, IL.
4.	iv.	HELENA BECHTEL, b. November 01, 1876, ILL.; d. June 24, 1953, Washington; m. SAMUEL L. LONGANECKER, May 16, 1903, Whiteside co., IL; b. December 24, 1875; d. December 22, 1946, Orville, WA.

Notes for HELENA BECHTEL:
COUSIN ONCE REMOVED OF RONALD REAGAN

Notes for SAMUEL L. LONGANECKER:
Wside co. marriage record #11,484, she is listed as Helen

Generation No. 3

3. JOHN WILSON[3] BECHTEL *(EPHRAIM MYERS[2], BENJAMIN R[1])* was born February 17, 1862 in Wside co., Clydetwp, IL, and died February 22, 1933 in Wside co., Clydetwp, IL. He married SARAH E. DETER 1886 in Whiteside co., IL. She was born August 28, 1858 in PA, and died March 28, 1908 in Wside co., Clydetwp, IL.

Notes for JOHN WILSON BECHTEL:
1870 WsideUstcen 95, age 8, IL
1910 WsidecoUsttwpIL census 47/49, age 48, widowed, IL OH IL
1920 WsidecoMorrisonIL census 152/156, age57, widowed IL OH IL, farm laborer
Bd. Malvern cemetery in plot with parents and wife, Sara E.
COUSIN ONCE REMOVED OF RONALD REAGAN

Notes for SARAH E. DETER:
Bd. Malvern cemetery

Children of JOHN BECHTEL and SARAH DETER are:
      i. ALBERT[4] BECHTEL, b. August 12, 1887, Whiteside co., IL.

      Notes for ALBERT BECHTEL:
      Whiteside co., IL marriage record: #5385 & & 104,677
      1880 Wsideco, 103 Genesee Ave., Morrison, IL age 32, IL IL PA
      1910 Wsideco cen 49, age 22, single, IL IL PA, as `Bert D.'. Farmer
      Never married
      SECOND COUSIN OF RONALD REAGAN

5.	ii.	WILLIAM DETER BECHTEL, b. March 11, 1891, Wside co., Clydetwp, IL.
	iii.	GEORGE DETER BECHTEL 2, b. March 29, 1892, Wside co., Clydetwp, IL; m. ELOISE; b. 1906, ILL..

      Notes for GEORGE DETER BECHTEL 2:
      WsidecoIL birth record #93,973.
      1910 Wsideco UsticktwpIL cen 49, age 18, farm laborer.
      1920 WsidecoUsttwpIL cen150/154 with wife Eloise
      SECOND COUSIN OF RONALD REAGAN

      Notes for ELOISE:
      1920 WsidecoUsttwpIL census 150/54 , age 24 IL IL IL, wife

6.	iv.	IVY MAY BECHTEL, b. May 1898.

4. ELLEN W.[3] BECHTEL *(EPHRAIM MYERS[2], BENJAMIN R[1])* was born July 01, 1866 in Wside co., Clydetwp, IL. She married DAVID EDMOND GERDES January 08, 1888 in Whiteside co., IL, son of HENRY GERDES and REBECCA KALLENOR. He was born December 1864 in Whiteside co., IL, and died January 13, 1934 in Whiteside co., IL.

Notes for ELLEN W. BECHTEL:
1870 WsidecoIL cen95, age 4, IL
1910 Wside census 163 age 43, IL OH IL
COUSIN ONCE REMOVED OF RONALD REAGAN

Notes for DAVID EDMOND GERDES:
WsidcoIL marriage record #7289. Minister of the Dunkard Church, Clyde & Rock Creek, ILL.
1910 WsidecoUsttwpIL census 61/63. David 45, farmer, IL Gr PA
1920 WsidecoClytwpIL. census119/121m age 55, farmer, IL Gr PA
1920 census has Ephraim Bechtel, 86, f in law, OH PA PA and Sarah (Wilson), his wife, 78, IL Sc Sc with David's family
The Clyde Twp. farm was in the family since 1863.

Children of ELLEN BECHTEL and DAVID GERDES are:

7.   i. EPHRAIM LAWRENCE[4] GERDES, b. October 11, 1888, Wside co., Clydetwp, IL.

    ii. REBECCA H GERDES, b. December 05, 1889, WSide co., Clydetwp, IL; d. April 28, 1981, Whiteside co., IL.

Notes for REBECCA H GERDES:
WsidecoIL birth record #6,315.
1910 Wside census 163, age 20, single, servant
Did not marry.
1920 Wside Clyde census, with father, 30, servant, IL IL IL
She lived on the family farm all her life, never married, kept house for her brothers.

More About REBECCA H GERDES:
Burial: Malvern cemetery

    iii. EDMUND WAYNE GERDES, b. March 02, 1892, Wside co., Clydetwp, IL; d. July 10, 1969, WHiteside co., IL.

Notes for EDMUND WAYNE GERDES:
WsidecoIL birth rcd #7,402
1910 WsideIL census 163, age 17, farm laborer, 'Wayne'
Living at RFD 2, Dixon, IL Feb. 1981, minister
WsidecoIL death records

8.   iv. GALEN GLENN GERDES, b. January 1894, Wside co., Clydetwp, IL; d. September 01, 1976, N. Manchester, IN.

    v. HENRY RALPH GERDES, b. November 03, 1899, Wside co., Clydetwp, IL; d. February 07, 1981, Morrison, IL.

Notes for HENRY RALPH GERDES:
1910 WsidecoIL, cen 163, age 10
1920 WsidecoIL, cen 121, age 20, laborer
Never married, lived on family farm all his life.

More About HENRY RALPH GERDES:
Burial: Malvern cemetery

    vi. LLOYD GERDES, b. August 02, 1903, Wside co., Clydetwp, IL.

Notes for LLOYD GERDES:
WsidecoIL birth record #10,211 as 'boy'. 1920 census lists him as 16.
1910 WsidecoIL census age 6
1920 WsidecoIL cen 121, age 16
Died in truck accident, not married.

    vii. VIRGIL E. GERDES, b. August 25, 1905, Wside co., Clydetwp, IL; d. April 23, 1987, Whiteside co., IL.

Notes for VIRGIL E. GERDES:
WsidecoIL birth record #12,024
1910 WsidecoIL cen163 age 4

1920 WsidecoIL cen 121, age 14
WsidecoIL death records
The author has a taped conversation with Virgil in which he reminisces about playing with Ronald Reagan as a child.
Lived on the family farm all his life, enjoyed antique farm machinery, never married.

More About VIRGIL E. GERDES:
Burial: Malvern cemetery

Generation No. 4

5. WILLIAM DETER[4] BECHTEL *(JOHN WILSON[3], EPHRAIM MYERS[2], BENJAMIN R[1])* was born March 11, 1891 in Wside co., Clydetwp, IL. He married WINNIE MILNES, daughter of FRANK MILNES and MINNIE PAPE. She was born 1894 in ILL..

Notes for WILLIAM DETER BECHTEL:
WsidecoIL birth record #6,845.
1910 WsidecoIL cen 49, age 19, IL IL PA. Farm laborer
1920 WsidecoUsttwpIL census 152/156, age 29 farmer, IL IL PA, Winnie F 26 md wife IL IL IL, Lucille f 5 S cau IL IL IL, Everett M 1 S son IL IL IL. [This does not agree with earlier records, perhaps Everett (1) died, another new son was named Everett)
SECOND COUSIN OF RONALD REAGAN

Notes for WINNIE MILNES:
1920 WsideUsttwpcoIL cen156, age 24, wife, IL IL IL

Children of WILLIAM BECHTEL and WINNIE MILNES are:
9.   i.   EVERETT[5] BECHTEL, b. 1905, ILL..
10. ii. LUCILLE FERN BECHTEL, b. March 09, 1914, Whiteside co., IL.
11. iii. GLENN BECHTEL.

6. IVY MAY[4] BECHTEL *(JOHN WILSON[3], EPHRAIM MYERS[2], BENJAMIN R[1])* was born May 1898. She married WILLIAM LANE.

Notes for IVY MAY BECHTEL:
1910 WsidecoIL cen 49, age 12, farm laborer
SECOND COUSIN OF RONALD REAGAN

Children of IVY BECHTEL and WILLIAM LANE are:
   i.   MILDRED[5] LANE.
   ii. DOROTHY ANN LANE.
   iii. WILLIAM LANE.

7. EPHRAIM LAWRENCE[4] GERDES *(ELLEN W.[3] BECHTEL, EPHRAIM MYERS[2], BENJAMIN R[1])* was born October 11, 1888 in Wside co., Clydetwp, IL.

Notes for EPHRAIM LAWRENCE GERDES:
WsidecoIL birth #5,888. Married, 2 boys, lived near Dixon.

Child of EPHRAIM LAWRENCE GERDES is:
   i.   WAYNE[5] GERDES, b. 1904.

        Notes for WAYNE GERDES:
        Living in Dixon in 1998 at 94, not married

8. GALEN GLENN[4] GERDES *(ELLEN W.[3] BECHTEL, EPHRAIM MYERS[2], BENJAMIN R[1])* was born January 1894 in Wside co., Clydetwp, IL, and died September 01, 1976 in N. Manchester, IN. He married (1) IDA FIKE September 02, 1923. She died September 12, 1923. He married (2) MARETA SHRIDER August 05, 1951.

Notes for GALEN GLENN GERDES:
Children per obituary
Minister, retired.

More About GALEN GLENN GERDES:
Burial: Yellow Creek Cemetery, Pearl City

Children of GALEN GERDES and MARETA SHRIDER are:
    i. ROBERT[5] GERDES.
    ii. RUTH GERDES.

Generation No. 5

9. EVERETT[5] BECHTEL *(WILLIAM DETER[4], JOHN WILSON[3], EPHRAIM MYERS[2], BENJAMIN R[1])* was born 1905 in ILL.. He married CARLENE MCKEE.

Notes for EVERETT BECHTEL:
1920 WsidecoIL cen 156 Ustick

Children of EVERETT BECHTEL and CARLENE MCKEE are:
    i. GARY[6] BECHTEL, m. PATRICIA WIERSEMA.
    ii. BONNIE BECHTEL, m. DOUGLAS BUSH.

10. LUCILLE FERN[5] BECHTEL *(WILLIAM DETER[4], JOHN WILSON[3], EPHRAIM MYERS[2], BENJAMIN R[1])* was born March 09, 1914 in Whiteside co., IL. She married LYLE NICE.

Notes for LUCILLE FERN BECHTEL:
WsidecoIL birth record # 17,783.
SECOND COUSIN ONCE REMOVED OF RONALD REAGAN

Children of LUCILLE BECHTEL and LYLE NICE are:
12.   i. ELWIN[6] NICE.
13.   ii. MARJORIE NICE.

11. GLENN[5] BECHTEL *(WILLIAM DETER[4], JOHN WILSON[3], EPHRAIM MYERS[2], BENJAMIN R[1])* He married RHEA GREEN.

Children of GLENN BECHTEL and RHEA GREEN are:
    i. GLENDA[6] BECHTEL, m. DARREL NICKE.
    ii. ELLEN BECHTEL, m. GREG PESSMAN.
    iii. SCOTT BECHTEL, m. SANDRA WALTERS.
    iv. CAROL BECHTEL, m. JOSEPH HIGH, July 17, 1876, Whiteside co., IL.

    Notes for CAROL BECHTEL:
    Whiteside co., IL marriage record #4216.

Generation No. 6

12. ELWIN[6] NICE *(LUCILLE FERN[5] BECHTEL, WILLIAM DETER[4], JOHN WILSON[3], EPHRAIM MYERS[2], BENJAMIN R[1])* He married SHIRLEY ENRIGHT.

Notes for ELWIN NICE:
SECOND COUSIN TWICE REMOVED OF RONALD REAGAN

Children of ELWIN NICE and SHIRLEY ENRIGHT are:
- i. WILLIAM[7] NICE, m. PATRICIA PETTICORD.
- ii. LINDA NICE.
- iii. PAM NICE.
- iv. JUDY NICE, m. JEFF MEINSMA.

13. MARJORIE[6] NICE *(LUCILLE FERN[5] BECHTEL, WILLIAM DETER[4], JOHN WILSON[3], EPHRAIM MYERS[2], BENJAMIN R[1])* She married ROBERT TRAUM.

Children of MARJORIE NICE and ROBERT TRAUM are:
- i. SUSAN[7] TRAUM.
- ii. JOHN TRAUM.
- iii. DAVID TRAUM.

Kinship of Benjamin R Bechtel

Name	Relationship with Benjamin Bechtel	Civil	Canon
Bechtel, Albert	Great-grandson	III	3
Bechtel, Benjamin R	Self		0
Bechtel, Bonnie	3rd great-granddaughter	V	5
Bechtel, Carol	3rd great-granddaughter	V	5
Bechtel, Ellen	3rd great-granddaughter	V	5
Bechtel, Ellen W.	Granddaughter	II	2
Bechtel, Ephraim Myers	Son	I	1
Bechtel, Everett	2nd great-grandson	IV	4
Bechtel, Gary	3rd great-grandson	V	5
Bechtel, Glenda	3rd great-granddaughter	V	5
Bechtel, Glenn	2nd great-grandson	IV	4
Bechtel, Helena	Granddaughter	II	2
Bechtel, Ivy May	Great-granddaughter	III	3
Bechtel, John Wilson	Grandson	II	2
Bechtel, Lucille Fern	2nd great-granddaughter	IV	4
Bechtel, Rebecca Jane	Granddaughter	II	2
Bechtel, Scott	3rd great-grandson	V	5
Bechtel, William Deter	Great-grandson	III	3
Bush, Douglas	Husband of the 3rd great-granddaughter		
C., Henry	Great-grandson	III	3
Deter, Sarah E.	Wife of the grandson		
Ella	Granddaughter	II	2
Enright, Shirley	Wife of the 3rd great-grandson		
Fike, Ida	Wife of the great-grandson		
Gerdes, David Edmond	Husband of the granddaughter		
Gerdes, Ephraim Lawrence	Great-grandson	III	3
Gerdes, Galen Glenn	Great-grandson	III	3
Gerdes, Henry Ralph	Great-grandson	III	3
Gerdes, Lloyd	Great-grandson	III	3
Gerdes, Robert	2nd great-grandson	IV	4
Gerdes, Ruth	2nd great-granddaughter	IV	4
Gerdes, Virgil E.	Great-grandson	III	3
Gerdes, Wayne	2nd great-grandson	IV	4
Green, Rhea	Wife of the 2nd great-grandson		
High, Joseph	Husband of the 3rd great-granddaughter		
Lane, Dorothy Ann	2nd great-granddaughter	IV	4
Lane, Mildred	2nd great-granddaughter	IV	4
Lane, William	Husband of the great-granddaughter		
Lane, William	2nd great-grandson	IV	4
Longanecker, Samuel L.	Husband of the granddaughter		
May, Iva	Great-granddaughter	III	3
McKee, Carlene	Wife of the 2nd great-grandson		
Meinsma, Jeff	Husband of the 4th great-granddaughter		
Milnes, Winnie	Wife of the great-grandson		
Myers, Rebecca	Wife		
Nice, Elwin	3rd great-grandson	V	5
Nice, Judy	4th great-granddaughter	VI	6
Nice, Linda	4th great-granddaughter	VI	6
Nice, Lyle	Husband of the 2nd great-granddaughter		
Nice, Marjorie	3rd great-granddaughter	V	5
Nice, Pam	4th great-granddaughter	VI	6

Name	Relationship with Benjamin Bechtel	Civil	Canon
Nice, William	4th great-grandson	VI	6
Nicke, Darrel	Husband of the 3rd great-granddaughter		
Pessman, Greg	Husband of the 3rd great-granddaughter		
Petticord, Patricia	Wife of the 4th great-grandson		
Shrider, Mareta	Wife of the great-grandson		
Traum, David	4th great-grandson	VI	6
Traum, John	4th great-grandson	VI	6
Traum, Robert	Husband of the 3rd great-granddaughter		
Traum, Susan	4th great-granddaughter	VI	6
Walters, Sandra	Wife of the 3rd great-grandson		
Wiersema, Patricia	Wife of the 3rd great-grandson		
Wilson, Sara	Daughter-in-law		

Descendants of Johnnie Blue

Generation No. 1

1. JOHNNIE[1] BLUE was born Bet. 1750 - 1775, and died in Kintyre, Argyll, Scotland.

Notes for JOHNNIE BLUE:
Family data from Merna Janvrin-Muschal, Blue/Smith.   He was a notorious bootlegger.

Child of JOHNNIE BLUE is:
2.   i.   DONALD DANIEL[2]BLUE, SR, b. January 18, 1799, Argyl, Scotland; d. January 14, 1888, Whiteside co., Clyde twp., IL.

Generation No. 2

2. DONALD DANIEL[2]BLUE, SR *(JOHNNIE[1] BLUE)* was born January 18, 1799 in Argyl, Scotland, and died January 14, 1888 in Whiteside co., Clyde twp., IL. He married CATHERINE MCFARLANE January 15, 1815 in Scotland, daughter of JOHN MCFARLANE and CUNNINGHAM FORSYTH. She was born January 01, 1801 in Scotland, and died February 21, 1883 in Whiteside co., Clyde twp., IL.

Notes for DONALD DANIELBLUE, SR:
Emigrated to New Brunswick, Canada, March 1820.   Moved in 1828 near Toronto.   He took part in the "Patriot War" in Canada.   Emigrated to Clyde twp., Section 17, 1839.   They were in California from 1852-5.   Bd, next to wife, Grove Hill cem., Morrison, Lot 46E, resident Clyde, age 91 yrs..
1830 WsidecoClytwpIL cen. Arrived 1839, 10 / 2
1840 Whiteside co., IL census: 1M uner 5, 1 age 5-10, 110-15, 1 20-30, 1 40-50// 1 F under 5, 1 5-10, 1 15-20, 1 40-50 [wife of head], 1 60-70.
1850 Wsideco 37th dist IL census 483/483, Daniel, 53, b. 1797, farmer, Sc, Katharine 58 F SC, Daniel 16 M Canada, Isabel 14 F Can, Charles 13 M Can, Katharine 10 F Can.
1860 WsidcoClydtwpIL census 482/470. $4,400/$1,000. Age58, Catherine 56, Dan'l 25, Catherine 20.
1870 WsidecoMorrisonIL census27/28, $1500/$500, age 67, Scotland, farm laborer, with wife `Kate', 66, Scotland, daughter Elizabeth, age 13 IL, and McKay, Robert, age 28, Scotland, blacksmith, wife Catharine 30, Canada, son Daniel, age 2, IL
1880 Wsideco Morrison, IL census 178/187, age 83, retired farmer, Sc Sc Sc, Catharine F 81 F wife Sc Sc Sc.
 Ronald V. Jackson, 'Reagan/Davis Ancestry', gives death as 1881/3.

More About DONALD DANIELBLUE, SR:
Burial: Grove Hill, Morrison, IL

Notes for CATHERINE MCFARLANE:
Bd. Grove Hill cem., Morrison, Lot46E, resident Morrison, deaths Whiteside co., IL, #928, age 84 yrs., lot 46E, residence Morrison.
1880 Wside Morrison IL census/187, age 81, Sc Sc Sc
History of Whiteside County, ILL, by Bent-Wilson, p. 145.   Biography of Daniel Blue.
Three children died in infancy, 11 in all.
1850 Wsideco 37dist IL cen483, age 58, born 1792, Sc., with Dan, Isabel, Charles, Kath.
Ronald V. Jackson, 'Reagan/Davis Ancestry', gives birth place as Paisley, Renfrow, Scotland, date as Jan. 10, 1801.

Children of DONALD BLUE, SR and CATHERINE MCFARLANE are:
3.   i.   JANE³ BLUE, b. April 01, 1821, Nova Scotia, Canada; d. June 01, 1894, Morrison, IL.
      ii.   JOHNBLUE, I, b. 1822; d. 1839, Clyde twp., Whiteside co., IL.

           Notes for JOHNBLUE, I:
           Bent, p. 142 tells of the death of John and Margaret shortly arrival in ILL.

4.   iii.   ALEXANDER BLUE, b. Abt. 1827, Nova Scotia; d. April 18, 1859, see notes.
      iv.   MARGARET BLUE, b. 1828, Canada; d. 1839, WSide co., Clydetwp, IL.

           Notes for MARGARET BLUE:
           Died in Clyde twp.. per Bent.
           Not in 1850 census
           Death information from Elizabeth Carroll notes to Mrs. D. Wilson

      v.   DONALD DANIELBLUE, JR., b. Abt. 1834, Canada; m. (1) ELLA BIRT; b. 1854, Wside co., Usttwp, IL; d. Independence, Iowa; m. (2) HELEN MAY BENJAMIN, November 05, 1860, Whiteside co., IL.

           Notes for DONALD DANIELBLUE, JR.:
           Author of 'Thrilling Narrative of Pike's Peak Gold Settlers' which details a trip west where they ran into a snow storm, insufficient rations, lack of heat, killed all the party except Daniel. He subsisted on a body until found by friendly Indians. They were going to Pikes Peak to hunt for gold.
           WsidecoIL marriage record #505.
           Daniel had one child with Ella Birt
           1850 WsidecoIL cen483, age 16, laborer, Canada
           1870 WSidecoIL cen 27/28 Morrison. Daniel Blue, 67 M Scotland, farm laborer, Kate 66 F Sc, Elizabeth 13 F IL, McKay, Robert 28 M Sc blacksmith, Catharine 30 F Can, Daniel 2 M IL. [Catharine daughter of Daniel/Kate]

           More About DONALD DANIELBLUE, JR.:
           Burial: Grove Hill cemetery, Morrison

           Notes for ELLA BIRT:
           See S J Clarke, publisher, 'The Biographical Record', Whiteside county, IL,, p. 26. She is the daughter of George W. Birt, b. Feb1, 1858, Clyde township, of Henry J. Birt, who was a son of George W. Birt, both of Gloucestershire, England. Ella is second child and had two children by her marriage to Harn, one child by marriage to Daniel Blue. She was widowed a second time.
           1870 Whiteside co., Ustick twp, IL cen164/164: as daughter of Henry J. , Helen 16 F IL.
           1880 WsidecoUsttwpIL census 185, age 24, daughter of Henry, IL EN VT, with Otis, Ida Harn.

           Notes for HELEN MAY BENJAMIN:
           Married by Rev. J. W. White at Morrison, per Wside Sentinel 8Nov1860
           Middle name from marriage record, Whiteside co., #505
           Death Dates prior to 1916, loose paper file, Odell Library, Morrison, IL, :
           E3 Mrs. David Blue, to city of Morrison Feb. 4, 1913. Digging grave $5. Approved Mar. 10, 1913. 7th Feb. Coffin and Box $18. Died at Mrs Julia Shepard.

5.   vi.   ISABELL BLUE, b. 1836, Canada.
      vii.   CHARLES BLUE, b. Abt. 1839, Canada; d. Abt. April 18, 1859.

           Notes for CHARLES BLUE:
           Died shortly after date given on trail to Pike's Peak, Smoky Hill route.
           1850 WsidecoIL census, age 13, Canada

6.   viii.   CATHARINE BLUE, b. August 17, 1839, Toronto, Canada.
      ix.   JOHN BLUE, 2, b. March 29, 1842; d. 1920, Wside co., Clydetwp, IL; m. E. M. BECHTEL, February 22, 1861.
      x.   <UNNAMED>.

Generation No. 3

3. JANE³ BLUE *(DONALD DANIEL²BLUE, SR, JOHNNIE¹ BLUE)* was born April 01, 1821 in Nova Scotia,

Canada, and died June 01, 1894 in Morrison, IL. She married JOHN WILSON November 23, 1841 in Whiteside co., IL, son of ANDREW WILSON and AMEILIA GLASGOW. He was born February 09, 1812 in Paisley, Renfrewshire, Scotland, and died March 09, 1883 in Wside co., Clydetwp., IL.

Notes for JANE BLUE:
Bd. Center Clyde cem. age 71 years. (Born 1823?)
1850 Wsideco37th D IL census 484, Nova Scotia, age 25.
1860 WsidecoClytwpIL census476/464. Jane 34, John 50, Sarah 16, Thos. 14, John 12.
1870 WsidecoClytwpIL cen 168, age 44, Parent foreign born, born New Brunswick.
Ronald V. Jackson, 'Reagan/Davis Ancestry', gives birth date as abt. 1824 at Queens, New Brunswick, Canada, marriage as Nov. 28, 1841, death as abt. 1880.
Birth also given as 1823
2 children died in infancy. Chapman Whiteside co. History, p. 63 'of Scotch parentage.
Donald E. Farr email of 19 Oct. 2002 gives her birth place as Queens, New Brunswick, Canada, and death date as June 3, 1894.
GREAT GRANDMOTHER OF RONALD REAGAN

More About JANE BLUE:
Burial: North Clyde cemetery

Notes for JOHN WILSON:
To Nova Scotia in 1832. Probably met his wife in Canada. He took part in the "Patriot War". He came to Clyde twp in 1839. Married in Whiteside co. Nov. 23, 1841 per marriage record # 54, not the 28th per Heritage Quest article.
Willson in marriage record Whiteside co., IL #54.
1860 Whitesideco37thDistIL census 4854/484, age 40, farmer, Scotland
1860 WsidecoIL Clyde twp census 476/464. Age 50, Scotland, Farmer, $8,000,$1,000, Jane 34 F Nova Scotia, Sarah 16 F IL, Thos. 14 M IL, John 12 M IL, Wilson, Alexander 10 M IL, Margrer 3 M? IL Catherine 7mo. F IL
1870 WsidecoClytwpIL census 168/168, $16,000, age 58, nat citizen, Scotland, Farmer
WsidecoIL death record #930
Original land grants:
6-24-1845. FD NWSW S9 22N 5E. 40 acres. $1.25 $50.00. V. 714, p. 131 014622.
7-19-1848. NWSW S17, 22N, 5E 40 acres, S$50.00 014623
12-30- 1853. 40 acres, $50.00. 091044
FD NWNE S23 22N 4E 40 acres. $50.00 091045
12-30-1853. FD NWNE S23 22N 4E 40 acres, $50.00. 091045
Ronald V. Jackson, 'Reagan/Davis Ancestry', gives father as Andrew Wilson, mother as Ameila Glassgow. He also gives deathdate as 6 February 1879. This does not agree with County records.
    Per Eliz. Carroll: Four men emigrated to Canada together. Donald Blue, Richard Beswick, John Wilson and William Wilson. William went to CA, possibly a brother of John?
ASSUMPTION: Claudio, b. 1786 as one of triplets, came to Clyde after emigration to MA and Mexico for some years.
Funeral at Clyde ME church
GREAT GRANDFATHER OF RONALD WILSON

More About JOHN WILSON:
Burial: North Clyde Cemetery

Children of JANE BLUE and JOHN WILSON are:
7.   i. SARA[4] WILSON, b. March 29, 1841, Wside co., Clydetwp, IL; d. November 17, 1920, Wside co., Clydetwp, IL.
8.   ii. THOMAS WILSON, b. April 28, 1844, Wside co., Clydetwp, IL; d. December 10, 1909, WSide co., Clydetwp, IL.
9.   iii. JOHN WILSON, b. July 11, 1846, Whiteside co., Clydetwp, IL; d. February 15, 1909, Morrison, IL.
10. iv. ALEXANDER B WILSON, b. February 21, 1848, WSide co., Clydetwp, IL; d. May 25, 1932.

11.	v.	MARGARET MAE WILSON, b. April 28, 1857, Whiteside co., Clydetwp, IL; d. March 12, 1944, Whiteside co., Clydetwp, IL.
12.	vi.	CATHERINE WILSON, b. November 09, 1859, Wside co., Clydetwp, IL; d. July 13, 1932, Highland Park, IL.
13.	vii.	ELIZABETH EVELYN WILSON, b. December 10, 1861, Whiteside co., Clyde twp., IL; d. November 19, 1945.
14.	viii.	REV. CHARLES DESMOND WILSON, b. November 10, 1865; d. 1937.

4. ALEXANDER[3] BLUE *(DONALD DANIEL[2] BLUE, SR, JOHNNIE[1] BLUE)* was born Abt. 1827 in Nova Scotia, and died April 18, 1859 in see notes. He married MARY BESWICK Abt. 1850. She was born Abt. 1829 in England, and died April 1863.

Notes for ALEXANDER BLUE:
Died en route to Pike's Peak Gold mines in 1859. Daniel Blue wrote a pamphlet regarding this trip.
1850 WsidcoIL cen485, age 23, Nova Scotia, farmer, with wife, Mary, 22, England

Notes for MARY BESWICK:
Three later children died in infancy, not listed.
Johnson marriage, record #630, Whiteside co., IL
1860 WsidecoClytwpIL cen483/471, 31 Eng. Children, Geo 9, John 7, Rich'd 5 also Elizabeth 22 IL. Have not located Elizabeth, not listed in the 1850 census either as Blue or Beswick.

Children of ALEXANDER BLUE and MARY BESWICK are:
    i. GEORGE[4] BLUE, b. Abt. 1851, ILL..

    Notes for GEORGE BLUE:
    1860 WsidecoClytwpIL cen 471 9 Eng
    1870 WsidecoClytwpIL census 72/72, age 19, IL, farm laborer, with James Stapleton, 40, England, farmer.

15.   ii. JOHN A. BLUE, b. Abt. 1853, ILL..
16.   iii. RICHARD BESWICK BLUE, b. November 07, 1855, ILL..
    iv. ELIZABETH BLUE, b. Abt. 1857, ILL..

    Notes for ELIZABETH BLUE:
    In 1870 census, Morrison, IL, with grandfather Donald Daniel Blue, Sr.
    Wside co., IL marriage record #5945 "Elizabeth Evelyn"

5. ISABELL[3] BLUE *(DONALD DANIEL[2] BLUE, SR, JOHNNIE[1] BLUE)* was born 1836 in Canada. She married JOHN BRETT February 27, 1852 in WHiteside co., IL. He was born 1833 in England.

Notes for ISABELL BLUE:
WsidecoIL marriage record #463.
1850 WsidecoIL cen. age 14, b. 1836.

Notes for JOHN BRETT:
1860 Whiteside co., Clyde twp., IL census480/468: Brett, John 27 M Farmer $1000/$250 Eng, Isabella 24 F Can, Kate 3 F IL, Charles 1 M IL, Ainsworth, Benj. 13 M En. [Perhaps a brother of Isabella?]
1880 Whiteside, Ustick twp., IL cen54/55: Brett, John M 51 Md Farmer En En En, Isabell F 47 wife, En Sc Sc, 7 children 23 to 5 yrs., Blue, Stella F 13 S niece IL CN NY. [Have not located Stella, nor Nettie A. Blue F 17 S Cn Sc Sc with John W. Kent, Union Grove twp.,]

Children of ISABELL BLUE and JOHN BRETT are:
    i. KATE[4] BRETT, b. 1857, Whiteside co, Clyde twp., IL.
    ii. CHARLES BRETT, b. 1859, Whiteside co, Clyde twp., IL.
    iii. ALEXANDER BRETT, b. 1861, Whiteside co., Ustick twp., IL.
    iv. GEORGE BRETT, b. 1864, Whiteside co., Ustick twp., IL.
    v. DONALD BRETT, b. 1866, Whiteside co., Ustick twp., IL.

vi. JOHN W. BRETT, b. 1871, Whiteside co., Ustick twp., IL.
vii. THOMAS C. BRETT, b. 1875, Whiteside co., Ustick twp., IL.

6. CATHARINE[3] BLUE *(DONALD DANIEL[2] BLUE, SR, JOHNNIE[1] BLUE)* was born August 17, 1839 in Toronto, Canada. She married (1) D. G. ACKERMAN, son of GARRET ACKERMAN and ELIZABETH WATSON. He was born February 13, 1832 in Paterson, NJ. She married (2) ROBERT MCKAY November 24, 1867 in Whiteside co., IL. He was born 1842 in Scotland.

Notes for CATHARINE BLUE:
WsidcoIL Marriage record #1928
Death cert. #928, Wside co IL
1850 WsidecoIL cen, age 10, 1870 census with father, Daniel, Kate, Elizabeth, Robert McKay 28 M Scotland Blacksmith, Catharine 30 F Canada, Daniel 2 M IL.

Notes for D. G. ACKERMAN:
He is the lone survivor of 5 children, came to ILL in 1876, mason & builder, later farmer, per Chapman 'Biog. & Portrait Album of Whiteside co., IL' p. 677.

Notes for ROBERT MCKAY:
WsidecoIL birth records do not show any children.
1870 WsidecoIL cen27/28 with father in law, Donald (Daniel) Blue.

Child of CATHARINE BLUE and ROBERT MCKAY is:
i. DANIEL[4] MCKAY, b. Abt. 1868.

Notes for DANIEL MCKAY:
Whiteside co., IL birth record: Robert McKay/Catherine Blue, Nov. 24, 1867, #1928, BUT no child listed, probably this Daniel.

Generation No. 4

7. SARA[4] WILSON *(JANE[3] BLUE, DONALD DANIEL[2] BLUE, SR, JOHNNIE[1] BLUE)* was born March 29, 1841 in Wside co., Clydetwp, IL, and died November 17, 1920 in Wside co., Clydetwp, IL. She married EPHRAIM MYERS BECHTEL February 22, 1861 in Whiteside co., IL, son of BENJAMIN BECHTEL and REBECCA MYERS. He was born March 23, 1833 in Columbiana Co., OH, and died January 16, 1928 in Wside co., Clydetwp, IL.

Notes for SARA WILSON:
1850 WsidecoIL census484, age 8, IL
1870 WsidecoIL census95, age 36, I
1910 WsideClytwpIL census, age 68, IL Sc Sc
1920 WsideClytwpcoIL census with David E Gerdes, age 78, with husband Ephraim Bechtel, 86
Bd. Malvern cemetery next to husband
Married by Rev. J. W. White, in Ustick twp., in her parent's home., Wside Sentinel 26 Feb1861
GREAT AUNT OF RONALD WILSON

More About SARA WILSON:
Burial: Malvern cemetery

Notes for EPHRAIM MYERS BECHTEL:
He came to Clyde Twp. at 19 with his parents.
1870 WsideUsttwpIL census 95/95, age 32, farmer, OH, Sarah 36 F IL, John 8 M IL, Rebecca 6 F IL, Ella 4 F IL. [Only Bechtel in census]
1880 WsideClydetwpIL census 119/121 with son in law David E. Gerdes, dau. Ella (Ellen)
1910 WsideClytwpIL census 56/58, age77, own income, IL Gr PA, Sarah F 68 wf IL Sc Sc
Whiteside marriage record #563. Ephraim N. on marriage record.

Bd. Malvern cemetery.
He died at the home of his daughter, Mrs. David (Ellen) Gerdes. He had been blind for a number of years. He was the last of 11 children to die.
COUSIN OF RONALD REAGAN

More About EPHRAIM MYERS BECHTEL:
Burial: Malvern cemetery

Children of SARA WILSON and EPHRAIM BECHTEL are:

17.   i.   JOHN WILSON[5] BECHTEL, b. February 17, 1862, Wside co., Clydetwp, IL; d. February 22, 1933, Wside co., Clydetwp, IL.
          ii.   REBECCA JANE BECHTEL, b. 1864; d. March 11, 1878, WSide co., Clydetwp, IL.

               Notes for REBECCA JANE BECHTEL:
               Bd. Malvern cemetery with parents, died at 14 years. 'Buried from the Franklin School House' from the Sentinel of May 11, 1878. Whiteside co. death certificate #88.
               1870 WsidecoIL cen95, age 6, IL
               COUSIN ONCE REMOVED OF RONALD REAGAN

18.   iii.   ELLEN W. BECHTEL, b. July 01, 1866, Wside co., Clydetwp, IL.
          iv.   HELENA BECHTEL, b. November 01, 1876, ILL.; d. June 24, 1953, Washington; m. SAMUEL L. LONGANECKER, May 16, 1903, Whiteside co., IL; b. December 24, 1875; d. December 22, 1946, Orville, WA.

               Notes for HELENA BECHTEL:
               COUSIN ONCE REMOVED OF RONALD REAGAN

               Notes for SAMUEL L. LONGANECKER:
               Wside co. marriage record #11,484, she is listed as Helen

8. THOMAS[4] WILSON *(JANE[3] BLUE, DONALD DANIEL[2] BLUE, SR, JOHNNIE[1] BLUE)* was born April 28, 1844 in Wside co., Clydetwp, IL, and died December 10, 1909 in WSide co., Clydetwp, IL. He married MARY ANN ELSEY January 25, 1866 in Whiteside co., IL, daughter of ROBERT ELSEY and MARY BAKER. She was born December 28, 1843 in Epsom, County Surrey, England, and died October 06, 1900 in Fulton, Whiteside Co., IL.

Notes for THOMAS WILSON:
Thomas was a prosperous farmer in Whiteside County.
Bd. N. Clyde cem., Wside co.. Place of death uncertain.
WsidecoIL mar rcd #1454
1850 WsidecoIL census484, age 6.
1880 Clyde twp. Whiteside co., IL census: Thomas Wilson 36 farmer IL En En, Mary A. 36 En En En, Emily dau 13 IL, John son 10 IL Jennie dau 8 IL, Alexande 7 IL, George son 4 IL, Mary dau 2 IL.
Not in 1900 census. Absent from home for periods of time, perhaps at this time.
Farmed near White Pigeon, Whiteside co., IL
GRANDFATHER OF RONALD REAGAN

More About THOMAS WILSON:
Burial: North Clyde cemetery

Notes for MARY ANN ELSEY:
Bd. Fulton Cem.
Married by Rev. George T. Crissman, per Sentinel 1Feb1860, Whiteside co. marriage record #1454.
1900 Fulton twp., Whiteside co., IL census: Mary Wilson, Dec 1843, En En En, Alexander son Mar 1874, IL, factory worker, Vina dau Apr 18ll80 IL, Nellie dau 16 July 1883 IL
GRANDMOTHER OF RONALD REAGAN

More About MARY ANN ELSEY:
Burial: Fulton Catholic cemetery

Children of THOMAS WILSON and MARY ELSEY are:
    i. EMILY G.[5] WILSON, b. November 12, 1867, Fulton, Whiteside Co., IL; d. February 21, 1947, O'Fallon, St. Clair, IL; m. STEPHEN A. RUSH, June 03, 1884, Morrison, Whiteside co., IL; b. April 1865, Fulton, Whiteside Co., IL; d. April 05, 1936, O'Fallon, IL.

    Notes for EMILY G. WILSON:
    1900 Wsideco Fulton ILL cen 165, age 31 IL IL En
    They had no children.
    AUNT OF RONALD REAGAN

    More About EMILY G. WILSON:
    Burial: February 25, 1947, Shilo cemetery

    Notes for STEPHEN A. RUSH:
    They had no children.
    Wside co IL marriage record #6376
    1900 Wsideco., Fulton, IL census 165/165, age 35, IL PA PA, boarding house, next door is a long listing of of occupants, probably his boarding house. Also lists: Pannell, Lawra F 20 S IL IL IL servant, domestic.
    1870 WsidecoAlbanyIL census 92/92. Stephen is 8, IL, in family of Henry W. Rush, age. 40, PA wife Marybea, age 37, NY, 8 children.
    Tavern owner, death date from wife's obituary.

19.   ii. JOHN CHARLES WILSON, b. October 09, 1870, Wsideco, Clyde twp, IL; d. June 21, 1942, Clinton, IA.
20.   iii. SARA JANE WILSON, b. June 16, 1871, Clyde twp, Whiteside co., IL; d. March 08, 1920, White Pigeon, Clyde twp, Whiteside Co., IL.
    iv. ALEXANDER THOMAS WILSON, b. March 30, 1874, Whiteside Co., Clyde twp., IL; d. April 26, 1962, Quincy, Adams co., IL; m. (1) MAYME AITKEN; m. (2) MAYME HELMS, June 12, 1912.

    Notes for ALEXANDER THOMAS WILSON:
    They had no children. Obituary in (unnamed) newspaper gives birth as March 30, 1876. Employed 44 years at Monroe Chemical Co., foreman of the mill rooom. Member First Christian Church and Quincy Lodge of Masons.
    UNCLE OF RONALD REAGAN

    More About ALEXANDER THOMAS WILSON:
    Burial: Greenmount cemetery, Quincy, IL

21.   v. GEORGE ORVILLE WILSON, b. March 02, 1876, Cordova, Whiteside co., IL; d. April 03, 1951, Clinton, IA.
22.   vi. MARY LAVINA WILSON, b. April 06, 1879, Wside co., Clydetwp, IL; d. September 06, 1951, Minneapolis, Hennepin co., MN.
23.   vii. NELLIE CLYDE WILSON, b. July 24, 1883, Fulton, Whiteside co., IL; d. July 25, 1962, Santa Monica, Los Angeles co., CA.

9. JOHN[4] WILSON *(JANE[3] BLUE, DONALD DANIEL[2] BLUE, SR, JOHNNIE[1] BLUE)* was born July 11, 1846 in Whiteside co., Clydetwp, IL, and died February 15, 1909 in Morrison, IL. He married ISABELLE MARY LIGGETT March 14, 1872. She was born October 1850 in OH.

Notes for JOHN WILSON:
1850 Wsideco37thDisIL census 484, age 4, IL
Citizenship paper, Whiteside co., IL, circuit court, 7 Dec. 1877, renounces Victoria, Queen of England.
Bd. Grove Hill cem., Morrison, Lot 7M, age 65 years.
1870 WsidecoClytwpIL cen73, age 23, IL
1880 Whiteside co., Ustick twp., IL cen110/112: Wilson, John M 34 md. Farmer IL Sc Sc, Isabell F 29 wf md OH OH OH, Fannie J. F 7 S IL IL OH.
1920 Whitesideco

John R. Wilson, land grant:
793,372. 12-30-1871. RR SESE S34 21N 7E 40 acres @$15. $600.00
GREAT UNCLE OF RONALD REAGAN

More About JOHN WILSON:
Burial: Grove Hill cemetery, Morrison

Notes for ISABELLE MARY LIGGETT:
1910 WsidecoMorrisonIL census 11/11, age 54, widow, OH OH OH, has 'own income'. Fannie dau 36 S IL IL OH, and Alexander 66 widowed,, her 'brother in law', IL Sc Sc 'own income'.

Children of JOHN WILSON and ISABELLE LIGGETT are:
    i. FRANCES JANE^5 WILSON, b. January 1873, Whiteside co., IL; d. November 07, 1968, Morrison, IL.

    Notes for FRANCES JANE WILSON:
    Birth date from Heritage Quest
    1910 Wsideco Morrison, IL census 11/11, age 36, single, IL IL OH
    School teacher.
    Died: 95 years, 7 months

    More About FRANCES JANE WILSON:
    Burial: Grove Hill cemetery, Morrison

24.   ii. MARGARET MAY WILSON, b. June 10, 1883, Whiteside co., IL.

10. ALEXANDER B^4 WILSON (*JANE^3 BLUE, DONALD DANIEL^2 BLUE, SR, JOHNNIE^1 BLUE*) was born February 21, 1848 in WSide co., Clydetwp, IL, and died May 25, 1932. He married DEBORAH A. FLETCHER June 14, 1876 in Whiteside co., IL, daughter of ISAAC FLETCHER and ELIZABETH SMITH. She was born March 08, 1853 in Chautauqua Co., NY, and died 1899.

Notes for ALEXANDER B WILSON:
WsidecoUGtwpIL cen 186 gives age 65, widowed, father of Paul, IL SC SC
1850 WsidcoIL cen 484, age 1
1860 WsidcoClytwpIL cen464 with John, Margaret 3, Catharine 7mo.
1870 WsidecoClytwpIL census 73, age 21, IL
1880 Whitesid co., Ustick twp., IL cen111/113: Wilson, Alexander M 28 md. IL Sc Sc, Debbie A. F 26 wf md. NY Eng Eng, Green, Lewis md in yr. M 24 md. Farmer IL OH NJ, Clara md in yr. F 19 wf md CA VA OH, Probuscaj, Gracie F 12 sister S CA VA OH
1910 Wsideco Morrison, ILL census 11/11 with Isabel, as brother in law, age 66, widowed, has 'own income', IL Sc Sc
Also on the 1910 census with Paul Wilson as Alex, father, age 67, NY NY NY.
Birth date also given as 21 Feb. 1849, Mrs. Dwight Wilson
Lot 109B, cemetery

More About ALEXANDER B WILSON:
Burial: Grove Hill, Morrison, IL

Notes for DEBORAH A. FLETCHER:
Chapman, History of Whiteside County, ILL, p. 437: 'Debbie A. Fletcher b. March 8, 1853 md. Alexander Wilson June 15, 1876, resides Ustick. She was a teacher for many years. Daughter of Isaac Fletcher, Eng., April 23, 1826 and Betsy Smith'   Whiteside co., IL marriage record #4191 gives June 14, 1876, Alexander R. Wilson md. Debbie A. Fletcher.

Child of ALEXANDER WILSON and DEBORAH FLETCHER is:
25.   i. PAUL FLETCHER^5 WILSON, b. January 1883, Whiteside co., IL; d. 1964.

11. MARGARET MAE[4] WILSON *(JANE[3] BLUE, DONALD DANIEL[2] BLUE, SR, JOHNNIE[1] BLUE)* was born April 28, 1857 in Whiteside co., Clydetwp, IL, and died March 12, 1944 in Whiteside co., Clydetwp, IL. She married DAVID B. GSELL February 25, 1879 in Mt. Carroll, Carroll Co., IL, son of WILLIAM GSELL and MARIA BARKHART. He was born December 15, 1852 in Letterkenny twp, Franklin co., PA, and died January 01, 1907 in Whiteside co., Clydetwp, IL.

Notes for MARGARET MAE WILSON:
Bd. N. Clyde Cem.
1870 WsidecoClyTwpIL cen73, age 13, IL
Married by Rev. J. P. Phillips, per Sentinel 27Feb1879
Death date from Mrs. D. Wilson. Member Methodist Episcopal church.

More About MARGARET MAE WILSON:
Burial: North Clyde Cemetery

Notes for DAVID B. GSELL:
Bd. N. Clyde cem.
Came west in 1864, per Carroll. Lived Section 7, Clyde Twp.. He was a Republican. See p. 389 of Chapman, Portrait and Biographical Album of Whiteside County, IL.

More About DAVID B. GSELL:
Burial: North Clyde Cemetery

Children of MARGARET WILSON and DAVID GSELL are:
- 26. i. CLIFFORD LEROY[5] GSELL, b. November 17, 1880, Whiteside co, Clyde twp., IL; d. August 11, 1951, Clinton, Iowa.
- 27. ii. MAUDE MAE GSELL, b. November 18, 1884, WsidClytwpIL; d. August 26, 1966, Fulton, IL.
- 28. iii. ESTELLA JANE GSELL, b. May 27, 1894, Whiteside co, Clyde twp., IL.

12. CATHERINE[4] WILSON *(JANE[3] BLUE, DONALD DANIEL[2] BLUE, SR, JOHNNIE[1] BLUE)* was born November 09, 1859 in Wside co., Clydetwp, IL, and died July 13, 1932 in Highland Park, IL. She married WILLIAM B. GSELL October 07, 1879 in Sterling, Whiteside co., IL, son of WILLIAM GSELL and MARIA BARKHART. He was born February 15, 1854 in Letterkenny twp, Franklin co., PA, and died April 02, 1921 in Highland Park, IL.

Notes for CATHERINE WILSON:
WsidecoIL marriage record #5104, Katie Wilson
1860 WsidecoClytwpIL cen464 7mo., census taken 15 June 1860.
1870 WsidecoClytwpIL census73, age 10, IL
Married at Sterling, IL, at the residence of Rev. J. T. Mason.
Buried Lot 31R; 72 yrs, 10 m, 1 d.. Chapman gives her birth as Nov. 9, 1861.

More About CATHERINE WILSON:
Burial: Grove Hill cemetery, Morrison

Notes for WILLIAM B. GSELL:
Died at 67 yrs., 1 mo., 17 d.. Lot 31R. Lived Section 30, Clyde Twp.. Came there in 1864. See p. 463 of Chapman, Port. & Biog. Album of Whiteside County, IL.

More About WILLIAM B. GSELL:
Burial: Grove Hill cemetery, Morrison

Child of CATHERINE WILSON and WILLIAM GSELL is:
- i. EARL WILSON[5] GSELL, b. August 18, 1882, WsidecoUsttwpIL; d. January 25, 1960, Highland Park, IL; m. FRANCIS LOUISE CUTLER; b. 1888; d. 1961.

Notes for EARL WILSON GSELL:
WsidecoIL birth record #2,733
Death date from Grove Hill records
Died at 77 yrs, bd. Lot 31R

More About EARL WILSON GSELL:
Burial: Grove Hill cemetery, Morrison

13. ELIZABETH EVELYN[4] WILSON (JANE[3] BLUE, DONALD DANIEL[2] BLUE, SR, JOHNNIE[1] BLUE) was born December 10, 1861 in Whiteside co., Clyde twp., IL, and died November 19, 1945. She married WILLIAM G. HIGH December 19, 1882 in Whiteside Co., IL.

Notes for ELIZABETH EVELYN WILSON:
1919 WsideRockFalls ILL census 38, age 46   IL NY NY
1870 WsidecoClytwpIL cen73, age 7, `Lizzie', IL
1900 WsideCoItwpIL census 487, age 35, IL VA IL
WsidcoIL marriage record # 5945, as Lizzie E..
Whiteside co., IL birth record #84,728.
Mother died at her home in Morrison, leaving her home in Chicago about April 1, ill.   Jane Wilson obituary

Child of ELIZABETH WILSON and WILLIAM HIGH is:
    i. BESSIE LUELLA JANE[5] HIGH, b. October 15, 1887, Wside co., IL; m. WILLIAM HOWELL, 1945; d. Boston, MA.

        Notes for BESSIE LUELLA JANE HIGH:
        WsidecoIL birth record #84728

14. REV. CHARLES DESMOND[4] WILSON (JANE[3] BLUE, DONALD DANIEL[2] BLUE, SR, JOHNNIE[1] BLUE) was born November 10, 1865, and died 1937. He married JENIE ALICE SMITH June 26, 1896. She was born March 24, 1873, and died 1927.

Notes for REV. CHARLES DESMOND WILSON:
1870 WsidecoClytwpIL cen 73, age 4, IL
Methodist minister.

Children of CHARLES WILSON and JENIE SMITH are:
29.   i. ALICE JANE[5] WILSON, b. April 15, 1897; d. July 05, 1952.
30.   ii. PHOEBE MAE WILSON, b. May 10, 1899; d. May 10, 1960.
31.   iii. WINIFRED M. WILSON, b. September 15, 1901.
      iv. CHARLES ABRAM WILSON, b. December 29, 1903; d. 1928.
      v. GEORGE JOHN WILSON, b. September 08, 1903; d. 1979; m. (1) MARGARET WILKINSON; m. (2) DOROTHY NELSON.

15. JOHN A.[4] BLUE (ALEXANDER[3], DONALD DANIEL[2] BLUE, SR, JOHNNIE[1] BLUE) was born Abt. 1853 in ILL.. He married ELLA A. KENT February 17, 1876 in Whiteside co., IL.

Notes for JOHN A. BLUE:
1860 WsidecoClytwpIL cen471, 7 IL

Notes for ELLA A. KENT:
Marriage records 4103, Wside co. IL
Married by Rev. George T. Crissman, both of Union Grove, per Wside Sentinel 24 Feb 1876

Child of JOHN BLUE and ELLA KENT is:

i. MARY ELIZABETH[5] BLUE, b. March 16, 1877, Whiteside co., IL.

Notes for MARY ELIZABETH BLUE:
WsidecoIL birth record # 81,374., Ella.

16. RICHARD BESWICK[4] BLUE *(ALEXANDER[3], DONALD DANIEL[2] BLUE, SR, JOHNNIE[1] BLUE)* was born November 07, 1855 in ILL.. He married EMMA A. ALLDRITT December 25, 1877 in Wside co., Clydetwp, IL, daughter of THOMAS ALLDRITT and LAVINA HEACOX. She was born August 13, 1859 in Clyde twp., Whiteside Co., IL.

Notes for RICHARD BESWICK BLUE:
Born in S 17 Clyde twp, Whiteside co., IL
1860 WsidecoClytwpIL cen 471 Rich'd 5 IL
1870 WsidecoClytwpIL cen168/168, age 14, IL, with Richard Beswick, age 59, England, farmer, and uncle of Richard Blue.
1880 WsidecoClytwpIL cen/144, this is with Thom. Alldritt, 138/143. His age 24, IL NS En
The couple lived in Mitchell, SD, then moved to Iroquois, SD.
Chapman History of Whiteside county, p. 487: lived S. 22, Clyde twp.. born on S. 17 Clyde twp..

Notes for EMMA A. ALLDRITT:
WsidecoIL marriage record #4621, Aldritt on marriage index.
1880 WsideCly cen/144, age 21, IL MA En
Married by Rev. George T. Crissman, both of Clyde twp., per Sentinel 27Dec1877
WS issue of 9 Jan. 1879 gave birth of son, not named, (Wilford)

Children of RICHARD BLUE and EMMA ALLDRITT are:
i. WILFORD T.[5] BLUE, b. December 16, 1878, Wside co., Clydetwp, IL.

Notes for WILFORD T. BLUE:
WsidecoIL birth record #714, as 'boy'. Birth mentioned in the 9 Jan. 1879 Whiteside Sentinel, Morrison, IL, a boy.
1880 WsidecoClytwpIL cen/144, age 1, IL IL IL

ii. SAMUEL A BLUE, b. January 06, 1885, Wside co., Clydetwp, IL.

Notes for SAMUEL A BLUE:
WsidecoIL birth record #4433, listed as 'boy'.

iii. GIRL BLUE, b. December 27, 1887, Wside co., Clydetwp, IL.

Notes for GIRL BLUE:
WsidecoIL birth record # 5,566, listed as 'Girl'.

Generation No. 5

17. JOHN WILSON[5] BECHTEL *(SARA[4] WILSON, JANE[3] BLUE, DONALD DANIEL[2] BLUE, SR, JOHNNIE[1] BLUE)* was born February 17, 1862 in Wside co., Clydetwp, IL, and died February 22, 1933 in Wside co., Clydetwp, IL. He married SARAH E. DETER 1886 in Whiteside co., IL. She was born August 28, 1858 in PA, and died March 28, 1908 in Wside co., Clydetwp, IL.

Notes for JOHN WILSON BECHTEL:
1870 WsideUstcen 95, age 8, IL
1910 WsidecoUsttwpIL census 47/49, age 48, widowed, IL OH IL
1920 WsidecoMorrisonIL census 152/156, age57, widowed IL OH IL, farm laborer
Bd. Malvern cemetery in plot with parents and wife, Sara E.
COUSIN ONCE REMOVED OF RONALD REAGAN

Notes for SARAH E. DETER:
Bd. Malvern cemetery

Children of JOHN BECHTEL and SARAH DETER are:
    i. ALBERT[6] BECHTEL, b. August 12, 1887, Whiteside co., IL.

        Notes for ALBERT BECHTEL:
        Whiteside co., IL marriage record: #5385 & & 104,677
        1880 Wsideco, 103 Genesee Ave., Morrison, IL age 32, IL IL PA
        1910 Wsideco cen 49, age 22, single, IL IL PA, as `Bert D.'. Farmer
        Never married
        SECOND COUSIN OF RONALD REAGAN

32.   ii. WILLIAM DETER BECHTEL, b. March 11, 1891, Wside co., Clydetwp, IL.
    iii. GEORGE DETER BECHTEL 2, b. March 29, 1892, Wside co., Clydetwp, IL; m. ELOISE; b. 1906, ILL..

        Notes for GEORGE DETER BECHTEL 2:
        WsidecoIL birth record #93,973.
        1910 Wsideco UsticktwpIL cen 49, age 18, farm laborer.
        1920 WsidecoUsttwpIL cen150/154 with wife Eloise
        SECOND COUSIN OF RONALD REAGAN

        Notes for ELOISE:
        1920 WsidecoUsttwpIL census 150/54 , age 24 IL IL IL, wife

33.   iv. IVY MAY BECHTEL, b. May 1898.

18. ELLEN W.[5] BECHTEL (SARA[4] WILSON, JANE[3] BLUE, DONALD DANIEL[2] BLUE, SR, JOHNNIE[1] BLUE) was born July 01, 1866 in Wside co., Clydetwp, IL. She married DAVID EDMOND GERDES January 08, 1888 in Whiteside co., IL, son of HENRY GERDES and REBECCA KALLENOR. He was born December 1864 in Whiteside co., IL, and died January 13, 1934 in Whiteside co., IL.

Notes for ELLEN W. BECHTEL:
1870 WsidecoIL cen95, age 4, IL
1910 Wside census 163 age 43, IL OH IL
COUSIN ONCE REMOVED OF RONALD REAGAN

Notes for DAVID EDMOND GERDES:
WsidcoIL marriage record #7289. Minister of the Dunkard Church, Clyde & Rock Creek, ILL.
1910 WsidecoUsttwpIL census 61/63. David 45, farmer, IL Gr PA
1920 WsidecoClytwpIL. census119/121m age 55, farmer, IL Gr PA
1920 census has Ephraim Bechtel, 86, f in law, OH PA PA and Sarah (Wilson), his wife, 78, IL Sc Sc with David's family
The Clyde Twp. farm was in the family since 1863.

Children of ELLEN BECHTEL and DAVID GERDES are:
34.   i. EPHRAIM LAWRENCE[6] GERDES, b. October 11, 1888, Wside co., Clydetwp, IL.
    ii. REBECCA H GERDES, b. December 05, 1889, WSide co., Clydetwp, IL; d. April 28, 1981, Whiteside co., IL.

        Notes for REBECCA H GERDES:
        WsidecoIL birth record #6,315.
        1910 Wside census 163, age 20, single, servant
        Did not marry.
        1920 Wside Clyde census, with father, 30, servant, IL IL IL
        She lived on the family farm all her life, never married, kept house for her brothers.

        More About REBECCA H GERDES:
        Burial: Malvern cemetery

iii. EDMUND WAYNE GERDES, b. March 02, 1892, Wside co., Clydetwp, IL; d. July 10, 1969, WHiteside co., IL.

Notes for EDMUND WAYNE GERDES:
WsidecoIL birth rcd #7,402
1910 WsideIL census 163, age 17, farm laborer, 'Wayne'
Living at RFD 2, Dixon, IL Feb. 1981, minister
WsidecoIL death records

35. iv. GALEN GLENN GERDES, b. January 1894, Wside co., Clydetwp, IL; d. September 01, 1976, N. Manchester, IN.
v. HENRY RALPH GERDES, b. November 03, 1899, Wside co., Clydetwp, IL; d. February 07, 1981, Morrison, IL.

Notes for HENRY RALPH GERDES:
1910 WsidecoIL, cen 163, age 10
1920 WsidecoIL, cen 121, age 20, laborer
Never married, lived on family farm all his life.

More About HENRY RALPH GERDES:
Burial: Malvern cemetery

vi. LLOYD GERDES, b. August 02, 1903, Wside co., Clydetwp, IL.

Notes for LLOYD GERDES:
WsidecoIL birth record #10,211 as 'boy'. 1920 census lists him as 16.
1910 WsidecoIL census age 6
1920 WsidecoIL cen 121, age 16
Died in truck accident, not married.

vii. VIRGIL E. GERDES, b. August 25, 1905, Wside co., Clydetwp, IL; d. April 23, 1987, Whiteside co., IL.

Notes for VIRGIL E. GERDES:
WsidecoIL birth record #12,024
1910 WsidecoIL cen163 age 4
1920 WsidecoIL cen 121, age 14
WsidecoIL death records
The author has a taped conversation with Virgil in which he remenisces about playing with Ronald Reagan as a child.
Lived on the family farm all his life, enjoyed antique farm machinery, never married.

More About VIRGIL E. GERDES:
Burial: Malvern cemetery

19. JOHN CHARLES[5] WILSON (THOMAS[4], JANE[3] BLUE, DONALD DANIEL[2] BLUE, SR, JOHNNIE[1] BLUE) was born October 09, 1870 in Wsideco, Clyde twp, IL, and died June 21, 1942 in Clinton, IA. He married (1) THELMA LILLIAN KEITH, daughter of HERBERT KEITH and JULIA KRAMER. She was born 1911 in Freeport, Stephenson co., IL. He married (2) CATHERINE STARCK January 16, 1893 in Fulton, Whiteside co., IL, daughter of MATHEW STARCK and ELIZABETH BONZLET. She was born November 1873 in Fulton, Whiteside Co., IL.

Notes for JOHN CHARLES WILSON:
WsidecoIL mar records #8634 for middle name, Katie Stark
Mrs. D Wilson gives death date as 21 June 1942
Death certificate, Hunt/Wiebenga material, night watchman, Mfg. plant
UNCLE OF RONALD REAGAN

Notes for CATHERINE STARCK:
Katie on marriage record, Katherine and Kate on birth records
4 sons, 5 girls, lived in Clinton, Iowa

Children of JOHN WILSON and CATHERINE STARCK are:

i. CHARLES LEROY[6] WILSON, b. August 10, 1894, Whiteside co., IL.

Notes for CHARLES LEROY WILSON:
WsidecoIL birth rcd #8,050
COUSIN OF RONALD REAGAN

36. ii. ELIZABETH MARY WILSON, b. December 15, 1895, Fulton, Whiteside co., IL; d. August 18, 1984, Estes Park, Larimer co., CO.
37. iii. MARY MARGARET WILSON, b. December 19, 1897, Whiteside co., IL; d. February 17, 1985, Clinton, Iowa.
38. iv. EARL CLYDE WILSON, b. November 16, 1902, Muscatine, IA; d. December 20, 1971, Rockford, Winnebago co., IL.
39. v. LEO VERNON WILSON, SR., b. September 16, 1908, Chadwick, Whiteside co., IL; d. February 16, 1975, Key West, FL.
40. vi. JOHN JAMES WILSON, b. May 25, 1905, Iowa; d. March 30, 1970, Freeport, Stephenson co., IL.
vii. JEANETTE WILSON, b. April 22, 1910, Chadwick, Whiteside co., IL; d. August 20, 1925, Sterling, Whiteside co., IL.

Notes for JEANETTE WILSON:
'Explosion started fire with kerosene. Accidently burned to death. Home not destroyed' on death certificate.
COUSIN OF RONALD REAGAN

20. SARA JANE[5] WILSON (THOMAS[4], JANE[3] BLUE, DONALD DANIEL[2] BLUE, SR, JOHNNIE[1] BLUE) was born June 16, 1871 in Clyde twp, Whiteside co., IL, and died March 08, 1920 in White Pigeon, Clyde twp, Whiteside Co., IL. She married (1) HORACE C. SMITH October 30, 1889 in Fulton, Whiteside co., IL, son of JACOB SMITH and MARTHA SIMONDS. He was born 1866 in Maquoketa, Iowa. She married (2) WALTER S. PIERCE January 20, 1904 in Morrison, Whiteside co., IL, son of NATHANIEL PIERCE and ESTHER HUGGETT. He was born January 03, 1865 in Wateska, WI, and died January 04, 1932 in Morrison, IL.

Notes for SARA JANE WILSON:
Place of death not known, but buried in Fulton.
Divorced 31 May 1897. Death certificate says birthdate is June 16, 1871, age at death 48 yrs., 8 mos. 22 days. Cause of death: cerebral hemorrhage.
AUNT OF RONALD REAGAN

More About SARA JANE WILSON:
Burial: Fulton cemetery. Fulton, IL

Notes for HORACE C SMITH:
Wside co IL marriage record #7748
Divorced May 31, 1897. Holley is used in all legal documents.
Teamster at time of marriage to Sarah Jane. Marriage license gives Maquoketa.
Perhaps 'Horace'?
UNCLE OF RONALD REAGAN

Notes for WALTER S. PIERCE:
1900 Clyde twp., Whiteside co., IL census: William Pierce, farmer, Jan. 1865 WI IL En, Eliza wife Dec 1871, md , IL Can VT, Walter S. Pierce, twin brother, farmer Jan 1865 WI
1910 Clyde twp., Whiteside co., IL census: Walter Pierce, retail grocer, 44 WI En En, Jennie wf 318 IL md 6yrs., 5 children living, IL EN, Elsey dau. 5 IL, Vera dau 2 NE

More About WALTER S. PIERCE:
Burial: West Genesee cem, Coleta, IL

Children of SARA WILSON and HORACE SMITH are:
41. i. CHARLES ALFRED[6] SMITH, b. August 22, 1890, Fulton, Whiteside Co., IL; d. December 30, 1968, Sterling,

		Whiteside co., IL.
42.	ii.	HORACE VERNON SMITH, b. August 18, 1892, Fulton, Whiteside Co., IL; d. October 19, 1968, Walden, CO.
43.	iii.	HARRY WILSON SMITH, b. January 11, 1895, Fulton, Whiteside Co., IL; d. December 12, 1967, Morrison, IL.

Children of SARA WILSON and WALTER PIERCE are:

44.	iv.	ELSEY MAE[6] PIERCE, b. September 17, 1904, White Pigeon, Whiteside co., IL; d. November 30, 1993, Whiteside co, Clyde twp., IL.
45.	v.	VERA MARIE PIERCE, b. February 16, 1908, Tekamah, Burt, Nebraska; d. January 30, 1986, White Pigeon, Whiteside co., IL.
	vi.	MARIE MUNDT, b. November 04, 1911; d. September 27, 1978; Foster child; m. GEORGE ERNST.

Notes for MARIE MUNDT:
Foster daughter

21. GEORGE ORVILLE[5] WILSON *(THOMAS[4], JANE[3] BLUE, DONALD DANIEL[2] BLUE, SR, JOHNNIE[1] BLUE)* was born March 02, 1876 in Cordova, Whiteside co., IL, and died April 03, 1951 in Clinton, IA. He married NORA KLOSTERMAN August 03, 1904 in Lyons, Clinton co., IA. She was born 1882.

Notes for GEORGE ORVILLE WILSON:
UNCLE OF RONALD REAGAN

Notes for NORA KLOSTERMAN:
Age 22 at marriage, per certificate

Child of GEORGE WILSON and NORA KLOSTERMAN is:
    i. GERTRUDE[6] WILSON, Adopted child; m. FRANCIS BURMEISTER, Clinton, Iowa.

    Notes for GERTRUDE WILSON:
    Adopted
    COUSIN OF RONALD REAGAN

22. MARY LAVINA[5] WILSON *(THOMAS[4], JANE[3] BLUE, DONALD DANIEL[2] BLUE, SR, JOHNNIE[1] BLUE)* was born April 06, 1879 in Wside co., Clydetwp, IL, and died September 06, 1951 in Minneapolis, Hennepin co., MN. She married LOUIS HERMAN HUNT September 23, 1903 in Fulton, Whiteside co., IL, son of HERMAN HUNT and MINNIE SCHAUB. He was born October 1879 in Aurora, Adams co., IL.

Notes for MARY LAVINA WILSON:
WsidecoIL marriage record #11586 as Mary Lavina. Also on Social Security application of Donald.
AUNT OF RONALD REAGAN

More About MARY LAVINA WILSON:
Burial: Fulton, IL

Notes for LOUIS HERMAN HUNT:
Wside co., IL marriage record #11588
Name from Social Security application of Donald
1880 census shows him 8/12, taken June 1880
AUNT OF RONALD REAGAN

Child of MARY WILSON and LOUIS HUNT is:
    i. DONALD WILSON[6] HUNT, b. March 30, 1909, Quincy, Adams co., IL; d. April 15, 1991, Los Angeles, CA; m. PAULINE CATHERINE BROOKS, June 18, 1944, Los Angeles, CA; b. 1911, New York, NY.

    Notes for DONALD WILSON HUNT:
    Final decree of divorce July 30, 1946.

He died intestate, widower, no children so the court ordered a genealogical search for heirs. The result: A lengthy document to the Superior Court of the State of California, undated in this file, details the relationships of Donald Hunt and the shares to be alloted to the relatives. A genealogy chart is also appended. From this and related material I have entered the various people listed, supplementing genealogy previously shared with me by members of the families and research by me in various county records. Curt J. Gronner, DDS
Birth certificate, Adams co., IL. Ronald Reagan witnessed the wedding.
COUSIN OF RONALD REAGAN

More About DONALD WILSON HUNT:
Burial: Rosedale cemetery, Los Angeles, CA

Notes for PAULINE CATHERINE BROOKS:
Decree of divorce granted her 25 July 1945.

23. NELLIE CLYDE[5] WILSON (*THOMAS[4], JANE[3] BLUE, DONALD DANIEL[2] BLUE, SR, JOHNNIE[1] BLUE*) was born July 24, 1883 in Fulton, Whiteside co., IL, and died July 25, 1962 in Santa Monica, Los Angeles co., CA. She married JOHN EDWARD REAGAN November 18, 1904 in Fulton, Whiteside Co., IL, son of JOHN REAGAN and JENNIE CUSICK. He was born July 13, 1883 in Fulton, Whiteside Co., IL, and died 1941.

Notes for NELLIE CLYDE WILSON:
Marriage date from WsidecoIL marriage rcd #11878

More About NELLIE CLYDE WILSON:
Burial: Calvary cemetery, Santa Monica, CA

Notes for JOHN EDWARD REAGAN:
   Lived with his aunt Margaret Reagan Baldwin after her marriage in 1895 at Buchanan, Iowa. Later Marguerite Chapman also came there after the death of her parents.
   Married in St. Emanuel's Catholic Church, Fulton. Marriage application says 'Jack', marriage certificate says 'John'.
   1910 Tampico twp., Whiteside co., IL census: John E. Reagan 26 IL En IL clerk in store, Nellie C. sife 26 IL IL En md 5 yrs. 1 ch living, Neal son 1 IL.

Children of NELLIE WILSON and JOHN REAGAN are:
      i. JOHN NEIL[6] REAGAN, b. September 16, 1908, Tampico, Wside Co., IL; d. California; m. RUTH HOFFMAN, August 31, 1935, Adel, Dallas Co., IA; b. February 23, 1908, Des Moines, Polk Co., Iowa.

      Notes for JOHN NEIL REAGAN:
      They have no children.

46.   ii. RONALD WILSON REAGAN, b. February 06, 1911, Tampico, Wside Co., IL.

24. MARGARET MAY[5] WILSON (*JOHN[4], JANE[3] BLUE, DONALD DANIEL[2] BLUE, SR, JOHNNIE[1] BLUE*) was born June 10, 1883 in Whiteside co., IL. She married GLENN OTTO WHISTLER October 06, 1908 in WHiteside co., IL. He died June 15, 1962 in Sterling, Whiteside co., IL.

Notes for MARGARET MAY WILSON:
Wside co., IL birth record #4,043, as Maggie May.

Notes for GLENN OTTO WHISTLER:
WsidecoIL marriage record #12,899.
Bd. Lot 7M

More About GLENN OTTO WHISTLER:
Burial: Grove Hill, Morrison, IL

Children of MARGARET WILSON and GLENN WHISTLER are:
47. i. LOIS W.[6] WHISTLER.
48. ii. FLORENCE I. WHISTLER, b. 1912; d. Peoria, IL.

25. PAUL FLETCHER[5] WILSON (*ALEXANDER B[4], JANE[3] BLUE, DONALD DANIEL[2] BLUE, SR, JOHNNIE[1] BLUE*) was born January 1883 in Whiteside co., IL, and died 1964. He married ETTA MAY BRISTLE October 11, 1905 in Whiteside co., IL, daughter of JOHN BRISTLE and ADDIE BODY. She was born November 27, 1883, and died May 14, 1956 in Morrison, IL.

Notes for PAUL FLETCHER WILSON:
Heritage Quest gives his connection. 1920 WsidecoUGrovetwpIL cen186/186 gives age 36, IL IL NY, farmer. His father, Alexander is with them, age 65, IL Sc Sc
1910 WsidecoUGrtwpIL census 60/63, Age 27, IL NY NY, wife May 26 IL IL IL, father Alex 67 Widower NY NY NY 'own income'.
Xerox of Sentinel, Oct. 12, 1905.

Notes for ETTA MAY BRISTLE:
1900 WsidecoIL census277, age 16, as Mary, IL IL IL
1910 WsidecoUGrIL census 60/63, age 26, IL IL IL
WsidecoIL birth certificate #4,020, mother as Addie F. Boda
Whiteside co., IL marriage record #2117.0.

More About ETTA MAY BRISTLE:
Burial: Grove Hill cemetery, Morrison

Children of PAUL WILSON and ETTA BRISTLE are:
49. i. DWIGHT ALVIN[6] WILSON, b. January 24, 1914; d. December 05, 1993, Sterling, Whiteside co., IL.
50. ii. ROBERT BRISTLE WILSON, b. September 12, 1917; d. May 07, 1942.

26. CLIFFORD LEROY[5] GSELL (*MARGARET MAE[4] WILSON, JANE[3] BLUE, DONALD DANIEL[2] BLUE, SR, JOHNNIE[1] BLUE*) was born November 17, 1880 in Whiteside co, Clyde twp., IL, and died August 11, 1951 in Clinton, Iowa. He married EDNA JULIA HAMMER. She was born 1890, and died 1981.

Notes for CLIFFORD LEROY GSELL:
WsidecoIL birth record #1,859, as 'boy'.
Buried lot 31HE

More About CLIFFORD LEROY GSELL:
Burial: Grove Hill cemetery, Morrison

Children of CLIFFORD GSELL and EDNA HAMMER are:
51. i. CLAIR LE ROY[6] GSELL, b. December 30, 1918.
     ii. HOWARD WILSON GSELL, b. June 23, 1920.

27. MAUDE MAE[5] GSELL (*MARGARET MAE[4] WILSON, JANE[3] BLUE, DONALD DANIEL[2] BLUE, SR, JOHNNIE[1] BLUE*) was born November 18, 1884 in WsidClytwpIL, and died August 26, 1966 in Fulton, IL. She married WALTER RICHARD MILNES January 16, 1902 in Whiteside co., IL. He was born July 29, 1877, and died March 05, 1953.

Notes for MAUDE MAE GSELL:
WsidecoIL birth record #3,547 as Maude Mae. Whiteside co., IL marriage record #11,091. Died at Harbor Crest, Fulton. Buried Lot 22W.

More About MAUDE MAE GSELL:

Burial: Grove Hill cemetery, Morrison

Children of MAUDE GSELL and WALTER MILNES are:
- 52. i. LEPHA MAE[6] MILNES, b. April 22, 1903; d. November 30, 1963.
- 53. ii. MARGARET ELIZABETH MILNES, b. June 07, 1913.
- 54. iii. WALTER MILNES, b. June 17, 1919.

28. ESTELLA JANE[5] GSELL *(MARGARET MAE[4] WILSON, JANE[3] BLUE, DONALD DANIEL[2] BLUE, SR, JOHNNIE[1] BLUE)* was born May 27, 1894 in Whiteside co, Clyde twp., IL. She married WILLIAM STAPLETON.

Notes for ESTELLA JANE GSELL:
WsidecoIL birth record #8,060 as Estella Jane.
Day of birth from Carroll

Children of ESTELLA GSELL and WILLIAM STAPLETON are:
- 55. i. GLADYS ELOISE[6] STAPLETON.
- ii. GLEN STAPLETON.

    Notes for GLEN STAPLETON:
    Died at birth

29. ALICE JANE[5] WILSON *(CHARLES DESMOND[4], JANE[3] BLUE, DONALD DANIEL[2] BLUE, SR, JOHNNIE[1] BLUE)* was born April 15, 1897, and died July 05, 1952. She married JAMES WARNER.

Child of ALICE WILSON and JAMES WARNER is:
- 56. i. ROBERT WILSON[6] WARNER.

30. PHOEBE MAE[5] WILSON *(CHARLES DESMOND[4], JANE[3] BLUE, DONALD DANIEL[2] BLUE, SR, JOHNNIE[1] BLUE)* was born May 10, 1899, and died May 10, 1960. She married LLOYD HERROLD.

Notes for LLOYD HERROLD:
Probably another son, also

Children of PHOEBE WILSON and LLOYD HERROLD are:
- i. EDITH[6] HERROLD.
- ii. LLOYD WILSON HERROLD.

31. WINIFRED M.[5] WILSON *(CHARLES DESMOND[4], JANE[3] BLUE, DONALD DANIEL[2] BLUE, SR, JOHNNIE[1] BLUE)* was born September 15, 1901. She married CLARENCE FLACK.

Children of WINIFRED WILSON and CLARENCE FLACK are:
- 57. i. THOMAS OLIVER[6] FLACK, d. 1981.
- 58. ii. TIMOTHY CONRAD FLACK.

Generation No. 6

32. WILLIAM DETER[6] BECHTEL *(JOHN WILSON[5], SARA[4] WILSON, JANE[3] BLUE, DONALD DANIEL[2] BLUE, SR, JOHNNIE[1] BLUE)* was born March 11, 1891 in Wside co., Clydetwp, IL. He married WINNIE MILNES, daughter of FRANK MILNES and MINNIE PAPE. She was born 1894 in ILL..

Notes for WILLIAM DETER BECHTEL:
WsidecoIL birth record #6,845.
1910 WsidecoIL cen 49, age 19, IL IL PA. Farm laborer
1920 WsidecoUsttwpIL census 152/156, age 29 farmer, IL IL PA, Winnie F 26 md wife IL IL IL,

Lucille f 5 S cau IL IL IL, Everett M 1 S son IL IL IL.   [This does not agree with earlier records, perhaps Everett (1) died, another new son was named Everett)
SECOND COUSIN OF RONALD REAGAN

Notes for WINNIE MILNES:
1920 WsideUsttwpcoIL cen156, age 24, wife, IL IL IL

Children of WILLIAM BECHTEL and WINNIE MILNES are:
59.   i.   EVERETT[7] BECHTEL, b. 1905, ILL..
60.   ii.   LUCILLE FERN BECHTEL, b. March 09, 1914, Whiteside co., IL.
61.   iii.   GLENN BECHTEL.

33.   IVY MAY[6] BECHTEL *(JOHN WILSON[5], SARA[4] WILSON, JANE[3] BLUE, DONALD DANIEL[2] BLUE, SR, JOHNNIE[1] BLUE)* was born May 1898. She married WILLIAM LANE.

Notes for IVY MAY BECHTEL:
1910 WsidecoIL cen 49, age 12, farm laborer
SECOND COUSIN OF RONALD REAGAN

Children of IVY BECHTEL and WILLIAM LANE are:
     i.   MILDRED[7] LANE.
     ii.   DOROTHY ANN LANE.
     iii.   WILLIAM LANE.

34.   EPHRAIM LAWRENCE[6] GERDES *(ELLEN W.[5] BECHTEL, SARA[4] WILSON, JANE[3] BLUE, DONALD DANIEL[2] BLUE, SR, JOHNNIE[1] BLUE)* was born October 11, 1888 in Wside co., Clydetwp, IL.

Notes for EPHRAIM LAWRENCE GERDES:
WsidecoIL birth #5,888.   Married, 2 boys, lived near Dixon.

Child of EPHRAIM LAWRENCE GERDES is:
     i.   WAYNE[7] GERDES, b. 1904.

         Notes for WAYNE GERDES:
         Living in Dixon in 1998 at 94, not married

35.   GALEN GLENN[6] GERDES *(ELLEN W.[5] BECHTEL, SARA[4] WILSON, JANE[3] BLUE, DONALD DANIEL[2] BLUE, SR, JOHNNIE[1] BLUE)* was born January 1894 in Wside co., Clydetwp, IL, and died September 01, 1976 in N. Manchester, IN. He married (1) IDA FIKE September 02, 1923. She died September 12, 1923. He married (2) MARETA SHRIDER August 05, 1951.

Notes for GALEN GLENN GERDES:
Children per obituary
Minister, retired.

More About GALEN GLENN GERDES:
Burial: Yellow Creek Cemetery, Pearl City

Children of GALEN GERDES and MARETA SHRIDER are:
     i.   ROBERT[7] GERDES.
     ii.   RUTH GERDES.

36.   ELIZABETH MARY[6] WILSON *(JOHN CHARLES[5], THOMAS[4], JANE[3] BLUE, DONALD DANIEL[2] BLUE, SR, JOHNNIE[1] BLUE)* was born December 15, 1895 in Fulton, Whiteside co., IL, and died August 18, 1984 in Estes Park, Larimer co., CO. She married RAYMOND JAMES DILLON August 24, 1918 in

Chicago, Cook co., ILL. He was born 1898 in Iowa, and died in Chicago, Cook co., IL.

Notes for ELIZABETH MARY WILSON:
Whiteside co., IL birth certificate #101765, #8,416
Death certificate, Hunt material, Wiebenga
COUSIN OF RONALD REAGAN

Notes for RAYMOND JAMES DILLON:
Birth date from birth certificate of child, Katherine
Brakeman , birth cert. 2nd child.
Raymond W. on marriage certificate
COUSIN OF RONALD REAGAN

Children of ELIZABETH WILSON and RAYMOND DILLON are:

    i. MARGARET ELIZA[7] DILLON, b. December 28, 1918, Chicago, Cook co., IL; m. CONANT.

        Notes for MARGARET ELIZA DILLON:
        Twin of Raymond
        COUSIN ONCE REMOVED OF RONALD REAGAN

    ii. RAYMOND JAMES DILLON, b. December 26, 1918, Chicago, Cook co., IL; d. May 15, 1942, Denmark.

        Notes for RAYMOND JAMES DILLON:
        Twin of Margaret, killed in action 18 May 1942 while serving on overseas air operations with 408 (RCAF)
        Squadron. Buried in Vaerlose Churchyard,, Vaerlose, Denmark. From Wiebenga material, Hunt descendants.
        COUSIN ONCE REMOVED OF RONALD REAGAN

        More About RAYMOND JAMES DILLON:
        Burial: Vearlose Churchyard, Vearlose, Denmark

    iii. KATHERINE ANNABELLE DILLON, b. July 03, 1924, Chicago, Cook co., IL.

        Notes for KATHERINE ANNABELLE DILLON:
        COUSIN ONCE REMOVED OF RONALD REAGAN

62.   iv. JOHN CHARLES DILLON, b. October 14, 1921, Clinton, ILL; d. December 21, 1963, Rockford, Winnebago co., IL.

37. MARY MARGARET[6] WILSON *(JOHN CHARLES[5], THOMAS[4], JANE[3] BLUE, DONALD DANIEL[2] BLUE, SR, JOHNNIE[1] BLUE)* was born December 19, 1897 in Whiteside co., IL, and died February 17, 1985 in Clinton, Iowa. She married HARRY JOHN HICKS. He was born 1892 in Morrison, IL, and died Bef. 1985.

Notes for MARY MARGARET WILSON:
WsidecoIL birth rcd #8,769
Death certificate, Clinton co., Iowa, bk 3-7-85, p. 3.
Widowed at time of death
COUSIN OF RONALD REAGAN

More About MARY MARGARET WILSON:
Burial: Grove Hill cemetery, Morrison

Notes for HARRY JOHN HICKS:
Birth certificate shows him as salesman

Children of MARY WILSON and HARRY HICKS are:

    i. EARL CLYDE[7] HICKS, b. September 15, 1929, Freeport, Stephenson co., IL.

        Notes for EARL CLYDE HICKS:

COUSIN, ONCE REMOVED, OF RONALD REAGAN

63. ii. KATHERINE JANE HICKS, b. January 09, 1917, Garden Plain Twp., Whiteside co., IL; d. November 05, 1986, Garden Plain Twp., Whiteside co., IL.
    iii. HARRIET HICKS.

    Notes for HARRIET HICKS:
    COUSIN ONCE REMOVED OF REAGAN REAGAN

38. EARL CLYDE[6] WILSON *(JOHN CHARLES[5], THOMAS[4], JANE[3] BLUE, DONALD DANIEL[2] BLUE, SR, JOHNNIE[1] BLUE)* was born November 16, 1902 in Muscatine, IA, and died December 20, 1971 in Rockford, Winnebago co., IL. He married HELEN MARIE NELSON November 03, 1923 in Crown Point, Lake co., IN, daughter of ELMER NELSON and EDITH JOHANNSEN. She was born December 26, 1904 in Clinton, Clinton co., IA.

Notes for EARL CLYDE WILSON:
Birth certificate gives birth 1902, marriage certificate gives 1901.
Widowed
COUSIN OF RONALD REAGAN

More About EARL CLYDE WILSON:
Burial: Dakota cemetery, Dakota, IL

Children of EARL WILSON and HELEN NELSON are:
  i. EARL CHARLES[7] WILSON, b. February 10, 1925, Chicago, Cook co., IL.

      Notes for EARL CHARLES WILSON:
      COUSIN ONCE REMOVED OF RONALD REAGAN

  ii. JANET MAE WILSON, b. September 29, 1931, Chicago, Cook co., IL; m. (1) 'MALE' WITZ, Bef. 1969; m. (2) DONALD LEROY JOHNSON, July 25, 1970, Rockford, Winnebago co., IL; b. 1937.

      Notes for JANET MAE WILSON:
      Name correction of birth certificate dated 21 April 1976 by Janet.
      Janet md. previous to Johnson marriage, a Witz.
      COUSIN ONCE REMOVED OF RONALD REAGAN

  iii. VAUGHN FAE WILSON, b. November 24, 1936, Freeport, Stephenson co., IL; m. EUGENE UFKEN, November 19, 1955, Dubuque, Dubuque co., IA; b. August 05, 1921, Huron, SD.

      Notes for VAUGHN FAE WILSON:
      COUSIN ONCE REMOVED OF RONALD REAGAN

  iv. RONALD STANLEY WILSON, b. March 30, 1942, Freeport, Stephenson co., IL.

      Notes for RONALD STANLEY WILSON:
      COUSIN ONCE REMOVED OF RONALD REAGAN

39. LEO VERNON[6] WILSON, SR. *(JOHN CHARLES[5], THOMAS[4], JANE[3] BLUE, DONALD DANIEL[2] BLUE, SR, JOHNNIE[1] BLUE)* was born September 16, 1908 in Chadwick, Whiteside co., IL, and died February 16, 1975 in Key West, FL. He married (1) THELMA LILLIAN KEITH, daughter of HERBERT KEITH and JULIA KRAMER. She was born 1911 in Freeport, Stephenson co., IL. He married (2) IONA MAE HOWARD. She was born 1916 in Sheldon Grove, IL. He married (3) IONA JEAN THOMAS February 08, 1957 in Quincy, Adams co., ILL, daughter of CHARLES THOMAS and EMMA MELVIN. She was born 1934 in Kellysville, WV.

Notes for LEO VERNON WILSON, SR.:
His first marriage to Iona Howard??

Business man, Sterling, ILL at time of marriage to Norma jean, age 49, his 3rd marriage. He owned 'Recreation Vehicles Agency' at time of death.
Owned 'Lunch Room' Sterling when Marc was born.
At the time of Marilyn's birth, 1931, he lived at Marion, OH, Thelma at Freeport.
1930 lived at Freeport, ILL
Chadwick birth place from Linda Kay birth certificate
COUSIN OF RONALD REAGAN

More About LEO VERNON WILSON, SR.:
Burial: Oak Knoll cemetery, Sterling, IL

Notes for IONA JEAN THOMAS:
Marriage to Wilson, her first

Children of LEO WILSON and THELMA KEITH are:
  i. JAMES KEITH[7] WILSON, b. January 30, 1938, Galesburg, ILL.

     Notes for JAMES KEITH WILSON:
     Birth certificate #29769, V. 1938, Knox co., IL

  ii. MARILYN JOAN WILSON, b. September 24, 1941, Freeport, Stephenson co., IL; d. December 17, 1951, Beloit, Rock co., IL.

     Notes for MARILYN JOAN WILSON:
     Died in an auto accident

  iii. NAOMI JEAN WILSON, b. February 12, 1930, Freeport, Stephenson co., IL; m. JAMES A CAPONE, September 19, 1954, Freeport, Stephenson co., IL; b. 1921.

Children of LEO WILSON and IONA HOWARD are:
  iv. JEANNETTE LYNN[7] WILSON, b. August 03, 1938, Galesburg, Knox co., ILL; m. JAMES H. PIERCE, October 05, 1956, Rock Falls, Whiteside co., IL; b. 1935, Sterling, Whiteside co., IL.

     Notes for JEANNETTE LYNN WILSON:
     Age 19 at marriage to James Pierce
     Birth certificate, Knox co., IL #40686, V. 1944

     Notes for JAMES H. PIERCE:
     Laborer, Prince Castle Manufactury

  v. TRUDY JEAN WILSON, b. May 18, 1945, Sterling, Whiteside co., IL; m. (1) RANDY GALE GALLENTINE; b. September 06, 1947, Morrison, IL; m. (2) 'MALE' STEVENS.
  vi. LINDA KAY WILSON, b. June 20, 1947, Sterling, Whiteside co., IL; m. (1) 'MALE' TUCKER; m. (2) JAMES JERRY VAN HORN, October 04, 1974, Sterling, Whiteside co., IL; b. 1946, Sterling, Whiteside co., IL; m. (3) DANIEL JOSEPH RYAN, December 18, 1982, Sterling, Whiteside co., IL; b. 1944.

     Notes for LINDA KAY WILSON:
     COUSIN ONCE REMOVED OF RONALD REAGAN

     Notes for DANIEL JOSEPH RYAN:
     Lived at Erie, IL at time of marriage to Linda Kay

  vii. KATHY ELIZABETH WILSON, b. February 24, 1949, Sterling, Whiteside co., IL; m. GAIL A. JELLERICHS, March 28, 1970, Sterling, Whiteside co., IL; b. February 18, 1949, Sterling, Whiteside co., IL.

     Notes for KATHY ELIZABETH WILSON:
     COUSIN ONCE REMOVED OF RONALD REAGAN

     Notes for GAIL A. JELLERICHS:

In military service when married to Kathy

viii. GLENDA JOYCE WILSON, b. September 23, 1957, Sterling, Whiteside co., IL; m. MICHAEL GRANT GIBSON, August 28, 1978, Sterling, Whiteside co., IL; b. September 17, 1957, Sterling, Whiteside co., IL.

Notes for GLENDA JOYCE WILSON:
Married at First Christian Church, Sterling, IL
COUSIN ONCE REMOVED OF RONALD REAGAN

Children of LEO WILSON and IONA THOMAS are:
ix. MARC LEE[7] WILSON, b. October 12, 1940, Sterling, Whiteside co., IL.

Notes for MARC LEE WILSON:
COUSIN ONCE REMOVED OF RONALD REAGAN

x. KIMBERLY ANN WILSON, b. April 05, 1960, Sterling, Whiteside co., IL; m. MATHEW LEE SMITH, August 04, 1979, Rock Falls, Whiteside co., IL; b. February 03, 1960, ILL.
xi. JODY ALLEN WILSON, b. January 24, 1967, Sterling, Whiteside co., IL.

40. JOHN JAMES[6] WILSON (*JOHN CHARLES[5], THOMAS[4], JANE[3] BLUE, DONALD DANIEL[2] BLUE, SR, JOHNNIE[1] BLUE*) was born May 25, 1905 in Iowa, and died March 30, 1970 in Freeport, Stephenson co., IL. He married MARGIE HOMERDING February 04, 1928 in Chicago, Cook co., ILL.

Notes for JOHN JAMES WILSON:
COUSIN OF RONALD REAGAN

More About JOHN JAMES WILSON:
Burial: Calvary cemetery, Freeport, IL

Children of JOHN WILSON and MARGIE HOMERDING are:
i. MARIE[7] WILSON.

Notes for MARIE WILSON:
Signed Father's death certificate, more of signature is unreadable.
COUSIN ONCE REMOVED OF RONALD REAGAN

64. ii. JOHN CHARLES WILSON, JR, b. December 14, 1928, IL; d. October 30, 1983, Mesa, Maricopa co., AZ.

41. CHARLES ALFRED[6] SMITH (*SARA JANE[5] WILSON, THOMAS[4], JANE[3] BLUE, DONALD DANIEL[2] BLUE, SR, JOHNNIE[1] BLUE*) was born August 22, 1890 in Fulton, Whiteside Co., IL, and died December 30, 1968 in Sterling, Whiteside co., IL. He married MABEL MAY SWEIGERT June 26, 1912 in Sterling, Whiteside co., IL, daughter of MILTON SWEIGERT and EVELYN REES. She was born September 18, 1888 in Elroy, Stephenson co., IL, and died February 17, 1972 in Rock Falls, Whiteside co., IL.

Notes for CHARLES ALFRED SMITH:
Retired in 1959 as Manager of Johnston Lumber co., Rock Falls after 50 years of service.
COUSIN OF RONALD REAGAN

More About CHARLES ALFRED SMITH:
Burial: January 02, 1969, Oak Knoll cemetery, Sterling, IL

Notes for MABEL MAY SWEIGERT:
WsidecoIL marriage record # 139760.0

More About MABEL MAY SWEIGERT:
Burial: Oak Knoll cemetery, Sterling, IL

Children of CHARLES SMITH and MABEL SWEIGERT are:
65. i. MILFORD L.⁷ SMITH, b. February 21, 1916, Rock Falls, Whiteside co., IL; d. October 29, 1980, Sterling, Whiteside co., IL.
66. ii. RAYMOND SMITH, b. February 07, 1918, Sterling, Whiteside co., IL; d. March 07, 1997.

42. HORACE VERNON⁶ SMITH *(SARA JANE⁵ WILSON, THOMAS⁴, JANE³ BLUE, DONALD DANIEL²BLUE, SR, JOHNNIE¹ BLUE)* was born August 18, 1892 in Fulton, Whiteside Co., IL, and died October 19, 1968 in Walden, CO. He married DOSSIE MAY MEAKINS February 20, 1915 in Morrison, IL. She was born July 17, 1890 in Coleta, Whiteside co., IL, and died December 03, 1972.

Notes for HORACE VERNON SMITH:
WsidecolL birth record #7,422, Supt. of Public Aid Department, Whiteside co..
COUSIN OF RONALD REAGAN

More About HORACE VERNON SMITH:
Burial: Grove Hill cemetery, Morrison

Notes for DOSSIE MAY MEAKINS:
School teacher

More About DOSSIE MAY MEAKINS:
Burial: Grove Hill cemetery, Morrison

Children of HORACE SMITH and DOSSIE MEAKINS are:
67. i. ROBERT CLARE⁷ SMITH, b. November 05, 1917, Sterling, Whiteside co., IL.
68. ii. GENE MEAKIN SMITH, b. March 27, 1922, Sterling, Whiteside co., IL; d. July 09, 1995.

43. HARRY WILSON⁶ SMITH *(SARA JANE⁵ WILSON, THOMAS⁴, JANE³ BLUE, DONALD DANIEL²BLUE, SR, JOHNNIE¹ BLUE)* was born January 11, 1895 in Fulton, Whiteside Co., IL, and died December 12, 1967 in Morrison, IL. He married HULDA PHILENA GOFF January 26, 1916 in Fulton, Whiteside co., IL, daughter of LYMAN GOFF and DELLA BULL. She was born April 20, 1893, and died December 14, 1974.

Notes for HARRY WILSON SMITH:
Owned auto body and paint shop
At time of marriage, lived at Ashton, IL, railroad employee. In 1922 he lived at Elmhurst, Il and was a signal maintainer, C&NW Ry..
COUSIN OF RONALD REAGAN

More About HARRY WILSON SMITH:
Burial: Grove Hill cemetery, Morrison

More About HULDA PHILENA GOFF:
Burial: Grove Hill cemetery, Morrison

Child of HARRY SMITH and HULDA GOFF is:
69. i. HARRY WILSON⁷ SMITH, JR, b. January 20, 1922, Oak Park, Cook co., IL.

44. ELSEY MAE⁶ PIERCE *(SARA JANE⁵ WILSON, THOMAS⁴, JANE³ BLUE, DONALD DANIEL²BLUE, SR, JOHNNIE¹ BLUE)* was born September 17, 1904 in White Pigeon, Whiteside co., IL, and died November 30, 1993 in Whiteside co, Clyde twp., IL. She married CARL B. WALTERS May 20, 1925 in Jordan, Whiteside co., IL. He was born October 22, 1901 in White Pigeon, Whiteside co., IL, and died August 07, 1987.

Notes for ELSEY MAE PIERCE:

Birth certificate says '4th child of this mother'. Vicky Wiebenga / Hunt material, 3 half brothers from Mother's Smith marriage.
She provided much of the information to the Heritage Quest author, Michael F. Pollock.

More About ELSEY MAE PIERCE:
Burial: West Genesee cem., Whiteside co.

More About CARL B. WALTERS:
Burial: West Genesee cem, Coleta, IL

Child of ELSEY PIERCE and CARL WALTERS is:
70.   i.   HAROLD EDWARD[7] WALTERS, b. December 02, 1925, White Pigeon, Whiteside co., IL; d. February 19, 1988, Morrison, IL.

45. VERA MARIE[6] PIERCE (*SARA JANE[5] WILSON, THOMAS[4], JANE[3] BLUE, DONALD DANIEL[2] BLUE, SR, JOHNNIE[1] BLUE*) was born February 16, 1908 in Tekamah, Burt, Nebraska, and died January 30, 1986 in White Pigeon, Whiteside co., IL. She married REINHARD F. HABBEN April 03, 1933 in Somonauk, DeKalb co., IL, son of EILT HABBEN and MARIE HOLMRICK. He was born April 30, 1902 in Frisia, nr. Bremerhaven, Germany, and died March 22, 1980 in Morrison, IL.

Notes for VERA MARIE PIERCE:
Married at St. Johns Lutheran Church, Somonauk, IL.
COUSIN OF RONALD REAGAN

More About VERA MARIE PIERCE:
Burial: West Genesee cem, Coleta, IL

Notes for REINHARD F. HABBEN:
Became a US citizen 9 Oct. 1931, Chicago, IL.

More About REINHARD F. HABBEN:
Burial: West Genesee cem, Coleta, IL

Children of VERA PIERCE and REINHARD HABBEN are:
71.   i.   MERNA JOY[7] HABBEN, b. October 12, 1933, Coleta, Whiteside co., IL.
72.   ii.   NORMAN WALTER HABBEN, b. September 10, 1935, Coleta, Whiteside co., IL.
73.   iii.   RONALD LEE HABBEN, b. July 17, 1938, Coleta, Whiteside co., IL.
74.   iv.   MILFORD GENE HABBEN, b. July 04, 1940, Coleta, Whiteside co., IL.
75.   v.   VELMA JANE HABBEN, b. April 10, 1943, Morrison, IL.
76.   vi.   JUDITH MAY HABBEN, b. April 28, 1946, Morrison, IL.
77.   vii.   CAROL ANN HABBEN, b. June 04, 1948, Morrison, IL.
78.   viii.   BEVERLY JOAN HABBEN, b. July 10, 1952, Morrison, IL.
79.   ix.   DONNA ELAINE HABBEN, b. August 04, 1954, Morrison, IL.

46. RONALD WILSON[6] REAGAN (*NELLIE CLYDE[5] WILSON, THOMAS[4], JANE[3] BLUE, DONALD DANIEL[2] BLUE, SR, JOHNNIE[1] BLUE*) was born February 06, 1911 in Tampico, Wside Co., IL. He married (1) SARA JANE FULKS January 16, 1940 in Glendale, CA. She was born January 04, 1914 in St. Joseph, MO. He married (2) ANNE FRANCES ROBBINS March 04, 1952 in North Hollywood, CA, daughter of KENNETH ROBBINS and EDITH LUCKETT. She was born July 06, 1923 in New York, NY.

Notes for RONALD WILSON REAGAN:
    They were divorced June 28, 1948. Michael was adopted. A daughter died in infancy.
    During his 1981 visit to Scotland, Reagan became an Honorary Keeper of the Keepers of the Quaich, a society of connoisseurs of Scotch whiskey. He was unaware of his relationship to Johnnie Blue, the last moonshine distiller on the Scottish peninsula of Kintyre. From the Chicago Tribune of Oct 21, 1981. This article also gives Claudio Wilson, a weaver [whom see] and Peggy Downey [Downie] whom he married in 1807 as the parents of John Wilson,

grandparents of Thomas. Claudio married a second time. [see Claudio 1787]

Notes for SARA JANE FULKS:
Also known as Jane Durrell and Jane Wyman

Notes for ANNE FRANCES ROBBINS:
Her legal name was 'Nancy Davis' through adoption.

Children of RONALD REAGAN and SARA FULKS are:
       i. MAUREEN ELIZABETH⁷ REAGAN, b. January 04, 1941, Los Angeles, CA.
80.   ii. MICHAEL REAGAN, b. March 18, 1945.

Children of RONALD REAGAN and ANNE ROBBINS are:
       iii. PATRICIA⁷ REAGAN, b. October 21, 1952.
       iv. RONALD PRESCOTT REAGAN, b. May 20, 1958; m. DORIA PALMIER, November 24, 1980.

47. LOIS W.⁶ WHISTLER *(MARGARET MAY⁵ WILSON, JOHN⁴, JANE³ BLUE, DONALD DANIEL²BLUE, SR, JOHNNIE¹ BLUE)* She married WHITFORD MITCHELL.

Children of LOIS WHISTLER and WHITFORD MITCHELL are:
81.   i. MARTHA ANN⁷ MITCHELL.
82.   ii. JOHN WILSON MITCHELL.
83.   iii. JANE WHITFORD MITCHELL.

48. FLORENCE I.⁶ WHISTLER *(MARGARET MAY⁵ WILSON, JOHN⁴, JANE³ BLUE, DONALD DANIEL²BLUE, SR, JOHNNIE¹ BLUE)* was born 1912, and died in Peoria, IL. She married GEORGE L MARR. He died in Peoria, IL.

Children of FLORENCE WHISTLER and GEORGE MARR are:
84.   i. BARBARA⁷ MARR.
       ii. GEORGE MICHAEL MARR.

49. DWIGHT ALVIN⁶ WILSON *(PAUL FLETCHER⁵, ALEXANDER B⁴, JANE³ BLUE, DONALD DANIEL²BLUE, SR, JOHNNIE¹ BLUE)* was born January 24, 1914, and died December 05, 1993 in Sterling, Whiteside co., IL. He married JANICE LUCILLE MATHEW December 25, 1937 in Sterling, Whiteside co., IL. She was born November 30, 1917.

Notes for DWIGHT ALVIN WILSON:
WsidecoUGtwpIL census 186
WsidecoIL birth record #17,965
Retired from 1st National Bank, Sterling, Jan. 1, 1978.

More About DWIGHT ALVIN WILSON:
Burial: Grove Hill cemetery, Morrison

Children of DWIGHT WILSON and JANICE MATHEW are:
85.   i. JUDITH SUZANE⁷ WILSON, b. November 21, 1942.
86.   ii. ROBERT THOMAS WILSON, b. June 29, 1944.

50. ROBERT BRISTLE⁶ WILSON *(PAUL FLETCHER⁵, ALEXANDER B⁴, JANE³ BLUE, DONALD DANIEL²BLUE, SR, JOHNNIE¹ BLUE)* was born September 12, 1917, and died May 07, 1942. He married MAXINE JOY BARRETT March 22, 1940, daughter of HARVEY BARRETT and EDNA LAWTON. She was born August 01, 1920, and died April 11, 1997 in Cedar Rapids, Iowa.

More About ROBERT BRISTLE WILSON:
Burial: Grove Hill cemetery, Morrison

Child of ROBERT WILSON and MAXINE BARRETT is:
87.   i.   DEBORAH ANN[7] WILSON, b. February 09, 1941.

51. CLAIR LE ROY[6] GSELL *(CLIFFORD LEROY[5], MARGARET MAE[4] WILSON, JANE[3] BLUE, DONALD DANIEL[2] BLUE, SR, JOHNNIE[1] BLUE)* was born December 30, 1918. He married MARY WATSON.

Children of CLAIR GSELL and MARY WATSON are:
88.   i.   STEVEN ALLEN[7] GSELL, b. April 24, 1939.
        ii.   RICHARD LEE GSELL, b. December 17, 1945; m. SHIRLEY MANNING.
89.   iii.   SUE ELLEN GSELL, b. September 25, 1955.

52. LEPHA MAE[6] MILNES *(MAUDE MAE[5] GSELL, MARGARET MAE[4] WILSON, JANE[3] BLUE, DONALD DANIEL[2] BLUE, SR, JOHNNIE[1] BLUE)* was born April 22, 1903, and died November 30, 1963. She married ANDREW F. WITT. He was born December 16, 1898.

Children of LEPHA MILNES and ANDREW WITT are:
90.   i.   DONNA JEAN[7] WITT, b. April 09, 1933.
        ii.   MAJOR SANDRA MAE WITT, b. April 13, 1938.

            Notes for MAJOR SANDRA MAE WITT:
            Major

91.   iii.   DR. HARLAN ANDREW WITT, b. April 27, 1946.

53. MARGARET ELIZABETH[6] MILNES *(MAUDE MAE[5] GSELL, MARGARET MAE[4] WILSON, JANE[3] BLUE, DONALD DANIEL[2] BLUE, SR, JOHNNIE[1] BLUE)* was born June 07, 1913. She married IVAN RALPH CARROLL. He was born October 12, 1907, and died June 25, 1950.

Children of MARGARET MILNES and IVAN CARROLL are:
92.   i.   DAVID IVAN[7] CARROLL, b. January 02, 1938.
93.   ii.   TERRY DEE CARROLL, b. January 03, 1946.

54. WALTER[6] MILNES *(MAUDE MAE[5] GSELL, MARGARET MAE[4] WILSON, JANE[3] BLUE, DONALD DANIEL[2] BLUE, SR, JOHNNIE[1] BLUE)* was born June 17, 1919. He married BEULAH VEY NAFTZGER. She was born July 03, 1918.

Children of WALTER MILNES and BEULAH NAFTZGER are:
        i.   WANDA VEY[7] MILNES, b. December 29, 1943.

            Notes for WANDA VEY MILNES:
            Never married.

94.   ii.   DIANE LOUISE MILNES, b. September 04, 1945.
95.   iii.   THOMAS BRENT MILNES, b. September 01, 1950.

55. GLADYS ELOISE[6] STAPLETON *(ESTELLA JANE[5] GSELL, MARGARET MAE[4] WILSON, JANE[3] BLUE, DONALD DANIEL[2] BLUE, SR, JOHNNIE[1] BLUE)* She married ERNEST VOS.

Children of GLADYS STAPLETON and ERNEST VOS are:
96.   i.   ARLYN[7] VOS, b. May 03, 1940.
97.   ii.   LARRY VOS.
        iii.   LAURI ANN VOS, m. ROBIN N GOLDSMITH.

56. ROBERT WILSON[6] WARNER *(ALICE JANE[5] WILSON, CHARLES DESMOND[4], JANE[3] BLUE, DONALD DANIEL[2] BLUE, SR, JOHNNIE[1] BLUE)*

Children of ROBERT WILSON WARNER are:
  i. JAMES[7] WARNER.
  ii. CATHERINE WARNER.

57. THOMAS OLIVER[6] FLACK *(WINIFRED M.[5] WILSON, CHARLES DESMOND[4], JANE[3] BLUE, DONALD DANIEL[2] BLUE, SR, JOHNNIE[1] BLUE)* died 1981.

Child of THOMAS OLIVER FLACK is:
  i. PAMELA[7] FLACK.

58. TIMOTHY CONRAD[6] FLACK *(WINIFRED M.[5] WILSON, CHARLES DESMOND[4], JANE[3] BLUE, DONALD DANIEL[2] BLUE, SR, JOHNNIE[1] BLUE)*

Children of TIMOTHY CONRAD FLACK are:
  i. KATHRYN[7] FLACK.
  ii. WILLIAM C. FLACK.

Generation No. 7

59. EVERETT[7] BECHTEL *(WILLIAM DETER[6], JOHN WILSON[5], SARA[4] WILSON, JANE[3] BLUE, DONALD DANIEL[2] BLUE, SR, JOHNNIE[1] BLUE)* was born 1905 in ILL.. He married CARLENE MCKEE.

Notes for EVERETT BECHTEL:
1920 WsidecoIL cen 156 Ustick

Children of EVERETT BECHTEL and CARLENE MCKEE are:
  i. GARY[8] BECHTEL, m. PATRICIA WIERSEMA.
  ii. BONNIE BECHTEL, m. DOUGLAS BUSH.

60. LUCILLE FERN[7] BECHTEL *(WILLIAM DETER[6], JOHN WILSON[5], SARA[4] WILSON, JANE[3] BLUE, DONALD DANIEL[2] BLUE, SR, JOHNNIE[1] BLUE)* was born March 09, 1914 in Whiteside co., IL. She married LYLE NICE.

Notes for LUCILLE FERN BECHTEL:
WsidecoIL birth record # 17,783.
SECOND COUSIN ONCE REMOVED OF RONALD REAGAN

Children of LUCILLE BECHTEL and LYLE NICE are:
98. i. ELWIN[8] NICE.
99. ii. MARJORIE NICE.

61. GLENN[7] BECHTEL *(WILLIAM DETER[6], JOHN WILSON[5], SARA[4] WILSON, JANE[3] BLUE, DONALD DANIEL[2] BLUE, SR, JOHNNIE[1] BLUE)* He married RHEA GREEN.

Children of GLENN BECHTEL and RHEA GREEN are:
  i. GLENDA[8] BECHTEL, m. DARREL NICKE.
  ii. ELLEN BECHTEL, m. GREG PESSMAN.
  iii. SCOTT BECHTEL, m. SANDRA WALTERS.
  iv. CAROL BECHTEL, m. JOSEPH HIGH, July 17, 1876, Whiteside co., IL.

Notes for CAROL BECHTEL:
Whiteside co., IL marriage record #4216.

62. JOHN CHARLES[7] DILLON *(ELIZABETH MARY[6] WILSON, JOHN CHARLES[5], THOMAS[4], JANE[3] BLUE, DONALD DANIEL[2] BLUE, SR, JOHNNIE[1] BLUE)* was born October 14, 1921 in Clinton, ILL, and died December 21, 1963 in Rockford, Winnebago co., IL. He married AMY ADELE ANDERSON July 11, 1942 in Peoria, Peoria co., ILL, daughter of ALEX ANDERSON and EDNA CLARK. She was born 1924 in Freeport, Stephenson co., IL.

Notes for JOHN CHARLES DILLON:
Died in Highway accident.
COUSIN ONCE REMOVED OF RONALD REAGAN

Child of JOHN DILLON and AMY ANDERSON is:
  i. JACKLYN ANN[8] DILLON, b. August 27, 1943, Freeport, Stephenson co., IL; m. DAVID ROBERT SPRINGMAN, October 13, 1978, Freeport, Stephenson co., IL; b. June 20, 1944, Freeport, Stephenson co., IL.

   Notes for JACKLYN ANN DILLON:
   COUSIN, ONCE REMOVED, OF RONALD REAGAN

63. KATHERINE JANE[7] HICKS *(MARY MARGARET[6] WILSON, JOHN CHARLES[5], THOMAS[4], JANE[3] BLUE, DONALD DANIEL[2] BLUE, SR, JOHNNIE[1] BLUE)* was born January 09, 1917 in Garden Plain Twp., Whiteside co., IL, and died November 05, 1986 in Garden Plain Twp., Whiteside co., IL. She married (1) ADOLPH G. KUNAVICH. She married (2) THEODORE DINGMAN Aft. 1946.

Notes for KATHERINE JANE HICKS:
Divorced from Kunavich 1946.
Divorced from Dingman 1960 and resumed her maiden name, Kay J. Hicks, per Ronald G. Kunavich affidavit.
COUSIN, ONCE REMOVED, OF RONALD REAGAN

Notes for ADOLPH G. KUNAVICH:
Divorce 1946 per affidavit of Ronald G. Kunavich

Children of KATHERINE HICKS and ADOLPH KUNAVICH are:
  i. RONALD GEORGE[8] KUNAVICH, b. April 25, 1942, Clinton, Clinton co., IA.

   Notes for RONALD GEORGE KUNAVICH:
   Was 'DPCM Ronald G. Kunavich CM/C' aboard the USS O'Brien DD-975' in Oct. 1987.
   COUSIN TWICE REMOVED FROM RONALD REAGAN

100. ii. JAMES JOSEPH KUNAVICH, b. October 22, 1943, Clinton, Clinton co., IA; d. April 24, 1971, Oaklawn, Cook co., IL.

64. JOHN CHARLES[7] WILSON, JR *(JOHN JAMES[6], JOHN CHARLES[5], THOMAS[4], JANE[3] BLUE, DONALD DANIEL[2] BLUE, SR, JOHNNIE[1] BLUE)* was born December 14, 1928 in IL, and died October 30, 1983 in Mesa, Maricopa co., AZ. He married (1) O. DARLENE RAINS. He married (2) SHIRLEY GIBSON February 21, 1948 in Freeport, Stephenson co., IL. She was born 1930 in Freeport, Stephenson co., IL. He married (3) GLENDA REITER January 20, 1958 in Alcorn co, MS, daughter of RODNEY REITER and ZELDA. She was born 1937.

Notes for JOHN CHARLES WILSON, JR:
Cremated.
COUSIN ONCE REMOVED OF RONALD REAGAN

Notes for O DARLENE RAINS:
She gave the information on the death certificate of John, Jr.

Notes for GLENDA REITER:
Noeske marriage assumed from marriage application with John Wilson. Marriage certificate, Alcorn co., MS.

Child of JOHN WILSON and O. RAINS is:
    i. JOHN CHARLES[8] WILSON III, b. June 09, 1948, Freeport, Stephenson co., IL.

    Notes for JOHN CHARLES WILSON III:
    Listed as 'Jr.' on his birth certificate.
    COUSIN TWICE REMOVED OF RONALD REAGAN

65. MILFORD L [7] SMITH *(CHARLES ALFRED[6], SARA JANE[5] WILSON, THOMAS[4], JANE[3] BLUE, DONALD DANIEL[2]BLUE, SR, JOHNNIE[1] BLUE)* was born February 21, 1916 in Rock Falls, Whiteside co., IL, and died October 29, 1980 in Sterling, Whiteside co., IL. He married MARIAN D. SCHNEIDER June 01, 1938 in Sterling, Whiteside co., IL, daughter of JOSEPH SCHNEIDER and DELLA MACQUAY. She was born 1916 in Coleta, Whiteside co., IL.

Notes for MILFORD L. SMITH:
Served in the military WW II. Cashier, International Harvester.
COUSIN ONCE REMOVED OF RONALD REAGAN

More About MILFORD L. SMITH:
Burial: Oak Knoll cemetery, Sterling, IL

More About MARIAN D. SCHNEIDER:
Burial: Oak Knoll cemetery, Sterling, IL

Children of MILFORD SMITH and MARIAN SCHNEIDER are:
    i. GORDON M.[8] SMITH, b. October 31, 1940, Rock Falls, Whiteside co., IL; d. September 10, 1971, Rock Falls, Whiteside co., IL.

    Notes for GORDON M SMITH:
    Not married
    COUSIN TWICE REMOVED OF RONALD REAGAN

    More About GORDON M SMITH:
    Burial: Oak Knoll cemetery, Sterling, IL

    ii. DENNIS SMITH, b. September 14, 1943, Rock Falls, Whiteside co., IL; d. January 28, 1983, Morrison, Whiteside co., IL.

    Notes for DENNIS SMITH:
    Not married
    COUSIN TWICE REMOVED OF RONALD REAGAN

    More About DENNIS SMITH:
    Burial: Oak Knoll cem.

66. RAYMOND[7] SMITH *(CHARLES ALFRED[6], SARA JANE[5] WILSON, THOMAS[4], JANE[3] BLUE, DONALD DANIEL[2]BLUE, SR, JOHNNIE[1] BLUE)* was born February 07, 1918 in Sterling, Whiteside co., IL, and died March 07, 1997. He married MADELINE WEYRAUCH August 27, 1942.

Notes for RAYMOND SMITH:
FIRST COUSIN ONCE REMOVED OF RONALD REAGAN

More About RAYMOND SMITH:
Burial: Oak Knoll cemetery, Sterling, IL

Children of RAYMOND SMITH and MADELINE WEYRAUCH are:
    i. HUDSON B.[8] SMITH, b. March 12, 1944.

        Notes for HUDSON B. SMITH:
        COUSIN TWICE REMOVED OF RONALD REAGAN

    ii. KAREN SMITH, b. April 1947.

        Notes for KAREN SMITH:
        COUSIN TWICE REMOVED OF RONALD REAGAN

    iii. SALLY SMITH, b. May 1950.

        Notes for SALLY SMITH:
        COUSIN TWICE REMOVED OF RONALD REAGAN

67. ROBERT CLARE[7] SMITH (*HORACE VERNON*[6], *SARA JANE*[5] *WILSON*, *THOMAS*[4], *JANE*[3] *BLUE*, *DONALD DANIEL*[2]*BLUE, SR, JOHNNIE*[1] *BLUE*) was born November 05, 1917 in Sterling, Whiteside co., IL. He married (1) DOROTHY BRICKLEY. She was born June 20, 1920, and died May 17, 1984. He married (2) JEANNE WEBB January 11, 1935.

Notes for ROBERT CLARE SMITH:
COUSIN ONCE REMOVED OF RONALD REAGAN

Children of ROBERT SMITH and DOROTHY BRICKLEY are:
101.   i. TERRY[8] SMITH, b. November 20, 1946.
102.   ii. VICKI SMITH, b. March 01, 1952.

68. GENE MEAKIN[7] SMITH (*HORACE VERNON*[6], *SARA JANE*[5] *WILSON*, *THOMAS*[4], *JANE*[3] *BLUE*, *DONALD DANIEL*[2]*BLUE, SR, JOHNNIE*[1] *BLUE*) was born March 27, 1922 in Sterling, Whiteside co., IL, and died July 09, 1995. He married JANET JANKE February 09, 1946 in Morrison, IL, daughter of HERBERT JANKE and EMMA KLEIST. She was born September 20, 1919 in Weyauwega, WI, and died October 24, 1989 in Sterling, Whiteside co., IL.

Notes for GENE MEAKIN SMITH:
COUSIN ONCE REMOVED OF RONALD REAGAN

Children of GENE SMITH and JANET JANKE are:
103.   i. DAVID[8] SMITH, b. May 21, 1948.
104.   ii. THOMAS SMITH, b. February 25, 1952.
105.   iii. NANCY SMITH, b. October 12, 1955.

69. HARRY WILSON[7] SMITH, JR (*HARRY WILSON*[6], *SARA JANE*[5] *WILSON*, *THOMAS*[4], *JANE*[3] *BLUE*, *DONALD DANIEL*[2]*BLUE, SR, JOHNNIE*[1] *BLUE*) was born January 20, 1922 in Oak Park, Cook co., IL. He married JEAN.

Notes for HARRY WILSON SMITH, JR:
Living in TN, 2000.
COUSIN ONCE REMOVED OF RONALD REAGAN

Children of HARRY SMITH and JEAN are:
    i. DALE[8] SMITH, m. NANCY LEE SPRAGUE, July 02, 1960.

Notes for DALE SMITH:
COUSIN TWICE REMOVED OF RONALD REAGAN

  ii. BARBARA SMITH.

Notes for BARBARA SMITH:
COUSIN TWICE REMOVED OF RONALD REAGAN

  iii. DEAN SMITH.

Notes for DEAN SMITH:
COUSIN TWICE REMOVED OF RONALD REAGAN

70. HAROLD EDWARD[7] WALTERS *(ELSEY MAE[6] PIERCE, SARA JANE[5] WILSON, THOMAS[4], JANE[3] BLUE, DONALD DANIEL[2] BLUE, SR, JOHNNIE[1] BLUE)* was born December 02, 1925 in White Pigeon, Whiteside co., IL, and died February 19, 1988 in Morrison, IL. He married RUTH JANE STUART October 22, 1945 in Morrison, IL. She was born July 07, 1924 in Morrison, IL.

More About HAROLD EDWARD WALTERS:
Burial: West Genesee cem., Whiteside co.

Children of HAROLD WALTERS and RUTH STUART are:
106. i. PAUL EDWARD[8] WALTERS, b. May 03, 1946, Morrison, IL.
107. ii. HARLAN GENE WALTERS, b. February 05, 1948, Morrison, IL.
108. iii. JANE KAYE WALTERS, b. April 16, 1950, Morrison, IL.
  iv. RHONDA RUTH WALTERS, b. September 15, 1952, Morrison, IL; m. DANNY KENNEDY, December 02, 1977, Morrison, IL; b. August 27, 1946.

Notes for RHONDA RUTH WALTERS:
Divorced Aug. 30, 1978

Notes for DANNY KENNEDY:
Divorced Aug. 30, 1978

109. v. DAWN GAIL WALTERS, b. March 19, 1962, Morrison, IL.
110. vi. PHILIP DALE WALTERS, b. July 15, 1968, Morrison, IL.

71. MERNA JOY[7] HABBEN *(VERA MARIE[6] PIERCE, SARA JANE[5] WILSON, THOMAS[4], JANE[3] BLUE, DONALD DANIEL[2] BLUE, SR, JOHNNIE[1] BLUE)* was born October 12, 1933 in Coleta, Whiteside co., IL. She married (1) CLYDE ELMER JANVRIN September 02, 1956 in Sterling, Whiteside co., IL. He was born August 24, 1925 in Morrison, IL, and died May 20, 1970 in Morrison, IL. She married (2) ROBERT MICHAEL MUSCHAL Aft. 1971, son of NICHOLAS MUSCHAL and KATHERINE MARX. He was born June 20, 1940 in Chicago, IL.

Notes for MERNA JOY HABBEN:
Md. in St. Johns Lutheran Church, Sterling
Dairy farmer.
Mrs. Merna Habben-Muschal has been of tremendous help in furnishing material and in proofreading my pages. If there are errors, blame me. CJG
COUSIN ONCE REMOVED OF RONALD REAGAN

Notes for CLYDE ELMER JANVRIN:
Dairy farmer, served in the Army.

More About CLYDE ELMER JANVRIN:
Burial: South Clyde cemetery

Notes for ROBERT MICHAEL MUSCHAL:

Painter. Marriage to Merna was his second marriage, also her 2nd.
Auditor and Inspector.   Married in United Methodist Church, Morrison, IL.

Children of MERNA HABBEN and CLYDE JANVRIN are:
- i. ERIC PAUL[8] JANVRIN, b. August 31, 1958, Morrison, IL; m. CAROL TRIMBLE, October 10, 1986, Fulton, Whiteside co., IL; b. November 06, 1956, Fulton, IL.
- 111. ii. KURT REINHARD JANVRIN, b. August 04, 1960, Morrison, IL.
- 112. iii. BRUCE CLYDE JANVRIN, b. December 22, 1961, Morrison, IL.
- 113. iv. ARON KYLE JANVRIN, b. November 13, 1964, Morrison, IL.

72. NORMAN WALTER[7] HABBEN *(VERA MARIE[6] PIERCE, SARA JANE[5] WILSON, THOMAS[4], JANE[3] BLUE, DONALD DANIEL[2] BLUE, SR, JOHNNIE[1] BLUE)* was born September 10, 1935 in Coleta, Whiteside co., IL. He married NORMA JEAN COOK June 02, 1956 in Rock Falls, Whiteside co., IL. She was born June 02, 1937 in Rock Falls, Whiteside co., IL.

Notes for NORMAN WALTER HABBEN:
COUSIN ONCE REMOVED OF RONALD REAGAN

Children of NORMAN HABBEN and NORMA COOK are:
- 114. i. RHONDA JANE[8] HABBEN, b. June 24, 1957.
- ii. ROBERT ALLEN HABBEN, b. August 02, 1958, Morrison, IL.
- 115. iii. GENE LEROY HABBEN, b. July 07, 1960, Morrison, IL.
- 116. iv. SARA LEANNE HABBEN, b. March 09, 1967, Morrison, IL.

73. RONALD LEE[7] HABBEN *(VERA MARIE[6] PIERCE, SARA JANE[5] WILSON, THOMAS[4], JANE[3] BLUE, DONALD DANIEL[2] BLUE, SR, JOHNNIE[1] BLUE)* was born July 17, 1938 in Coleta, Whiteside co., IL. He married NANCY JOAN BIELEMA September 02, 1961 in Fulton, Whiteside co., IL. She was born November 15, 1940 in Fulton, IL.

Notes for RONALD LEE HABBEN:
COUSIN ONCE REMOVED OF RONALD REAGAN

Children of RONALD HABBEN and NANCY BIELEMA are:
- 117. i. DANIEL LEE[8] HABBEN, b. June 26, 1962, Morrison, IL.
- 118. ii. DEBRA LOU HABBEN, b. September 17, 1964, Morrison, IL.
- iii. DAVID ALLEN HABBEN, b. November 08, 1978, Morrison, IL.

74. MILFORD GENE[7] HABBEN *(VERA MARIE[6] PIERCE, SARA JANE[5] WILSON, THOMAS[4], JANE[3] BLUE, DONALD DANIEL[2] BLUE, SR, JOHNNIE[1] BLUE)* was born July 04, 1940 in Coleta, Whiteside co., IL. He married JOANNE PATRICK July 06, 1964 in San Jose, Santa Clara co., CA. She was born May 23, 1943 in Santa Clara, CA.

Notes for MILFORD GENE HABBEN:
COUSIN ONCE REMOVED OF RONALD REAGAN

Children of MILFORD HABBEN and JOANNE PATRICK are:
- 119. i. CATHERINE JEAN[8] HABBEN, b. May 08, 1966, Morrison, IL.
- ii. DONALD PATRICK HABBEN, b. April 08, 1969, Morrison, IL; m. LISA FREDRICK, November 10, 1990, Dixon, Lee co., IL.

   Notes for DONALD PATRICK HABBEN:
   Divorced, no children.

75. VELMA JANE[7] HABBEN *(VERA MARIE[6] PIERCE, SARA JANE[5] WILSON, THOMAS[4], JANE[3] BLUE, DONALD DANIEL[2] BLUE, SR, JOHNNIE[1] BLUE)* was born April 10, 1943 in Morrison, IL. She married WILLIAM

RICHARD NORTON, JR December 07, 1963 in Freeport, Stephenson co., IL, son of WILLIAM NORTON and EDNA LOTT. He was born October 20, 1938 in Rockford, ILL.

Notes for VELMA JANE HABBEN:
COUSIN ONCE REMOVED OF RONALD REAGAN

Notes for WILLIAM RICHARD NORTON, JR:
Railroad telegrapher at time of marriage, later truck driver.

Children of VELMA HABBEN and WILLIAM NORTON are:
      i. JAMES RICHARD[8] NORTON, b. June 30, 1967, Freport, Stephenson co., IL.
120.   ii. JEFFERY MICHAEL NORTON, b. December 23, 1971, Freport, Stephenson co., IL.

76. JUDITH MAY[7] HABBEN *(VERA MARIE[6] PIERCE, SARA JANE[5] WILSON, THOMAS[4], JANE[3] BLUE, DONALD DANIEL[2] BLUE, SR, JOHNNIE[1] BLUE)* was born April 28, 1946 in Morrison, IL. She married DONALD RAY BURMEISTER August 28, 1976 in Dewitt, Clinton co., Iowa. He was born January 23, 1939 in Dewitt, Clinton co., IA.

Notes for JUDITH MAY HABBEN:
COUSIN ONCE REMOVED OF RONALD REAGAN

Notes for DONALD RAY BURMEISTER:
His second marriage.

Children of JUDITH HABBEN and DONALD BURMEISTER are:
      i. JOHN BRANDON[8] BURMEISTER, b. August 25, 1977, Dewitt, Clinton co., IA.
     ii. BRIAN DOUGLAS BURMEISTER, b. October 09, 1980, Dewitt, Clinton co., IA.

77. CAROL ANN[7] HABBEN *(VERA MARIE[6] PIERCE, SARA JANE[5] WILSON, THOMAS[4], JANE[3] BLUE, DONALD DANIEL[2] BLUE, SR, JOHNNIE[1] BLUE)* was born June 04, 1948 in Morrison, IL. She met CHARLES ROBERT ALBRECHT March 01, 1969 in Belvidere, Boone co., IL, son of FRANK ALBRECHT and IRENE HOWE. He was born November 28, 1937.

Notes for CAROL ANN HABBEN:
Born at Morrison Community Hospital
COUSIN ONCE REMOVED OF RONALD REAGAN

Notes for CHARLES ROBERT ALBRECHT:
Married by Robert A. Blodgett, Magistrate, at Belvidere, Boone co., IL
He was an 'assembler' when married.
This was his second marriage. Data from marriage license/Wiebenga material

Children of CAROL HABBEN and CHARLES ALBRECHT are:
121.   i. CALE RICHARD[8] ALBRECHT, b. June 06, 1973, Freport, Stephenson co., IL.
     ii. CALEB WILLAIM ALBRECHT, b. May 17, 1975, Freport, Stephenson co., IL.

    Notes for CALEB WILLAIM ALBRECHT:
    Married 1999, one child b. April 2000

78. BEVERLY JOAN[7] HABBEN *(VERA MARIE[6] PIERCE, SARA JANE[5] WILSON, THOMAS[4], JANE[3] BLUE, DONALD DANIEL[2] BLUE, SR, JOHNNIE[1] BLUE)* was born July 10, 1952 in Morrison, IL. She married KENNETH ALDEN ETHRIDGE November 25, 1972 in Pearl City, Jo Davies co., IL. He was born 1939 in Freport, Stephenson co., IL.

Notes for BEVERLY JOAN HABBEN:
COUSIN ONCE REMOVED OF RONALD REAGAN

Children of BEVERLY HABBEN and KENNETH ETHRIDGE are:
- i. JEREMY M.[8] ETHRIDGE, b. July 08, 1978, Freport, Stephenson co., IL.
- ii. KEVIN MARSHALL ETHRIDGE, b. June 29, 1980, Freport, Stephenson co., IL.
- iii. LAURA MARIE ETHRIDGE, b. May 29, 1983, Freport, Stephenson co., IL.

    Notes for LAURA MARIE ETHRIDGE:

- iv. BRADLEY ETHRIDGE, b. March 18, 1988, Freport, Stephenson co., IL.

79. DONNA ELAINE[7] HABBEN *(VERA MARIE[6] PIERCE, SARA JANE[5] WILSON, THOMAS[4], JANE[3] BLUE, DONALD DANIEL[2] BLUE, SR, JOHNNIE[1] BLUE)* was born August 04, 1954 in Morrison, IL. She married THOMAS MICHAEL ARDWIN November 02, 1982 in North Glenn, Adams co., CO, son of DETER ARDWIN and ANNA GAFKA. He was born January 15, 1942 in Detroit, MI.

Notes for DONNA ELAINE HABBEN:
Divorced Jan. 29, 1971, per marriage application, Detroit, MI
COUSIN ONCE REMOVED OF RONALD REAGAN

Notes for THOMAS MICHAEL ARDWIN:
Divorced: Jan. 29, 1971, per marriage application, Detroit, MI

Children of DONNA HABBEN and THOMAS ARDWIN are:
- i. DONNA MARIE[8] ARDWIN, b. March 28, 1987, Denver, Adams co., CO.
- ii. MICHAEL THOMAS ARDWIN, b. January 19, 1989, Denver, Adams co., CO.
- iii. LISA ARDWIN.

80. MICHAEL[7] REAGAN *(RONALD WILSON[6], NELLIE CLYDE[5] WILSON, THOMAS[4], JANE[3] BLUE, DONALD DANIEL[2] BLUE, SR, JOHNNIE[1] BLUE)* was born March 18, 1945. He married COLLEEN STEARNS.

Notes for COLLEEN STEARNS:
Information from Mrs. Vickie Wiebenga

Child of MICHAEL REAGAN and COLLEEN STEARNS is:
- i. CAMERON MICHAEL[8] REAGAN, b. May 30, 1978.

81. MARTHA ANN[7] MITCHELL *(LOIS W.[6] WHISTLER, MARGARET MAY[5] WILSON, JOHN[4], JANE[3] BLUE, DONALD DANIEL[2] BLUE, SR, JOHNNIE[1] BLUE)* She married DAVID DEUTERMANN.

Children of MARTHA MITCHELL and DAVID DEUTERMANN are:
- i. DAVID WHITFORD[8] DEUTERMANN.
- ii. JULIA ANN DEUTERMANN.

82. JOHN WILSON[7] MITCHELL *(LOIS W.[6] WHISTLER, MARGARET MAY[5] WILSON, JOHN[4], JANE[3] BLUE, DONALD DANIEL[2] BLUE, SR, JOHNNIE[1] BLUE)* He married NAOMI YATES.

Child of JOHN MITCHELL and NAOMI YATES is:
- i. WHITFORD KIMBALL[8] MITCHELL.

83. JANE WHITFORD[7] MITCHELL *(LOIS W.[6] WHISTLER, MARGARET MAY[5] WILSON, JOHN[4], JANE[3] BLUE, DONALD DANIEL[2] BLUE, SR, JOHNNIE[1] BLUE)* She married DONALD GORZNEY.

Children of JANE MITCHELL and DONALD GORZNEY are:

    i. JOHN[8] GORZNEY.
    ii. JAMES GORZNEY.
    iii. SUSAN JANE GORZNEY.
    iv. GLEN GORZNEY.

84. BARBARA[7] MARR *(FLORENCE I.[6] WHISTLER, MARGARET MAY[5] WILSON, JOHN[4], JANE[3] BLUE, DONALD DANIEL[2] BLUE, SR, JOHNNIE[1] BLUE)* She married 'MALE' DOUGHERTY.

Children of BARBARA MARR and 'MALE' DOUGHERTY are:
    i. DENNIE[8] DOUGHERTY.
    ii. TIMOTHY DOUGHERTY.
    iii. DOUGLAS DOUGHERTY.
    iv. BRIAN DOUGHERTY.
    v. PATRICK DOUGHERTY.

85. JUDITH SUZANE[7] WILSON *(DWIGHT ALVIN[6], PAUL FLETCHER[5], ALEXANDER B[4], JANE[3] BLUE, DONALD DANIEL[2] BLUE, SR, JOHNNIE[1] BLUE)* was born November 21, 1942. She married JAMES KEITH ROWE June 13, 1964, son of V. ROWE and MARY. He was born November 25, 1941.

Notes for JUDITH SUZANE WILSON:
Teacher

Notes for JAMES KEITH ROWE:
Teacher
Divorced August, 1994

Children of JUDITH WILSON and JAMES ROWE are:
    i. DAVID KEITH[8] ROWE, b. March 17, 1968; m. RHONDA KAY BAYLES, November 23, 1996; b. April 14, 1967.
122. ii. ROBERT MATHEW ROWE, b. September 06, 1970.

86. ROBERT THOMAS[7] WILSON *(DWIGHT ALVIN[6], PAUL FLETCHER[5], ALEXANDER B[4], JANE[3] BLUE, DONALD DANIEL[2] BLUE, SR, JOHNNIE[1] BLUE)* was born June 29, 1944. He married GEORGIANNE HUMMEL March 21, 1972. She was born August 10, 1949.

Notes for GEORGIANNE HUMMEL:
Legal secretary

Children of ROBERT WILSON and GEORGIANNE HUMMEL are:
    i. THOMAS ROBERT[8] WILSON, b. August 24, 1984, Danville, IL.
    ii. PAUL MATHEW WILSON, b. October 27, 1985, Danville, IL.

87. DEBORAH ANN[7] WILSON *(ROBERT BRISTLE[6], PAUL FLETCHER[5], ALEXANDER B[4], JANE[3] BLUE, DONALD DANIEL[2] BLUE, SR, JOHNNIE[1] BLUE)* was born February 09, 1941. She married MICHAEL MORAN September 02, 1961, son of DON MORAN and LIENNE VITE. He was born January 26, 1941.

Children of DEBORAH WILSON and MICHAEL MORAN are:
    i. CHRISTINE ELIZABETH[8] MORAN, b. April 18, 1963; m. 'MALE' FOSTER.
123. ii. KIMBERLY JANE MORAN, b. February 27, 1965.
    iii. STEPHEN MICHAEL MORAN, b. December 08, 1968.

88. STEVEN ALLEN[7] GSELL *(CLAIR LE ROY[6], CLIFFORD LEROY[5], MARGARET MAE[4] WILSON, JANE[3] BLUE, DONALD DANIEL[2] BLUE, SR, JOHNNIE[1] BLUE)* was born April 24, 1939. He married DARLENE E. VEIHL.

Children of STEVEN GSELL and DARLENE VEIHL are:
    i. BRIAN DAVID[8] GSELL.

       Notes for BRIAN DAVID GSELL:
       Twin of Dawn

    ii. DAWN ELIZABETH GSELL.

       Notes for DAWN ELIZABETH GSELL:
       Twin of Brian

    iii. BLYTHE ANN GSELL.

89. SUE ELLEN[7] GSELL *(CLAIR LE ROY[6], CLIFFORD LEROY[5], MARGARET MAE[4] WILSON, JANE[3] BLUE, DONALD DANIEL[2] BLUE, SR, JOHNNIE[1] BLUE)* was born September 25, 1955. She married JOHN KIMBERLIN.

Notes for JOHN KIMBERLIN:
2 other children

Child of SUE GSELL and JOHN KIMBERLIN is:
    i. CORINNE[8] KIMBERLIN.

90. DONNA JEAN[7] WITT *(LEPHA MAE[6] MILNES, MAUDE MAE[5] GSELL, MARGARET MAE[4] WILSON, JANE[3] BLUE, DONALD DANIEL[2] BLUE, SR, JOHNNIE[1] BLUE)* was born April 09, 1933. She married GEORGE MEDEMA. He was born July 17, 1933.

Children of DONNA WITT and GEORGE MEDEMA are:
124.   i. JHODY JEAN[8] MEDEMA, b. March 11, 1952.
125.   ii. JULIE MARIE MEDEMA, b. June 09, 1953.
    iii. JEANIE LARIE MEDEMA, b. May 31, 1954.
    iv. JANICE LYNE MEDEMA, b. November 27, 1956; m. CHARLES SWANSON.
    v. JERRY ALLEN MEDEMA, b. August 27, 1963.
    vi. JON CRAIG MEDEMA, b. November 29, 1966.
    vii. JAMES GREG MEDEMA, b. December 03, 1969.

91. DR. HARLAN ANDREW[7] WITT *(LEPHA MAE[6] MILNES, MAUDE MAE[5] GSELL, MARGARET MAE[4] WILSON, JANE[3] BLUE, DONALD DANIEL[2] BLUE, SR, JOHNNIE[1] BLUE)* was born April 27, 1946. He married VERLEE ANN SILVIS.

Children of HARLAN WITT and VERLEE SILVIS are:
    i. JEFFREY ANDREW[8] WITT, b. October 19, 1967.
    ii. KIMBERLY LYNN WITT.

       Notes for KIMBERLY LYNN WITT:
       Twin of Kristen

    iii. KRISTEN LES WITT.

       Notes for KRISTEN LES WITT:
       Twin of Kimberly

92. DAVID IVAN[7] CARROLL *(MARGARET ELIZABETH[6] MILNES, MAUDE MAE[5] GSELL, MARGARET MAE[4] WILSON, JANE[3] BLUE, DONALD DANIEL[2] BLUE, SR, JOHNNIE[1] BLUE)* was born January 02, 1938. He married SALLY ANN ONKEN. She was born December 12, 1938.

Children of DAVID CARROLL and SALLY ONKEN are:

i. TROY ANDREW[8] CARROLL, b. April 13, 1965.
   ii. ERICK PAUL CARROLL, b. May 20, 1967.
   iii. LYNN ANDREA CARROLL, b. July 01, 1971.
   iv. LISA PAMELA CARROLL, b. December 27, 1973.

93. TERRY DEE[7] CARROLL *(MARGARET ELIZABETH[6] MILNES, MAUDE MAE[5] GSELL, MARGARET MAE[4] WILSON, JANE[3] BLUE, DONALD DANIEL[2] BLUE, SR, JOHNNIE[1] BLUE)* was born January 03, 1946. He married VIRGINIA KAY BUSH. She was born April 15, 1947.

Children of TERRY CARROLL and VIRGINIA BUSH are:
   i. CHRISTINE LEA[8] CARROLL, b. December 17, 1968.
   ii. KARLA JEAN CARROLL, b. October 13, 1975.
   iii. MATTHEW THOMAS CARROLL, b. July 04, 1980.

94. DIANE LOUISE[7] MILNES *(WALTER[6], MAUDE MAE[5] GSELL, MARGARET MAE[4] WILSON, JANE[3] BLUE, DONALD DANIEL[2] BLUE, SR, JOHNNIE[1] BLUE)* was born September 04, 1945. She married PAUL GLISPIE.

Child of DIANE MILNES and PAUL GLISPIE is:
   i. JOHN WESLEY[8] GLISPIE.

   Notes for JOHN WESLEY GLISPIE:
   Married 1999

95. THOMAS BRENT[7] MILNES *(WALTER[6], MAUDE MAE[5] GSELL, MARGARET MAE[4] WILSON, JANE[3] BLUE, DONALD DANIEL[2] BLUE, SR, JOHNNIE[1] BLUE)* was born September 01, 1950. He married (1) PATRICIA RICK 1976. He married (2) PENNY SMITH 1980.

Notes for THOMAS BRENT MILNES:
Divorced from Patricia.
Dairy farmer

Child of THOMAS MILNES and PATRICIA RICK is:
   i. TINA ELIZABETH[8] MILNES, b. March 02, 1977.

   Notes for TINA ELIZABETH MILNES:
   School teacher, no children, not married (2000)

Children of THOMAS MILNES and PENNY SMITH are:
   ii. SCOTT T.[8] MILNES, b. October 31, 1981.
   iii. BRYAN THOMAS MILNES, b. January 22, 1985.
   iv. SHAUN MATHEW MILNES, b. April 13, 1986.

96. ARLYN[7] VOS *(GLADYS ELOISE[6] STAPLETON, ESTELLA JANE[5] GSELL, MARGARET MAE[4] WILSON, JANE[3] BLUE, DONALD DANIEL[2] BLUE, SR, JOHNNIE[1] BLUE)* was born May 03, 1940. He married MARY BUIKEMA. She was born November 20, 1939.

Children of ARLYN VOS and MARY BUIKEMA are:
   i. KATHY LYNN[8] VOS.
   ii. ARLYN DALE VOS.
   iii. DEBRA JANE VOS.
   iv. MARLA ANN VOS.

97. LARRY[7] VOS *(GLADYS ELOISE[6] STAPLETON, ESTELLA JANE[5] GSELL, MARGARET MAE[4] WILSON, JANE[3] BLUE,*

DONALD DANIEL[2] BLUE, SR, JOHNNIE[1] BLUE) He married LINDA FRANCIS.

Children of LARRY VOS and LINDA FRANCIS are:
  i. KARI SUE[8] VOS.
  ii. TERI ANN VOS.

Generation No. 8

98. ELWIN[8] NICE *(LUCILLE FERN[7] BECHTEL, WILLIAM DETER[6], JOHN WILSON[5], SARA[4] WILSON, JANE[3] BLUE, DONALD DANIEL[2] BLUE, SR, JOHNNIE[1] BLUE)* He married SHIRLEY ENRIGHT.

Notes for ELWIN NICE:
SECOND COUSIN TWICE REMOVED OF RONALD REAGAN

Children of ELWIN NICE and SHIRLEY ENRIGHT are:
  i. WILLIAM[9] NICE, m. PATRICIA PETTICORD.
  ii. LINDA NICE.
  iii. PAM NICE.
  iv. JUDY NICE, m. JEFF MEINSMA.

99. MARJORIE[8] NICE *(LUCILLE FERN[7] BECHTEL, WILLIAM DETER[6], JOHN WILSON[5], SARA[4] WILSON, JANE[3] BLUE, DONALD DANIEL[2] BLUE, SR, JOHNNIE[1] BLUE)* She married ROBERT TRAUM.

Children of MARJORIE NICE and ROBERT TRAUM are:
  i. SUSAN[9] TRAUM.
  ii. JOHN TRAUM.
  iii. DAVID TRAUM.

100. JAMES JOSEPH[8] KUNAVICH *(KATHERINE JANE[7] HICKS, MARY MARGARET[6] WILSON, JOHN CHARLES[5], THOMAS[4], JANE[3] BLUE, DONALD DANIEL[2] BLUE, SR, JOHNNIE[1] BLUE)* was born October 22, 1943 in Clinton, Clinton co., IA, and died April 24, 1971 in Oaklawn, Cook co., IL. He married ALBERTA LYNN YONKERS January 10, 1963 in Chicago, Cook co., ILL. She was born 1945 in Chicago, Cook co., IL.

Notes for JAMES JOSEPH KUNAVICH:
Divorced before death. Accidental injury, car, Palos Hill, Cook co, IL.
COUSIN TWICE REMOVED OF RONALD REAGAN

More About JAMES JOSEPH KUNAVICH:
Burial: Grove Hill, Morrison, IL

Notes for ALBERTA LYNN YONKERS:
Divorce from Kunavich September, 1969. Married Curtis

Child of JAMES KUNAVICH and ALBERTA YONKERS is:
  i. JAMES JOSEPH[9] KUNAVICH, JR., b. March 29, 1963, Chicago, Cook co., IL.

    Notes for JAMES JOSEPH KUNAVICH, JR :
    Because his Mother divorced Kunavich and married Curtis, John Kunavich, Jr. assumed the surname 'Curtis' to carry the same name as his Mother, affidavit of 20 Aug. 1992, Fulton, IL in the Donald Hunt estate case.
    COUSIN 3 TIMES REMOVED FROM RONALD REAGAN

101. TERRY[8] SMITH *(ROBERT CLARE[7], HORACE VERNON[6], SARA JANE[5] WILSON, THOMAS[4], JANE[3] BLUE, DONALD DANIEL[2] BLUE, SR, JOHNNIE[1] BLUE)* was born November 20, 1946. He married (1) DONNA ANN RURY January 13, 1967. He married (2) MARIA MARTINEZ August 14, 1983. He married

(3) MARGARITA MARISEAL August 17, 1996.

Notes for TERRY SMITH:
Divorced 1981, from Donna, divorced from Maria.
COUSIN TWICE REMOVED OF RONALD REAGAN

Notes for DONNA ANN RURY:
Divorced 1981

Children of TERRY SMITH and DONNA RURY are:
    i. CHRISTOPHER SCOTT[9] SMITH, b. January 29, 1968.

        Notes for CHRISTOPHER SCOTT SMITH:
        COUSIN 3 TIMES REMOVED FROM RONALD REAGAN

    ii. JAMIE SMITH, b. January 23, 1973.

        Notes for JAMIE SMITH:
        Twin of Corie
        COUSIN 3 TIMES REMOVED OF RONALD REAGAN

    iii. CORY SMITH, b. January 23, 1973.

        Notes for CORY SMITH:
        Twin of Jamie
        COUSIN 3 TIMES REMOVED OF RONALD REAGAN

    iv. JENIFER ERIN SMITH, b. January 24, 1978.

        Notes for JENIFER ERIN SMITH:
        COUSIN 3 TIMES REMOVED OF RONALD REAGAN

102. VICKI[8] SMITH (ROBERT CLARE[7], HORACE VERNON[6], SARA JANE[5] WILSON, THOMAS[4], JANE[3] BLUE, DONALD DANIEL[2] BLUE, SR, JOHNNIE[1] BLUE) was born March 01, 1952. She married (1) BRUCE UNGER August 07, 1971 in Morrison, IL. He died March 17, 1974. She married (2) RON WIEBENGA October 24, 1975.

Notes for VICKI SMITH:
COUSIN TWICE REMOVED OF RONALD REAGAN

Notes for BRUCE UNGER:
Deceased

More About BRUCE UNGER:
Burial: Grove Hill cemetery, Morrison

Child of VICKI SMITH and BRUCE UNGER is:
    i. BRUCE EDWIN[9] UNGER, JR., b. July 04, 1974; m. KAREN GEORGE, November 06, 1999, Peoria, IL.

        Notes for BRUCE EDWIN UNGER, JR.:
        COUSIN 3 TIMES REMOVED OF RONALD REAGAN

Child of VICKI SMITH and RON WIEBENGA is:
    ii. LESLEY DAWN[9] WIEBENGA, b. April 24, 1977, Morrison, IL; m. CHAD PAUL DEVER, June 06, 1998, Morrison, IL.

        Notes for LESLEY DAWN WIEBENGA:
        COUSIN 3 TIMES REMOVED OF RONALD REAGAN

103. DAVID[8] SMITH *(GENE MEAKIN[7], HORACE VERNON[6], SARA JANE[5] WILSON, THOMAS[4], JANE[3] BLUE, DONALD DANIEL[2] BLUE, SR, JOHNNIE[1] BLUE)* was born May 21, 1948. He married DEE ANN BILDSTEIN August 09, 1975.

Notes for DAVID SMITH:
Lives in Iowa, divorced.
COUSIN TWICE REMOVED OF RONALD REAGAN

Child of DAVID SMITH and DEE BILDSTEIN is:
i. CHELSEY[9] SMITH, b. May 20, 1982.

104. THOMAS[8] SMITH *(GENE MEAKIN[7], HORACE VERNON[6], SARA JANE[5] WILSON, THOMAS[4], JANE[3] BLUE, DONALD DANIEL[2] BLUE, SR, JOHNNIE[1] BLUE)* was born February 25, 1952. He married (1) CHRISTINE PYRON July 07, 1973. He married (2) DAWN SCHRYVER March 31, 1978. He married (3) CINDY OSTEMA March 09, 1984.

Notes for THOMAS SMITH:
Divorced Feb. 1975 - Christine
Divorced - Dawn - Dec. 1979
COUSIN TWICE REMOVED OF RONALD REAGAN

Notes for CHRISTINE PYRON:
Divorced Feb. 1975

Child of THOMAS SMITH and DAWN SCHRYVER is:
i. THOMAS S.[9] SMITH, m. CINDY.

Children of THOMAS SMITH and CINDY OSTEMA are:
ii. MARSHALL[9] SMITH, b. August 22, 1984.
iii. TAYLOR SMITH, b. December 17, 1996.

105. NANCY[8] SMITH *(GENE MEAKIN[7], HORACE VERNON[6], SARA JANE[5] WILSON, THOMAS[4], JANE[3] BLUE, DONALD DANIEL[2] BLUE, SR, JOHNNIE[1] BLUE)* was born October 12, 1955. She married (1) MITCHELL FOREMAN January 04, 1975. She married (2) STEVE MERRILL Aft. January 1980.

Notes for NANCY SMITH:
Divorced Steve Jan. 5, 1980
COUSIN TWICE REMOVED OF RONALD REAGAN

Child of NANCY SMITH and MITCHELL FOREMAN is:
i. CAMERON RYAN[9] FOREMAN, b. July 14, 1978.

Notes for CAMERON RYAN FOREMAN:
COUSIN 3 TIMES REMOVED OF RONALD REAGAN

Child of NANCY SMITH and STEVE MERRILL is:
ii. DUSTIN[9] MERRILL, b. May 05, 1982.

106. PAUL EDWARD[8] WALTERS *(HAROLD EDWARD[7], ELSEY MAE[6] PIERCE, SARA JANE[5] WILSON, THOMAS[4], JANE[3] BLUE, DONALD DANIEL[2] BLUE, SR, JOHNNIE[1] BLUE)* was born May 03, 1946 in Morrison, IL. He married (1) PATRICIA BARTZ February 26, 1965 in Morrison, IL. She was born May 11, 1949 in Morrison, IL. He married (2) SHARON TIESMAN March 19, 1970 in Lyndon, Whiteside co., IL.

She was born April 27, 1945.

Notes for PAUL EDWARD WALTERS:
Divorce 1970

Notes for PATRICIA BARTZ:
Divorced 1970

Child of PAUL WALTERS and PATRICIA BARTZ is:
    i. WENDY LEE[9] WALTERS, b. August 21, 1965, Morrison, IL; m. WILLIAM CHARLES HUTCHINSON; b. September 08, 1964, Carroll co., IL.

    Notes for WILLIAM CHARLES HUTCHINSON:
    Divorced

Children of PAUL WALTERS and SHARON TIESMAN are:
    ii. BABY[9] WALTERS, b. March 19, 1973; d. March 19, 1973.

    Notes for BABY WALTERS:
    Stillborn

    More About BABY WALTERS:
    Burial: Fulton cemetery. Fulton, IL

126.   iii. TORI CHERYL WALTERS, b. April 25, 1974, Morrison, IL.
127.   iv. TROY J. WALTERS, b. November 05, 1975, Morrison, IL.

107. HARLAN GENE[8] WALTERS (*HAROLD EDWARD[7], ELSEY MAE[6] PIERCE, SARA JANE[5] WILSON, THOMAS[4], JANE[3] BLUE, DONALD DANIEL[2] BLUE, SR, JOHNNIE[1] BLUE*) was born February 05, 1948 in Morrison, IL. He married (1) MARIE SHARER February 24, 1967 in Fulton, Whiteside co., IL. She was born May 25, 1947. He married (2) BETH RICK August 31, 1974 in Morrison, IL. She was born January 27, 1945. He married (3) LINDA ROBINSON December 02, 1983 in TX.

Notes for HARLAN GENE WALTERS:
Divorced from Marie 1974
Divorced from Beth Rick
Divorced from Linda 2002

Notes for MARIE SHARER:
Divorce 1974

Notes for BETH RICK:
Divorced

Notes for LINDA ROBINSON:
She has two children, Carolyn and Rebecca. They are children of her previous marriage.

Children of HARLAN WALTERS and MARIE SHARER are:
    i. TERRY HARLAN[9] WALTERS, b. June 06, 1968, Morrison, IL.
    ii. MARK DOUGLAS WALTERS, b. June 16, 1969, Morrison, IL.
    iii. DAVID GENE WALTERS, b. August 26, 1971, Morrison, IL.

Children of HARLAN WALTERS and LINDA ROBINSON are:
    iv. CAROLYN[9].

Notes for CAROLYN:
Child of Mother's previous marriage.

   v.   REBECCA.

Notes for REBECCA:
Child of Mother's previous marriage.

108. JANE KAYE[8] WALTERS *(HAROLD EDWARD[7], ELSEY MAE[6] PIERCE, SARA JANE[5] WILSON, THOMAS[4], JANE[3] BLUE, DONALD DANIEL[2]BLUE, SR, JOHNNIE[1] BLUE)* was born April 16, 1950 in Morrison, IL. She married (1) LEONARD PRITCHARD March 07, 1969 in Morrison, IL. He was born November 16, 1946. She married (2) FRANK MATCHIE October 07, 1972 in Morrison, IL. He was born June 07, 1947. She married (3) WALTER G. HEATH October 22, 1990 in Morrison, IL.

Notes for JANE KAYE WALTERS:
Divorced 3 Aug 1970 from Pritchard
Divorced from Matchie

Notes for LEONARD PRITCHARD:
Divorced from Jane Kaye 3 Aug. 1970

Notes for FRANK MATCHIE:
Divorced

Child of JANE WALTERS and LEONARD PRITCHARD is:
    i. TIMOTHY ALLEN[9] PRITCHARD, b. September 22, 1969, Morrison, IL; m. ANGELA KAY MACHIE, May 1987, Morrison, IL; b. December 22, 1974, Morrison, IL.

Child of JANE WALTERS and FRANK MATCHIE is:
128.   ii. ANGELA[9] MATCHIE, b. December 22, 1974.

109. DAWN GAIL[8] WALTERS *(HAROLD EDWARD[7], ELSEY MAE[6] PIERCE, SARA JANE[5] WILSON, THOMAS[4], JANE[3] BLUE, DONALD DANIEL[2]BLUE, SR, JOHNNIE[1] BLUE)* was born March 19, 1962 in Morrison, IL. She married ROBERT JAMES BAUER May 02, 1981 in Morrison, IL. He was born August 06, 1960 in Morrison, IL.

Children of DAWN WALTERS and ROBERT BAUER are:
    i. AMANDA GAIL[9] BAUER, b. July 31, 1991, Clinton, Clinton Co., IA.
    ii. LAYLA MARIE BAUER, b. August 27, 1994, Clinton, Clinton Co., IA.

110. PHILIP DALE[8] WALTERS *(HAROLD EDWARD[7], ELSEY MAE[6] PIERCE, SARA JANE[5] WILSON, THOMAS[4], JANE[3] BLUE, DONALD DANIEL[2]BLUE, SR, JOHNNIE[1] BLUE)* was born July 15, 1968 in Morrison, IL. He married CHRISTINE KRAUSE May 30, 1989 in Dixon, Lee co., IL.

Notes for CHRISTINE KRAUSE:
Adopted by Baughman

Children of PHILIP WALTERS and CHRISTINE KRAUSE are:
    i. STEPHANIE ANNE[9] WALTERS, b. February 11, 1988, Dixon, Lee co., IL.
    ii. TIFFANY MARIE WALTERS, b. May 22, 1990, Dallas, TX.
    iii. MATTHEW WALTERS, b. September 15, 1992.

111. KURT REINHARD[8] JANVRIN *(MERNA JOY[7] HABBEN, VERA MARIE[6] PIERCE, SARA JANE[5] WILSON, THOMAS[4], JANE[3] BLUE, DONALD DANIEL[2]BLUE, SR, JOHNNIE[1] BLUE)* was born August 04, 1960 in

Morrison, IL. He married YVONNE AMMON June 16, 1984 in Long Grove, Lake co., IL. She was born December 19, 1961 in Decatur, Macon co., IL.

Children of KURT JANVRIN and YVONNE AMMON are:
    i. REBECCA LINDSEY[9] JANVRIN, b. May 23, 1988, Trenton, Mercer co., NJ.
    ii. HANNAH KATE JANVRIN, b. October 07, 1990, Trenton, Mercer co., NJ.
    iii. GENEVIEVE JANVRIN, b. 1993.
    iv. MABELINE JANVRIN, b. 1997.

112. BRUCE CLYDE[8] JANVRIN *(MERNA JOY[7] HABBEN, VERA MARIE[6] PIERCE, SARA JANE[5] WILSON, THOMAS[4], JANE[3] BLUE, DONALD DANIEL[2] BLUE, SR, JOHNNIE[1] BLUE)* was born December 22, 1961 in Morrison, IL. He married DIANE MEHLHAUS August 11, 1990 in Dysart, Benton co., IA. She was born February 20, 1961 in Dysart, Benton co., Iowa.

Children of BRUCE JANVRIN and DIANE MEHLHAUS are:
    i. BRICE[9] JANVRIN, b. 1993.
    ii. BRYLEIGH JANVRIN, b. 1998.

113. ARON KYLE[8] JANVRIN *(MERNA JOY[7] HABBEN, VERA MARIE[6] PIERCE, SARA JANE[5] WILSON, THOMAS[4], JANE[3] BLUE, DONALD DANIEL[2] BLUE, SR, JOHNNIE[1] BLUE)* was born November 13, 1964 in Morrison, IL. He married CAROLYN BROWN June 28, 1998.

Child of ARON JANVRIN and CAROLYN BROWN is:
    i. TYLER[9] JANVRIN, b. February 29, 2000.

114. RHONDA JANE[8] HABBEN *(NORMAN WALTER[7], VERA MARIE[6] PIERCE, SARA JANE[5] WILSON, THOMAS[4], JANE[3] BLUE, DONALD DANIEL[2] BLUE, SR, JOHNNIE[1] BLUE)* was born June 24, 1957. She married (1) ALLEN GREELEY June 10, 1978 in Morrison, IL. He was born August 05, 1951 in Morrison, IL. She married (2) ALLEN RAY GREELEY June 10, 1978 in Morrison, IL. He was born August 05, 1951 in Morrison, IL.

Children of RHONDA HABBEN and ALLEN GREELEY are:
    i. MELLISSA JEAN[9] GREELEY, b. December 08, 1980, Morrison, IL.
    ii. WILLIAM NORMAN GREELEY, b. June 19, 1983, Morrison, IL.
    iii. MARLA JANE GREELEY, b. September 04, 1984, Morrison, IL.

115. GENE LEROY[8] HABBEN *(NORMAN WALTER[7], VERA MARIE[6] PIERCE, SARA JANE[5] WILSON, THOMAS[4], JANE[3] BLUE, DONALD DANIEL[2] BLUE, SR, JOHNNIE[1] BLUE)* was born July 07, 1960 in Morrison, IL. He married KAREN ROENIKE February 25, 1989 in Clinton, Iowa.

Children of GENE HABBEN and KAREN ROENIKE are:
    i. TRAVIS[9] HABBEN, b. 1993.
    ii. RYAN HABBEN, b. 1996.
    iii. KRISTIN, b. 1999.

116. SARA LEANNE[8] HABBEN *(NORMAN WALTER[7], VERA MARIE[6] PIERCE, SARA JANE[5] WILSON, THOMAS[4], JANE[3] BLUE, DONALD DANIEL[2] BLUE, SR, JOHNNIE[1] BLUE)* was born March 09, 1967 in Morrison, IL. She married (1) COONAN DICKMAN March 29, 1986 in Morrison, IL. He was born March 24, 1967. She married (2) RANDY FAUST September 1990 in Mo--.

Notes for SARA LEANNE HABBEN:
Divorced Dickman 1990, no children with him.

Notes for COONAN DICKMAN:

Divorced 1990, no children.

Children of SARA HABBEN and RANDY FAUST are:
    i. ADAM CHARLES[9] FAUST, b. March 23, 1991, Virginia Beach, VA.
    ii. ASHLEY FAUST, b. 1994.

117. DANIEL LEE[8] HABBEN *(RONALD LEE[7], VERA MARIE[6] PIERCE, SARA JANE[5] WILSON, THOMAS[4], JANE[3] BLUE, DONALD DANIEL[2] BLUE, SR, JOHNNIE[1] BLUE)* was born June 26, 1962 in Morrison, IL. He married BETH HACKER June 20, 1987 in Morrison, IL. She was born January 10, 1962.

Children of DANIEL HABBEN and BETH HACKER are:
    i. LOGAN DANIEL[9] HABBEN, b. May 14, 1989, Sterling, Whiteside co., IL.
    ii. ABBEY HABBEN, b. 1994.

118. DEBRA LOU[8] HABBEN *(RONALD LEE[7], VERA MARIE[6] PIERCE, SARA JANE[5] WILSON, THOMAS[4], JANE[3] BLUE, DONALD DANIEL[2] BLUE, SR, JOHNNIE[1] BLUE)* was born September 17, 1964 in Morrison, IL. She married JAMES LEE SNYDER June 11, 1983 in Morrison, IL. He was born October 30, 1963 in Morrison, IL.

Notes for DEBRA LOU HABBEN:
Divorced 1988

Notes for JAMES LEE SNYDER:
Divorced 1988

Children of DEBRA HABBEN and JAMES SNYDER are:
    i. BRANDON[9] SNYDER, b. October 31, 1985, Germany.
    ii. TIMOTHY SNYDER, b. February 12, 1987, Sterling, Whiteside co., IL.

119. CATHERINE JEAN[8] HABBEN *(MILFORD GENE[7], VERA MARIE[6] PIERCE, SARA JANE[5] WILSON, THOMAS[4], JANE[3] BLUE, DONALD DANIEL[2] BLUE, SR, JOHNNIE[1] BLUE)* was born May 08, 1966 in Morrison, IL. She married MARK BENNET June 27, 1987 in Dixon, Lee co., IL.

Notes for CATHERINE JEAN HABBEN:
Divorced

Children of CATHERINE HABBEN and MARK BENNET are:
    i. JENNIFER ANN[9] BENNET, b. October 06, 1990, Sterling, Whiteside co., IL.
    ii. AMANDA BENNET, b. 1994.

120. JEFFERY MICHAEL[8] NORTON *(VELMA JANE[7] HABBEN, VERA MARIE[6] PIERCE, SARA JANE[5] WILSON, THOMAS[4], JANE[3] BLUE, DONALD DANIEL[2] BLUE, SR, JOHNNIE[1] BLUE)* was born December 23, 1971 in Freport, Stephenson co., IL. He married ANGIE.

Child of JEFFERY NORTON and ANGIE is:
    i. GRACE[9] NORTON, b. 1999.

121. CALE RICHARD[8] ALBRECHT *(CAROL ANN[7] HABBEN, VERA MARIE[6] PIERCE, SARA JANE[5] WILSON, THOMAS[4], JANE[3] BLUE, DONALD DANIEL[2] BLUE, SR, JOHNNIE[1] BLUE)* was born June 06, 1973 in Freport, Stephenson co., IL. He married CHRIS.

Notes for CALE RICHARD ALBRECHT:
3rd Great-grandson of John Wilson.
Divorced, 2000

Child of CALE ALBRECHT and CHRIS is:
    i. CARRIE[9] ALBRECHT, b. 1995.

122. ROBERT MATHEW[8] ROWE *(JUDITH SUZANE[7] WILSON, DWIGHT ALVIN[6], PAUL FLETCHER[5], ALEXANDER B[4], JANE[3] BLUE, DONALD DANIEL[2] BLUE, SR, JOHNNIE[1] BLUE)* was born September 06, 1970. He married HEIDI ANN HULBERT October 10, 1992, daughter of STEPHEN HULBERT and DIANE. She was born March 22, 1969.

Children of ROBERT ROWE and HEIDI HULBERT are:
    i. AMANDA[9] ROWE, b. April 29, 1995.
    ii. LUCAS MATHEW ROWE, b. February 10, 1998.

123. KIMBERLY JANE[8] MORAN *(DEBORAH ANN[7] WILSON, ROBERT BRISTLE[6], PAUL FLETCHER[5], ALEXANDER B[4], JANE[3] BLUE, DONALD DANIEL[2] BLUE, SR, JOHNNIE[1] BLUE)* was born February 27, 1965. She married 'MALE' KIDWELL.

Children of KIMBERLY MORAN and 'MALE' KIDWELL are:
    i. TYLER[9] KIDWELL.
    ii. JACOB KIDWELL.
    iii. STEVEN KIDWELL.

124. JHODY JEAN[8] MEDEMA *(DONNA JEAN[7] WITT, LEPHA MAE[6] MILNES, MAUDE MAE[5] GSELL, MARGARET MAE[4] WILSON, JANE[3] BLUE, DONALD DANIEL[2] BLUE, SR, JOHNNIE[1] BLUE)* was born March 11, 1952. He married KATHY DITTMAR.

Child of JHODY MEDEMA and KATHY DITTMAR is:
    i. JACOB[9] MEDEMA.

125. JULIE MARIE[8] MEDEMA *(DONNA JEAN[7] WITT, LEPHA MAE[6] MILNES, MAUDE MAE[5] GSELL, MARGARET MAE[4] WILSON, JANE[3] BLUE, DONALD DANIEL[2] BLUE, SR, JOHNNIE[1] BLUE)* was born June 09, 1953. She married THOMAS SCHUMACHER.

Children of JULIE MEDEMA and THOMAS SCHUMACHER are:
    i. MATTHEW COLLIN[9] SCHUMACHER.
    ii. LUCAS SCHUMACHER.

Generation No. 9

126. TORI CHERYL[9] WALTERS *(PAUL EDWARD[8], HAROLD EDWARD[7], ELSEY MAE[6] PIERCE, SARA JANE[5] WILSON, THOMAS[4], JANE[3] BLUE, DONALD DANIEL[2] BLUE, SR, JOHNNIE[1] BLUE)* was born April 25, 1974 in Morrison, IL. She married JUSTIN EADS January 13, 1996.

Children of TORI WALTERS and JUSTIN EADS are:
    i. CHELSEA CHERYL[10] EADS, b. June 20, 1996, Sterling, IL.
    ii. JOSEPH JAMES EADS, b. December 29, 1998, Sterling, IL.
    iii. ZACHARY PHILIP EADS, b. March 07, 2003, Davenport, IA.

127. TROY J.[9] WALTERS *(PAUL EDWARD[8], HAROLD EDWARD[7], ELSEY MAE[6] PIERCE, SARA JANE[5] WILSON, THOMAS[4], JANE[3] BLUE, DONALD DANIEL[2] BLUE, SR, JOHNNIE[1] BLUE)* was born November 05, 1975 in Morrison, IL. He married CHRISTINA.

Notes for TROY J. WALTERS:

Divorced 2002

Notes for CHRISTINA:
Divorced 2002

Children of TROY WALTERS and CHRISTINA are:
    i. JULIA ANNA[10] WALTERS, b. September 26, 1999, Sterling, IL.
    ii. DREW PHILIP WALTERS, b. December 23, 2000, Sterling, IL.

128. ANGELA[9] MATCHIE *(JANE KAYE[8] WALTERS, HAROLD EDWARD[7], ELSEY MAE[6] PIERCE, SARA JANE[5] WILSON, THOMAS[4], JANE[3] BLUE, DONALD DANIEL[2] BLUE, SR, JOHNNIE[1] BLUE)* was born December 22, 1974. She married SHANE FERGUSON August 31, 1996.

Children of ANGELA MATCHIE and SHANE FERGUSON are:
    i. MIRISSA JANE[10], b. March 10, 1995.
    ii. HUNTER MICHAEL FERGUSON, b. January 03, 1997, Sterling, IL.

Kinship of Johnnie Blue

Name	Relationship with Johnnie Blue	Civil	Canon
<Unnamed>	Granddaughter	II	2
Ackerman, D. G.	Husband of the granddaughter		
Aitken, Mayme	Wife of the 2nd great-grandson		
Aldritt	Wife of the great-grandson		
Alex	2nd great-grandson	IV	4
Alldritt, Emma A.	Wife of the great-grandson		
Ammon, Yvonne	Wife of the 5th great-grandson		
Anderson, Amy Adele	Wife of the 4th great-grandson		
Barrett, Maxine Joy	Wife of the 3rd great-grandson		
Bartz, Patricia	Wife of the 5th great-grandson		
Bauer, Amanda Gail	6th great-granddaughter	VIII	8
Bauer, Robert James	Husband of the 5th great-granddaughter		
Bayles, Rhonda Kay	Wife of the 5th great-grandson		
Bechtel, Albert	3rd great-grandson	V	5
Bechtel, Bonnie	5th great-granddaughter	VII	7
Bechtel, Carol	5th great-granddaughter	VII	7
Bechtel, E. M.	Wife of the grandson		
Bechtel, Ellen	5th great-granddaughter	VII	7
Bechtel, Ellen W.	2nd great-granddaughter	IV	4
Bechtel, Ephraim Myers	Husband of the great-granddaughter		
Bechtel, Everett	4th great-grandson	VI	6
Bechtel, Gary	5th great-grandson	VII	7
Bechtel, Glenda	5th great-granddaughter	VII	7
Bechtel, Glenn	4th great-grandson	VI	6
Bechtel, Helena	2nd great-granddaughter	IV	4
Bechtel, Ivy May	3rd great-granddaughter	V	5
Bechtel, John Wilson	2nd great-grandson	IV	4
Bechtel, Lucille Fern	4th great-granddaughter	VI	6
Bechtel, Rebecca Jane	2nd great-granddaughter	IV	4
Bechtel, Scott	5th great-grandson	VII	7
Bechtel, William Deter	3rd great-grandson	V	5
Belle	Wife of the great-grandson		
Benjamin, Helen May	Wife of the grandson		
Bennet, Amanda	6th great-granddaughter	VIII	8
Bennet, Jennifer Ann	6th great-granddaughter	VIII	8
Bennet, Mark	Husband of the 5th great-granddaughter		
Bessie	3rd great-granddaughter	V	5
Beswick, Mary	Wife of the grandson		
Bildstein, Dee Ann	Wife of the 5th great-grandson		
Birt, Ella	Wife of the grandson		
Blue, Alexander	Grandson	II	2
Blue, Catharine	Granddaughter	II	2
Blue, Charles	Grandson	II	2
Blue, Elizabeth	Great-granddaughter	III	3
Blue, George	Great-grandson	III	3
Blue, Girl	2nd great-grandson	IV	4
Blue, I, John	Grandson	II	2
Blue, Isabell	Granddaughter	II	2
Blue, Jane	Granddaughter	II	2
Blue, John A.	Great-grandson	III	3
Blue, John, 2	Grandson	II	2

Name	Relationship with Johnnie Blue	Civil	Canon
Blue, Johnnie	Self		0
Blue, Jr., Donald Daniel	Grandson	II	2
Blue, Margaret	Granddaughter	II	2
Blue, Mary Elizabeth	2nd great-granddaughter	IV	4
Blue, Richard Beswick	Great-grandson	III	3
Blue, Samuel A	2nd great-grandson	IV	4
Blue, Sr, Donald Daniel	Son	I	1
Blue, Wilford T.	2nd great-grandson	IV	4
Brett, Alexander	Great-grandson	III	3
Brett, Charles	Great-grandson	III	3
Brett, Donald	Great-grandson	III	3
Brett, George	Great-grandson	III	3
Brett, John	Husband of the granddaughter		
Brett, John W.	Great-grandson	III	3
Brett, Kate	Great-granddaughter	III	3
Brett, Thomas C.	Great-grandson	III	3
Brickley, Dorothy	Wife of the 4th great-grandson		
Bristle, Etta May	Wife of the 2nd great-grandson		
Brooks, Pauline Catherine	Wife of the 3rd great-grandson		
Brown, Carolyn	Wife of the 5th great-grandson		
Buikema, Mary	Wife of the 4th great-grandson		
Bush, Douglas	Husband of the 5th great-granddaughter		
Bush, Virginia Kay	Wife of the 4th great-grandson		
C., Henry	3rd great-grandson	V	5
Capone, James A	Husband of the 4th great-granddaughter		
Carolyn	6th great-granddaughter	VIII	8
Carroll, Christine Lea	5th great-granddaughter	VII	7
Carroll, David Ivan	4th great-grandson	VI	6
Carroll, Erick Paul	5th great-grandson	VII	7
Carroll, Ivan Ralph	Husband of the 3rd great-granddaughter		
Carroll, Karla Jean	5th great-granddaughter	VII	7
Carroll, Lisa Pamela	5th great-granddaughter	VII	7
Carroll, Lynn Andrea	5th great-granddaughter	VII	7
Carroll, Matthew Thomas	5th great-grandson	VII	7
Carroll, Terry Dee	4th great-grandson	VI	6
Carroll, Troy Andrew	5th great-grandson	VII	7
Christina	Wife of the 6th great-grandson		
Cindy	Wife of the 6th great-grandson		
Conant	Husband of the 4th great-granddaughter		
Cook, Norma Jean	Wife of the 4th great-grandson		
Curtis, James J.	6th great-grandson	VIII	8
Cutler, Francis Louise	Wife of the 2nd great-grandson		
Daniel	Son	I	1
Daniel	Grandson	II	2
Davis, Nancy	Wife of the 3rd great-grandson		
Debbie	Wife of the great-grandson		
Deter, Sarah E.	Wife of the 2nd great-grandson		
Deutermann, David	Husband of the 4th great-granddaughter		
Deutermann, David Whitford	5th great-grandson	VII	7
Deutermann, Julia Ann	5th great-granddaughter	VII	7
Dever, Chad Paul	Husband of the 6th great-granddaughter		
Dickman, Coonan	Husband of the 5th great-granddaughter		
Dillon, Jacklyn Ann	5th great-granddaughter	VII	7

Name	Relationship with Johnnie Blue	Civil	Canon
Dillon, John Charles	4th great-grandson	VI	6
Dillon, Katherine Annabelle	4th great-granddaughter	VI	6
Dillon, Margaret Eliza	4th great-granddaughter	VI	6
Dillon, Raymond James	Husband of the 3rd great-granddaughter		
Dillon, Raymond James	4th great-grandson	VI	6
Dingman, Theodore	Husband of the 4th great-granddaughter		
Dittmar, Kathy	Wife of the 5th great-grandson		
Dougherty, Brian	5th great-grandson	VII	7
Dougherty, Dennie	5th great-grandson	VII	7
Dougherty, Douglas	5th great-grandson	VII	7
Dougherty, 'Male'	Husband of the 4th great-granddaughter		
Dougherty, Patrick	5th great-grandson	VII	7
Dougherty, Timothy	5th great-grandson	VII	7
Dutch	3rd great-grandson	V	5
Eads, Chelsea Cheryl	7th great-granddaughter	IX	9
Eads, Joseph James	7th great-grandson	IX	9
Eads, Justin	Husband of the 6th great-granddaughter		
Eads, Zachary Philip	7th great-grandson	IX	9
Ella	2nd great-granddaughter	IV	4
Ella	2nd great-granddaughter	IV	4
Elsey, Mary Ann	Wife of the great-grandson		
Enright, Shirley	Wife of the 5th great-grandson		
Fannie	2nd great-granddaughter	IV	4
Faust, Adam Charles	6th great-grandson	VIII	8
Faust, Ashley	6th great-granddaughter	VIII	8
Faust, Randy	Husband of the 5th great-granddaughter		
Ferguson, Hunter Michael	7th great-grandson	IX	9
Ferguson, Shane	Husband of the 6th great-granddaughter		
Fike, Ida	Wife of the 3rd great-grandson		
Flack, Clarence	Husband of the 2nd great-granddaughter		
Flack, Kathryn	4th great-granddaughter	VI	6
Flack, Pamela	4th great-granddaughter	VI	6
Flack, Thomas Oliver	3rd great-grandson	V	5
Flack, Timothy Conrad	3rd great-grandson	V	5
Flack, William C.	4th great-grandson	VI	6
Fletcher, Deborah A.	Wife of the great-grandson		
Foreman, Cameron Ryan	6th great-grandson	VIII	8
Foreman, Mitchell	Husband of the 5th great-granddaughter		
Foster, 'Male'	Husband of the 5th great-granddaughter		
Francis, Linda	Wife of the 4th great-grandson		
Fredrick, Lisa	Wife of the 5th great-grandson		
Fulks, Sara Jane	Wife of the 3rd great-grandson		
Gallentine, Randy Gale	Husband of the 4th great-granddaughter		
George, Karen	Wife of the 6th great-grandson		
Gerdes, David Edmond	Husband of the 2nd great-granddaughter		
Gerdes, Ephraim Lawrence	3rd great-grandson	V	5
Gerdes, Galen Glenn	3rd great-grandson	V	5
Gerdes, Henry Ralph	3rd great-grandson	V	5
Gerdes, Lloyd	3rd great-grandson	V	5
Gerdes, Robert	4th great-grandson	VI	6
Gerdes, Ruth	4th great-granddaughter	VI	6
Gerdes, Virgil E.	3rd great-grandson	V	5
Gerdes, Wayne	4th great-grandson	VI	6

Name	Relationship with Johnnie Blue	Civil	Canon
Gibson, Shirley	Wife of the 4th great-grandson		
Glispie, John Wesley	5th great-grandson	VII	7
Glispie, Paul	Husband of the 4th great-granddaughter		
Goff, Hulda Philena	Wife of the 3rd great-grandson		
Goldsmith, Robin N.	Husband of the 4th great-granddaughter		
Gorzney, Donald	Husband of the 4th great-granddaughter		
Gorzney, Glen	5th great-grandson	VII	7
Gorzney, James	5th great-grandson	VII	7
Gorzney, John	5th great-grandson	VII	7
Gorzney, Susan Jane	5th great-granddaughter	VII	7
Greeley, Allen	Husband of the 5th great-granddaughter		
Greeley, Allen Ray	Husband of the 5th great-granddaughter		
Greeley, Marla Jane	6th great-granddaughter	VIII	8
Greeley, Mellissa Jean	6th great-granddaughter	VIII	8
Greeley, William Norman	6th great-grandson	VIII	8
Green, Rhea	Wife of the 4th great-grandson		
Gsell, Blythe Ann	5th great-granddaughter	VII	7
Gsell, Brian David	5th great-grandson	VII	7
Gsell, Clair Le Roy	3rd great-grandson	V	5
Gsell, Clifford Leroy	2nd great-grandson	IV	4
Gsell, David B.	Husband of the great-granddaughter		
Gsell, Dawn Elizabeth	5th great-granddaughter	VII	7
Gsell, Earl Wilson	2nd great-grandson	IV	4
Gsell, Estella Jane	2nd great-granddaughter	IV	4
Gsell, Howard Wilson	3rd great-grandson	V	5
Gsell, Maude Mae	2nd great-granddaughter	IV	4
Gsell, Richard Lee	4th great-grandson	VI	6
Gsell, Steven Allen	4th great-grandson	VI	6
Gsell, Sue Ellen	4th great-granddaughter	VI	6
Gsell, William B.	Husband of the great-granddaughter		
Habben, Catherine Jean	5th great-granddaughter	VII	7
Habben, Donald Patrick	5th great-grandson	VII	7
Habben, Gene LeRoy	5th great-grandson	VII	7
Habben, Merna Joy	4th great-granddaughter	VI	6
Habben, Milford Gene	4th great-grandson	VI	6
Habben, Norman Walter	4th great-grandson	VI	6
Habben, Reinhard F.	Husband of the 3rd great-granddaughter		
Habben, Rhonda Jane	5th great-granddaughter	VII	7
Habben, Robert Allen	5th great-grandson	VII	7
Habben, Ryan	6th great-grandson	VIII	8
Habben, Sara Leanne	5th great-granddaughter	VII	7
Habben, Travis	6th great-grandson	VIII	8
Hammer, Edna Julia	Wife of the 2nd great-grandson		
Heath, Walter G.	Husband of the 5th great-granddaughter		
Helms, Mayme	Wife of the 2nd great-grandson		
Herrold, Edith	3rd great-granddaughter	V	5
Herrold, Lloyd	Husband of the 2nd great-granddaughter		
Herrold, Lloyd Wilson	3rd great-grandson	V	5
Hicks, Earl Clyde	4th great-grandson	VI	6
Hicks, Harriet	4th great-granddaughter	VI	6
Hicks, Harry John	Husband of the 3rd great-granddaughter		
Hicks, Katherine Jane	4th great-granddaughter	VI	6
High, Bessie Luella Jane	2nd great-granddaughter	IV	4

Name	Relationship with Johnnie Blue	Civil	Canon
High, Joseph	Husband of the 5th great-granddaughter		
High, William G.	Husband of the great-granddaughter		
Hoffman, Ruth	Wife of the 3rd great-grandson		
Holly	Husband of the 2nd great-granddaughter		
Homerding, Margie	Wife of the 3rd great-grandson		
Howard, Iona Mae	Wife of the 3rd great-grandson		
Howell, William	Husband of the 2nd great-granddaughter		
Hulbert, Heidi Ann	Wife of the 5th great-grandson		
Hulda	Wife of the 3rd great-grandson		
Hummel, Georgianne	Wife of the 4th great-grandson		
Hunt, Donald Wilson	3rd great-grandson	V	5
Hunt, Louis Herman	Husband of the 2nd great-granddaughter		
Hutchinson, William Charles	Husband of the 6th great-granddaughter		
J., Katie	Great-granddaughter	III	3
Jack	Husband of the 2nd great-granddaughter		
Janke, Janet	Wife of the 4th great-grandson		
Janvrin, Aron Kyle	5th great-grandson	VII	7
Janvrin, Brice	6th great-grandson	VIII	8
Janvrin, Bruce Clyde	5th great-grandson	VII	7
Janvrin, Bryleigh	6th great-granddaughter	VIII	8
Janvrin, Clyde Elmer	Husband of the 4th great-granddaughter		
Janvrin, Eric Paul	5th great-grandson	VII	7
Janvrin, Genevieve	6th great-granddaughter	VIII	8
Janvrin, Hannah Kate	6th great-granddaughter	VIII	8
Janvrin, Kurt Reinhard	5th great-grandson	VII	7
Janvrin, Mabeline	6th great-granddaughter	VIII	8
Janvrin, Rebecca Lindsey	6th great-granddaughter	VIII	8
Janvrin, Tyler	6th great-grandson	VIII	8
Jean	Wife of the 4th great-grandson		
Jellerichs, Gail A.	Husband of the 4th great-granddaughter		
Jennie	2nd great-granddaughter	IV	4
Joe	5th great-grandson	VII	7
Johnson, Donald LeRoy	Husband of the 4th great-granddaughter		
Jr.	3rd great-grandson	V	5
Jr.	4th great-grandson	VI	6
Katherine	Granddaughter	II	2
Keith, Thelma Lillian	Wife of the 2nd great-grandson		
	Wife of the 3rd great-grandson		
Kennedy, Danny	Husband of the 5th great-granddaughter		
Kent, Ella A.	Wife of the great-grandson		
Kidwell, Jacob	6th great-grandson	VIII	8
Kidwell, 'Male'	Husband of the 5th great-granddaughter		
Kidwell, Steven	6th great-grandson	VIII	8
Kidwell, Tyler	6th great-grandson	VIII	8
Kimberlin, Corinne	5th great-granddaughter	VII	7
Kimberlin, John	Husband of the 4th great-granddaughter		
Klosterman, Nora	Wife of the 2nd great-grandson		
Krause, Christine	Wife of the 5th great-grandson		
Kristin	6th great-granddaughter	VIII	8
Kunavich, Adolph G.	Husband of the 4th great-granddaughter		
Kunavich, James Joseph	5th great-grandson	VII	7
Kunavich, James Joseph, Jr.	6th great-grandson	VIII	8
Kunavich, Ronald George	5th great-grandson	VII	7

Name	Relationship with Johnnie Blue	Civil	Canon
Lane, Dorothy Ann	4th great-granddaughter	VI	6
Lane, Mildred	4th great-granddaughter	VI	6
Lane, William	Husband of the 3rd great-granddaughter		
Lane, William	4th great-grandson	VI	6
Layla Marie Bauer	6th great-granddaughter	VIII	8
Lewis	Husband of the 2nd great-granddaughter		
Liggett, Isabelle Mary	Wife of the great-grandson		
Lizzie	Great-granddaughter	III	3
Longanecker, Samuel L.	Husband of the 2nd great-granddaughter		
Machie, Angela Kay	Wife of the 6th great-grandson		
Maggie	Great-granddaughter	III	3
Maggie	2nd great-granddaughter	IV	4
Manning, Shirley	Wife of the 4th great-grandson		
Mariseal, Margarita	Wife of the 5th great-grandson		
Marr, Barbara	4th great-granddaughter	VI	6
Marr, George L.	Husband of the 3rd great-granddaughter		
Marr, George Michael	4th great-grandson	VI	6
Martinez, Maria	Wife of the 5th great-grandson		
Mary	Wife of the 2nd great-grandson		
Matchie, Angela	6th great-granddaughter	VIII	8
Matchie, Frank	Husband of the 5th great-granddaughter		
Mathew, Janice Lucille	Wife of the 3rd great-grandson		
May, Denzie	Wife of the 3rd great-grandson		
May, Iva	3rd great-granddaughter	V	5
Mayme	3rd great-granddaughter	V	5
McFarlain, Katharine	Daughter-in-law		
McFarlane, Catherine	Daughter-in-law		
McKay, Daniel	Great-grandson	III	3
McKay, Robert	Husband of the granddaughter		
McKee, Carlene	Wife of the 4th great-grandson		
Meakins, Dossie May	Wife of the 3rd great-grandson		
Medema, George	Husband of the 4th great-granddaughter		
Medema, Jacob	6th great-grandson	VIII	8
Medema, James Greg	5th great-grandson	VII	7
Medema, Janice Lyne	5th great-granddaughter	VII	7
Medema, Jeanie Larie	5th great-granddaughter	VII	7
Medema, Jerry Allen	5th great-grandson	VII	7
Medema, Jhody Jean	5th great-grandson	VII	7
Medema, Jon Craig	5th great-grandson	VII	7
Medema, Julie Marie	5th great-granddaughter	VII	7
Mehlhaus, Diane	Wife of the 5th great-grandson		
Meinsma, Jeff	Husband of the 6th great-granddaughter		
Merrill, Dustin	6th great-grandson	VIII	8
Merrill, Steve	Husband of the 5th great-granddaughter		
Milnes, Bryan Thomas	5th great-grandson	VII	7
Milnes, Diane Louise	4th great-granddaughter	VI	6
Milnes, Lepha Mae	3rd great-granddaughter	V	5
Milnes, Margaret Elizabeth	3rd great-granddaughter	V	5
Milnes, Scott T.	5th great-grandson	VII	7
Milnes, Shaun Mathew	5th great-grandson	VII	7
Milnes, Thomas Brent	4th great-grandson	VI	6
Milnes, Tina Elizabeth	5th great-granddaughter	VII	7
Milnes, Walter	3rd great-grandson	V	5

Name	Relationship with Johnnie Blue	Civil	Canon
Milnes, Walter Richard	Husband of the 2nd great-granddaughter		
Milnes, Wanda Vey	4th great-granddaughter	VI	6
Milnes, Winnie	Wife of the 3rd great-grandson		
Mirissa Jane	7th great-granddaughter	IX	9
Mitchell, Jane Whitford	4th great-granddaughter	VI	6
Mitchell, John Wilson	4th great-grandson	VI	6
Mitchell, Martha Ann	4th great-granddaughter	VI	6
Mitchell, Whitford	Husband of the 3rd great-granddaughter		
Mitchell, Whitford Kimball	5th great-grandson	VII	7
Moon	3rd great-grandson	V	5
Moran, Christine Elizabeth	5th great-granddaughter	VII	7
Moran, Kimberly Jane	5th great-granddaughter	VII	7
Moran, Michael	Husband of the 4th great-granddaughter		
Moran, Stephen Michael	5th great-grandson	VII	7
Muschal, Robert Michael	Husband of the 4th great-granddaughter		
Naftzger, Beulah Vey	Wife of the 3rd great-grandson		
Nellie, Helen	Wife of the grandson		
Nelson, Dorothy	Wife of the 2nd great-grandson		
Nelson, Helen Marie	Wife of the 3rd great-grandson		
Nice, Elwin	5th great-grandson	VII	7
Nice, Judy	6th great-granddaughter	VIII	8
Nice, Linda	6th great-granddaughter	VIII	8
Nice, Lyle	Husband of the 4th great-granddaughter		
Nice, Marjorie	5th great-granddaughter	VII	7
Nice, Pam	6th great-granddaughter	VIII	8
Nice, William	6th great-grandson	VIII	8
Nicke, Darrel	Husband of the 5th great-granddaughter		
Onken, Sally Ann	Wife of the 4th great-grandson		
Ostema, Cindy	Wife of the 5th great-grandson		
Palmier, Doria	Wife of the 4th great-grandson		
Patrick, JoAnne	Wife of the 4th great-grandson		
Patti	4th great-granddaughter	VI	6
Pessman, Greg	Husband of the 5th great-granddaughter		
Petticord, Patricia	Wife of the 6th great-grandson		
Pierce, Elsey Mae	3rd great-granddaughter	V	5
Pierce, James H.	Husband of the 4th great-granddaughter		
Pierce, Vera Marie	3rd great-granddaughter	V	5
Pierce, Walter S.	Husband of the 2nd great-granddaughter		
Pritchard, Leonard	Husband of the 5th great-granddaughter		
Pritchard, Timothy Allen	6th great-grandson	VIII	8
Pyron, Christine	Wife of the 5th great-grandson		
Rains, O. Darlene	Wife of the 4th great-grandson		
Reagan, Cameron Michael	5th great-grandson	VII	7
Reagan, John Edward	Husband of the 2nd great-granddaughter		
Reagan, John Neil	3rd great-grandson	V	5
Reagan, Maureen Elizabeth	4th great-granddaughter	VI	6
Reagan, Michael	4th great-grandson	VI	6
Reagan, Patricia	4th great-granddaughter	VI	6
Reagan, Ronald Prescott	4th great-grandson	VI	6
Reagan, Ronald Wilson	3rd great-grandson	V	5
Rebecca	6th great-granddaughter	VIII	8
Reinhardt	Husband of the 3rd great-granddaughter		
Reiter, Glenda	Wife of the 4th great-grandson		

Name	Relationship with Johnnie Blue	Civil	Canon
Rick, Beth	Wife of the 5th great-grandson		
Rick, Patricia	Wife of the 4th great-grandson		
Robbins, Anne Frances	Wife of the 3rd great-grandson		
Robinson, Linda	Wife of the 5th great-grandson		
Roenike, Karen	Wife of the 5th great-grandson		
Rowe, Amanda	6th great-granddaughter	VIII	8
Rowe, David Keith	5th great-grandson	VII	7
Rowe, James Keith	Husband of the 4th great-granddaughter		
Rowe, Lucas Mathew	6th great-grandson	VIII	8
Rowe, Robert Mathew	5th great-grandson	VII	7
Rury, Donna Ann	Wife of the 5th great-grandson		
Rush, Stephen A.	Husband of the 2nd great-granddaughter		
Ryan, Daniel Joseph	Husband of the 4th great-granddaughter		
Schneider, Marian D.	Wife of the 4th great-grandson		
Schryver, Dawn	Wife of the 5th great-grandson		
Schumacher, Lucas	6th great-grandson	VIII	8
Schumacher, Matthew Collin	6th great-grandson	VIII	8
Schumacher, Thomas	Husband of the 5th great-granddaughter		
Sharer, Marie	Wife of the 5th great-grandson		
Shrider, Mareta	Wife of the 3rd great-grandson		
Silvis, Verlee Ann	Wife of the 4th great-grandson		
Smith, Barbara	5th great-granddaughter	VII	7
Smith, Charles Alfred	3rd great-grandson	V	5
Smith, Chelsey	6th great-granddaughter	VIII	8
Smith, Christopher Scott	6th great-grandson	VIII	8
Smith, Cory	6th great-granddaughter	VIII	8
Smith, Dale	5th great-grandson	VII	7
Smith, David	5th great-grandson	VII	7
Smith, Dean	5th great-grandson	VII	7
Smith, Dennis	5th great-grandson	VII	7
Smith, Gene Meakin	4th great-grandson	VI	6
Smith, Gordon M.	5th great-grandson	VII	7
Smith, Harry Wilson	3rd great-grandson	V	5
Smith, Harry Wilson, Jr	4th great-grandson	VI	6
Smith, Horace C.	Husband of the 2nd great-granddaughter		
Smith, Horace Vernon	3rd great-grandson	V	5
Smith, Hudson B.	5th great-grandson	VII	7
Smith, Jamie	6th great-grandson	VIII	8
Smith, Jenie Alice	Wife of the great-grandson		
Smith, Jenifer Erin	6th great-granddaughter	VIII	8
Smith, Karen	5th great-granddaughter	VII	7
Smith, Marshall	6th great-grandson	VIII	8
Smith, Mathew Lee	Husband of the 4th great-granddaughter		
Smith, Milford L.	4th great-grandson	VI	6
Smith, Nancy	5th great-granddaughter	VII	7
Smith, Penny	Wife of the 4th great-grandson		
Smith, Raymond	4th great-grandson	VI	6
Smith, Robert Clare	4th great-grandson	VI	6
Smith, Sally	5th great-granddaughter	VII	7
Smith, Taylor	6th great-grandson	VIII	8
Smith, Terry	5th great-grandson	VII	7
Smith, Thomas	5th great-grandson	VII	7
Smith, Thomas S.	6th great-grandson	VIII	8

Name	Relationship with Johnnie Blue	Civil	Canon
Smith, Vicki	5th great-granddaughter	VII	7
Sprague, Nancy Lee	Wife of the 5th great-grandson		
Springman, David Robert	Husband of the 5th great-granddaughter		
Stapleton, Gladys Eloise	3rd great-granddaughter	V	5
Stapleton, Glen	3rd great-grandson	V	5
Stapleton, William	Husband of the 2nd great-granddaughter		
Starck, Catherine	Wife of the 2nd great-grandson		
Stark, Katie	Wife of the 2nd great-grandson		
Stearns, Colleen	Wife of the 4th great-grandson		
Stella	2nd great-granddaughter	IV	4
Steven	Husband of the 2nd great-granddaughter		
Stevens, 'Male'	Husband of the 4th great-granddaughter		
Stuart, Ruth Jane	Wife of the 4th great-grandson		
Swanson, Charles	Husband of the 5th great-granddaughter		
Sweigert, Mabel May	Wife of the 3rd great-grandson		
Thomas, Iona Jean	Wife of the 3rd great-grandson		
Tiesman, Sharon	Wife of the 5th great-grandson		
Traum, David	6th great-grandson	VIII	8
Traum, John	6th great-grandson	VIII	8
Traum, Robert	Husband of the 5th great-granddaughter		
Traum, Susan	6th great-granddaughter	VIII	8
Trimble, Carol	Wife of the 5th great-grandson		
Tucker, 'Male'	Husband of the 4th great-granddaughter		
Tug	2nd great-grandson	IV	4
Ufken, Eugene	Husband of the 4th great-granddaughter		
Unger, Bruce	Husband of the 5th great-granddaughter		
Unger, Bruce Edwin, Jr.	6th great-grandson	VIII	8
Van Horn, James Jerry	Husband of the 4th great-granddaughter		
Veihl, Darlene E.	Wife of the 4th great-grandson		
Vina	2nd great-granddaughter	IV	4
Vos, Arlyn	4th great-grandson	VI	6
Vos, Arlyn Dale	5th great-grandson	VII	7
Vos, Debra Jane	5th great-granddaughter	VII	7
Vos, Ernest	Husband of the 3rd great-granddaughter		
Vos, Kari Sue	5th great-granddaughter	VII	7
Vos, Kathy Lynn	5th great-granddaughter	VII	7
Vos, Larry	4th great-grandson	VI	6
Vos, Lauri Ann	4th great-granddaughter	VI	6
Vos, Marla Ann	5th great-granddaughter	VII	7
Vos, Teri Ann	5th great-granddaughter	VII	7
Walters, Baby	6th great-granddaughter	VIII	8
Walters, Carl B.	Husband of the 3rd great-granddaughter		
Walters, David Gene	6th great-grandson	VIII	8
Walters, Dawn Gail	5th great-granddaughter	VII	7
Walters, Drew Philip	7th great-grandson	IX	9
Walters, Harlan Gene	5th great-grandson	VII	7
Walters, Harold Edward	4th great-grandson	VI	6
Walters, Jane Kaye	5th great-granddaughter	VII	7
Walters, Julia Anna	7th great-granddaughter	IX	9
Walters, Mark Douglas	6th great-grandson	VIII	8
Walters, Matthew	6th great-grandson	VIII	8
Walters, Paul Edward	5th great-grandson	VII	7
Walters, Philip Dale	5th great-grandson	VII	7

Name	Relationship with Johnnie Blue	Civil	Canon
Walters, Rhonda Ruth	5th great-granddaughter	VII	7
Walters, Sandra	Wife of the 5th great-grandson		
Walters, Stephanie Anne	6th great-granddaughter	VIII	8
Walters, Terry Harlan	6th great-grandson	VIII	8
Walters, Tiffany Marie	6th great-granddaughter	VIII	8
Walters, Tori Cheryl	6th great-granddaughter	VIII	8
Walters, Troy J.	6th great-grandson	VIII	8
Walters, Wendy Lee	6th great-granddaughter	VIII	8
Warner, Catherine	4th great-granddaughter	VI	6
Warner, James	Husband of the 2nd great-granddaughter		
Warner, James	4th great-grandson	VI	6
Warner, Robert Wilson	3rd great-grandson	V	5
Watson, Mary	Wife of the 3rd great-grandson		
Webb, Jeanne	Wife of the 4th great-grandson		
Weyrauch, Madeline	Wife of the 4th great-grandson		
Whistler, Florence I.	3rd great-granddaughter	V	5
Whistler, Glenn Otto	Husband of the 2nd great-granddaughter		
Whistler, Lois W.	3rd great-granddaughter	V	5
Wiebenga, Lesley Dawn	6th great-granddaughter	VIII	8
Wiebenga, Ron	Husband of the 5th great-granddaughter		
Wiersema, Patricia	Wife of the 5th great-grandson		
Wilkinson, Margaret	Wife of the 2nd great-grandson		
Willson	Husband of the granddaughter		
Wilson, Alexander B	Great-grandson	III	3
Wilson, Alexander Thomas	2nd great-grandson	IV	4
Wilson, Alice Jane	2nd great-granddaughter	IV	4
Wilson, Catherine	Great-granddaughter	III	3
Wilson, Charles Abram	2nd great-grandson	IV	4
Wilson, Charles Desmond	Great-grandson	III	3
Wilson, Charles LeRoy	3rd great-grandson	V	5
Wilson, Deborah Ann	4th great-granddaughter	VI	6
Wilson, Dwight Alvin	3rd great-grandson	V	5
Wilson, Earl Charles	4th great-grandson	VI	6
Wilson, Earl Clyde	3rd great-grandson	V	5
Wilson, Elizabeth Evelyn	Great-granddaughter	III	3
Wilson, Elizabeth Mary	3rd great-granddaughter	V	5
Wilson, Emily G.	2nd great-granddaughter	IV	4
Wilson, Frances Jane	2nd great-granddaughter	IV	4
Wilson, George John	2nd great-grandson	IV	4
Wilson, George Orville	2nd great-grandson	IV	4
Wilson, Janet Mae	4th great-granddaughter	VI	6
Wilson, Jeanette	3rd great-granddaughter	V	5
Wilson, Jeannette Lynn	4th great-granddaughter	VI	6
Wilson, Jody Allen	4th great-grandson	VI	6
Wilson, John	Husband of the granddaughter		
Wilson, John	Great-grandson	III	3
Wilson, John Charles	2nd great-grandson	IV	4
Wilson, John Charles III	5th great-grandson	VII	7
Wilson, John Charles, Jr	4th great-grandson	VI	6
Wilson, John James	3rd great-grandson	V	5
Wilson, Judith Suzane	4th great-granddaughter	VI	6
Wilson, Kathy Elizabeth	4th great-granddaughter	VI	6
Wilson, Kimberly Ann	4th great-granddaughter	VI	6

Name	Relationship with Johnnie Blue	Civil	Canon
Wilson, Leo Vernon, Sr.	3rd great-grandson	V	5
Wilson, Linda Kay	4th great-granddaughter	VI	6
Wilson, Marc Lee	4th great-grandson	VI	6
Wilson, Margaret Mae	Great-granddaughter	III	3
Wilson, Margaret May	2nd great-granddaughter	IV	4
Wilson, Marie	4th great-granddaughter	VI	6
Wilson, Marilyn Joan	4th great-granddaughter	VI	6
Wilson, Mary LaVina	2nd great-granddaughter	IV	4
Wilson, Mary Margaret	3rd great-granddaughter	V	5
Wilson, Naomi Jean	4th great-granddaughter	VI	6
Wilson, Nellie Clyde	2nd great-granddaughter	IV	4
Wilson, Paul Fletcher	2nd great-grandson	IV	4
Wilson, Paul Mathew	5th great-grandson	VII	7
Wilson, Phoebe Mae	2nd great-granddaughter	IV	4
Wilson, Robert Bristle	3rd great-grandson	V	5
Wilson, Robert Thomas	4th great-grandson	VI	6
Wilson, Ronald Stanley	4th great-grandson	VI	6
Wilson, Sara	Great-granddaughter	III	3
Wilson, Sara Jane	2nd great-granddaughter	IV	4
Wilson, Thomas	Great-grandson	III	3
Wilson, Thomas Robert	5th great-grandson	VII	7
Wilson, Trudy Jean	4th great-granddaughter	VI	6
Wilson, Vaughn Fae	4th great-granddaughter	VI	6
Wilson, Winifred M.	2nd great-granddaughter	IV	4
Witt, Andrew F.	Husband of the 3rd great-granddaughter		
Witt, Donna Jean	4th great-granddaughter	VI	6
Witt, Harlan Andrew	4th great-grandson	VI	6
Witt, Jeffrey Andrew	5th great-grandson	VII	7
Witt, Kimberly Lynn	5th great-granddaughter	VII	7
Witt, Kristen Les	5th great-granddaughter	VII	7
Witt, Sandra Mae	4th great-granddaughter	VI	6
Witz, 'Male'	Husband of the 4th great-granddaughter		
Yates, Naomi	Wife of the 4th great-grandson		
Yonkers, Alberta Lynn	Wife of the 5th great-grandson		

Descendants of George Bristle

Generation No. 1

1. GEORGE[1] BRISTLE was born 1829 in Baden, Germany. He married DOROTHA. She was born 1833 in Baden, Germany.

Notes for GEORGE BRISTLE:
1880 WsidecoClytwpIL census 48/50, age 51, Baden Baden Baden, Dorotha F 47 Baden Baden Baden, John M 21 IL Baden Baden.

Notes for DOROTHA:
1880 WsidecoClytwpIL cen50, age 47, Ba Ba Ba

Child of GEORGE BRISTLE and DOROTHA is:
2. i. JOHN J.[2] BRISTLE, b. October 04, 1859, Wside co., Clydetwp, IL; d. April 19, 1939, WHiteside co., IL.

Generation No. 2

2. JOHN J.[2] BRISTLE *(GEORGE[1])* was born October 04, 1859 in Wside co., Clydetwp, IL, and died April 19, 1939 in WHiteside co., IL. He married ADDIE FRANCES BODY December 25, 1882 in Whiteside co., IL, daughter of ISAAC BODY and CYRENA DYSON. She was born 1861, and died October 17, 1935 in Morrison, IL.

Notes for JOHN J. BRISTLE:
1880 WsidecoClytwpIL cen50, age 21, IL Ba Ba
WsidecoIL marriage #5955
1900 WsidecoMorrisonIL census215/277, age 40, IL Gr Gr, landlord
Bd. Grove Hill cem., Morrison, Lot 7E, residence Morrison, age 80yrs, 6mos, 15d.
Birth date estimated.

Notes for ADDIE FRANCES BODY:
1900 WsidecoMorrisonIL cen277, IL IL IL
Bd. Grove Hill cem., Morrison, Lot 7EE, age 74 years, middle name from cem. records.

Children of JOHN BRISTLE and ADDIE BODY are:
3. i. ETTA MAY[3] BRISTLE, b. November 27, 1883; d. May 14, 1956, Morrison, IL.
    ii. GEORGE EARL BRISTLE, b. December 05, 1889, Whiteside co., IL; d. September 02, 1961, WHiteside co., IL.

> Notes for GEORGE EARL BRISTLE:
> WsidecoIL birth certificate #6,314
> 1900 WsidecoIL cen277, George E., age 10, IL IL IL
> Bd. Grove Hill cem., Morrison, Lot 14S, age 71 years.

Generation No. 3

3. ETTA MAY[3] BRISTLE *(JOHN J.[2], GEORGE[1])* was born November 27, 1883, and died May 14, 1956 in Morrison, IL. She married PAUL FLETCHER WILSON October 11, 1905 in Whiteside co., IL, son of ALEXANDER WILSON and DEBORAH FLETCHER. He was born January 1883 in Whiteside co., IL, and died 1964.

Notes for ETTA MAY BRISTLE:

1900 WsidecoIL census277, age 16, as Mary, IL IL IL
1910 WsidecoUGrIL census 60/63, age 26, IL IL IL
WsidecoIL birth certificate #4,020, mother as Addie F. Boda
Whiteside co., IL marriage record #2117.0.

More About ETTA MAY BRISTLE:
Burial: Grove Hill cemetery, Morrison

Notes for PAUL FLETCHER WILSON:
Heritage Quest gives his connection. 1920 WsidecoUGrovetwpIL cen186/186 gives age 36, IL IL NY, farmer. His father, Alexander is with them, age 65, IL Sc Sc
1910 WsidecoUGrtwpIL census 60/63, Age 27, IL NY NY, wife May 26 IL IL IL, father Alex 67 Widower NY NY NY 'own income'.
Xerox of Sentinel, Oct. 12, 1905.

Children of ETTA BRISTLE and PAUL WILSON are:
4.   i. DWIGHT ALVIN[4] WILSON, b. January 24, 1914; d. December 05, 1993, Sterling, Whiteside co., IL.
5.   ii. ROBERT BRISTLE WILSON, b. September 12, 1917; d. May 07, 1942.

Generation No. 4

4. DWIGHT ALVIN[4] WILSON (*ETTA MAY[3] BRISTLE, JOHN J.[2], GEORGE[1]*) was born January 24, 1914, and died December 05, 1993 in Sterling, Whiteside co., IL. He married JANICE LUCILLE MATHEW December 25, 1937 in Sterling, Whiteside co., IL. She was born November 30, 1917.

Notes for DWIGHT ALVIN WILSON:
WsidecoUGtwpIL census 186
WsidecoIL birth record #17,965
Retired from 1st National Bank, Sterling, Jan. 1, 1978.

More About DWIGHT ALVIN WILSON:
Burial: Grove Hill cemetery, Morrison

Children of DWIGHT WILSON and JANICE MATHEW are:
6.   i. JUDITH SUZANE[5] WILSON, b. November 21, 1942.
7.   ii. ROBERT THOMAS WILSON, b. June 29, 1944.

5. ROBERT BRISTLE[4] WILSON (*ETTA MAY[3] BRISTLE, JOHN J.[2], GEORGE[1]*) was born September 12, 1917, and died May 07, 1942. He married MAXINE JOY BARRETT March 22, 1940, daughter of HARVEY BARRETT and EDNA LAWTON. She was born August 01, 1920, and died April 11, 1997 in Cedar Rapids, Iowa.

More About ROBERT BRISTLE WILSON:
Burial: Grove Hill cemetery, Morrison

Child of ROBERT WILSON and MAXINE BARRETT is:
8.   i. DEBORAH ANN[5] WILSON, b. February 09, 1941.

Generation No. 5

6. JUDITH SUZANE[5] WILSON (*DWIGHT ALVIN[4], ETTA MAY[3] BRISTLE, JOHN J.[2], GEORGE[1]*) was born November 21, 1942. She married JAMES KEITH ROWE June 13, 1964, son of V. ROWE and MARY. He was born November 25, 1941.

Notes for JUDITH SUZANE WILSON:

Teacher

Notes for JAMES KEITH ROWE:
Teacher
Divorced August, 1994

Children of JUDITH WILSON and JAMES ROWE are:
        i. DAVID KEITH[6] ROWE, b. March 17, 1968; m. RHONDA KAY BAYLES, November 23, 1996; b. April 14, 1967.
9.   ii. ROBERT MATHEW ROWE, b. September 06, 1970.

7. ROBERT THOMAS[5] WILSON *(DWIGHT ALVIN[4], ETTA MAY[3] BRISTLE, JOHN J.[2], GEORGE[1])* was born June 29, 1944. He married GEORGIANNE HUMMEL March 21, 1972. She was born August 10, 1949.

Notes for GEORGIANNE HUMMEL:
Legal secretary

Children of ROBERT WILSON and GEORGIANNE HUMMEL are:
        i. THOMAS ROBERT[6] WILSON, b. August 24, 1984, Danville, IL.
        ii. PAUL MATHEW WILSON, b. October 27, 1985, Danville, IL.

8. DEBORAH ANN[5] WILSON *(ROBERT BRISTLE[4], ETTA MAY[3] BRISTLE, JOHN J.[2], GEORGE[1])* was born February 09, 1941. She married MICHAEL MORAN September 02, 1961, son of DON MORAN and LIENNE VITE. He was born January 26, 1941.

Children of DEBORAH WILSON and MICHAEL MORAN are:
        i. CHRISTINE ELIZABETH[6] MORAN, b. April 18, 1963; m. 'MALE' FOSTER.
10.   ii. KIMBERLY JANE MORAN, b. February 27, 1965.
        iii. STEPHEN MICHAEL MORAN, b. December 08, 1968.

Generation No. 6

9. ROBERT MATHEW[6] ROWE *(JUDITH SUZANE[5] WILSON, DWIGHT ALVIN[4], ETTA MAY[3] BRISTLE, JOHN J.[2], GEORGE[1])* was born September 06, 1970. He married HEIDI ANN HULBERT October 10, 1992, daughter of STEPHEN HULBERT and DIANE. She was born March 22, 1969.

Children of ROBERT ROWE and HEIDI HULBERT are:
        i. AMANDA[7] ROWE, b. April 29, 1995.
        ii. LUCAS MATHEW ROWE, b. February 10, 1998.

10. KIMBERLY JANE[6] MORAN *(DEBORAH ANN[5] WILSON, ROBERT BRISTLE[4], ETTA MAY[3] BRISTLE, JOHN J.[2], GEORGE[1])* was born February 27, 1965. She married 'MALE' KIDWELL.

Children of KIMBERLY MORAN and 'MALE' KIDWELL are:
        i. TYLER[7] KIDWELL.
        ii. JACOB KIDWELL.
        iii. STEVEN KIDWELL.

Kinship of George Bristle

Name	Relationship with George Bristle	Civil	Canon
Barrett, Maxine Joy	Wife of the great-grandson		
Bayles, Rhonda Kay	Wife of the 3rd great-grandson		
Body, Addie F. Boda/Ada F	Daughter-in-law		
Body, Addie Frances	Daughter-in-law		
Bristle, Etta May	Granddaughter	II	2
Bristle, George	Self		0
Bristle, George Earl	Grandson	II	2
Bristle, John J.	Son	I	1
Dorotha	Wife		
Foster, 'Male'	Husband of the 3rd great-granddaughter		
Hulbert, Heidi Ann	Wife of the 3rd great-grandson		
Hummel, Georgianne	Wife of the 2nd great-grandson		
Kidwell, Jacob	4th great-grandson	VI	6
Kidwell, 'Male'	Husband of the 3rd great-granddaughter		
Kidwell, Steven	4th great-grandson	VI	6
Kidwell, Tyler	4th great-grandson	VI	6
Mary	Granddaughter	II	2
Mathew, Janice Lucille	Wife of the great-grandson		
Moran, Christine Elizabeth	3rd great-granddaughter	V	5
Moran, Kimberly Jane	3rd great-granddaughter	V	5
Moran, Michael	Husband of the 2nd great-granddaughter		
Moran, Stephen Michael	3rd great-grandson	V	5
Rowe, Amanda	4th great-granddaughter	VI	6
Rowe, David Keith	3rd great-grandson	V	5
Rowe, James Keith	Husband of the 2nd great-granddaughter		
Rowe, Lucas Mathew	4th great-grandson	VI	6
Rowe, Robert Mathew	3rd great-grandson	V	5
Wilson, Deborah Ann	2nd great-granddaughter	IV	4
Wilson, Dwight Alvin	Great-grandson	III	3
Wilson, Judith Suzane	2nd great-granddaughter	IV	4
Wilson, Paul Fletcher	Husband of the granddaughter		
Wilson, Paul Mathew	3rd great-grandson	V	5
Wilson, Robert Bristle	Great-grandson	III	3
Wilson, Robert Thomas	2nd great-grandson	IV	4
Wilson, Thomas Robert	3rd great-grandson	V	5

Descendants of Henry E. Gerdes

Generation No. 1

1. HENRY E.[1] GERDES was born Abt. 1840 in Germany, and died August 26, 1908 in Whiteside co., IL. He married REBECCA KALLENOR. She was born Abt. 1840 in Germany, and died February 08, 1905 in Wside co., Clydetwp, IL.

Notes for HENRY E. GERDES:
Birth date for clarification. Information from Heritage Quest.
WsidecoIL death record #5,336.

Notes for REBECCA KALLENOR:
Death date from death rcds WsidecoIL #4317. Also 'Cohenauer'.

Child of HENRY GERDES and REBECCA KALLENOR is:
2.   i.   DAVID EDMOND[2] GERDES, b. December 1864, Whiteside co., IL; d. January 13, 1934, Whiteside co., IL.

Generation No. 2

2. DAVID EDMOND[2] GERDES *(HENRY E.[1])* was born December 1864 in Whiteside co., IL, and died January 13, 1934 in Whiteside co., IL. He married ELLEN W. BECHTEL January 08, 1888 in Whiteside co., IL, daughter of EPHRAIM BECHTEL and SARA WILSON. She was born July 01, 1866 in Wside co., Clydetwp, IL.

Notes for DAVID EDMOND GERDES:
WsidcoIL marriage record #7289. Minister of the Dunkard Church, Clyde & Rock Creek, ILL.
1910 WsidecoUsttwpIL census 61/63. David 45, farmer, IL Gr PA
1920 WsidecoClytwpIL. census119/121m age 55, farmer, IL Gr PA
1920 census has Ephraim Bechtel, 86, f in law, OH PA PA and Sarah (Wilson), his wife, 78, IL Sc Sc with David's family
The Clyde Twp. farm was in the family since 1863.

Notes for ELLEN W. BECHTEL:
1870 WsidecoIL cen95, age 4, IL
1910 Wside census 163 age 43, IL OH IL
COUSIN ONCE REMOVED OF RONALD REAGAN

Children of DAVID GERDES and ELLEN BECHTEL are:
3.   i.   EPHRAIM LAWRENCE[3] GERDES, b. October 11, 1888, Wside co., Clydetwp, IL.
    ii.   REBECCA H GERDES, b. December 05, 1889, WSide co., Clydetwp, IL; d. April 28, 1981, Whiteside co., IL.

        Notes for REBECCA H GERDES:
        WsidecoIL birth record #6,315.
        1910 Wside census 163, age 20, single, servant
        Did not marry.
        1920 Wside Clyde census, with father, 30, servant, IL IL IL
        She lived on the family farm all her life, never married, kept house for her brothers.

        More About REBECCA H GERDES:
        Burial: Malvern cemetery

    iii.   EDMUND WAYNE GERDES, b. March 02, 1892, Wside co., Clydetwp, IL; d. July 10, 1969, WHiteside co., IL.

Notes for EDMUND WAYNE GERDES:
WsidecoIL birth rcd #7,402
1910 WsideIL census 163, age 17, farm laborer, 'Wayne'
Living at RFD 2, Dixon, IL Feb. 1981, minister
WsidecoIL death records

4.   iv.   GALEN GLENN GERDES, b. January 1894, Wside co., Clydetwp, IL; d. September 01, 1976, N. Manchester, IN.

         v.   HENRY RALPH GERDES, b. November 03, 1899, Wside co., Clydetwp, IL; d. February 07, 1981, Morrison, IL.

Notes for HENRY RALPH GERDES:
1910 WsidecoIL, cen 163, age 10
1920 WsidecoIL, cen 121, age 20, laborer
Never married, lived on family farm all his life.

More About HENRY RALPH GERDES:
Burial: Malvern cemetery

        vi.   LLOYD GERDES, b. August 02, 1903, Wside co., Clydetwp, IL.

Notes for LLOYD GERDES:
WsidecoIL birth record #10,211 as 'boy'. 1920 census lists him as 16.
1910 WsidecoIL census age 6
1920 WsidecoIL cen 121, age 16
Died in truck accident, not married.

       vii.   VIRGIL E. GERDES, b. August 25, 1905, Wside co., Clydetwp, IL; d. April 23, 1987, Whiteside co., IL.

Notes for VIRGIL E. GERDES:
WsidecoIL birth record #12,024
1910 WsidecoIL cen163 age 4
1920 WsidecoIL cen 121, age 14
WsidecoIL death records
The author has a taped conversation with Virgil in which he remenisces about playing with Ronald Reagan as a child.
Lived on the family farm all his life, enjoyed antique farm machinery, never married.

More About VIRGIL E. GERDES:
Burial: Malvern cemetery

Generation No. 3

3. EPHRAIM LAWRENCE[3] GERDES *(DAVID EDMOND[2], HENRY E.[1])* was born October 11, 1888 in Wside co., Clydetwp, IL.

Notes for EPHRAIM LAWRENCE GERDES:
WsidecoIL birth #5,888. Married, 2 boys, lived near Dixon.

Child of EPHRAIM LAWRENCE GERDES is:
         i.   WAYNE[4] GERDES, b. 1904.

Notes for WAYNE GERDES:
Living in Dixon in 1998 at 94, not married

4. GALEN GLENN[3] GERDES *(DAVID EDMOND[2], HENRY E.[1])* was born January 1894 in Wside co., Clydetwp, IL, and died September 01, 1976 in N. Manchester, IN. He married (1) IDA FIKE September 02, 1923. She died September 12, 1923. He married (2) MARETA SHRIDER August 05, 1951.

Notes for GALEN GLENN GERDES:
Children per obituary
Minister, retired.

More About GALEN GLENN GERDES:
Burial: Yellow Creek Cemetery, Pearl City

Children of GALEN GERDES and MARETA SHRIDER are:
     i. ROBERT[4] GERDES.
    ii. RUTH GERDES.

Kinship of Henry E. Gerdes

Name	Relationship with Henry Gerdes	Civil	Canon
Bechtel, Ellen W.	Daughter-in-law		
C., Henry	Grandson	II	2
Cohenauer	Wife		
Ella	Daughter-in-law		
Fike, Ida	Wife of the grandson		
Gerdes, David Edmond	Son	I	1
Gerdes, Ephraim Lawrence	Grandson	II	2
Gerdes, Galen Glenn	Grandson	II	2
Gerdes, Henry E.	Self		0
Gerdes, Henry Ralph	Grandson	II	2
Gerdes, Lloyd	Grandson	II	2
Gerdes, Robert	Great-grandson	III	3
Gerdes, Ruth	Great-granddaughter	III	3
Gerdes, Virgil E.	Grandson	II	2
Gerdes, Wayne	Great-grandson	III	3
Kallenor, Rebecca	Wife		
Shrider, Mareta	Wife of the grandson		

Descendants of Eilt Habben

Generation No. 1

1. EILT[1] HABBEN was born in Germany, and died in Germany. He married MARIE HOLMRICK.

Notes for EILT HABBEN:
Probably lived in Frisia, near Bremerhaven, Germany. His son born there.

Child of EILT HABBEN and MARIE HOLMRICK is:
2.   i. REINHARD F.[2] HABBEN, b. April 30, 1902, Frisia, nr. Bremerhaven, Germany; d. March 22, 1980, Morrison, IL.

Generation No. 2

2. REINHARD F.[2] HABBEN *(EILT[1])* was born April 30, 1902 in Frisia, nr. Bremerhaven, Germany, and died March 22, 1980 in Morrison, IL. He married VERA MARIE PIERCE April 03, 1933 in Somonauk, DeKalb co., IL, daughter of WALTER PIERCE and SARA WILSON. She was born February 16, 1908 in Tekamah, Burt, Nebraska, and died January 30, 1986 in White Pigeon, Whiteside co., IL.

Notes for REINHARD F. HABBEN:
Became a US citizen 9 Oct. 1931, Chicago, IL.

More About REINHARD F. HABBEN:
Burial: West Genesee cem, Coleta, IL

Notes for VERA MARIE PIERCE:
Married at St. Johns Lutheran Church, Somonauk, IL.
COUSIN OF RONALD REAGAN

More About VERA MARIE PIERCE:
Burial: West Genesee cem, Coleta, IL

Children of REINHARD HABBEN and VERA PIERCE are:
3.   i. MERNA JOY[3] HABBEN, b. October 12, 1933, Coleta, Whiteside co., IL.
4.   ii. NORMAN WALTER HABBEN, b. September 10, 1935, Coleta, Whiteside co., IL.
5.   iii. RONALD LEE HABBEN, b. July 17, 1938, Coleta, Whiteside co., IL.
6.   iv. MILFORD GENE HABBEN, b. July 04, 1940, Coleta, Whiteside co., IL.
7.   v. VELMA JANE HABBEN, b. April 10, 1943, Morrison, IL.
8.   vi. JUDITH MAY HABBEN, b. April 28, 1946, Morrison, IL.
9.   vii. CAROL ANN HABBEN, b. June 04, 1948, Morrison, IL.
10.   viii. BEVERLY JOAN HABBEN, b. July 10, 1952, Morrison, IL.
11.   ix. DONNA ELAINE HABBEN, b. August 04, 1954, Morrison, IL.

Generation No. 3

3. MERNA JOY[3] HABBEN *(REINHARD F.[2], EILT[1])* was born October 12, 1933 in Coleta, Whiteside co., IL. She married (1) CLYDE ELMER JANVRIN September 02, 1956 in Sterling, Whiteside co., IL. He was born August 24, 1925 in Morrison, IL, and died May 20, 1970 in Morrison, IL. She married (2) ROBERT MICHAEL MUSCHAL Aft. 1971, son of NICHOLAS MUSCHAL and KATHERINE MARX. He was born June 20, 1940 in Chicago, IL.

Notes for MERNA JOY HABBEN:
Md. in St. Johns Lutheran Church, Sterling
Dairy farmer.
Mrs. Merna Habben-Muschal has been of tremendous help in furnishing material and in proofreading my pages. If there are errors, blame me. CJG
COUSIN ONCE REMOVED OF RONALD REAGAN

Notes for CLYDE ELMER JANVRIN:
Dairy farmer, served in the Army.

More About CLYDE ELMER JANVRIN:
Burial: South Clyde cemetery

Notes for ROBERT MICHAEL MUSCHAL:
Painter. Marriage to Merna was his second marriage, also her 2nd.
Auditor and Inspector. Married in United Methodist Church, Morrison, IL.

Children of MERNA HABBEN and CLYDE JANVRIN are:
      i. ERIC PAUL^4 JANVRIN, b. August 31, 1958, Morrison, IL; m. CAROL TRIMBLE, October 10, 1986, Fulton, Whiteside co., IL; b. November 06, 1956, Fulton, IL.
12. ii. KURT REINHARD JANVRIN, b. August 04, 1960, Morrison, IL.
13. iii. BRUCE CLYDE JANVRIN, b. December 22, 1961, Morrison, IL.
14. iv. ARON KYLE JANVRIN, b. November 13, 1964, Morrison, IL.

4. NORMAN WALTER^3 HABBEN *(REINHARD F.^{2}, EILT^1)* was born September 10, 1935 in Coleta, Whiteside co., IL. He married NORMA JEAN COOK June 02, 1956 in Rock Falls, Whiteside co., IL. She was born June 02, 1937 in Rock Falls, Whiteside co., IL.

Notes for NORMAN WALTER HABBEN:
COUSIN ONCE REMOVED OF RONALD REAGAN

Children of NORMAN HABBEN and NORMA COOK are:
15. i. RHONDA JANE^4 HABBEN, b. June 24, 1957.
      ii. ROBERT ALLEN HABBEN, b. August 02, 1958, Morrison, IL.
16. iii. GENE LEROY HABBEN, b. July 07, 1960, Morrison, IL.
17. iv. SARA LEANNE HABBEN, b. March 09, 1967, Morrison, IL.

5. RONALD LEE^3 HABBEN *(REINHARD F.^{2}, EILT^1)* was born July 17, 1938 in Coleta, Whiteside co., IL. He married NANCY JOAN BIELEMA September 02, 1961 in Fulton, Whiteside co., IL. She was born November 15, 1940 in Fulton, IL.

Notes for RONALD LEE HABBEN:
COUSIN ONCE REMOVED OF RONALD REAGAN

Children of RONALD HABBEN and NANCY BIELEMA are:
18. i. DANIEL LEE^4 HABBEN, b. June 26, 1962, Morrison, IL.
19. ii. DEBRA LOU HABBEN, b. September 17, 1964, Morrison, IL.
      iii. DAVID ALLEN HABBEN, b. November 08, 1978, Morrison, IL.

6. MILFORD GENE^3 HABBEN *(REINHARD F.^{2}, EILT^1)* was born July 04, 1940 in Coleta, Whiteside co., IL. He married JOANNE PATRICK July 06, 1964 in San Jose, Santa Clara co., CA. She was born May 23, 1943 in Santa Clara, CA.

Notes for MILFORD GENE HABBEN:
COUSIN ONCE REMOVED OF RONALD REAGAN

Children of MILFORD HABBEN and JOANNE PATRICK are:
20.   i. CATHERINE JEAN[4] HABBEN, b. May 08, 1966, Morrison, IL.
    ii. DONALD PATRICK HABBEN, b. April 08, 1969, Morrison, IL; m. LISA FREDRICK, November 10, 1990, Dixon, Lee co., IL.

Notes for DONALD PATRICK HABBEN:
Divorced, no children.

7. VELMA JANE[3] HABBEN *(REINHARD F.[2], EILT[1])* was born April 10, 1943 in Morrison, IL. She married WILLIAM RICHARD NORTON, JR December 07, 1963 in Freeport, Stephenson co., IL, son of WILLIAM NORTON and EDNA LOTT. He was born October 20, 1938 in Rockford, ILL.

Notes for VELMA JANE HABBEN:
COUSIN ONCE REMOVED OF RONALD REAGAN

Notes for WILLIAM RICHARD NORTON, JR:
Railroad telegrapher at time of marriage, later truck driver.

Children of VELMA HABBEN and WILLIAM NORTON are:
    i. JAMES RICHARD[4] NORTON, b. June 30, 1967, Freport, Stephenson co., IL.
21.   ii. JEFFERY MICHAEL NORTON, b. December 23, 1971, Freport, Stephenson co., IL.

8. JUDITH MAY[3] HABBEN *(REINHARD F.[2], EILT[1])* was born April 28, 1946 in Morrison, IL. She married DONALD RAY BURMEISTER August 28, 1976 in Dewitt, Clinton co., Iowa. He was born January 23, 1939 in Dewitt, Clinton co., IA.

Notes for JUDITH MAY HABBEN:
COUSIN ONCE REMOVED OF RONALD REAGAN

Notes for DONALD RAY BURMEISTER:
His second marriage.

Children of JUDITH HABBEN and DONALD BURMEISTER are:
    i. JOHN BRANDON[4] BURMEISTER, b. August 25, 1977, Dewitt, Clinton co., IA.
    ii. BRIAN DOUGLAS BURMEISTER, b. October 09, 1980, Dewitt, Clinton co., IA.

9. CAROL ANN[3] HABBEN *(REINHARD F.[2], EILT[1])* was born June 04, 1948 in Morrison, IL. She met CHARLES ROBERT ALBRECHT March 01, 1969 in Belvidere, Boone co., IL, son of FRANK ALBRECHT and IRENE HOWE. He was born November 28, 1937.

Notes for CAROL ANN HABBEN:
Born at Morrison Community Hospital
COUSIN ONCE REMOVED OF RONALD REAGAN

Notes for CHARLES ROBERT ALBRECHT:
Married by Robert A. Blodgett, Magistrate, at Belvidere, Boone co., IL
He was an 'assembler' when married.
This was his second marriage. Data from marriage license/Wiebenga material

Children of CAROL HABBEN and CHARLES ALBRECHT are:
22.   i. CALE RICHARD[4] ALBRECHT, b. June 06, 1973, Freport, Stephenson co., IL.
    ii. CALEB WILLAIM ALBRECHT, b. May 17, 1975, Freport, Stephenson co., IL.

Notes for CALEB WILLAIM ALBRECHT:
Married 1999, one child b. April 2000

10. BEVERLY JOAN[3] HABBEN *(REINHARD F.[2], EILT[1])* was born July 10, 1952 in Morrison, IL. She married KENNETH ALDEN ETHRIDGE November 25, 1972 in Pearl City, Jo Davies co., IL. He was born 1939 in Freport, Stephenson co., IL.

Notes for BEVERLY JOAN HABBEN:
COUSIN ONCE REMOVED OF RONALD REAGAN

Children of BEVERLY HABBEN and KENNETH ETHRIDGE are:
    i. JEREMY M.[4] ETHRIDGE, b. July 08, 1978, Freport, Stephenson co., IL.
    ii. KEVIN MARSHALL ETHRIDGE, b. June 29, 1980, Freport, Stephenson co., IL.
    iii. LAURA MARIE ETHRIDGE, b. May 29, 1983, Freport, Stephenson co., IL.

    Notes for LAURA MARIE ETHRIDGE:

    iv. BRADLEY ETHRIDGE, b. March 18, 1988, Freport, Stephenson co., IL.

11. DONNA ELAINE[3] HABBEN *(REINHARD F.[2], EILT[1])* was born August 04, 1954 in Morrison, IL. She married THOMAS MICHAEL ARDWIN November 02, 1982 in North Glenn, Adams co., CO, son of DETER ARDWIN and ANNA GAFKA. He was born January 15, 1942 in Detroit, MI.

Notes for DONNA ELAINE HABBEN:
Divorced Jan. 29, 1971, per marriage application, Detroit, MI
COUSIN ONCE REMOVED OF RONALD REAGAN

Notes for THOMAS MICHAEL ARDWIN:
Divorced: Jan. 29, 1971, per marriage application, Detroit, MI

Children of DONNA HABBEN and THOMAS ARDWIN are:
    i. DONNA MARIE[4] ARDWIN, b. March 28, 1987, Denver, Adams co., CO.
    ii. MICHAEL THOMAS ARDWIN, b. January 19, 1989, Denver, Adams co., CO.
    iii. LISA ARDWIN.

Generation No. 4

12. KURT REINHARD[4] JANVRIN *(MERNA JOY[3] HABBEN, REINHARD F.[2], EILT[1])* was born August 04, 1960 in Morrison, IL. He married YVONNE AMMON June 16, 1984 in Long Grove, Lake co., IL. She was born December 19, 1961 in Decatur, Macon co., IL.

Children of KURT JANVRIN and YVONNE AMMON are:
    i. REBECCA LINDSEY[5] JANVRIN, b. May 23, 1988, Trenton, Mercer co., NJ.
    ii. HANNAH KATE JANVRIN, b. October 07, 1990, Trenton, Mercer co., NJ.
    iii. GENEVIEVE JANVRIN, b. 1993.
    iv. MABELINE JANVRIN, b. 1997.

13. BRUCE CLYDE[4] JANVRIN *(MERNA JOY[3] HABBEN, REINHARD F.[2], EILT[1])* was born December 22, 1961 in Morrison, IL. He married DIANE MEHLHAUS August 11, 1990 in Dysart, Benton co., IA. She was born February 20, 1961 in Dysart, Benton co., Iowa.

Children of BRUCE JANVRIN and DIANE MEHLHAUS are:
    i. BRICE[5] JANVRIN, b. 1993.
    ii. BRYLEIGH JANVRIN, b. 1998.

14. ARON KYLE[4] JANVRIN *(MERNA JOY[3] HABBEN, REINHARD F.[2], EILT[1])* was born November 13, 1964 in Morrison, IL. He married CAROLYN BROWN June 28, 1998.

Child of ARON JANVRIN and CAROLYN BROWN is:
    i. TYLER[5] JANVRIN, b. February 29, 2000.

15. RHONDA JANE[4] HABBEN *(NORMAN WALTER[3], REINHARD F.[2], EILT[1])* was born June 24, 1957. She married (1) ALLEN GREELEY June 10, 1978 in Morrison, IL. He was born August 05, 1951 in Morrison, IL. She married (2) ALLEN RAY GREELEY June 10, 1978 in Morrison, IL. He was born August 05, 1951 in Morrison, IL.

Children of RHONDA HABBEN and ALLEN GREELEY are:
    i. MELLISSA JEAN[5] GREELEY, b. December 08, 1980, Morrison, IL.
    ii. WILLIAM NORMAN GREELEY, b. June 19, 1983, Morrison, IL.
    iii. MARLA JANE GREELEY, b. September 04, 1984, Morrison, IL.

16. GENE LEROY[4] HABBEN *(NORMAN WALTER[3], REINHARD F.[2], EILT[1])* was born July 07, 1960 in Morrison, IL. He married KAREN ROENIKE February 25, 1989 in Clinton, Iowa.

Children of GENE HABBEN and KAREN ROENIKE are:
    i. TRAVIS[5] HABBEN, b. 1993.
    ii. RYAN HABBEN, b. 1996.
    iii. KRISTIN, b. 1999.

17. SARA LEANNE[4] HABBEN *(NORMAN WALTER[3], REINHARD F.[2], EILT[1])* was born March 09, 1967 in Morrison, IL. She married (1) COONAN DICKMAN March 29, 1986 in Morrison, IL. He was born March 24, 1967. She married (2) RANDY FAUST September 1990 in Mo-.

Notes for SARA LEANNE HABBEN:
Divorced Dickman 1990, no children with him.

Notes for COONAN DICKMAN:
Divorced 1990, no children.

Children of SARA HABBEN and RANDY FAUST are:
    i. ADAM CHARLES[5] FAUST, b. March 23, 1991, Virginia Beach, VA.
    ii. ASHLEY FAUST, b. 1994.

18. DANIEL LEE[4] HABBEN *(RONALD LEE[3], REINHARD F.[2], EILT[1])* was born June 26, 1962 in Morrison, IL. He married BETH HACKER June 20, 1987 in Morrison, IL. She was born January 10, 1962.

Children of DANIEL HABBEN and BETH HACKER are:
    i. LOGAN DANIEL[5] HABBEN, b. May 14, 1989, Sterling, Whiteside co., IL.
    ii. ABBEY HABBEN, b. 1994.

19. DEBRA LOU[4] HABBEN *(RONALD LEE[3], REINHARD F.[2], EILT[1])* was born September 17, 1964 in Morrison, IL. She married JAMES LEE SNYDER June 11, 1983 in Morrison, IL. He was born October 30, 1963 in Morrison, IL.

Notes for DEBRA LOU HABBEN:
Divorced 1988

Notes for JAMES LEE SNYDER:
Divorced 1988

Children of DEBRA HABBEN and JAMES SNYDER are:
- i. BRANDON[5] SNYDER, b. October 31, 1985, Germany.
- ii. TIMOTHY SNYDER, b. February 12, 1987, Sterling, Whiteside co., IL.

20. CATHERINE JEAN[4] HABBEN *(MILFORD GENE[3], REINHARD F.[2], EILT[1])* was born May 08, 1966 in Morrison, IL. She married MARK BENNET June 27, 1987 in Dixon, Lee co., IL.

Notes for CATHERINE JEAN HABBEN:
Divorced

Children of CATHERINE HABBEN and MARK BENNET are:
- i. JENNIFER ANN[5] BENNET, b. October 06, 1990, Sterling, Whiteside co., IL.
- ii. AMANDA BENNET, b. 1994.

21. JEFFERY MICHAEL[4] NORTON *(VELMA JANE[3] HABBEN, REINHARD F.[2], EILT[1])* was born December 23, 1971 in Freport, Stephenson co., IL. He married ANGIE.

Child of JEFFERY NORTON and ANGIE is:
- i. GRACE[5] NORTON, b. 1999.

22. CALE RICHARD[4] ALBRECHT *(CAROL ANN[3] HABBEN, REINHARD F.[2], EILT[1])* was born June 06, 1973 in Freport, Stephenson co., IL. He married CHRIS.

Notes for CALE RICHARD ALBRECHT:
3rd Great-grandson of John Wilson.
Divorced, 2000

Child of CALE ALBRECHT and CHRIS is:
- i. CARRIE[5] ALBRECHT, b. 1995.

Kinship of Eilt Habben

Name	Relationship with Eilt Habben	Civil	Canon
Ammon, Yvonne	Wife of the great-grandson		
Bennet, Amanda	2nd great-granddaughter	IV	4
Bennet, Jennifer Ann	2nd great-granddaughter	IV	4
Bennet, Mark	Husband of the great-granddaughter		
Brown, Carolyn	Wife of the great-grandson		
Cook, Norma Jean	Wife of the grandson		
Dickman, Coonan	Husband of the great-granddaughter		
Faust, Adam Charles	2nd great-grandson	IV	4
Faust, Ashley	2nd great-granddaughter	IV	4
Faust, Randy	Husband of the great-granddaughter		
Fredrick, Lisa	Wife of the great-grandson		
Greeley, Allen	Husband of the great-granddaughter		
Greeley, Allen Ray	Husband of the great-granddaughter		
Greeley, Marla Jane	2nd great-granddaughter	IV	4
Greeley, Mellissa Jean	2nd great-granddaughter	IV	4
Greeley, William Norman	2nd great-grandson	IV	4
Habben, Catherine Jean	Great-granddaughter	III	3
Habben, Donald Patrick	Great-grandson	III	3
Habben, Eilt	Self		0
Habben, Gene LeRoy	Great-grandson	III	3
Habben, Merna Joy	Granddaughter	II	2
Habben, Milford Gene	Grandson	II	2
Habben, Norman Walter	Grandson	II	2
Habben, Reinhard F.	Son	I	1
Habben, Rhonda Jane	Great-granddaughter	III	3
Habben, Robert Allen	Great-grandson	III	3
Habben, Ryan	2nd great-grandson	IV	4
Habben, Sara Leanne	Great-granddaughter	III	3
Habben, Travis	2nd great-grandson	IV	4
Holmrick, Marie	Wife		
Janvrin, Aron Kyle	Great-grandson	III	3
Janvrin, Brice	2nd great-grandson	IV	4
Janvrin, Bruce Clyde	Great-grandson	III	3
Janvrin, Bryleigh	2nd great-granddaughter	IV	4
Janvrin, Clyde Elmer	Husband of the granddaughter		
Janvrin, Eric Paul	Great-grandson	III	3
Janvrin, Genevieve	2nd great-granddaughter	IV	4
Janvrin, Hannah Kate	2nd great-granddaughter	IV	4
Janvrin, Kurt Reinhard	Great-grandson	III	3
Janvrin, Mabeline	2nd great-granddaughter	IV	4
Janvrin, Rebecca Lindsey	2nd great-granddaughter	IV	4
Janvrin, Tyler	2nd great-grandson	IV	4
Kristin	2nd great-granddaughter	IV	4
Mehlhaus, Diane	Wife of the great-grandson		
Muschal, Robert Michael	Husband of the granddaughter		
Patrick, JoAnne	Wife of the grandson		
Pierce, Vera Marie	Daughter-in-law		
Reinhardt	Son	I	1
Roenike, Karen	Wife of the great-grandson		
Trimble, Carol	Wife of the great-grandson		

Descendants of Samuel Luckett

Generation No. 1

1. SAMUEL[1] LUCKETT He married ELIZABETH HUSSEY 1684 in Kent Co., England.

Notes for SAMUEL LUCKETT:
This family information from Ronald V. Jackson, 'Reagan/Davis Ancestry'.

Child of SAMUEL LUCKETT and ELIZABETH HUSSEY is:
2. i. SAMUEL[2] LUCKETT, b. October 10, 1685, Port Tabacco, Charles Co., MD.

Generation No. 2

2. SAMUEL[2] LUCKETT *(SAMUEL[1])* was born October 10, 1685 in Port Tabacco, Charles Co., MD. He married ANN SMOOT.

Notes for SAMUEL LUCKETT:
This family information from Ronald V. Jackson, 'Reagan/Davis Ancestry'.

Child of SAMUEL LUCKETT and ANN SMOOT is:
3. i. WILLIAM[3] LUCKETT, b. 1717, Frederick Co., MD; d. 1783.

Generation No. 3

3. WILLIAM[3] LUCKETT *(SAMUEL[2], SAMUEL[1])* was born 1717 in Frederick Co., MD, and died 1783. He married CHARITY MIDDLETON, daughter of JOHN MIDDLETON and MARY WHEELER. She was born 1717 in Charles Co., MD.

Child of WILLIAM LUCKETT and CHARITY MIDDLETON is:
4. i. LEVI[4] LUCKETT, b. December 20, 1762, Frederick Co., MD; d. 1829, Loundon Co., KY.

Generation No. 4

4. LEVI[4] LUCKETT *(WILLIAM[3], SAMUEL[2], SAMUEL[1])* was born December 20, 1762 in Frederick Co., MD, and died 1829 in Loundon Co., KY. He married LETITIA PAYTON, daughter of FRANCIS PAYTON and FRANCES DATE. She died December 26, 1821 in Loundon Co., KY.

Child of LEVI LUCKETT and LETITIA PAYTON is:
5. i. ALFRED PAXTON[5] LUCKETT, b. May 12, 1801, Loundon Co., KY; d. April 17, 1828, Seages Creek, Barren Co., KY.

Generation No. 5

5. ALFRED PAXTON[5] LUCKETT *(LEVI[4], WILLIAM[3], SAMUEL[2], SAMUEL[1])* was born May 12, 1801 in Loundon Co., KY, and died April 17, 1828 in Seages Creek, Barren Co., KY. He married SUSAN EVALINE HOBBS February 01, 1828. She was born June 03, 1809 in Charles Co., MD.

Child of ALFRED LUCKETT and SUSAN HOBBS is:
6. i. DR. EDWARD HOBBS[6] LUCKETT, b. January 03, 1833, Jefferson Co., KY; d. May 10, 1858, Owensbow, KY.

Generation No. 6

6. DR. EDWARD HOBBS[6] LUCKETT *(ALFRED PAXTON[5], LEVI[4], WILLIAM[3], SAMUEL[2], SAMUEL[1])* was born January 03, 1833 in Jefferson Co., KY, and died May 10, 1858 in Owensbow, KY. He married ANN HARTLEY MURRY May 10, 1858.

Child of EDWARD LUCKETT and ANN MURRY is:
7. i. CHARLES EDWARD[7] LUCKETT, b. 1860, Jefferson Co., KY.

Generation No. 7

7. CHARLES EDWARD[7] LUCKETT *(EDWARD HOBBS[6], ALFRED PAXTON[5], LEVI[4], WILLIAM[3], SAMUEL[2], SAMUEL[1])* was born 1860 in Jefferson Co., KY. He married SARAH FRANCIS WHITLOCK, daughter of BENJAMIN WHITLOCK and ELIZABETH. She was born 1849 in Russeville, Franklin Co., AL.

Child of CHARLES LUCKETT and SARAH WHITLOCK is:
8. i. EDITH[8] LUCKETT, b. Petersburg VA.

Generation No. 8

8. EDITH[8] LUCKETT *(CHARLES EDWARD[7], EDWARD HOBBS[6], ALFRED PAXTON[5], LEVI[4], WILLIAM[3], SAMUEL[2], SAMUEL[1])* was born in Petersburg VA. She married (1) KENNETH ROBBINS, son of GEORGE ROBBINS and ANNE. He was born November 1890 in Pittsfield, MA, and died in NJ. She married (2) DR. LOYAL EDWARD DAVIS.

Notes for EDITH LUCKETT:
Robbins & Luckett information from Ronald V. Jackson, 'Reagan/Davis Ancestry'.

Notes for DR. LOYAL EDWARD DAVIS:
Physician. He adopted Nancy.

Child of EDITH LUCKETT and KENNETH ROBBINS is:
   i. ANNE FRANCES[9] ROBBINS, b. July 06, 1923, New York, NY; m. RONALD WILSON REAGAN, March 04, 1952, North Hollywood, CA; b. February 06, 1911, Tampico, Wside Co., IL.

   Notes for ANNE FRANCES ROBBINS:
   Her legal name was 'Nancy Davis' through adoption.

   Notes for RONALD WILSON REAGAN:
   They were divorced June 28, 1948. Michael was adopted. A daughter died in infancy.
   During his 1981 visit to Scotland, Reagan became an Honorary Keeper of the Keepers of the Quaich, a society of connoisseurs of Scotch whiskey. He was unaware of his relationship to Johnnie Blue, the last moonshine distiller on the Scottish peninsula of Kintyre. From the Chicago Tribune of Oct 21, 1981. This article also gives Claudio Wilson, a weaver [whom see] and Peggy Downey [Downie] whom he married in 1807 as the parents of John Wilson, grandparents of Thomas. Claudio married a second time. [see Claudio 1787]

Kinship of Samuel Luckett

Name	Relationship with Samuel Luckett	Civil	Canon
Davis, Loyal Edward	Husband of the 5th great-granddaughter		
Davis, Nancy	6th great-granddaughter	VIII	8
Dee, Ede or Dee	5th great-granddaughter	VII	7
Dutch	Husband of the 6th great-granddaughter		
Hobbs, Susan Evaline	Wife of the 2nd great-grandson		
Hussey, Elizabeth	Wife		
Levin	Great-grandson	III	3
Luckett, Alfred Paxton	2nd great-grandson	IV	4
Luckett, Charles Edward	4th great-grandson	VI	6
Luckett, Edith	5th great-granddaughter	VII	7
Luckett, Edward Hobbs	3rd great-grandson	V	5
Luckett, Levi	Great-grandson	III	3
Luckett, Samuel	Self		0
Luckett, Samuel	Son	I	1
Luckett, William	Grandson	II	2
Middleton, Charity	Wife of the grandson		
Murry, Ann Hartley	Wife of the 3rd great-grandson		
Palmier, Doria	Wife of the 7th great-grandson		
Patti	7th great-granddaughter	IX	9
Payton, Letitia	Wife of the great-grandson		
Reagan, Patricia	7th great-granddaughter	IX	9
Reagan, Ronald Prescott	7th great-grandson	IX	9
Reagan, Ronald Wilson	Husband of the 6th great-granddaughter		
Robbins, Anne Frances	6th great-granddaughter	VIII	8
Robbins, Kenneth	Husband of the 5th great-granddaughter		
Smoot, Ann	Daughter-in-law		
Sr.	Self		0
Whitlock, Sarah Francis	Wife of the 4th great-grandson		

Descendants of William McFarlane

Generation No. 1

1. WILLIAM[1] MCFARLANE was born in Paisley, Renfrewshire, Scotland. He married ELIZABETH ALLISON.

Notes for WILLIAM MCFARLANE:
   R. V. Jackson, 'Reagan/Davis Ancestry', gives christened date as August, 1879, same as his son John.
   From Merna Habben: MacFarlane's Lantern! A popular name for the moon. According to Sir Walter Scott [1771-1832] the clan of MacFarlane, living on the mountainous slopes above Loch Lomond was notorious for raiding the lowlands and making off with the cattle and other livestock. Since the clan members moved by night, the moon came to be called their lantern.

Notes for ELIZABETH ALLISON:
Per Ronald V. Jackson, 'Reagan/Davis Ancestry'.

Child of WILLIAM MCFARLANE and ELIZABETH ALLISON is:
2.   i.   JOHN M.[2] MCFARLANE, b. August 02, 1869, Paisley, Renfrewshire, Scotland; d. February 21, 1883.

Generation No. 2

2. JOHN M.[2] MCFARLANE *(WILLIAM[1])* was born August 02, 1869 in Paisley, Renfrewshire, Scotland, and died February 21, 1883. He married CUNNINGHAM FORSYTH. She was born in Paisley, Renfrewshire, Scotland.

Notes for JOHN M. MCFARLANE:
Christened 2 Aug. 1869 per Ronald V. Jackson, 'Reagan/Davis Ancestry'.

Notes for CUNNINGHAM FORSYTH:
Per Ronald V. Jackson, 'Reagan/Davis Ancestry'.

Child of JOHN MCFARLANE and CUNNINGHAM FORSYTH is:
3.   i.   CATHERINE[3] MCFARLANE, b. January 01, 1801, Scotland; d. February 21, 1883, Whiteside co., Clyde twp., IL.

Generation No. 3

3. CATHERINE[3] MCFARLANE *(JOHN M.[2], WILLIAM[1])* was born January 01, 1801 in Scotland, and died February 21, 1883 in Whiteside co., Clyde twp., IL. She married DONALD DANIELBLUE, SR January 15, 1815 in Scotland, son of JOHNNIE BLUE. He was born January 18, 1799 in Argyl, Scotland, and died January 14, 1888 in Whiteside co., Clyde twp., IL.

Notes for CATHERINE MCFARLANE:
Bd. Grove Hill cem., Morrison, Lot46E, resident Morrison, deaths Whiteside co., IL, #928, age 84 yrs., lot 46E, residence Morrison.
1880 Wside Morrison IL census/187, age 81, Sc Sc Sc
History of Whiteside County, ILL, by Bent-Wilson, p. 145. Biography of Daniel Blue.
Three children died in infancy, 11 in all.
1850 Wsideco 37dist IL cen483, age 58, born 1792, Sc., with Dan, Isabel, Charles, Kath.
Ronald V. Jackson, 'Reagan/Davis Ancestry', gives birth place as Paisley, Renfrow, Scotland, date as Jan. 10, 1801.

Notes for DONALD DANIELBLUE, SR:
Emigrated to New Brunswick, Canada, March 1820. Moved in 1828 near Toronto. He took part in the "Patriot War" in Canada. Emigrated to Clyde twp., Section 17, 1839. They were in California from 1852-5. Bd, next to wife, Grove Hill cem., Morrison, Lot 46E, resident Clyde, age 91 yrs..
1830 WsidecoClytwpIL cen. Arrived 1839, 10 / 2
1840 Whiteside co., IL census: 1M uner 5, 1 age 5-10, 1 10-15, 1 20-30, 1 40-50// 1 F under 5, 1 5-10, 1 15-20, 1 40-50 [wife of head], 1 60-70.
1850 Wsideco 37th dist IL census 483/483, Daniel, 53, b. 1797, farmer, Sc, Katharine 58 F SC, Daniel 16 M Canada, Isabel 14 F Can, Charles 13 M Can, Katharine 10 F Can.
1860 WsidcoClydtwpIL census 482/470. $4,400/$1,000. Age58, Catherine 56, Dan'l 25, Catherine 20.
1870 WsidecoMorrisonIL census27/28, $1500/$500, age 67, Scotland, farm laborer, with wife `Kate', 66, Scotland, daughter Elizabeth, age 13 IL, and McKay, Robert, age 28, Scotland, blacksmith, wife Catharine 30, Canada, son Daniel, age 2, IL
1880 Wsideco Morrison, IL census 178/187, age 83, retired farmer, Sc Sc Sc, Catharine F 81 F wife Sc Sc Sc.
Ronald V. Jackson, 'Reagan/Davis Ancestry', gives death as 1881/3.

More About DONALD DANIELBLUE, SR:
Burial: Grove Hill, Morrison, IL

Children of CATHERINE MCFARLANE and DONALD BLUE, SR are:
4.   i.   JANE[4] BLUE, b. April 01, 1821, Nova Scotia, Canada; d. June 01, 1894, Morrison, IL.
        ii.   JOHNBLUE, I, b. 1822; d. 1839, Clyde twp., Whiteside co., IL.

          Notes for JOHNBLUE, I:
          Bent, p. 142 tells of the death of John and Margaret shortly arrival in ILL.

5.   iii.   ALEXANDER BLUE, b. Abt. 1827, Nova Scotia; d. April 18, 1859, see notes.
        iv.   MARGARET BLUE, b. 1828, Canada; d. 1839, WSide co., Clydetwp, IL.

          Notes for MARGARET BLUE:
          Died in Clyde twp.. per Bent.
          Not in 1850 census
          Death information from Elizabeth Carroll notes to Mrs. D. Wilson

        v.   DONALD DANIELBLUE, JR., b. Abt. 1834, Canada; m. (1) ELLA BIRT; b. 1854, Wside co., Usttwp, IL; d. Independence, Iowa; m. (2) HELEN MAY BENJAMIN, November 05, 1860, Whiteside co., IL.

          Notes for DONALD DANIELBLUE, JR.:
          Author of `Thrilling Narrative of Pike's Peak Gold Settlers' which details a trip west where they ran into a snow storm, insufficient rations, lack of heat, killed all the party except Daniel. He subsisted on a body until found by friendly Indians. They were going to Pikes Peak to hunt for gold.
          WsidecoIL marriage record #505.
          Daniel had one child with Ella Birt
          1850 WsidecoIL cen483, age 16, laborer, Canada
          1870 WSidecoIL cen 27/28 Morrison. Daniel Blue, 67 M Scotland, farm laborer, Kate 66 F Sc, Elizabeth 13 F IL, McKay, Robert 28 M Sc blacksmith, Catharine 30 F Can, Daniel 2 M IL. [Catharine daughter of Daniel/Kate]

          More About DONALD DANIELBLUE, JR.:
          Burial: Grove Hill cemetery, Morrison

          Notes for ELLA BIRT:
          See S J Clarke, publisher, `The Biographical Record', Whiteside county, IL,, p. 26. She is the daughter of George W. Birt, b. Feb 1, 1858, Clyde township, of Henry J. Birt, who was a son of George W. Birt, both of Gloucestershire, England. Ella is second child and had two children by her marriage to Harn, one child by marriage to Daniel Blue. She was widowed a second time.

1870 Whiteside co., Ustick twp, IL cen164/164: as daughter of Henry J., Helen 16 F IL.
1880 WsidecoUsttwpIL census 185, age 24, daughter of Henry, IL EN VT, with Otis, Ida Harn.

Notes for HELEN MAY BENJAMIN:
Married by Rev. J. W. White at Morrison, per Wside Sentinel 8Nov1860
Middle name from marriage record, Whiteside co., #505
Death Dates prior to 1916, loose paper file, Odell Library, Morrison, IL, :
E3 Mrs. David Blue, to city of Morrison Feb. 4, 1913. Digging grave $5. Approved Mar. 10, 1913. 7th Feb. Coffin and Box $18. Died at Mrs Julia Shepard.

6. vi. ISABELL BLUE, b. 1836, Canada.
vii. CHARLES BLUE, b. Abt. 1839, Canada; d. Abt. April 18, 1859.

Notes for CHARLES BLUE:
Died shortly after date given on trail to Pike's Peak, Smoky Hill route.
1850 WsidecoIL census, age 13, Canada

7. viii. CATHARINE BLUE, b. August 17, 1839, Toronto, Canada.
ix. JOHN BLUE, 2, b. March 29, 1842; d. 1920, Wside co., Clydetwp, IL; m. E. M. BECHTEL, February 22, 1861.
x. <UNNAMED>.

Generation No. 4

4. JANE[4] BLUE *(CATHERINE[3] McFARLANE, JOHN M.[2], WILLIAM[1])* was born April 01, 1821 in Nova Scotia, Canada, and died June 01, 1894 in Morrison, IL. She married JOHN WILSON November 23, 1841 in Whiteside co., IL, son of ANDREW WILSON and AMEILIA GLASGOW. He was born February 09, 1812 in Paisley, Renfrewshire, Scotland, and died March 09, 1883 in Wside co., Clydetwp., IL.

Notes for JANE BLUE:
Bd. Center Clyde cem. age 71 years. (Born 1823?)
1850 Wsideco37th D IL census 484, Nova Scotia, age 25.
1860 WsidecoClytwpIL census476/464. Jane 34, John 50, Sarah 16, Thos. 14, John 12.
1870 WsidecoClytwpIL cen 168, age 44, Parent foreign born, born New Brunswick.
Ronald V. Jackson, 'Reagan/Davis Ancestry', gives birth date as abt. 1824 at Queens, New Brunswick, Canada, marriage as Nov. 28, 1841, death as abt. 1880.
Birth also given as 1823
2 children died in infancy. Chapman Whiteside co. History, p. 63 'of Scotch parentage.
Donald E. Farr email of 19 Oct. 2002 gives her birth place as Queens, New Brunswick, Canada, and death date as June 3, 1894.
GREAT GRANDMOTHER OF RONALD REAGAN

More About JANE BLUE:
Burial: North Clyde cemetery

Notes for JOHN WILSON:
To Nova Scotia in 1832. Probably met his wife in Canada. He took part in the "Patriot War". He came to Clyde twp in 1839. Married in Whiteside co. Nov. 23, 1841 per marriage record # 54, not the 28th per Heritage Quest article.
Willson in marriage record Whiteside co., IL #54.
1860 Whitesideco37thDistIL census 4854/484, age 40, farmer, Scotland
1860 WsidecoIL Clyde twp census 476/464. Age 50, Scotland, Farmer, $8,000,$1,000, Jane 34 F Nova Scotia, Sarah 16 F IL, Thos. 14 M IL, John 12 M IL, Wilson, Alexander 10 M IL, Margrer 3 M? IL Catherine 7mo. F IL
1870 WsidecoClytwpIL census 168/168, $16,000, age 58, nat citizen, Scotland, Farmer
WsidecoIL death record #930
Original land grants:
6-24-1845. FD NWSW S9 22N 5E. 40 acres. $1.25 $50.00. V. 714, p. 131

014622.
7-19-1848. NWSW S17, 22N, 5E 40 acres, S$50.00 014623
12-30- 1853. 40 acres, $50.00. 091044
FD NWNE S23 22N 4E 40 acres. $50.00 091045
12-30-1853. FD NWNE S23 22N 4E 40 acres, $50.00. 091045
Ronald V. Jackson, 'Reagan/Davis Ancestry', gives father as Andrew Wilson, mother as Ameila Glassgow. He also gives deathdate as 6 February 1879. This does not agree with County records.

Per Eliz. Carroll: Four men emigrated to Canada together. Donald Blue, Richard Beswick, John Wilson and William Wilson. William went to CA, possibly a brother of John?
ASSUMPTION: Claudio, b. 1786 as one of triplets, came to Clyde after emigration to MA and Mexico for some years.
Funeral at Clyde ME church
GREAT GRANDFATHER OF RONALD WILSON

More About JOHN WILSON:
Burial: North Clyde Cemetery

Children of JANE BLUE and JOHN WILSON are:
8.   i. SARA[5] WILSON, b. March 29, 1841, Wside co., Clydetwp, IL; d. November 17, 1920, Wside co., Clydetwp, IL.
9.   ii. THOMAS WILSON, b. April 28, 1844, Wside co., Clydetwp, IL; d. December 10, 1909, WSide co., Clydetwp, IL.
10.   iii. JOHN WILSON, b. July 11, 1846, Whiteside co., Clydetwp, IL; d. February 15, 1909, Morrison, IL.
11.   iv. ALEXANDER B WILSON, b. February 21, 1848, WSide co., Clydetwp, IL; d. May 25, 1932.
12.   v. MARGARET MAE WILSON, b. April 28, 1857, Whiteside co., Clydetwp, IL; d. March 12, 1944, Whiteside co., Clydetwp, IL.
13.   vi. CATHERINE WILSON, b. November 09, 1859, Wside co., Clydetwp, IL; d. July 13, 1932, Highland Park, IL.
14.   vii. ELIZABETH EVELYN WILSON, b. December 10, 1861, Whiteside co., Clyde twp., IL; d. November 19, 1945.
15.   viii. REV. CHARLES DESMOND WILSON, b. November 10, 1865; d. 1937.

5. ALEXANDER[4] BLUE (CATHERINE[3] MCFARLANE, JOHN M.[2], WILLIAM[1]) was born Abt. 1827 in Nova Scotia, and died April 18, 1859 in see notes. He married MARY BESWICK Abt. 1850. She was born Abt. 1829 in England, and died April 1863.

Notes for ALEXANDER BLUE:
Died en route to Pike's Peak Gold mines in 1859. Daniel Blue wrote a pamphlet regarding this trip.
1850 WsidcolL cen485, age 23, Nova Scotia, farmer, with wife, Mary, 22, England

Notes for MARY BESWICK:
Three later children died in infancy, not listed.
Johnson marriage, record #630, Whiteside co., IL
1860 WsidecoClytwpIL cen483/471, 31 Eng. Children, Geo 9, John 7, Rich'd 5 also Elizabeth 22 IL. Have not located Elizabeth, not listed in the 1850 census either as Blue or Beswick.

Children of ALEXANDER BLUE and MARY BESWICK are:
   i. GEORGE[5] BLUE, b. Abt. 1851, ILL..

     Notes for GEORGE BLUE:
     1860 WsidecoClytwpIL cen 471 9 Eng
     1870 WsidecoClytwpIL census 72/72, age 19, IL, farm laborer, with James Stapleton, 40, England, farmer.

16.   ii. JOHN A. BLUE, b. Abt. 1853, ILL..
17.   iii. RICHARD BESWICK BLUE, b. November 07, 1855, ILL..
   iv. ELIZABETH BLUE, b. Abt. 1857, ILL..

     Notes for ELIZABETH BLUE:
     In 1870 census, Morrison, IL, with grandfather Donald Daniel Blue, Sr.
     Wside co., IL marriage record #5945 "Elizabeth Evelyn"

6. ISABELL[4] BLUE *(CATHERINE[3] MCFARLANE, JOHN M.[2], WILLIAM[1])* was born 1836 in Canada. She married JOHN BRETT February 27, 1852 in WHiteside co., IL. He was born 1833 in England.

Notes for ISABELL BLUE:
WsidecoIL marriage record #463.
1850 WsidecoIL cen. age 14, b. 1836.

Notes for JOHN BRETT:
1860 Whiteside co., Clyde twp., IL census480/468: Brett, John 27 M Farmer $1000/$250 Eng, Isabella 24 F Can, Kate 3 F IL, Charles 1 M IL, Ainsworth, Benj. 13 M En. [Perhaps a brother of Isabella?]
1880 Whiteside, Ustick twp., IL cen54/55: Brett, John M 51 Md Farmer En En En, Isabell F 47 wife, En Sc Sc, 7 children 23 to 5 yrs., Blue, Stella F 13 S niece IL CN NY. [Have not located Stella, nor Nettie A. Blue F 17 S Cn Sc Sc with John W. Kent, Union Grove twp.,]

Children of ISABELL BLUE and JOHN BRETT are:
    i. KATE[5] BRETT, b. 1857, Whiteside co, Clyde twp., IL.
    ii. CHARLES BRETT, b. 1859, Whiteside co, Clyde twp., IL.
    iii. ALEXANDER BRETT, b. 1861, Whiteside co., Ustick twp., IL.
    iv. GEORGE BRETT, b. 1864, Whiteside co., Ustick twp., IL.
    v. DONALD BRETT, b. 1866, Whiteside co., Ustick twp., IL.
    vi. JOHN W. BRETT, b. 1871, Whiteside co., Ustick twp., IL.
    vii. THOMAS C. BRETT, b. 1875, Whiteside co., Ustick twp., IL.

7. CATHARINE[4] BLUE *(CATHERINE[3] MCFARLANE, JOHN M.[2], WILLIAM[1])* was born August 17, 1839 in Toronto, Canada. She married (1) D. G. ACKERMAN, son of GARRET ACKERMAN and ELIZABETH WATSON. He was born February 13, 1832 in Paterson, NJ. She married (2) ROBERT MCKAY November 24, 1867 in Whiteside co., IL. He was born 1842 in Scotland.

Notes for CATHARINE BLUE:
WsidcoIL Marriage record #1928
Death cert. #928, Wside co IL
1850 WsidecoIL cen, age 10, 1870 census with father, Daniel, Kate, Elizabeth, Robert McKay 28 M Scotland Blacksmith, Catharine 30 F Canada, Daniel 2 M IL.

Notes for D. G. ACKERMAN:
He is the lone survivor of 5 children, came to ILL In 1876, mason & builder, later farmer, per Chapman 'Biog. & Portrait Album of Whiteside co., IL' p. 677.

Notes for ROBERT MCKAY:
WsidecoIL birth records do not show any children.
1870 WsidecoIL cen27/28 with father in law, Donald (Daniel) Blue.

Child of CATHARINE BLUE and ROBERT MCKAY is:
    i. DANIEL[5] MCKAY, b. Abt. 1868.

    Notes for DANIEL MCKAY:
    Whiteside co., IL birth record: Robert McKay/Catherine Blue, Nov. 24, 1867, #1928, BUT no child listed, probably this Daniel.

Generation No. 5

8. SARA[5] WILSON *(JANE[4] BLUE, CATHERINE[3] MCFARLANE, JOHN M.[2], WILLIAM[1])* was born March 29, 1841 in Wside co., Clydetwp, IL, and died November 17, 1920 in Wside co., Clydetwp, IL. She married EPHRAIM MYERS BECHTEL February 22, 1861 in Whiteside co., IL, son of BENJAMIN BECHTEL and REBECCA MYERS. He was born March 23, 1833 in Columbiana Co., OH, and died January 16, 1928 in Wside co., Clydetwp, IL.

Notes for SARA WILSON:
1850 WsidecoIL census484, age 8, IL
1870 WsidecoIL census95, age 36, I
1910 WsideClytwpIL census, age 68, IL Sc Sc
1920 WsideClytwpcoIL census with David E Gerdes, age 78, with husband Ephraim Bechtel, 86
Bd. Malvern cemetery next to husband
Married by Rev. J. W. White, in Ustick twp., in her parent's home., Wside Sentinel 26 Feb1861
GREAT AUNT OF RONALD WILSON

More About SARA WILSON:
Burial: Malvern cemetery

Notes for EPHRAIM MYERS BECHTEL:
He came to Clyde Twp. at 19 with his parents.
1870 WsideUsttwpIL census 95/95, age 32, farmer, OH, Sarah 36 F IL, John 8 M IL, Rebecca 6 F IL, Ella 4 F IL. [Only Bechtel in census]
1880 WsideClydetwpIL census 119/121 with son in law David E. Gerdes, dau. Ella (Ellen)
1910 WsideClytwpIL census 56/58, age77, own income, IL Gr PA, Sarah F 68 wf IL Sc Sc
Whiteside marriage record #563. Ephraim N. on marriage record.
Bd. Malvern cemetery.
He died at the home of his daughter, Mrs. David (Ellen) Gerdes. He had been blind for a number of years. He was the last of 11 children to die.
COUSIN OF RONALD REAGAN

More About EPHRAIM MYERS BECHTEL:
Burial: Malvern cemetery

Children of SARA WILSON and EPHRAIM BECHTEL are:
18.   i.   JOHN WILSON[6] BECHTEL, b. February 17, 1862, Wside co., Clydetwp, IL; d. February 22, 1933, Wside co., Clydetwp, IL.
    ii.   REBECCA JANE BECHTEL, b. 1864; d. March 11, 1878, WSide co., Clydetwp, IL.

Notes for REBECCA JANE BECHTEL:
Bd. Malvern cemetery with parents, died at 14 years. 'Buried from the Franklin School House' from the Sentinel of May 11, 1878. Whiteside co. death certificate #88.
1870 WsidecoIL cen95, age 6, IL
COUSIN ONCE REMOVED OF RONALD REAGAN

19.   iii.   ELLEN W. BECHTEL, b. July 01, 1866, Wside co., Clydetwp, IL.
    iv.   HELENA BECHTEL, b. November 01, 1876, ILL.; d. June 24, 1953, Washington; m. SAMUEL L. LONGANECKER, May 16, 1903, Whiteside co., IL; b. December 24, 1875; d. December 22, 1946, Orville, WA.

Notes for HELENA BECHTEL:
COUSIN ONCE REMOVED OF RONALD REAGAN

Notes for SAMUEL L. LONGANECKER:
Wside co. marriage record #11,484, she is listed as Helen

9. THOMAS[5] WILSON *(JANE[4] BLUE, CATHERINE[3] MCFARLANE, JOHN M.[2], WILLIAM[1])* was born April 28, 1844 in Wside co., Clydetwp, IL, and died December 10, 1909 in WSide co., Clydetwp, IL. He married MARY ANN ELSEY January 25, 1866 in Whiteside co., IL, daughter of ROBERT ELSEY and MARY BAKER. She was born December 28, 1843 in Epsom, County Surrey, England, and died October 06, 1900 in Fulton, Whiteside Co., IL.

Notes for THOMAS WILSON:
Thomas was a prosperous farmer in Whiteside County.
Bd. N. Clyde cem., Wside co.. Place of death uncertain.
WsidecoIL mar rcd #1454
1850 WsidecoIL census484, age 6.
1880 Clyde twp. Whiteside co., IL census: Thomas Wilson 36 farmer IL En En, Mary A. 36 En En En, Emily dau 13 IL, John son 10 IL Jennie dau 8 IL, Alexande 7 IL, George son 4 IL, Mary dau 2 IL.
Not in 1900 census. Absent from home for periods of time, perhaps at this time.
Farmed near White Pigeon, Whiteside co., IL
GRANDFATHER OF RONALD REAGAN

More About THOMAS WILSON:
Burial: North Clyde cemetery

Notes for MARY ANN ELSEY:
Bd. Fulton Cem.
Married by Rev. George T. Crissman, per Sentinel 1Feb1860, Whiteside co. marriage record #1454.
1900 Fulton twp., Whiteside co., IL census: Mary Wilson, Dec 1843, En En En, Alexander son Mar 1874, IL, factory worker, Vina dau Apr 18I180 IL, Nellie dau 16 July 1883 IL
GRANDMOTHER OF RONALD REAGAN

More About MARY ANN ELSEY:
Burial: Fulton Catholic cemetery

Children of THOMAS WILSON and MARY ELSEY are:
    i. EMILY G.6 WILSON, b. November 12, 1867, Fulton, Whiteside Co., IL; d. February 21, 1947, O'Fallon, St. Clair, IL; m. STEPHEN A. RUSH, June 03, 1884, Morrison, Whiteside co., IL; b. April 1865, Fulton, Whiteside Co., IL; d. April 05, 1936, O'Fallon, IL.

    Notes for EMILY G. WILSON:
    1900 Wsideco Fulton ILL cen 165, age 31 IL IL En
    They had no children.
    AUNT OF RONALD REAGAN

    More About EMILY G. WILSON:
    Burial: February 25, 1947, Shilo cemetery

    Notes for STEPHEN A. RUSH:
    They had no children.
    Wside co IL marriage record #6376
    1900 Wsideco., Fulton, IL census 165/165, age 35, IL PA PA, boarding house, next door is a long listing of of occupants, probably his boarding house. Also lists: Pannell, Lawra F 20 S IL IL IL servant, domestic.
    1870 WsidecoAlbanyIL census 92/92. Stephen is 8, IL, in family of Henry W. Rush, age. 40, PA wife Marybea, age 37, NY, 8 children.
    Tavern owner, death date from wife's obituary.

20.   ii. JOHN CHARLES WILSON, b. October 09, 1870, Wsideco, Clyde twp, IL; d. June 21, 1942, Clinton, IA.
21.   iii. SARA JANE WILSON, b. June 16, 1871, Clyde twp, Whiteside co., IL; d. March 08, 1920, White Pigeon, Clyde twp, Whiteside Co., IL.
    iv. ALEXANDER THOMAS WILSON, b. March 30, 1874, Whiteside Co., Clyde twp., IL; d. April 26, 1962, Quincy, Adams co., IL; m. (1) MAYME AITKEN; m. (2) MAYME HELMS, June 12, 1912.

    Notes for ALEXANDER THOMAS WILSON:
    They had no children. Obituary in (unnamed) newspaper gives birth as March 30, 1876. Employed 44 years at Monroe Chemical Co., foreman of the mill rooom. Member First Christian Church and Quincy Lodge of Masons.
    UNCLE OF RONALD REAGAN

22.	v.	GEORGE ORVILLE WILSON, b. March 02, 1876, Cordova, Whiteside co., IL; d. April 03, 1951, Clinton, IA.
23.	vi.	MARY LAVINA WILSON, b. April 06, 1879, Wside co., Clydetwp, IL; d. September 06, 1951, Minneapolis, Hennepin co., MN.
24.	vii.	NELLIE CLYDE WILSON, b. July 24, 1883, Fulton, Whiteside co., IL; d. July 25, 1962, Santa Monica, Los Angeles co., CA.

More About ALEXANDER THOMAS WILSON:
Burial: Greenmount cemetery, Quincy, IL

10. JOHN[5] WILSON *(JANE[4] BLUE, CATHERINE[3] MCFARLANE, JOHN M.[2], WILLIAM[1])* was born July 11, 1846 in Whiteside co., Clydetwp, IL, and died February 15, 1909 in Morrison, IL. He married ISABELLE MARY LIGGETT March 14, 1872. She was born October 1850 in OH.

Notes for JOHN WILSON:
1850 Wsideco37thDisIL census 484, age 4, IL
Citizenship paper, Whiteside co., IL, circuit court, 7 Dec. 1877, renounces Victoria, Queen of England.
Bd. Grove Hill cem., Morrison, Lot 7M, age 65 years.
1870 WsidecoClytwpIL cen73, age 23, IL
1880 Whiteside co., Ustick twp., IL cen110/112: Wilson, John M 34 md. Farmer IL Sc Sc, Isabell F 29 wf md OH OH OH, Fannie J. F 7 S IL IL OH.
1920 Whitesideco
John R. Wilson, land grant:
793,372. 12-30-1871. RR SESE S34 21N 7E 40 acres @$15. $600.00
GREAT UNCLE OF RONALD REAGAN

More About JOHN WILSON:
Burial: Grove Hill cemetery, Morrison

Notes for ISABELLE MARY LIGGETT:
1910 WsidecoMorrisonIL census 11/11, age 54, widow, OH OH OH, has `own income'. Fannie dau 36 S IL IL OH, and Alexander 66 widowed,, her `brother in law', IL Sc Sc 'own income'.

Children of JOHN WILSON and ISABELLE LIGGETT are:
    i. FRANCES JANE[6] WILSON, b. January 1873, Whiteside co., IL; d. November 07, 1968, Morrison, IL.

    Notes for FRANCES JANE WILSON:
    Birth date from Heritage Quest
    1910 Wsideco Morrison, IL census 11/11, age 36, single, IL IL OH
    School teacher.
    Died: 95 years, 7 months

    More About FRANCES JANE WILSON:
    Burial: Grove Hill cemetery, Morrison

25.   ii. MARGARET MAY WILSON, b. June 10, 1883, Whiteside co., IL.

11. ALEXANDER B[5] WILSON *(JANE[4] BLUE, CATHERINE[3] MCFARLANE, JOHN M.[2], WILLIAM[1])* was born February 21, 1848 in WSide co., Clydetwp, IL, and died May 25, 1932. He married DEBORAH A. FLETCHER June 14, 1876 in Whiteside co., IL, daughter of ISAAC FLETCHER and ELIZABETH SMITH. She was born March 08, 1853 in Chautauqua Co., NY, and died 1899.

Notes for ALEXANDER B WILSON:
WsidecoUGtwpIL cen 186 gives age 65, widowed, father of Paul, IL SC SC
1850 WsidcoIL cen 484, age 1
1860 WsidcoClytwpIL cen464 with John, Margaret 3, Catharine 7mo.

1870 WsidecoClytwpIL census 73, age 21, IL
1880 Whitesid co., Ustick twp., IL cen111/113: Wilson, Alexander M 28 md. IL Sc Sc, Debbie A. F 26 wf md. NY Eng Eng, Green, Lewis md in yr. M 24 md. Farmer IL OH NJ, Clara md in yr. F 19 wf md CA VA OH, Probuscaj, Gracie F 12 sister S CA VA OH
1910 Wsideco Morrison, ILL census 11/11 with Isabel, as brother in law, age 66, widowed, has `own income', IL Sc Sc
Also on the 1910 census with Paul Wilson as Alex, father, age 67, NY NY NY.
Birth date also given as 21 Feb. 1849, Mrs. Dwight Wilson
Lot 109B, cemetery

More About ALEXANDER B WILSON:
Burial: Grove Hill, Morrison, IL

Notes for DEBORAH A. FLETCHER:
Chapman, History of Whiteside County, ILL, p. 437: 'Debbie A. Fletcher b. March 8, 1853 md. Alexander Wilson June 15, 1876, resides Ustick. She was a teacher for many years. Daughter of Isaac Fletcher, Eng., April 23, 1826 and Betsy Smith'   Whiteside co., IL marriage record #4191 gives June 14, 1876, Alexander R. Wilson md. Debbie A. Fletcher.

Child of ALEXANDER WILSON and DEBORAH FLETCHER is:
26.   i.   PAUL FLETCHER[6] WILSON, b. January 1883, Whiteside co., IL; d. 1964.

12. MARGARET MAE[5] WILSON *(JANE[4] BLUE, CATHERINE[3] MCFARLANE, JOHN M.[2], WILLIAM[1])* was born April 28, 1857 in Whiteside co., Clydetwp, IL, and died March 12, 1944 in Whiteside co., Clydetwp, IL. She married DAVID B. GSELL February 25, 1879 in Mt. Carroll, Carroll Co., IL, son of WILLIAM GSELL and MARIA BARKHART. He was born December 15, 1852 in Letterkenny twp, Franklin co., PA, and died January 01, 1907 in Whiteside co., Clydetwp, IL.

Notes for MARGARET MAE WILSON:
Bd. N. Clyde Cem.
1870 WsidecoClyTwpIL cen73, age 13, IL
Married by Rev. J. P. Phillips, per Sentinel 27Feb1879
Death date from Mrs. D. Wilson.   Member Methodist Episcopal church.

More About MARGARET MAE WILSON:
Burial: North Clyde Cemetery

Notes for DAVID B. GSELL:
Bd. N. Clyde cem.
Came west in 1864, per Carroll. Lived Section 7, Clyde Twp.. He was a Republican. See p. 389 of Chapman, Portrait and Biographical Album of Whiteside County, IL.

More About DAVID B. GSELL:
Burial: North Clyde Cemetery

Children of MARGARET WILSON and DAVID GSELL are:
27.   i.   CLIFFORD LEROY[6] GSELL, b. November 17, 1880, Whiteside co, Clyde twp., IL; d. August 11, 1951, Clinton, Iowa.
28.   ii.   MAUDE MAE GSELL, b. November 18, 1884, WsidClytwpIL; d. August 26, 1966, Fulton, IL.
29.   iii.   ESTELLA JANE GSELL, b. May 27, 1894, Whiteside co, Clyde twp., IL.

13. CATHERINE[5] WILSON *(JANE[4] BLUE, CATHERINE[3] MCFARLANE, JOHN M.[2], WILLIAM[1])* was born November 09, 1859 in Wside co., Clydetwp, IL, and died July 13, 1932 in Highland Park, IL. She married WILLIAM B. GSELL October 07, 1879 in Sterling, Whiteside co., IL, son of WILLIAM

GSELL and MARIA BARKHART. He was born February 15, 1854 in Letterkenny twp, Franklin co., PA, and died April 02, 1921 in Highland Park, IL.

Notes for CATHERINE WILSON:
WsidecoIL marriage record #5104, Katie Wilson
1860 WsidecoClytwpIL cen464 7mo., census taken 15 June 1860.
1870 WsidecoClytwpIL census73, age 10, IL
Married at Sterling, IL, at the residence of Rev. J. T. Mason.
Buried Lot 31R; 72 yrs, 10 m, 1 d.. Chapman gives her birth as Nov. 9, 1861.

More About CATHERINE WILSON:
Burial: Grove Hill cemetery, Morrison

Notes for WILLIAM B. GSELL:
Died at 67 yrs., 1 mo., 17 d.. Lot 31R. Lived Section 30, Clyde Twp.. Came there in 1864. See p. 463 of Chapman, Port. & Biog. Album of Whiteside County, IL.

More About WILLIAM B. GSELL:
Burial: Grove Hill cemetery, Morrison

Child of CATHERINE WILSON and WILLIAM GSELL is:
  i. EARL WILSON[6] GSELL, b. August 18, 1882, WsidecoUsttwpIL; d. January 25, 1960, Highland Park, IL; m. FRANCIS LOUISE CUTLER; b. 1888; d. 1961.

  Notes for EARL WILSON GSELL:
  WsidecoIL birth record #2,733
  Death date from Grove Hill records
  Died at 77 yrs, bd. Lot 31R

  More About EARL WILSON GSELL:
  Burial: Grove Hill cemetery, Morrison

14. ELIZABETH EVELYN[5] WILSON (*JANE[4] BLUE, CATHERINE[3] MCFARLANE, JOHN M.[2], WILLIAM[1]*) was born December 10, 1861 in Whiteside co., Clyde twp., IL, and died November 19, 1945. She married WILLIAM G. HIGH December 19, 1882 in Whiteside Co., IL.

Notes for ELIZABETH EVELYN WILSON:
1919 WsideRockFalls ILL census 38, age 46 IL NY NY
1870 WsidecoClytwpIL cen73, age 7, `Lizzie', IL
1900 WsideColtwpIL census 487, age 35, IL VA IL
WsidcoIL marriage record # 5945, as Lizzie E..
Whiteside co., IL birth record #84,728.
Mother died at her home in Morrison, leaving her home in Chicago about April 1, ill. Jane Wilson obituary

Child of ELIZABETH WILSON and WILLIAM HIGH is:
  i. BESSIE LUELLA JANE[6] HIGH, b. October 15, 1887, Wside co., IL; m. WILLIAM HOWELL, 1945; d. Boston, MA.

  Notes for BESSIE LUELLA JANE HIGH:
  WsidecoIL birth record #84728

15. REV. CHARLES DESMOND[5] WILSON (*JANE[4] BLUE, CATHERINE[3] MCFARLANE, JOHN M.[2], WILLIAM[1]*) was born November 10, 1865, and died 1937. He married JENIE ALICE SMITH June 26, 1896. She was born March 24, 1873, and died 1927.

Notes for REV. CHARLES DESMOND WILSON:
1870 WsidecoClytwpIL cen 73, age 4, IL
Methodist minister.

Children of CHARLES WILSON and JENIE SMITH are:
30.   i. ALICE JANE[6] WILSON, b. April 15, 1897; d. July 05, 1952.
31.   ii. PHOEBE MAE WILSON, b. May 10, 1899; d. May 10, 1960.
32.   iii. WINIFRED M. WILSON, b. September 15, 1901.
        iv. CHARLES ABRAM WILSON, b. December 29, 1903; d. 1928.
        v. GEORGE JOHN WILSON, b. September 08, 1903; d. 1979; m. (1) MARGARET WILKINSON; m. (2) DOROTHY NELSON.

16. JOHN A.[5] BLUE *(ALEXANDER[4], CATHERINE[3] MCFARLANE, JOHN M.[2], WILLIAM[1])* was born Abt. 1853 in ILL.. He married ELLA A. KENT February 17, 1876 in Whiteside co., IL.

Notes for JOHN A. BLUE:
1860 WsidecoClytwpIL cen471, 7 IL

Notes for ELLA A. KENT:
Marriage records 4103, Wside co. IL
Married by Rev. George T. Crissman, both of Union Grove, per Wside Sentinel 24 Feb 1876

Child of JOHN BLUE and ELLA KENT is:
    i. MARY ELIZABETH[6] BLUE, b. March 16, 1877, Whiteside co., IL.

        Notes for MARY ELIZABETH BLUE:
        WsidecoIL birth record # 81,374., Ella.

17. RICHARD BESWICK[5] BLUE *(ALEXANDER[4], CATHERINE[3] MCFARLANE, JOHN M.[2], WILLIAM[1])* was born November 07, 1855 in ILL.. He married EMMA A. ALLDRITT December 25, 1877 in Wside co., Clydetwp, IL, daughter of THOMAS ALLDRITT and LAVINA HEACOX. She was born August 13, 1859 in Clyde twp., Whiteside Co., IL.

Notes for RICHARD BESWICK BLUE:
Born in S 17 Clyde twp, Whiteside co., IL
1860 WsidecoClytwpIL cen 471 Rich'd 5 IL
1870 WsidecoClytwpIL cen168/168, age 14, IL, with Richard Beswick, age 59, England, farmer, and uncle of Richard Blue.
1880 WsidecoClytwpIL cen/144, this is with Thom. Alldritt, 138/143. His age 24, IL NS En
The couple lived in Mitchell, SD, then moved to Iroquois, SD.
Chapman History of Whiteside county, p. 487: lived S. 22, Clyde twp.. born on S. 17 Clyde twp..

Notes for EMMA A. ALLDRITT:
WsidecoIL marriage record #4621, Aldritt on marriage index.
1880 WsideCly cen/144, age 21, IL MA En
Married by Rev. George T. Crissman, both of Clyde twp., per Sentinel 27Dec1877
WS issue of 9 Jan. 1879 gave birth of son, not named, (Wilford)

Children of RICHARD BLUE and EMMA ALLDRITT are:
    i. WILFORD T.[6] BLUE, b. December 16, 1878, Wside co., Clydetwp, IL.

        Notes for WILFORD T. BLUE:
        WsidecoIL birth record #714, as `boy'. Birth mentioned in the 9 Jan. 1879 Whiteside Sentinel, Morrison, IL, a boy.
        1880 WsidecoClytwpIL cen/144, age 1, IL IL IL

    ii. SAMUEL A BLUE, b. January 06, 1885, Wside co., Clydetwp, IL.

    Notes for SAMUEL A BLUE:
    WsidecoIL birth record #4433, listed as `boy'.

    iii. GIRL BLUE, b. December 27, 1887, Wside co., Clydetwp, IL.

    Notes for GIRL BLUE:
    WsidecoIL birth record # 5,566, listed as `Girl'.

Generation No. 6

18. JOHN WILSON[6] BECHTEL *(SARA[5] WILSON, JANE[4] BLUE, CATHERINE[3] MCFARLANE, JOHN M.[2], WILLIAM[1])* was born February 17, 1862 in Wside co., Clydetwp, IL, and died February 22, 1933 in Wside co., Clydetwp, IL. He married SARAH E. DETER 1886 in Whiteside co., IL. She was born August 28, 1858 in PA, and died March 28, 1908 in Wside co., Clydetwp, IL.

Notes for JOHN WILSON BECHTEL:
1870 WsideUstcen 95, age 8, IL
1910 WsidecoUsttwpIL census 47/49, age 48, widowed, IL OH IL
1920 WsidecoMorrisonIL census 152/156, age57, widowed IL OH IL, farm laborer
Bd. Malvern cemetery in plot with parents and wife, Sara E.
COUSIN ONCE REMOVED OF RONALD REAGAN

Notes for SARAH E. DETER:
Bd. Malvern cemetery

Children of JOHN BECHTEL and SARAH DETER are:
    i. ALBERT[7] BECHTEL, b. August 12, 1887, Whiteside co., IL.

    Notes for ALBERT BECHTEL:
    Whiteside co., IL marriage record: #5385 & & 104,677
    1880 Wsideco, 103 Genesee Ave., Morrison, IL age 32, IL IL PA
    1910 Wsideco cen 49, age 22, single, IL IL PA, as `Bert D.'. Farmer
    Never married
    SECOND COUSIN OF RONALD REAGAN

33.   ii. WILLIAM DETER BECHTEL, b. March 11, 1891, Wside co., Clydetwp, IL.
    iii. GEORGE DETER BECHTEL 2, b. March 29, 1892, Wside co., Clydetwp, IL; m. ELOISE; b. 1906, ILL..

    Notes for GEORGE DETER BECHTEL 2:
    WsidecoIL birth record #93,973.
    1910 Wsideco UsticktwpIL cen 49, age 18, farm laborer.
    1920 WsidecoUsttwpIL cen150/154 with wife Eloise
    SECOND COUSIN OF RONALD REAGAN

    Notes for ELOISE:
    1920 WsidecoUsttwpIL census 150/54 , age 24 IL IL IL, wife

34.   iv. IVY MAY BECHTEL, b. May 1898.

19. ELLEN W.[6] BECHTEL *(SARA[5] WILSON, JANE[4] BLUE, CATHERINE[3] MCFARLANE, JOHN M.[2], WILLIAM[1])* was born July 01, 1866 in Wside co., Clydetwp, IL. She married DAVID EDMOND GERDES January 08, 1888 in Whiteside co., IL, son of HENRY GERDES and REBECCA KALLENOR. He was born December 1864 in Whiteside co., IL, and died January 13, 1934 in Whiteside co., IL.

Notes for ELLEN W. BECHTEL:
1870 WsidecoIL cen95, age 4, IL

1910 Wside census 163 age 43, IL OH IL
COUSIN ONCE REMOVED OF RONALD REAGAN

Notes for DAVID EDMOND GERDES:
WsidcoIL marriage record #7289. Minister of the Dunkard Church, Clyde & Rock Creek, ILL.
1910 WsidecoUsttwpIL census 61/63. David 45, farmer, IL Gr PA
1920 WsidecoClytwpIL. census119/121m age 55, farmer, IL Gr PA
1920 census has Ephraim Bechtel, 86, f in law, OH PA PA and Sarah (Wilson), his wife, 78, IL Sc Sc with David's family
The Clyde Twp. farm was in the family since 1863.

Children of ELLEN BECHTEL and DAVID GERDES are:

35.   i. EPHRAIM LAWRENCE[7] GERDES, b. October 11, 1888, Wside co., Clydetwp, IL.
      ii. REBECCA H GERDES, b. December 05, 1889, WSide co., Clydetwp, IL; d. April 28, 1981, Whiteside co., IL.

          Notes for REBECCA H GERDES:
          WsidecoIL birth record #6,315.
          1910 Wside census 163, age 20, single, servant
          Did not marry.
          1920 Wside Clyde census, with father, 30, servant, IL IL IL
          She lived on the family farm all her life, never married, kept house for her brothers.

          More About REBECCA H GERDES:
          Burial: Malvern cemetery

      iii. EDMUND WAYNE GERDES, b. March 02, 1892, Wside co., Clydetwp, IL; d. July 10, 1969, WHiteside co., IL.

          Notes for EDMUND WAYNE GERDES:
          WsidecoIL birth rcd #7,402
          1910 WsideIL census 163, age 17, farm laborer, `Wayne'
          Living at RFD 2, Dixon, IL Feb. 1981, minister
          WsidecoIL death records

36.   iv. GALEN GLENN GERDES, b. January 1894, Wside co., Clydetwp, IL; d. September 01, 1976, N. Manchester, IN.
      v. HENRY RALPH GERDES, b. November 03, 1899, Wside co., Clydetwp, IL; d. February 07, 1981, Morrison, IL.

          Notes for HENRY RALPH GERDES:
          1910 WsidecoIL, cen 163, age 10
          1920 WsidecoIL, cen 121, age 20, laborer
          Never married, lived on family farm all his life.

          More About HENRY RALPH GERDES:
          Burial: Malvern cemetery

      vi. LLOYD GERDES, b. August 02, 1903, Wside co., Clydetwp, IL.

          Notes for LLOYD GERDES:
          WsidecoIL birth record #10,211 as `boy'. 1920 census lists him as 16.
          1910 WsidecoIL census age 6
          1920 WsidecoIL cen 121, age 16
          Died in truck accident, not married.

      vii. VIRGIL E. GERDES, b. August 25, 1905, Wside co., Clydetwp, IL; d. April 23, 1987, Whiteside co., IL.

          Notes for VIRGIL E. GERDES:
          WsidecoIL birth record #12,024
          1910 WsidecoIL cen163 age 4
          1920 WsidecoIL cen 121, age 14
          WsidecoIL death records

The author has a taped conversation with Virgil in which he remenisces about playing with Ronald Reagan as a child.
Lived on the family farm all his life, enjoyed antique farm machinery, never married.

More About VIRGIL E. GERDES:
Burial: Malvern cemetery

20. JOHN CHARLES[6] WILSON *(THOMAS[5], JANE[4] BLUE, CATHERINE[3] MCFARLANE, JOHN M.[2], WILLIAM[1])* was born October 09, 1870 in Wsideco, Clyde twp, IL, and died June 21, 1942 in Clinton, IA. He married (1) THELMA LILLIAN KEITH, daughter of HERBERT KEITH and JULIA KRAMER. She was born 1911 in Freeport, Stephenson co., IL. He married (2) CATHERINE STARCK January 16, 1893 in Fulton, Whiteside co., IL, daughter of MATHEW STARCK and ELIZABETH BONZLET. She was born November 1873 in Fulton, Whiteside Co., IL.

Notes for JOHN CHARLES WILSON:
WsidecoIL mar records #8634 for middle name, Katie Stark
 Mrs. D Wilson gives death date as 21 June 1942
Death certificate, Hunt/Wiebenga material, night watchman, Mfg. plant
UNCLE OF RONALD REAGAN

Notes for CATHERINE STARCK:
Katie on marriage record, Katherine and Kate on birth records
4 sons, 5 girls, lived in Clinton, Iowa

Children of JOHN WILSON and CATHERINE STARCK are:
    i. CHARLES LEROY[7] WILSON, b. August 10, 1894, Whiteside co., IL.

    Notes for CHARLES LEROY WILSON:
    WsidecoIL birth rcd #8,050
    COUSIN OF RONALD REAGAN

37.   ii. ELIZABETH MARY WILSON, b. December 15, 1895, Fulton, Whiteside co., IL; d. August 18, 1984, Estes Park, Larimer co., CO.
38.   iii. MARY MARGARET WILSON, b. December 19, 1897, Whiteside co., IL; d. February 17, 1985, Clinton, Iowa.
39.   iv. EARL CLYDE WILSON, b. November 16, 1902, Muscatine, IA; d. December 20, 1971, Rockford, Winnebago co., IL.
40.   v. LEO VERNON WILSON, SR., b. September 16, 1908, Chadwick, Whiteside co., IL; d. February 16, 1975, Key West, FL.
41.   vi. JOHN JAMES WILSON, b. May 25, 1905, Iowa; d. March 30, 1970, Freeport, Stephenson co., IL.
    vii. JEANETTE WILSON, b. April 22, 1910, Chadwick, Whiteside co., IL; d. August 20, 1925, Sterling, Whiteside co., IL.

    Notes for JEANETTE WILSON:
    'Explosion started fire with kerosene. Accidently burned to death. Home not destroyed' on death certificate.
    COUSIN OF RONALD REAGAN

21. SARA JANE[6] WILSON *(THOMAS[5], JANE[4] BLUE, CATHERINE[3] MCFARLANE, JOHN M.[2], WILLIAM[1])* was born June 16, 1871 in Clyde twp, Whiteside co., IL, and died March 08, 1920 in White Pigeon, Clyde twp, Whiteside Co., IL. She married (1) HORACE C. SMITH October 30, 1889 in Fulton, Whiteside co., IL, son of JACOB SMITH and MARTHA SIMONDS. He was born 1866 in Maquoketa, Iowa. She married (2) WALTER S PIERCE January 20, 1904 in Morrison, Whiteside co., IL, son of NATHANIEL PIERCE and ESTHER HUGGETT. He was born January 03, 1865 in Wateska, WI, and died January 04, 1932 in Morrison, IL.

Notes for SARA JANE WILSON:
Place of death not known, but buried in Fulton.
Divorced 31 May 1897. Death certificate says birthdate is June 16, 1871, age at death 48 yrs., 8 mos. 22 days. Cause of death: cerebral hemorrhage.

AUNT OF RONALD REAGAN

More About SARA JANE WILSON:
Burial: Fulton cemetery. Fulton, IL

Notes for HORACE C. SMITH:
Wside co IL marriage record #7748
Divorced May 31, 1897. Holley is used in all legal documents.
Teamster at time of marriage to Sarah Jane. Marriage license gives Maquoketa.
Perhaps 'Horace'?
UNCLE OF RONALD REAGAN

Notes for WALTER S. PIERCE:
1900 Clyde twp., Whiteside co., IL census: William Pierce, farmer, Jan. 1865 WI IL En, Eliza wife Dec 1871, md , IL Can VT, Walter S. Pierce, twin brother, farmer Jan 1865 WI
1910 Clyde twp., Whiteside co., IL census: Walter Pierce, retail grocer, 44 WI En En, Jennie wf 3I8 IL md 6yrs., 5 children living, IL EN, Elsey dau. 5 IL, Vera dau 2 NE

More About WALTER S. PIERCE:
Burial: West Genesee cem, Coleta, IL

Children of SARA WILSON and HORACE SMITH are:
42. i. CHARLES ALFRED[7] SMITH, b. August 22, 1890, Fulton, Whiteside Co., IL; d. December 30, 1968, Sterling, Whiteside co., IL.
43. ii. HORACE VERNON SMITH, b. August 18, 1892, Fulton, Whiteside Co., IL; d. October 19, 1968, Walden, CO.
44. iii. HARRY WILSON SMITH, b. January 11, 1895, Fulton, Whiteside Co., IL; d. December 12, 1967, Morrison, IL.

Children of SARA WILSON and WALTER PIERCE are:
45. iv. ELSEY MAE[7] PIERCE, b. September 17, 1904, White Pigeon, Whiteside co., IL; d. November 30, 1993, Whiteside co, Clyde twp., IL.
46. v. VERA MARIE PIERCE, b. February 16, 1908, Tekamah, Burt, Nebraska; d. January 30, 1986, White Pigeon, Whiteside co., IL.
     vi. MARIE MUNDT, b. November 04, 1911; d. September 27, 1978; Foster child; m. GEORGE ERNST.

     Notes for MARIE MUNDT:
     Foster daughter

22. GEORGE ORVILLE[6] WILSON (*THOMAS[5], JANE[4] BLUE, CATHERINE[3] MCFARLANE, JOHN M.[2], WILLIAM[1]*) was born March 02, 1876 in Cordova, Whiteside co., IL, and died April 03, 1951 in Clinton, IA. He married NORA KLOSTERMAN August 03, 1904 in Lyons, Clinton co., IA. She was born 1882.

Notes for GEORGE ORVILLE WILSON:
UNCLE OF RONALD REAGAN

Notes for NORA KLOSTERMAN:
Age 22 at marriage, per certificate

Child of GEORGE WILSON and NORA KLOSTERMAN is:
     i. GERTRUDE[7] WILSON, Adopted child; m. FRANCIS BURMEISTER, Clinton, Iowa.

     Notes for GERTRUDE WILSON:
     Adopted
     COUSIN OF RONALD REAGAN

23. MARY LAVINA[6] WILSON (*THOMAS[5], JANE[4] BLUE, CATHERINE[3] MCFARLANE, JOHN M.[2], WILLIAM[1]*) was born April 06, 1879 in Wside co., Clydetwp, IL, and died September 06, 1951 in Minneapolis,

Hennepin co., MN. She married LOUIS HERMAN HUNT September 23, 1903 in Fulton, Whiteside co., IL, son of HERMAN HUNT and MINNIE SCHAUB. He was born October 1879 in Aurora, Adams co., IL.

Notes for MARY LAVINA WILSON:
WsidecoIL marriage record #11586 as Mary Lavina. Also on Social Security application of Donald.
AUNT OF RONALD REAGAN

More About MARY LAVINA WILSON:
Burial: Fulton, IL

Notes for LOUIS HERMAN HUNT:
Wside co., IL marriage record #11588
Name from Social Security application of Donald
1880 census shows him 8/12, taken June 1880
AUNT OF RONALD REAGAN

Child of MARY WILSON and LOUIS HUNT is:
    i. DONALD WILSON[7] HUNT, b. March 30, 1909, Quincy, Adams co., IL; d. April 15, 1991, Los Angeles, CA; m. PAULINE CATHERINE BROOKS, June 18, 1944, Los Angeles, CA; b. 1911, New York, NY.

    Notes for DONALD WILSON HUNT:
    Final decree of divorce July 30, 1946.
    He died intestate, widower, no children so the court ordered a genealogical search for heirs. The result:
    A lengthy document to the Superior Court of the State of California, undated in this file, details the relationships of Donald Hunt and the shares to be alloted to the relatives. A genealogy chart is also appended. From this and related material I have entered the various people listed, supplementing genealogy previously shared with me by members of the families and research by me in various county records. Curt J. Gronner, DDS
    Birth certificate, Adams co., IL. Ronald Reagan witnessed the wedding.
    COUSIN OF RONALD REAGAN

    More About DONALD WILSON HUNT:
    Burial: Rosedale cemetery, Los Angeles, CA

    Notes for PAULINE CATHERINE BROOKS:
    Decree of divorce granted her 25 July 1945.

24. NELLIE CLYDE[6] WILSON (THOMAS[5], JANE[4] BLUE, CATHERINE[3] MCFARLANE, JOHN M.[2], WILLIAM[1]) was born July 24, 1883 in Fulton, Whiteside co., IL, and died July 25, 1962 in Santa Monica, Los Angeles co., CA. She married JOHN EDWARD REAGAN November 18, 1904 in Fulton, Whiteside Co., IL, son of JOHN REAGAN and JENNIE CUSICK. He was born July 13, 1883 in Fulton, Whiteside Co., IL, and died 1941.

Notes for NELLIE CLYDE WILSON:
Marriage date from WsidecoIL marriage rcd #11878

More About NELLIE CLYDE WILSON:
Burial: Calvary cemetery, Santa Monica, CA

Notes for JOHN EDWARD REAGAN:
    Lived with his aunt Margaret Reagan Baldwin after her marriage in 1895 at Buchanan, Iowa. Later Marguerite Chapman also came there after the death of her parents.
    Married in St. Emanuel's Catholic Church, Fulton. Marriage application says 'Jack', marriage certificate says 'John'.
    1910 Tampico twp., Whiteside co., IL census: John E. Reagan 26 IL En IL clerk in store, Nellie C. sife 26 IL IL En md 5 yrs. 1 ch living, Neal son 1 IL.

Children of NELLIE WILSON and JOHN REAGAN are:
    i. JOHN NEIL[7] REAGAN, b. September 16, 1908, Tampico, Wside Co., IL; d. California; m. RUTH HOFFMAN, August 31, 1935, Adel, Dallas Co., IA; b. February 23, 1908, Des Moines, Polk Co., Iowa.

    Notes for JOHN NEIL REAGAN:
    They have no children.

47.   ii. RONALD WILSON REAGAN, b. February 06, 1911, Tampico, Wside Co., IL.

25. MARGARET MAY[6] WILSON *(JOHN[5], JANE[4] BLUE, CATHERINE[3] MCFARLANE, JOHN M.[2], WILLIAM[1])* was born June 10, 1883 in Whiteside co., IL. She married GLENN OTTO WHISTLER October 06, 1908 in WHiteside co., IL. He died June 15, 1962 in Sterling, Whiteside co., IL.

Notes for MARGARET MAY WILSON:
Wside co., IL birth record #4,043, as Maggie May.

Notes for GLENN OTTO WHISTLER:
WsidecoIL marriage record #12,899.
Bd. Lot 7M

More About GLENN OTTO WHISTLER:
Burial: Grove Hill, Morrison, IL

Children of MARGARET WILSON and GLENN WHISTLER are:
48.   i. LOIS W[7] WHISTLER.
49.   ii. FLORENCE I. WHISTLER, b. 1912; d. Peoria, IL.

26. PAUL FLETCHER[6] WILSON *(ALEXANDER B[5], JANE[4] BLUE, CATHERINE[3] MCFARLANE, JOHN M.[2], WILLIAM[1])* was born January 1883 in Whiteside co., IL, and died 1964. He married ETTA MAY BRISTLE October 11, 1905 in Whiteside co., IL, daughter of JOHN BRISTLE and ADDIE BODY. She was born November 27, 1883, and died May 14, 1956 in Morrison, IL.

Notes for PAUL FLETCHER WILSON:
Heritage Quest gives his connection. 1920 WsidecoUGrovetwpIL cen186/186 gives age 36, IL IL NY, farmer. His father, Alexander is with them, age 65, IL Sc Sc
1910 WsidecoUGrtwpIL census 60/63, Age 27, IL NY NY, wife May 26 IL IL IL, father Alex 67 Widower NY NY NY 'own income'.
Xerox of Sentinel, Oct. 12, 1905.

Notes for ETTA MAY BRISTLE:
1900 WsidecoIL census277, age 16, as Mary, IL IL IL
1910 WsidecoUGrIL census 60/63, age 26, IL IL IL
WsidecoIL birth certificate #4,020, mother as Addie F. Boda
Whiteside co., IL marriage record #2117.0.

More About ETTA MAY BRISTLE:
Burial: Grove Hill cemetery, Morrison

Children of PAUL WILSON and ETTA BRISTLE are:
50.   i. DWIGHT ALVIN[7] WILSON, b. January 24, 1914; d. December 05, 1993, Sterling, Whiteside co., IL.
51.   ii. ROBERT BRISTLE WILSON, b. September 12, 1917; d. May 07, 1942.

27. CLIFFORD LEROY[6] GSELL *(MARGARET MAE[5] WILSON, JANE[4] BLUE, CATHERINE[3] MCFARLANE, JOHN M.[2], WILLIAM[1])* was born November 17, 1880 in Whiteside co, Clyde twp., IL, and died August 11, 1951 in Clinton, Iowa. He married EDNA JULIA HAMMER. She was born 1890, and died 1981.

Notes for CLIFFORD LEROY GSELL:
WsidecolL birth record #1,859, as 'boy'.
Buried lot 31HE

More About CLIFFORD LEROY GSELL:
Burial: Grove Hill cemetery, Morrison

Children of CLIFFORD GSELL and EDNA HAMMER are:
52.   i.   CLAIR LE ROY[7] GSELL, b. December 30, 1918.
      ii. HOWARD WILSON GSELL, b. June 23, 1920.

28. MAUDE MAE[6] GSELL *(MARGARET MAE[5] WILSON, JANE[4] BLUE, CATHERINE[3] MCFARLANE, JOHN M.[2], WILLIAM[1])* was born November 18, 1884 in WsidClytwpIL, and died August 26, 1966 in Fulton, IL. She married WALTER RICHARD MILNES January 16, 1902 in Whiteside co., IL. He was born July 29, 1877, and died March 05, 1953.

Notes for MAUDE MAE GSELL:
WsidecolL birth record #3,547 as Maude Mae.   Whiteside co., IL marriage record #11,091. Died at Harbor Crest, Fulton. Buried Lot 22W.

More About MAUDE MAE GSELL:
Burial: Grove Hill cemetery, Morrison

Children of MAUDE GSELL and WALTER MILNES are:
53.   i.   LEPHA MAE[7] MILNES, b. April 22, 1903; d. November 30, 1963.
54.   ii.   MARGARET ELIZABETH MILNES, b. June 07, 1913.
55.   iii. WALTER MILNES, b. June 17, 1919.

29. ESTELLA JANE[6] GSELL *(MARGARET MAE[5] WILSON, JANE[4] BLUE, CATHERINE[3] MCFARLANE, JOHN M.[2], WILLIAM[1])* was born May 27, 1894 in Whiteside co, Clyde twp., IL. She married WILLIAM STAPLETON.

Notes for ESTELLA JANE GSELL:
WsidecolL birth record #8,060 as Estella Jane.
Day of birth from Carroll

Children of ESTELLA GSELL and WILLIAM STAPLETON are:
56.   i.   GLADYS ELOISE[7] STAPLETON.
      ii. GLEN STAPLETON.

> Notes for GLEN STAPLETON:
> Died at birth

30. ALICE JANE[6] WILSON *(CHARLES DESMOND[5], JANE[4] BLUE, CATHERINE[3] MCFARLANE, JOHN M.[2], WILLIAM[1])* was born April 15, 1897, and died July 05, 1952. She married JAMES WARNER.

Child of ALICE WILSON and JAMES WARNER is:
57.   i.   ROBERT WILSON[7] WARNER.

31. PHOEBE MAE[6] WILSON *(CHARLES DESMOND[5], JANE[4] BLUE, CATHERINE[3] MCFARLANE, JOHN M.[2], WILLIAM[1])* was born May 10, 1899, and died May 10, 1960. She married LLOYD HERROLD.

Notes for LLOYD HERROLD:
Probably another son, also

Children of PHOEBE WILSON and LLOYD HERROLD are:
- i. EDITH[7] HERROLD.
- ii. LLOYD WILSON HERROLD.

32. WINIFRED M.[6] WILSON (*CHARLES DESMOND[5], JANE[4] BLUE, CATHERINE[3] MCFARLANE, JOHN M.[2], WILLIAM[1]*) was born September 15, 1901. She married CLARENCE FLACK.

Children of WINIFRED WILSON and CLARENCE FLACK are:
- 58. i. THOMAS OLIVER[7] FLACK, d. 1981.
- 59. ii. TIMOTHY CONRAD FLACK.

Generation No. 7

33. WILLIAM DETER[7] BECHTEL (*JOHN WILSON[6], SARA[5] WILSON, JANE[4] BLUE, CATHERINE[3] MCFARLANE, JOHN M.[2], WILLIAM[1]*) was born March 11, 1891 in Wside co., Clydetwp, IL. He married WINNIE MILNES, daughter of FRANK MILNES and MINNIE PAPE. She was born 1894 in ILL..

Notes for WILLIAM DETER BECHTEL:
WsidecoIL birth record #6,845.
1910 WsidecoIL cen 49, age 19, IL IL PA. Farm laborer
1920 WsidecoUsttwpIL census 152/156, age 29 farmer, IL IL PA, Winnie F 26 md wife IL IL IL, Lucille f 5 S cau IL IL IL, Everett M 1 S son IL IL IL.   [This does not agree with earlier records, perhaps Everett (1) died, another new son was named Everett)
SECOND COUSIN OF RONALD REAGAN

Notes for WINNIE MILNES:
1920 WsideUsttwpcoIL cen156, age 24, wife, IL IL IL

Children of WILLIAM BECHTEL and WINNIE MILNES are:
- 60. i. EVERETT[8] BECHTEL, b. 1905, ILL..
- 61. ii. LUCILLE FERN BECHTEL, b. March 09, 1914, Whiteside co., IL.
- 62. iii. GLENN BECHTEL.

34. IVY MAY[7] BECHTEL (*JOHN WILSON[6], SARA[5] WILSON, JANE[4] BLUE, CATHERINE[3] MCFARLANE, JOHN M.[2], WILLIAM[1]*) was born May 1898. She married WILLIAM LANE.

Notes for IVY MAY BECHTEL:
1910 WsidecoIL cen 49, age 12, farm laborer
SECOND COUSIN OF RONALD REAGAN

Children of IVY BECHTEL and WILLIAM LANE are:
- i. MILDRED[8] LANE.
- ii. DOROTHY ANN LANE.
- iii. WILLIAM LANE.

35. EPHRAIM LAWRENCE[7] GERDES (*ELLEN W.[6] BECHTEL, SARA[5] WILSON, JANE[4] BLUE, CATHERINE[3] MCFARLANE, JOHN M.[2], WILLIAM[1]*) was born October 11, 1888 in Wside co., Clydetwp, IL.

Notes for EPHRAIM LAWRENCE GERDES:
WsidecoIL birth #5,888. Married, 2 boys, lived near Dixon.

Child of EPHRAIM LAWRENCE GERDES is:
- i. WAYNE[8] GERDES, b. 1904.

Notes for WAYNE GERDES:
Living in Dixon in 1998 at 94, not married

36. GALEN GLENN[7] GERDES (ELLEN W.[6] BECHTEL, SARA[5] WILSON, JANE[4] BLUE, CATHERINE[3] MCFARLANE, JOHN M.[2], WILLIAM[1]) was born January 1894 in Wside co., Clydetwp, IL, and died September 01, 1976 in N. Manchester, IN. He married (1) IDA FIKE September 02, 1923. She died September 12, 1923. He married (2) MARETA SHRIDER August 05, 1951.

Notes for GALEN GLENN GERDES:
Children per obituary
Minister, retired.

More About GALEN GLENN GERDES:
Burial: Yellow Creek Cemetery, Pearl City

Children of GALEN GERDES and MARETA SHRIDER are:
    i. ROBERT[8] GERDES.
    ii. RUTH GERDES.

37. ELIZABETH MARY[7] WILSON (JOHN CHARLES[6], THOMAS[5], JANE[4] BLUE, CATHERINE[3] MCFARLANE, JOHN M.[2], WILLIAM[1]) was born December 15, 1895 in Fulton, Whiteside co., IL, and died August 18, 1984 in Estes Park, Larimer co., CO. She married RAYMOND JAMES DILLON August 24, 1918 in Chicago, Cook co., ILL. He was born 1898 in Iowa, and died in Chicago, Cook co., IL.

Notes for ELIZABETH MARY WILSON:
Whiteside co., IL birth certificate #101765, #8,416
Death certificate, Hunt material, Wiebenga
COUSIN OF RONALD REAGAN

Notes for RAYMOND JAMES DILLON:
Birth date from birth certificate of child, Katherine Brakeman, birth cert. 2nd child.
Raymond W. on marriage certificate
COUSIN OF RONALD REAGAN

Children of ELIZABETH WILSON and RAYMOND DILLON are:
    i. MARGARET ELIZA[8] DILLON, b. December 28, 1918, Chicago, Cook co., IL; m. CONANT.

    Notes for MARGARET ELIZA DILLON:
    Twin of Raymond
    COUSIN ONCE REMOVED OF RONALD REAGAN

    ii. RAYMOND JAMES DILLON, b. December 26, 1918, Chicago, Cook co., IL; d. May 15, 1942, Denmark.

    Notes for RAYMOND JAMES DILLON:
    Twin of Margaret, killed in action 18 May 1942 while serving on overseas air operations with 408 (RCAF) Squadron. Buried in Vaerlose Churchyard,, Vaerlose, Denmark. From Wiebenga material, Hunt descendants.
    COUSIN ONCE REMOVED OF RONALD REAGAN

    More About RAYMOND JAMES DILLON:
    Burial: Vearlose Churchyard, Vearlose, Denmark

    iii. KATHERINE ANNABELLE DILLON, b. July 03, 1924, Chicago, Cook co., IL.

    Notes for KATHERINE ANNABELLE DILLON:
    COUSIN ONCE REMOVED OF RONALD REAGAN

63.   iv. JOHN CHARLES DILLON, b. October 14, 1921, Clinton, ILL; d. December 21, 1963, Rockford, Winnebago

co., IL.

38. MARY MARGARET[7] WILSON (*JOHN CHARLES*[6], *THOMAS*[5], *JANE*[4] *BLUE*, *CATHERINE*[3] *MCFARLANE*, *JOHN M.*[2], *WILLIAM*[1]) was born December 19, 1897 in Whiteside co., IL, and died February 17, 1985 in Clinton, Iowa. She married HARRY JOHN HICKS. He was born 1892 in Morrison, IL, and died Bef. 1985.

Notes for MARY MARGARET WILSON:
WsidecoIL birth rcd #8,769
Death certificate, Clinton co., Iowa, bk 3-7-85, p. 3.
Widowed at time of death
COUSIN OF RONALD REAGAN

More About MARY MARGARET WILSON:
Burial: Grove Hill cemetery, Morrison

Notes for HARRY JOHN HICKS:
Birth certificate shows him as salesman

Children of MARY WILSON and HARRY HICKS are:
    i. EARL CLYDE[8] HICKS, b. September 15, 1929, Freeport, Stephenson co., IL.

    Notes for EARL CLYDE HICKS:
    COUSIN, ONCE REMOVED, OF RONALD REAGAN

64.   ii. KATHERINE JANE HICKS, b. January 09, 1917, Garden Plain Twp., Whiteside co., IL; d. November 05, 1986, Garden Plain Twp., Whiteside co., IL.
    iii. HARRIET HICKS.

    Notes for HARRIET HICKS:
    COUSIN ONCE REMOVED OF REAGAN REAGAN

39. EARL CLYDE[7] WILSON (*JOHN CHARLES*[6], *THOMAS*[5], *JANE*[4] *BLUE*, *CATHERINE*[3] *MCFARLANE*, *JOHN M.*[2], *WILLIAM*[1]) was born November 16, 1902 in Muscatine, IA, and died December 20, 1971 in Rockford, Winnebago co., IL. He married HELEN MARIE NELSON November 03, 1923 in Crown Point, Lake co., IN, daughter of ELMER NELSON and EDITH JOHANNSEN. She was born December 26, 1904 in Clinton, Clinton co., IA.

Notes for EARL CLYDE WILSON:
Birth certificate gives birth 1902, marriage certificate gives 1901.
Widowed
COUSIN OF RONALD REAGAN

More About EARL CLYDE WILSON:
Burial: Dakota cemetery, Dakota, IL

Children of EARL WILSON and HELEN NELSON are:
    i. EARL CHARLES[8] WILSON, b. February 10, 1925, Chicago, Cook co., IL.

    Notes for EARL CHARLES WILSON:
    COUSIN ONCE REMOVED OF RONALD REAGAN

    ii. JANET MAE WILSON, b. September 29, 1931, Chicago, Cook co., IL; m. (1) 'MALE' WITZ, Bef. 1969; m. (2) DONALD LEROY JOHNSON, July 25, 1970, Rockford, Winnebago co., IL; b. 1937.

    Notes for JANET MAE WILSON:
    Name correction of birth certificate dated 21 April 1976 by Janet.
    Janet md. previous to Johnson marriage, a Witz.

COUSIN ONCE REMOVED OF RONALD REAGAN

    iii. VAUGHN FAE WILSON, b. November 24, 1936, Freeport, Stephenson co., IL; m. EUGENE UFKEN, November 19, 1955, Dubuque, Dubuque co., IA; b. August 05, 1921, Huron, SD.

    Notes for VAUGHN FAE WILSON:
    COUSIN ONCE REMOVED OF RONALD REAGAN

    iv. RONALD STANLEY WILSON, b. March 30, 1942, Freeport, Stephenson co., IL.

    Notes for RONALD STANLEY WILSON:
    COUSIN ONCE REMOVED OF RONALD REAGAN

40. LEO VERNON[7] WILSON, SR *(JOHN CHARLES[6], THOMAS[5], JANE[4] BLUE, CATHERINE[3] MCFARLANE, JOHN M.[2], WILLIAM[1])* was born September 16, 1908 in Chadwick, Whiteside co., IL, and died February 16, 1975 in Key West, FL. He married (1) THELMA LILLIAN KEITH, daughter of HERBERT KEITH and JULIA KRAMER. She was born 1911 in Freeport, Stephenson co., IL. He married (2) IONA MAE HOWARD. She was born 1916 in Sheldon Grove, IL. He married (3) IONA JEAN THOMAS February 08, 1957 in Quincy, Adams co., ILL, daughter of CHARLES THOMAS and EMMA MELVIN. She was born 1934 in Kellysville, WV.

Notes for LEO VERNON WILSON, SR.:
His first marriage to Iona Howard??
Business man, Sterling, ILL at time of marriage to Norma jean, age 49, his 3rd marriage. He owned 'Recreation Vehicles Agency' at time of death.
Owned 'Lunch Room' Sterling when Marc was born.
At the time of Marilyn's birth, 1931, he lived at Marion, OH, Thelma at Freeport.
1930 lived at Freeport, ILL
Chadwick birth place from Linda Kay birth certificate
COUSIN OF RONALD REAGAN

More About LEO VERNON WILSON, SR.:
Burial: Oak Knoll cemetery, Sterling, IL

Notes for IONA JEAN THOMAS:
Marriage to Wilson, her first

Children of LEO WILSON and THELMA KEITH are:
    i. JAMES KEITH[8] WILSON, b. January 30, 1938, Galesburg, ILL.

    Notes for JAMES KEITH WILSON:
    Birth certificate #29769, V. 1938, Knox co., IL

    ii. MARILYN JOAN WILSON, b. September 24, 1941, Freeport, Stephenson co., IL; d. December 17, 1951, Beloit, Rock co., IL.

    Notes for MARILYN JOAN WILSON:
    Died in an auto accident

    iii. NAOMI JEAN WILSON, b. February 12, 1930, Freeport, Stephenson co., IL; m. JAMES A CAPONE, September 19, 1954, Freeport, Stephenson co., IL; b. 1921.

Children of LEO WILSON and IONA HOWARD are:
    iv. JEANNETTE LYNN[8] WILSON, b. August 03, 1938, Galesburg, Knox co., ILL; m. JAMES H. PIERCE, October 05, 1956, Rock Falls, Whiteside co., IL; b. 1935, Sterling, Whiteside co., IL.

    Notes for JEANNETTE LYNN WILSON:

Age 19 at marriage to James Pierce
Birth certificate, Knox co., IL #40686, V. 1944

Notes for JAMES H. PIERCE:
Laborer, Prince Castle Manufactury

v. TRUDY JEAN WILSON, b. May 18, 1945, Sterling, Whiteside co., IL; m. (1) RANDY GALE GALLENTINE; b. September 06, 1947, Morrison, IL; m. (2) 'MALE' STEVENS.
vi. LINDA KAY WILSON, b. June 20, 1947, Sterling, Whiteside co., IL; m. (1) 'MALE' TUCKER; m. (2) JAMES JERRY VAN HORN, October 04, 1974, Sterling, Whiteside co., IL; b. 1946, Sterling, Whiteside co., IL; m. (3) DANIEL JOSEPH RYAN, December 18, 1982, Sterling, Whiteside co., IL; b. 1944.

Notes for LINDA KAY WILSON:
COUSIN ONCE REMOVED OF RONALD REAGAN

Notes for DANIEL JOSEPH RYAN:
Lived at Erie, IL at time of marriage to Linda Kay

vii. KATHY ELIZABETH WILSON, b. February 24, 1949, Sterling, Whiteside co., IL; m. GAIL A. JELLERICHS, March 28, 1970, Sterling, Whiteside co., IL; b. February 18, 1949, Sterling, Whiteside co., IL.

Notes for KATHY ELIZABETH WILSON:
COUSIN ONCE REMOVED OF RONALD REAGAN

Notes for GAIL A. JELLERICHS:
In military service when married to Kathy

viii. GLENDA JOYCE WILSON, b. September 23, 1957, Sterling, Whiteside co., IL; m. MICHAEL GRANT GIBSON, August 28, 1978, Sterling, Whiteside co., IL; b. September 17, 1957, Sterling, Whiteside co., IL.

Notes for GLENDA JOYCE WILSON:
Married at First Christian Church, Sterling, IL
COUSIN ONCE REMOVED OF RONALD REAGAN

Children of LEO WILSON and IONA THOMAS are:
ix. MARC LEE[8] WILSON, b. October 12, 1940, Sterling, Whiteside co., IL.

Notes for MARC LEE WILSON:
COUSIN ONCE REMOVED OF RONALD REAGAN

x. KIMBERLY ANN WILSON, b. April 05, 1960, Sterling, Whiteside co., IL; m. MATHEW LEE SMITH, August 04, 1979, Rock Falls, Whiteside co., IL; b. February 03, 1960, ILL.
xi. JODY ALLEN WILSON, b. January 24, 1967, Sterling, Whiteside co., IL.

41. JOHN JAMES[7] WILSON (*JOHN CHARLES[6], THOMAS[5], JANE[4] BLUE, CATHERINE[3] MCFARLANE, JOHN M.[2], WILLIAM[1]*) was born May 25, 1905 in Iowa, and died March 30, 1970 in Freeport, Stephenson co., IL. He married MARGIE HOMERDING February 04, 1928 in Chicago, Cook co., ILL.

Notes for JOHN JAMES WILSON:
COUSIN OF RONALD REAGAN

More About JOHN JAMES WILSON:
Burial: Calvary cemetery, Freeport, IL

Children of JOHN WILSON and MARGIE HOMERDING are:
i. MARIE[8] WILSON.

Notes for MARIE WILSON:
Signed Father's death certificate, more of signature is unreadable.

COUSIN ONCE REMOVED OF RONALD REAGAN

65.   ii.   JOHN CHARLES WILSON, JR, b. December 14, 1928, IL; d. October 30, 1983, Mesa, Maricopa co., AZ.

42. CHARLES ALFRED[7] SMITH *(SARA JANE[6] WILSON, THOMAS[5], JANE[4] BLUE, CATHERINE[3] MCFARLANE, JOHN M.[2], WILLIAM[1])* was born August 22, 1890 in Fulton, Whiteside Co., IL, and died December 30, 1968 in Sterling, Whiteside co., IL. He married MABEL MAY SWEIGERT June 26, 1912 in Sterling, Whiteside co., IL, daughter of MILTON SWEIGERT and EVELYN REES. She was born September 18, 1888 in Elroy, Stephenson co., IL, and died February 17, 1972 in Rock Falls, Whiteside co., IL.

Notes for CHARLES ALFRED SMITH:
Retired in 1959 as Manager of Johnston Lumber co., Rock Falls after 50 years of service.
COUSIN OF RONALD REAGAN

More About CHARLES ALFRED SMITH:
Burial: January 02, 1969, Oak Knoll cemetery, Sterling, IL

Notes for MABEL MAY SWEIGERT:
WsidecoIL marriage record # 139760.0

More About MABEL MAY SWEIGERT:
Burial: Oak Knoll cemetery, Sterling, IL

Children of CHARLES SMITH and MABEL SWEIGERT are:
66.   i.   MILFORD L.[8] SMITH, b. February 21, 1916, Rock Falls, Whiteside co., IL; d. October 29, 1980, Sterling, Whiteside co., IL.
67.   ii.   RAYMOND SMITH, b. February 07, 1918, Sterling, Whiteside co., IL; d. March 07, 1997.

43. HORACE VERNON[7] SMITH *(SARA JANE[6] WILSON, THOMAS[5], JANE[4] BLUE, CATHERINE[3] MCFARLANE, JOHN M.[2], WILLIAM[1])* was born August 18, 1892 in Fulton, Whiteside Co., IL, and died October 19, 1968 in Walden, CO. He married DOSSIE MAY MEAKINS February 20, 1915 in Morrison, IL. She was born July 17, 1890 in Coleta, Whiteside co., IL, and died December 03, 1972.

Notes for HORACE VERNON SMITH:
WsidecoIL birth record #7,422,   Supt. of Public Aid Department, Whiteside co..
COUSIN OF RONALD REAGAN

More About HORACE VERNON SMITH:
Burial: Grove Hill cemetery, Morrison

Notes for DOSSIE MAY MEAKINS:
School teacher

More About DOSSIE MAY MEAKINS:
Burial: Grove Hill cemetery, Morrison

Children of HORACE SMITH and DOSSIE MEAKINS are:
68.   i.   ROBERT CLARE[8] SMITH, b. November 05, 1917, Sterling, Whiteside co., IL.
69.   ii.   GENE MEAKIN SMITH, b. March 27, 1922, Sterling, Whiteside co., IL; d. July 09, 1995.

44. HARRY WILSON[7] SMITH *(SARA JANE[6] WILSON, THOMAS[5], JANE[4] BLUE, CATHERINE[3] MCFARLANE, JOHN M.[2], WILLIAM[1])* was born January 11, 1895 in Fulton, Whiteside Co., IL, and died December 12, 1967 in Morrison, IL. He married HULDA PHILENA GOFF January 26, 1916 in Fulton, Whiteside co., IL, daughter of LYMAN GOFF and DELLA BULL. She was born April 20, 1893, and died December 14, 1974.

Notes for HARRY WILSON SMITH:
Owned auto body and paint shop
At time of marriage, lived at Ashton, IL, railroad employee. In 1922 he lived at Elmhurst, Il and was a signal maintainer, C&NW Ry..
COUSIN OF RONALD REAGAN

More About HARRY WILSON SMITH:
Burial: Grove Hill cemetery, Morrison

More About HULDA PHILENA GOFF:
Burial: Grove Hill cemetery, Morrison

Child of HARRY SMITH and HULDA GOFF is:
70.   i. HARRY WILSON[8] SMITH, JR, b. January 20, 1922, Oak Park, Cook co., IL.

45. ELSEY MAE[7] PIERCE (*SARA JANE[6] WILSON, THOMAS[5], JANE[4] BLUE, CATHERINE[3] MCFARLANE, JOHN M.[2], WILLIAM[1]*) was born September 17, 1904 in White Pigeon, Whiteside co., IL, and died November 30, 1993 in Whiteside co, Clyde twp., IL. She married CARL B. WALTERS May 20, 1925 in Jordan, Whiteside co., IL. He was born October 22, 1901 in White Pigeon, Whiteside co., IL, and died August 07, 1987.

Notes for ELSEY MAE PIERCE:
Birth certificate says '4th child of this mother'. Vicky Wiebenga / Hunt material, 3 half brothers from Mother's Smith marriage.
She provided much of the information to the Heritage Quest author, Michael F. Pollock.

More About ELSEY MAE PIERCE:
Burial: West Genesee cem., Whiteside co.

More About CARL B. WALTERS:
Burial: West Genesee cem, Coleta, IL

Child of ELSEY PIERCE and CARL WALTERS is:
71.   i. HAROLD EDWARD[8] WALTERS, b. December 02, 1925, White Pigeon, Whiteside co., IL; d. February 19, 1988, Morrison, IL.

46. VERA MARIE[7] PIERCE (*SARA JANE[6] WILSON, THOMAS[5], JANE[4] BLUE, CATHERINE[3] MCFARLANE, JOHN M.[2], WILLIAM[1]*) was born February 16, 1908 in Tekamah, Burt, Nebraska, and died January 30, 1986 in White Pigeon, Whiteside co., IL. She married REINHARD F. HABBEN April 03, 1933 in Somonauk, DeKalb co., IL, son of EILT HABBEN and MARIE HOLMRICK. He was born April 30, 1902 in Frisia, nr. Bremerhaven, Germany, and died March 22, 1980 in Morrison, IL.

Notes for VERA MARIE PIERCE:
Married at St. Johns Lutheran Church, Somonauk, IL.
COUSIN OF RONALD REAGAN

More About VERA MARIE PIERCE:
Burial: West Genesee cem, Coleta, IL

Notes for REINHARD F. HABBEN:
Became a US citizen 9 Oct. 1931, Chicago, IL.

More About REINHARD F. HABBEN:
Burial: West Genesee cem, Coleta, IL

Children of VERA PIERCE and REINHARD HABBEN are:

72.	i.	MERNA JOY[8] HABBEN, b. October 12, 1933, Coleta, Whiteside co., IL.
73.	ii.	NORMAN WALTER HABBEN, b. September 10, 1935, Coleta, Whiteside co., IL.
74.	iii.	RONALD LEE HABBEN, b. July 17, 1938, Coleta, Whiteside co., IL.
75.	iv.	MILFORD GENE HABBEN, b. July 04, 1940, Coleta, Whiteside co., IL.
76.	v.	VELMA JANE HABBEN, b. April 10, 1943, Morrison, IL.
77.	vi.	JUDITH MAY HABBEN, b. April 28, 1946, Morrison, IL.
78.	vii.	CAROL ANN HABBEN, b. June 04, 1948, Morrison, IL.
79.	viii.	BEVERLY JOAN HABBEN, b. July 10, 1952, Morrison, IL.
80.	ix.	DONNA ELAINE HABBEN, b. August 04, 1954, Morrison, IL.

47. RONALD WILSON[7] REAGAN *(NELLIE CLYDE[6] WILSON, THOMAS[5], JANE[4] BLUE, CATHERINE[3] MCFARLANE, JOHN M.[2], WILLIAM[1])* was born February 06, 1911 in Tampico, Wside Co., IL. He married (1) SARA JANE FULKS January 16, 1940 in Glendale, CA. She was born January 04, 1914 in St. Joseph, MO. He married (2) ANNE FRANCES ROBBINS March 04, 1952 in North Hollywood, CA, daughter of KENNETH ROBBINS and EDITH LUCKETT. She was born July 06, 1923 in New York, NY.

Notes for RONALD WILSON REAGAN:
They were divorced June 28, 1948. Michael was adopted. A daughter died in infancy.
During his 1981 visit to Scotland, Reagan became an Honorary Keeper of the Keepers of the Quaich, a society of connoisseurs of Scotch whiskey. He was unaware of his relationship to Johnnie Blue, the last moonshine distiller on the Scottish peninsula of Kintyre. From the Chicago Tribune of Oct 21, 1981. This article also gives Claudio Wilson, a weaver [whom see] and Peggy Downey [Downie] whom he married in 1807 as the parents of John Wilson, grandparents of Thomas. Claudio married a second time. [see Claudio 1787]

Notes for SARA JANE FULKS:
Also known as Jane Durrell and Jane Wyman

Notes for ANNE FRANCES ROBBINS:
Her legal name was 'Nancy Davis' through adoption.

Children of RONALD REAGAN and SARA FULKS are:
	i.	MAUREEN ELIZABETH[8] REAGAN, b. January 04, 1941, Los Angeles, CA.
81.	ii.	MICHAEL REAGAN, b. March 18, 1945.

Children of RONALD REAGAN and ANNE ROBBINS are:
	iii.	PATRICIA[8] REAGAN, b. October 21, 1952.
	iv.	RONALD PRESCOTT REAGAN, b. May 20, 1958; m. DORIA PALMIER, November 24, 1980.

48. LOIS W.[7] WHISTLER *(MARGARET MAY[6] WILSON, JOHN[5], JANE[4] BLUE, CATHERINE[3] MCFARLANE, JOHN M.[2], WILLIAM[1])* She married WHITFORD MITCHELL.

Children of LOIS WHISTLER and WHITFORD MITCHELL are:
82.	i.	MARTHA ANN[8] MITCHELL.
83.	ii.	JOHN WILSON MITCHELL.
84.	iii.	JANE WHITFORD MITCHELL.

49. FLORENCE I [7] WHISTLER *(MARGARET MAY[6] WILSON, JOHN[5], JANE[4] BLUE, CATHERINE[3] MCFARLANE, JOHN M.[2], WILLIAM[1])* was born 1912, and died in Peoria, IL. She married GEORGE L. MARR. He died in Peoria, IL.

Children of FLORENCE WHISTLER and GEORGE MARR are:
85.	i.	BARBARA[8] MARR.
	ii.	GEORGE MICHAEL MARR.

50. DWIGHT ALVIN[7] WILSON *(PAUL FLETCHER[6], ALEXANDER B[5], JANE[4] BLUE, CATHERINE[3] MCFARLANE, JOHN M.[2], WILLIAM[1])* was born January 24, 1914, and died December 05, 1993 in Sterling, Whiteside co., IL. He married JANICE LUCILLE MATHEW December 25, 1937 in Sterling, Whiteside co., IL. She was born November 30, 1917.

Notes for DWIGHT ALVIN WILSON:
WsidecoUGtwpIL census 186
WsidecoIL birth record #17,965
Retired from 1st National Bank, Sterling, Jan. 1, 1978.

More About DWIGHT ALVIN WILSON:
Burial: Grove Hill cemetery, Morrison

Children of DWIGHT WILSON and JANICE MATHEW are:
- 86. i. JUDITH SUZANE[8] WILSON, b. November 21, 1942.
- 87. ii. ROBERT THOMAS WILSON, b. June 29, 1944.

51. ROBERT BRISTLE[7] WILSON *(PAUL FLETCHER[6], ALEXANDER B[5], JANE[4] BLUE, CATHERINE[3] MCFARLANE, JOHN M.[2], WILLIAM[1])* was born September 12, 1917, and died May 07, 1942. He married MAXINE JOY BARRETT March 22, 1940, daughter of HARVEY BARRETT and EDNA LAWTON. She was born August 01, 1920, and died April 11, 1997 in Cedar Rapids, Iowa.

More About ROBERT BRISTLE WILSON:
Burial: Grove Hill cemetery, Morrison

Child of ROBERT WILSON and MAXINE BARRETT is:
- 88. i. DEBORAH ANN[8] WILSON, b. February 09, 1941.

52. CLAIR LE ROY[7] GSELL *(CLIFFORD LEROY[6], MARGARET MAE[5] WILSON, JANE[4] BLUE, CATHERINE[3] MCFARLANE, JOHN M.[2], WILLIAM[1])* was born December 30, 1918. He married MARY WATSON.

Children of CLAIR GSELL and MARY WATSON are:
- 89. i. STEVEN ALLEN[8] GSELL, b. April 24, 1939.
-     ii. RICHARD LEE GSELL, b. December 17, 1945; m. SHIRLEY MANNING.
- 90. iii. SUE ELLEN GSELL, b. September 25, 1955.

53. LEPHA MAF[7] MILNES *(MAUDE MAE[6] GSELL, MARGARET MAE[5] WILSON, JANE[4] BLUE, CATHERINE[3] MCFARLANE, JOHN M.[2], WILLIAM[1])* was born April 22, 1903, and died November 30, 1963. She married ANDREW F. WITT. He was born December 16, 1898.

Children of LEPHA MILNES and ANDREW WITT are:
- 91. i. DONNA JEAN[8] WITT, b. April 09, 1933.
-     ii. MAJOR SANDRA MAE WITT, b. April 13, 1938.

    Notes for MAJOR SANDRA MAE WITT:
    Major

- 92. iii. DR. HARLAN ANDREW WITT, b. April 27, 1946.

54. MARGARET ELIZABETH[7] MILNES *(MAUDE MAE[6] GSELL, MARGARET MAE[5] WILSON, JANE[4] BLUE, CATHERINE[3] MCFARLANE, JOHN M.[2], WILLIAM[1])* was born June 07, 1913. She married IVAN RALPH CARROLL. He was born October 12, 1907, and died June 25, 1950.

Children of MARGARET MILNES and IVAN CARROLL are:

93.	i.	DAVID IVAN[8] CARROLL, b. January 02, 1938.
94.	ii.	TERRY DEE CARROLL, b. January 03, 1946.

55. WALTER[7] MILNES *(MAUDE MAE[6] GSELL, MARGARET MAE[5] WILSON, JANE[4] BLUE, CATHERINE[3] MCFARLANE, JOHN M.[2], WILLIAM[1])* was born June 17, 1919. He married BEULAH VEY NAFTZGER. She was born July 03, 1918.

Children of WALTER MILNES and BEULAH NAFTZGER are:
    i. WANDA VEY[8] MILNES, b. December 29, 1943.

    Notes for WANDA VEY MILNES:
    Never married.

95.	ii.	DIANE LOUISE MILNES, b. September 04, 1945.
96.	iii.	THOMAS BRENT MILNES, b. September 01, 1950.

56. GLADYS ELOISE[7] STAPLETON *(ESTELLA JANE[6] GSELL, MARGARET MAE[5] WILSON, JANE[4] BLUE, CATHERINE[3] MCFARLANE, JOHN M.[2], WILLIAM[1])* She married ERNEST VOS.

Children of GLADYS STAPLETON and ERNEST VOS are:
97.	i.	ARLYN[8] VOS, b. May 03, 1940.
98.	ii.	LARRY VOS.
	iii.	LAURI ANN VOS, m. ROBIN N. GOLDSMITH.

57. ROBERT WILSON[7] WARNER *(ALICE JANE[6] WILSON, CHARLES DESMOND[5], JANE[4] BLUE, CATHERINE[3] MCFARLANE, JOHN M.[2], WILLIAM[1])*

Children of ROBERT WILSON WARNER are:
    i. JAMES[8] WARNER.
    ii. CATHERINE WARNER.

58. THOMAS OLIVER[7] FLACK *(WINIFRED M.[6] WILSON, CHARLES DESMOND[5], JANE[4] BLUE, CATHERINE[3] MCFARLANE, JOHN M.[2], WILLIAM[1])* died 1981.

Child of THOMAS OLIVER FLACK is:
    i. PAMELA[8] FLACK.

59. TIMOTHY CONRAD[7] FLACK *(WINIFRED M.[6] WILSON, CHARLES DESMOND[5], JANE[4] BLUE, CATHERINE[3] MCFARLANE, JOHN M.[2], WILLIAM[1])*

Children of TIMOTHY CONRAD FLACK are:
    i. KATHRYN[8] FLACK.
    ii. WILLIAM C. FLACK.

Generation No. 8

60. EVERETT[8] BECHTEL *(WILLIAM DETER[7], JOHN WILSON[6], SARA[5] WILSON, JANE[4] BLUE, CATHERINE[3] MCFARLANE, JOHN M.[2], WILLIAM[1])* was born 1905 in ILL.. He married CARLENE MCKEE.

Notes for EVERETT BECHTEL:
1920 WsidecolL cen 156 Ustick

Children of EVERETT BECHTEL and CARLENE MCKEE are:

i. GARY[9] BECHTEL, m. PATRICIA WIERSEMA.
ii. BONNIE BECHTEL, m. DOUGLAS BUSH.

61. LUCILLE FERN[8] BECHTEL *(WILLIAM DETER[7], JOHN WILSON[6], SARA[5] WILSON, JANE[4] BLUE, CATHERINE[3] MCFARLANE, JOHN M.[2], WILLIAM[1])* was born March 09, 1914 in Whiteside co., IL. She married LYLE NICE.

Notes for LUCILLE FERN BECHTEL:
WsidecoIL birth record # 17,783.
SECOND COUSIN ONCE REMOVED OF RONALD REAGAN

Children of LUCILLE BECHTEL and LYLE NICE are:
99. i. ELWIN[9] NICE.
100. ii. MARJORIE NICE.

62. GLENN[8] BECHTEL *(WILLIAM DETER[7], JOHN WILSON[6], SARA[5] WILSON, JANE[4] BLUE, CATHERINE[3] MCFARLANE, JOHN M.[2], WILLIAM[1])* He married RHEA GREEN.

Children of GLENN BECHTEL and RHEA GREEN are:
i. GLENDA[9] BECHTEL, m. DARREL NICKE.
ii. ELLEN BECHTEL, m. GREG PESSMAN.
iii. SCOTT BECHTEL, m. SANDRA WALTERS.
iv. CAROL BECHTEL, m. JOSEPH HIGH, July 17, 1876, Whiteside co., IL.

Notes for CAROL BECHTEL:
Whiteside co., IL marriage record #4216.

63. JOHN CHARLES[8] DILLON *(ELIZABETH MARY[7] WILSON, JOHN CHARLES[6], THOMAS[5], JANE[4] BLUE, CATHERINE[3] MCFARLANE, JOHN M.[2], WILLIAM[1])* was born October 14, 1921 in Clinton, ILL, and died December 21, 1963 in Rockford, Winnebago co., IL. He married AMY ADELE ANDERSON July 11, 1942 in Peoria, Peoria co., ILL, daughter of ALEX ANDERSON and EDNA CLARK. She was born 1924 in Freeport, Stephenson co., IL.

Notes for JOHN CHARLES DILLON:
Died in Highway accident.
COUSIN ONCE REMOVED OF RONALD REAGAN

Child of JOHN DILLON and AMY ANDERSON is:
i. JACKLYN ANN[9] DILLON, b. August 27, 1943, Freeport, Stephenson co., IL; m. DAVID ROBERT SPRINGMAN, October 13, 1978, Freeport, Stephenson co., IL; b. June 20, 1944, Freeport, Stephenson co., IL.

Notes for JACKLYN ANN DILLON:
COUSIN, ONCE REMOVED, OF RONALD REAGAN

64. KATHERINE JANE[8] HICKS *(MARY MARGARET[7] WILSON, JOHN CHARLES[6], THOMAS[5], JANE[4] BLUE, CATHERINE[3] MCFARLANE, JOHN M.[2], WILLIAM[1])* was born January 09, 1917 in Garden Plain Twp., Whiteside co., IL, and died November 05, 1986 in Garden Plain Twp., Whiteside co., IL. She married (1) ADOLPH G. KUNAVICH. She married (2) THEODORE DINGMAN Aft. 1946.

Notes for KATHERINE JANE HICKS:
Divorced from Kunavich 1946.
Divorced from Dingman 1960 and resumed her maiden name, Kay J. Hicks, per Ronald G. Kunavich affidavit.
COUSIN, ONCE REMOVED, OF RONALD REAGAN

Notes for ADOLPH G KUNAVICH:
Divorce 1946 per affidavit of Ronald G. Kunavich

Children of KATHERINE HICKS and ADOLPH KUNAVICH are:
    i. RONALD GEORGE[9] KUNAVICH, b. April 25, 1942, Clinton, Clinton co., IA.

    Notes for RONALD GEORGE KUNAVICH:
    Was 'DPCM Ronald G. Kunavich CM/C' aboard the USS O'Brien DD-975' in Oct. 1987.
    COUSIN TWICE REMOVED FROM RONALD REAGAN

101.   ii. JAMES JOSEPH KUNAVICH, b. October 22, 1943, Clinton, Clinton co., IA; d. April 24, 1971, Oaklawn, Cook co., IL.

65. JOHN CHARLES[8] WILSON, JR *(JOHN JAMES[7], JOHN CHARLES[6], THOMAS[5], JANE[4] BLUE, CATHERINE[3] MCFARLANE, JOHN M.[2], WILLIAM[1])* was born December 14, 1928 in IL, and died October 30, 1983 in Mesa, Maricopa co., AZ. He married (1) O. DARLENE RAINS. He married (2) SHIRLEY GIBSON February 21, 1948 in Freeport, Stephenson co., IL. She was born 1930 in Freeport, Stephenson co., IL. He married (3) GLENDA REITER January 20, 1958 in Alcorn co, MS, daughter of RODNEY REITER and ZELDA. She was born 1937.

Notes for JOHN CHARLES WILSON, JR:
Cremated.
COUSIN ONCE REMOVED OF RONALD REAGAN

Notes for O. DARLENE RAINS:
She gave the information on the death certificate of John, Jr.

Notes for GLENDA REITER:
Noeske marriage assumed from marriage application with John Wilson. Marriage certificate, Alcorn co., MS.

Child of JOHN WILSON and O. RAINS is:
    i. JOHN CHARLES[9] WILSON III, b. June 09, 1948, Freeport, Stephenson co., IL.

    Notes for JOHN CHARLES WILSON III:
    Listed as 'Jr.' on his birth certificate.
    COUSIN TWICE REMOVED OF RONALD REAGAN

66. MILFORD L.[8] SMITH *(CHARLES ALFRED[7], SARA JANE[6] WILSON, THOMAS[5], JANE[4] BLUE, CATHERINE[3] MCFARLANE, JOHN M.[2], WILLIAM[1])* was born February 21, 1916 in Rock Falls, Whiteside co., IL, and died October 29, 1980 in Sterling, Whiteside co., IL. He married MARIAN D. SCHNEIDER June 01, 1938 in Sterling, Whiteside co., IL, daughter of JOSEPH SCHNEIDER and DELLA MACQUAY. She was born 1916 in Coleta, Whiteside co., IL.

Notes for MILFORD L. SMITH:
Served in the military WW II. Cashier, International Harvester.
COUSIN ONCE REMOVED OF RONALD REAGAN

More About MILFORD L. SMITH:
Burial: Oak Knoll cemetery, Sterling, IL

More About MARIAN D SCHNEIDER:
Burial: Oak Knoll cemetery, Sterling, IL

Children of MILFORD SMITH and MARIAN SCHNEIDER are:
    i. GORDON M.[9] SMITH, b. October 31, 1940, Rock Falls, Whiteside co., IL; d. September 10, 1971, Rock Falls, Whiteside co., IL.

Notes for GORDON M. SMITH:
Not married
COUSIN TWICE REMOVED OF RONALD REAGAN

More About GORDON M. SMITH:
Burial: Oak Knoll cemetery, Sterling, IL

    ii. DENNIS SMITH, b. September 14, 1943, Rock Falls, Whiteside co., IL; d. January 28, 1983, Morrison, Whiteside co., IL.

Notes for DENNIS SMITH:
Not married
COUSIN TWICE REMOVED OF RONALD REAGAN

More About DENNIS SMITH:
Burial: Oak Knoll cem.

67. RAYMOND[8] SMITH (*CHARLES ALFRED*[7], *SARA JANE*[6] *WILSON*, *THOMAS*[5], *JANE*[4] *BLUE*, *CATHERINE*[3] *MCFARLANE*, *JOHN M.*[2], *WILLIAM*[1]) was born February 07, 1918 in Sterling, Whiteside co., IL, and died March 07, 1997. He married MADELINE WEYRAUCH August 27, 1942.

Notes for RAYMOND SMITH:
FIRST COUSIN ONCE REMOVED OF RONALD REAGAN

More About RAYMOND SMITH:
Burial: Oak Knoll cemetery, Sterling, IL

Children of RAYMOND SMITH and MADELINE WEYRAUCH are:
    i. HUDSON B.[9] SMITH, b. March 12, 1944.

Notes for HUDSON B. SMITH:
COUSIN TWICE REMOVED OF RONALD REAGAN

    ii. KAREN SMITH, b. April 1947.

Notes for KAREN SMITH:
COUSIN TWICE REMOVED OF RONALD REAGAN

    iii. SALLY SMITH, b. May 1950.

Notes for SALLY SMITH:
COUSIN TWICE REMOVED OF RONALD REAGAN

68. ROBERT CLARE[8] SMITH (*HORACE VERNON*[7], *SARA JANE*[6] *WILSON*, *THOMAS*[5], *JANE*[4] *BLUE*, *CATHERINE*[3] *MCFARLANE*, *JOHN M.*[2], *WILLIAM*[1]) was born November 05, 1917 in Sterling, Whiteside co., IL. He married (1) DOROTHY BRICKLEY. She was born June 20, 1920, and died May 17, 1984. He married (2) JEANNE WEBB January 11, 1935.

Notes for ROBERT CLARE SMITH:
COUSIN ONCE REMOVED OF RONALD REAGAN

Children of ROBERT SMITH and DOROTHY BRICKLEY are:
102.   i. TERRY[9] SMITH, b. November 20, 1946.
103.   ii. VICKI SMITH, b. March 01, 1952.

69. GENE MEAKIN[8] SMITH (*HORACE VERNON*[7], *SARA JANE*[6] *WILSON*, *THOMAS*[5], *JANE*[4] *BLUE*, *CATHERINE*[3]

McFarlane, John M.², William¹) was born March 27, 1922 in Sterling, Whiteside co., IL, and died July 09, 1995. He married Janet Janke February 09, 1946 in Morrison, IL, daughter of Herbert Janke and Emma Kleist. She was born September 20, 1919 in Weyauwega, WI, and died October 24, 1989 in Sterling, Whiteside co., IL.

Notes for Gene Meakin Smith:
COUSIN ONCE REMOVED OF RONALD REAGAN

Children of Gene Smith and Janet Janke are:
104.   i.   David⁹ Smith, b. May 21, 1948.
105.   ii.   Thomas Smith, b. February 25, 1952.
106.   iii.   Nancy Smith, b. October 12, 1955.

70. Harry Wilson⁸ Smith, Jr (Harry Wilson⁷, Sara Jane⁶ Wilson, Thomas⁵, Jane⁴ Blue, Catherine³ McFarlane, John M.², William¹) was born January 20, 1922 in Oak Park, Cook co., IL. He married Jean.

Notes for Harry Wilson Smith, Jr:
Living in TN, 2000.
COUSIN ONCE REMOVED OF RONALD REAGAN

Children of Harry Smith and Jean are:
     i.   Dale⁹ Smith, m. Nancy Lee Sprague, July 02, 1960.

         Notes for Dale Smith:
         COUSIN TWICE REMOVED OF RONALD REAGAN

    ii.   Barbara Smith.

         Notes for Barbara Smith:
         COUSIN TWICE REMOVED OF RONALD REAGAN

   iii.   Dean Smith.

         Notes for Dean Smith:
         COUSIN TWICE REMOVED OF RONALD REAGAN

71. Harold Edward⁸ Walters (Elsey Mae⁷ Pierce, Sara Jane⁶ Wilson, Thomas⁵, Jane⁴ Blue, Catherine³ McFarlane, John M.², William¹) was born December 02, 1925 in White Pigeon, Whiteside co., IL, and died February 19, 1988 in Morrison, IL. He married Ruth Jane Stuart October 22, 1945 in Morrison, IL. She was born July 07, 1924 in Morrison, IL.

More About Harold Edward Walters:
Burial: West Genesee cem., Whiteside co.

Children of Harold Walters and Ruth Stuart are:
107.   i.   Paul Edward⁹ Walters, b. May 03, 1946, Morrison, IL.
108.   ii.   Harlan Gene Walters, b. February 05, 1948, Morrison, IL.
109.   iii.   Jane Kaye Walters, b. April 16, 1950, Morrison, IL.
       iv.   Rhonda Ruth Walters, b. September 15, 1952, Morrison, IL; m. Danny Kennedy, December 02, 1977, Morrison, IL; b. August 27, 1946.

         Notes for Rhonda Ruth Walters:
         Divorced Aug. 30, 1978

         Notes for Danny Kennedy:
         Divorced Aug. 30, 1978

110.   v.   DAWN GAIL WALTERS, b. March 19, 1962, Morrison, IL.
111.   vi. PHILIP DALE WALTERS, b. July 15, 1968, Morrison, IL.

72. MERNA JOY[8] HABBEN *(VERA MARIE[7] PIERCE, SARA JANE[6] WILSON, THOMAS[5], JANE[4] BLUE, CATHERINE[3] MCFARLANE, JOHN M.[2], WILLIAM[1])* was born October 12, 1933 in Coleta, Whiteside co., IL. She married (1) CLYDE ELMER JANVRIN September 02, 1956 in Sterling, Whiteside co., IL. He was born August 24, 1925 in Morrison, IL, and died May 20, 1970 in Morrison, IL. She married (2) ROBERT MICHAEL MUSCHAL Aft. 1971, son of NICHOLAS MUSCHAL and KATHERINE MARX. He was born June 20, 1940 in Chicago, IL.

Notes for MERNA JOY HABBEN:
Md. in St. Johns Lutheran Church, Sterling
Dairy farmer.
Mrs. Merna Habben-Muschal has been of tremendous help in furnishing material and in proofreading my pages. If there are errors, blame me. CJG
COUSIN ONCE REMOVED OF RONALD REAGAN

Notes for CLYDE ELMER JANVRIN:
Dairy farmer, served in the Army.

More About CLYDE ELMER JANVRIN:
Burial: South Clyde cemetery

Notes for ROBERT MICHAEL MUSCHAL:
Painter. Marriage to Merna was his second marriage, also her 2nd.
Auditor and Inspector.   Married in United Methodist Church, Morrison, IL.

Children of MERNA HABBEN and CLYDE JANVRIN are:
         i.   ERIC PAUL[9] JANVRIN, b. August 31, 1958, Morrison, IL; m. CAROL TRIMBLE, October 10, 1986, Fulton, Whiteside co., IL; b. November 06, 1956, Fulton, IL.
112.   ii.   KURT REINHARD JANVRIN, b. August 04, 1960, Morrison, IL.
113.   iii.   BRUCE CLYDE JANVRIN, b. December 22, 1961, Morrison, IL.
114.   iv. ARON KYLE JANVRIN, b. November 13, 1964, Morrison, IL.

73. NORMAN WALTER[8] HABBEN *(VERA MARIE[7] PIERCE, SARA JANE[6] WILSON, THOMAS[5], JANE[4] BLUE, CATHERINE[3] MCFARLANE, JOHN M.[2], WILLIAM[1])* was born September 10, 1935 in Coleta, Whiteside co., IL. He married NORMA JEAN COOK June 02, 1956 in Rock Falls, Whiteside co., IL. She was born June 02, 1937 in Rock Falls, Whiteside co., IL.

Notes for NORMAN WALTER HABBEN:
COUSIN ONCE REMOVED OF RONALD REAGAN

Children of NORMAN HABBEN and NORMA COOK are:
115.   i.   RHONDA JANE[9] HABBEN, b. June 24, 1957.
        ii. ROBERT ALLEN HABBEN, b. August 02, 1958, Morrison, IL.
116.   iii. GENE LEROY HABBEN, b. July 07, 1960, Morrison, IL.
117.   iv. SARA LEANNE HABBEN, b. March 09, 1967, Morrison, IL.

74. RONALD LEE[8] HABBEN *(VERA MARIE[7] PIERCE, SARA JANE[6] WILSON, THOMAS[5], JANE[4] BLUE, CATHERINE[3] MCFARLANE, JOHN M.[2], WILLIAM[1])* was born July 17, 1938 in Coleta, Whiteside co., IL. He married NANCY JOAN BIELEMA September 02, 1961 in Fulton, Whiteside co., IL. She was born November 15, 1940 in Fulton, IL.

Notes for RONALD LEE HABBEN:
COUSIN ONCE REMOVED OF RONALD REAGAN

Children of RONALD HABBEN and NANCY BIELEMA are:
118. i. DANIEL LEE[9] HABBEN, b. June 26, 1962, Morrison, IL.
119. ii. DEBRA LOU HABBEN, b. September 17, 1964, Morrison, IL.
      iii. DAVID ALLEN HABBEN, b. November 08, 1978, Morrison, IL.

75. MILFORD GENE[8] HABBEN *(VERA MARIE[7] PIERCE, SARA JANE[6] WILSON, THOMAS[5], JANE[4] BLUE, CATHERINE[3] MCFARLANE, JOHN M.[2], WILLIAM[1])* was born July 04, 1940 in Coleta, Whiteside co., IL. He married JOANNE PATRICK July 06, 1964 in San Jose, Santa Clara co., CA. She was born May 23, 1943 in Santa Clara, CA.

Notes for MILFORD GENE HABBEN:
COUSIN ONCE REMOVED OF RONALD REAGAN

Children of MILFORD HABBEN and JOANNE PATRICK are:
120. i. CATHERINE JEAN[9] HABBEN, b. May 08, 1966, Morrison, IL.
      ii. DONALD PATRICK HABBEN, b. April 08, 1969, Morrison, IL; m. LISA FREDRICK, November 10, 1990, Dixon, Lee co., IL.

     Notes for DONALD PATRICK HABBEN:
     Divorced, no children.

76. VELMA JANE[8] HABBEN *(VERA MARIE[7] PIERCE, SARA JANE[6] WILSON, THOMAS[5], JANE[4] BLUE, CATHERINE[3] MCFARLANE, JOHN M.[2], WILLIAM[1])* was born April 10, 1943 in Morrison, IL. She married WILLIAM RICHARD NORTON, JR December 07, 1963 in Freeport, Stephenson co., IL, son of WILLIAM NORTON and EDNA LOTT. He was born October 20, 1938 in Rockford, ILL.

Notes for VELMA JANE HABBEN:
COUSIN ONCE REMOVED OF RONALD REAGAN

Notes for WILLIAM RICHARD NORTON, JR:
Railroad telegrapher at time of marriage, later truck driver.

Children of VELMA HABBEN and WILLIAM NORTON are:
      i. JAMES RICHARD[9] NORTON, b. June 30, 1967, Freport, Stephenson co., IL.
121. ii. JEFFERY MICHAEL NORTON, b. December 23, 1971, Freport, Stephenson co., IL.

77. JUDITH MAY[8] HABBEN *(VERA MARIE[7] PIERCE, SARA JANE[6] WILSON, THOMAS[5], JANE[4] BLUE, CATHERINE[3] MCFARLANE, JOHN M.[2], WILLIAM[1])* was born April 28, 1946 in Morrison, IL. She married DONALD RAY BURMEISTER August 28, 1976 in Dewitt,Clinton co., Iowa. He was born January 23, 1939 in Dewitt, Clinton co., IA.

Notes for JUDITH MAY HABBEN:
COUSIN ONCE REMOVED OF RONALD REAGAN

Notes for DONALD RAY BURMEISTER:
His second marriage.

Children of JUDITH HABBEN and DONALD BURMEISTER are:
      i. JOHN BRANDON[9] BURMEISTER, b. August 25, 1977, Dewitt, Clinton co., IA.
      ii. BRIAN DOUGLAS BURMEISTER, b. October 09, 1980, Dewitt, Clinton co., IA.

78. CAROL ANN[8] HABBEN *(VERA MARIE[7] PIERCE, SARA JANE[6] WILSON, THOMAS[5], JANE[4] BLUE, CATHERINE[3] MCFARLANE, JOHN M.[2], WILLIAM[1])* was born June 04, 1948 in Morrison, IL. She met CHARLES ROBERT ALBRECHT March 01, 1969 in Belvidere, Boone co., IL, son of FRANK ALBRECHT and IRENE HOWE. He was born November 28, 1937.

Notes for CAROL ANN HABBEN:
Born at Morrison Community Hospital
COUSIN ONCE REMOVED OF RONALD REAGAN

Notes for CHARLES ROBERT ALBRECHT:
Married by Robert A. Blodgett, Magistrate, at Belvidere, Boone co., IL
He was an 'assembler' when married.
This was his second marriage. Data from marriage license/Wiebenga material

Children of CAROL HABBEN and CHARLES ALBRECHT are:
122.   i. CALE RICHARD[9] ALBRECHT, b. June 06, 1973, Freport, Stephenson co., IL.
     ii. CALEB WILLAIM ALBRECHT, b. May 17, 1975, Freport, Stephenson co., IL.

        Notes for CALEB WILLAIM ALBRECHT:
        Married 1999, one child b. April 2000

79. BEVERLY JOAN[8] HABBEN *(VERA MARIE[7] PIERCE, SARA JANE[6] WILSON, THOMAS[5], JANE[4] BLUE, CATHERINE[3] MCFARLANE, JOHN M.[2], WILLIAM[1])* was born July 10, 1952 in Morrison, IL. She married KENNETH ALDEN ETHRIDGE November 25, 1972 in Pearl City, Jo Davies co., IL. He was born 1939 in Freport, Stephenson co., IL.

Notes for BEVERLY JOAN HABBEN:
COUSIN ONCE REMOVED OF RONALD REAGAN

Children of BEVERLY HABBEN and KENNETH ETHRIDGE are:
    i. JEREMY M.[9] ETHRIDGE, b. July 08, 1978, Freport, Stephenson co., IL.
    ii. KEVIN MARSHALL ETHRIDGE, b. June 29, 1980, Freport, Stephenson co., IL.
    iii. LAURA MARIE ETHRIDGE, b. May 29, 1983, Freport, Stephenson co., IL.

        Notes for LAURA MARIE ETHRIDGE:

    iv. BRADLEY ETHRIDGE, b. March 18, 1988, Freport, Stephenson co., IL.

80. DONNA ELAINE[8] HABBEN *(VERA MARIE[7] PIERCE, SARA JANE[6] WILSON, THOMAS[5], JANE[4] BLUE, CATHERINE[3] MCFARLANE, JOHN M.[2], WILLIAM[1])* was born August 04, 1954 in Morrison, IL. She married THOMAS MICHAEL ARDWIN November 02, 1982 in North Glenn, Adams co., CO, son of DETER ARDWIN and ANNA GAFKA. He was born January 15, 1942 in Detroit, MI.

Notes for DONNA ELAINE HABBEN:
Divorced Jan. 29, 1971, per marriage application, Detroit, MI
COUSIN ONCE REMOVED OF RONALD REAGAN

Notes for THOMAS MICHAEL ARDWIN:
Divorced: Jan. 29, 1971, per marriage application, Detroit, MI

Children of DONNA HABBEN and THOMAS ARDWIN are:
    i. DONNA MARIE[9] ARDWIN, b. March 28, 1987, Denver, Adams co., CO.
    ii. MICHAEL THOMAS ARDWIN, b. January 19, 1989, Denver, Adams co., CO.
    iii. LISA ARDWIN.

81. MICHAEL[8] REAGAN *(RONALD WILSON[7], NELLIE CLYDE[6] WILSON, THOMAS[5], JANE[4] BLUE, CATHERINE[3] MCFARLANE, JOHN M.[2], WILLIAM[1])* was born March 18, 1945. He married COLLEEN STEARNS.

Notes for COLLEEN STEARNS:

Information from Mrs. Vickie Wiebenga

Child of MICHAEL REAGAN and COLLEEN STEARNS is:
    i. CAMERON MICHAEL[9] REAGAN, b. May 30, 1978.

82. MARTHA ANN[8] MITCHELL *(LOIS W.[7] WHISTLER, MARGARET MAY[6] WILSON, JOHN[5], JANE[4] BLUE, CATHERINE[3] MCFARLANE, JOHN M.[2], WILLIAM[1])* She married DAVID DEUTERMANN.

Children of MARTHA MITCHELL and DAVID DEUTERMANN are:
    i. DAVID WHITFORD[9] DEUTERMANN.
    ii. JULIA ANN DEUTERMANN.

83. JOHN WILSON[8] MITCHELL *(LOIS W.[7] WHISTLER, MARGARET MAY[6] WILSON, JOHN[5], JANE[4] BLUE, CATHERINE[3] MCFARLANE, JOHN M.[2], WILLIAM[1])* He married NAOMI YATES.

Child of JOHN MITCHELL and NAOMI YATES is:
    i. WHITFORD KIMBALL[9] MITCHELL.

84. JANE WHITFORD[8] MITCHELL *(LOIS W.[7] WHISTLER, MARGARET MAY[6] WILSON, JOHN[5], JANE[4] BLUE, CATHERINE[3] MCFARLANE, JOHN M.[2], WILLIAM[1])* She married DONALD GORZNEY.

Children of JANE MITCHELL and DONALD GORZNEY are:
    i. JOHN[9] GORZNEY.
    ii. JAMES GORZNEY.
    iii. SUSAN JANE GORZNEY.
    iv. GLEN GORZNEY.

85. BARBARA[8] MARR *(FLORENCE I.[7] WHISTLER, MARGARET MAY[6] WILSON, JOHN[5], JANE[4] BLUE, CATHERINE[3] MCFARLANE, JOHN M.[2], WILLIAM[1])* She married 'MALE' DOUGHERTY.

Children of BARBARA MARR and 'MALE' DOUGHERTY are:
    i. DENNIE[9] DOUGHERTY.
    ii. TIMOTHY DOUGHERTY.
    iii. DOUGLAS DOUGHERTY.
    iv. BRIAN DOUGHERTY.
    v. PATRICK DOUGHERTY.

86. JUDITH SUZANE[8] WILSON *(DWIGHT ALVIN[7], PAUL FLETCHER[6], ALEXANDER B[5], JANE[4] BLUE, CATHERINE[3] MCFARLANE, JOHN M.[2], WILLIAM[1])* was born November 21, 1942. She married JAMES KEITH ROWE June 13, 1964, son of V. ROWE and MARY. He was born November 25, 1941.

Notes for JUDITH SUZANE WILSON:
Teacher

Notes for JAMES KEITH ROWE:
Teacher
Divorced August, 1994

Children of JUDITH WILSON and JAMES ROWE are:
    i. DAVID KEITH[9] ROWE, b. March 17, 1968; m. RHONDA KAY BAYLES, November 23, 1996; b. April 14, 1967.
123.   ii. ROBERT MATHEW ROWE, b. September 06, 1970.

87. ROBERT THOMAS[8] WILSON *(DWIGHT ALVIN[7], PAUL FLETCHER[6], ALEXANDER B[5], JANE[4] BLUE, CATHERINE[3] MCFARLANE, JOHN M.[2], WILLIAM[1])* was born June 29, 1944. He married GEORGIANNE HUMMEL March 21, 1972. She was born August 10, 1949.

Notes for GEORGIANNE HUMMEL:
Legal secretary

Children of ROBERT WILSON and GEORGIANNE HUMMEL are:
    i. THOMAS ROBERT[9] WILSON, b. August 24, 1984, Danville, IL.
    ii. PAUL MATHEW WILSON, b. October 27, 1985, Danville, IL.

88. DEBORAH ANN[8] WILSON *(ROBERT BRISTLE[7], PAUL FLETCHER[6], ALEXANDER B[5], JANE[4] BLUE, CATHERINE[3] MCFARLANE, JOHN M.[2], WILLIAM[1])* was born February 09, 1941. She married MICHAEL MORAN September 02, 1961, son of DON MORAN and LIENNE VITE. He was born January 26, 1941.

Children of DEBORAH WILSON and MICHAEL MORAN are:
    i. CHRISTINE ELIZABETH[9] MORAN, b. April 18, 1963; m. 'MALE' FOSTER.
124. ii. KIMBERLY JANE MORAN, b. February 27, 1965.
    iii. STEPHEN MICHAEL MORAN, b. December 08, 1968.

89. STEVEN ALLEN[8] GSELL *(CLAIR LE ROY[7], CLIFFORD LEROY[6], MARGARET MAE[5] WILSON, JANE[4] BLUE, CATHERINE[3] MCFARLANE, JOHN M.[2], WILLIAM[1])* was born April 24, 1939. He married DARLENE E. VEIHL.

Children of STEVEN GSELL and DARLENE VEIHL are:
    i. BRIAN DAVID[9] GSELL.

       Notes for BRIAN DAVID GSELL:
       Twin of Dawn

    ii. DAWN ELIZABETH GSELL.

       Notes for DAWN ELIZABETH GSELL:
       Twin of Brian

    iii. BLYTHE ANN GSELL.

90. SUE ELLEN[8] GSELL *(CLAIR LE ROY[7], CLIFFORD LEROY[6], MARGARET MAE[5] WILSON, JANE[4] BLUE, CATHERINE[3] MCFARLANE, JOHN M.[2], WILLIAM[1])* was born September 25, 1955. She married JOHN KIMBERLIN.

Notes for JOHN KIMBERLIN:
2 other children

Child of SUE GSELL and JOHN KIMBERLIN is:
    i. CORINNE[9] KIMBERLIN.

91. DONNA JEAN[8] WITT *(LEPHA MAE[7] MILNES, MAUDE MAE[6] GSELL, MARGARET MAE[5] WILSON, JANE[4] BLUE, CATHERINE[3] MCFARLANE, JOHN M.[2], WILLIAM[1])* was born April 09, 1933. She married GEORGE MEDEMA. He was born July 17, 1933.

Children of DONNA WITT and GEORGE MEDEMA are:
125. i. JHODY JEAN[9] MEDEMA, b. March 11, 1952.
126. ii. JULIE MARIE MEDEMA, b. June 09, 1953.
    iii. JEANIE LARIE MEDEMA, b. May 31, 1954.

    iv. JANICE LYNE MEDEMA, b. November 27, 1956; m. CHARLES SWANSON.
    v. JERRY ALLEN MEDEMA, b. August 27, 1963.
    vi. JON CRAIG MEDEMA, b. November 29, 1966.
    vii. JAMES GREG MEDEMA, b. December 03, 1969.

92. DR. HARLAN ANDREW[8] WITT (*LEPHA MAE[7] MILNES, MAUDE MAE[6] GSELL, MARGARET MAE[5] WILSON, JANE[4] BLUE, CATHERINE[3] MCFARLANE, JOHN M.[2], WILLIAM[1]*) was born April 27, 1946. He married VERLEE ANN SILVIS.

Children of HARLAN WITT and VERLEE SILVIS are:
    i. JEFFREY ANDREW[9] WITT, b. October 19, 1967.
    ii. KIMBERLY LYNN WITT.

        Notes for KIMBERLY LYNN WITT:
        Twin of Kristen

    iii. KRISTEN LES WITT.

        Notes for KRISTEN LES WITT:
        Twin of Kimberly

93. DAVID IVAN[8] CARROLL (*MARGARET ELIZABETH[7] MILNES, MAUDE MAE[6] GSELL, MARGARET MAE[5] WILSON, JANE[4] BLUE, CATHERINE[3] MCFARLANE, JOHN M.[2], WILLIAM[1]*) was born January 02, 1938. He married SALLY ANN ONKEN. She was born December 12, 1938.

Children of DAVID CARROLL and SALLY ONKEN are:
    i. TROY ANDREW[9] CARROLL, b. April 13, 1965.
    ii. ERICK PAUL CARROLL, b. May 20, 1967.
    iii. LYNN ANDREA CARROLL, b. July 01, 1971.
    iv. LISA PAMELA CARROLL, b. December 27, 1973.

94. TERRY DEE[8] CARROLL (*MARGARET ELIZABETH[7] MILNES, MAUDE MAE[6] GSELL, MARGARET MAE[5] WILSON, JANE[4] BLUE, CATHERINE[3] MCFARLANE, JOHN M.[2], WILLIAM[1]*) was born January 03, 1946. He married VIRGINIA KAY BUSH. She was born April 15, 1947.

Children of TERRY CARROLL and VIRGINIA BUSH are:
    i. CHRISTINE LEA[9] CARROLL, b. December 17, 1968.
    ii. KARLA JEAN CARROLL, b. October 13, 1975.
    iii. MATTHEW THOMAS CARROLL, b. July 04, 1980.

95. DIANE LOUISE[8] MILNES (*WALTER[7], MAUDE MAE[6] GSELL, MARGARET MAE[5] WILSON, JANE[4] BLUE, CATHERINE[3] MCFARLANE, JOHN M.[2], WILLIAM[1]*) was born September 04, 1945. She married PAUL GLISPIE.

Child of DIANE MILNES and PAUL GLISPIE is:
    i. JOHN WESLEY[9] GLISPIE.

        Notes for JOHN WESLEY GLISPIE:
        Married 1999

96. THOMAS BRENT[8] MILNES (*WALTER[7], MAUDE MAE[6] GSELL, MARGARET MAE[5] WILSON, JANE[4] BLUE, CATHERINE[3] MCFARLANE, JOHN M.[2], WILLIAM[1]*) was born September 01, 1950. He married (1) PATRICIA RICK 1976. He married (2) PENNY SMITH 1980.

Notes for THOMAS BRENT MILNES:

Divorced from Patricia.
Dairy farmer

Child of THOMAS MILNES and PATRICIA RICK is:
  i. TINA ELIZABETH[9] MILNES, b. March 02, 1977.

     Notes for TINA ELIZABETH MILNES:
     School teacher, no children, not married (2000)

Children of THOMAS MILNES and PENNY SMITH are:
  ii. SCOTT T.[9] MILNES, b. October 31, 1981.
  iii. BRYAN THOMAS MILNES, b. January 22, 1985.
  iv. SHAUN MATHEW MILNES, b. April 13, 1986.

97. ARLYN[8] VOS *(GLADYS ELOISE[7] STAPLETON, ESTELLA JANE[6] GSELL, MARGARET MAE[5] WILSON, JANE[4] BLUE, CATHERINE[3] MCFARLANE, JOHN M.[2], WILLIAM[1])* was born May 03, 1940. He married MARY BUIKEMA. She was born November 20, 1939.

Children of ARLYN VOS and MARY BUIKEMA are:
  i. KATHY LYNN[9] VOS.
  ii. ARLYN DALE VOS.
  iii. DEBRA JANE VOS.
  iv. MARLA ANN VOS.

98. LARRY[8] VOS *(GLADYS ELOISE[7] STAPLETON, ESTELLA JANE[6] GSELL, MARGARET MAE[5] WILSON, JANE[4] BLUE, CATHERINE[3] MCFARLANE, JOHN M.[2], WILLIAM[1])* He married LINDA FRANCIS.

Children of LARRY VOS and LINDA FRANCIS are:
  i. KARI SUE[9] VOS.
  ii. TERI ANN VOS.

Generation No. 9

99. ELWIN[9] NICE *(LUCILLE FERN[8] BECHTEL, WILLIAM DETER[7], JOHN WILSON[6], SARA[5] WILSON, JANE[4] BLUE, CATHERINE[3] MCFARLANE, JOHN M.[2], WILLIAM[1])* He married SHIRLEY ENRIGHT.

Notes for ELWIN NICE:
SECOND COUSIN TWICE REMOVED OF RONALD REAGAN

Children of ELWIN NICE and SHIRLEY ENRIGHT are:
  i. WILLIAM[10] NICE, m. PATRICIA PETTICORD.
  ii. LINDA NICE.
  iii. PAM NICE.
  iv. JUDY NICE, m. JEFF MEINSMA.

100. MARJORIE[9] NICE *(LUCILLE FERN[8] BECHTEL, WILLIAM DETER[7], JOHN WILSON[6], SARA[5] WILSON, JANE[4] BLUE, CATHERINE[3] MCFARLANE, JOHN M.[2], WILLIAM[1])* She married ROBERT TRAUM.

Children of MARJORIE NICE and ROBERT TRAUM are:
  i. SUSAN[10] TRAUM.
  ii. JOHN TRAUM.
  iii. DAVID TRAUM.

101. JAMES JOSEPH[9] KUNAVICH *(KATHERINE JANE[8] HICKS, MARY MARGARET[7] WILSON, JOHN CHARLES[6], THOMAS[5], JANE[4] BLUE, CATHERINE[3] MCFARLANE, JOHN M.[2], WILLIAM[1])* was born October 22, 1943 in Clinton, Clinton co., IA, and died April 24, 1971 in Oaklawn, Cook co., IL. He married ALBERTA LYNN YONKERS January 10, 1963 in Chicago, Cook co., ILL. She was born 1945 in Chicago, Cook co., IL.

Notes for JAMES JOSEPH KUNAVICH:
Divorced before death. Accidental injury, car, Palos Hill, Cook co, IL.
COUSIN TWICE REMOVED OF RONALD REAGAN

More About JAMES JOSEPH KUNAVICH:
Burial: Grove Hill, Morrison, IL

Notes for ALBERTA LYNN YONKERS:
Divorce from Kunavich September, 1969. Married Curtis

Child of JAMES KUNAVICH and ALBERTA YONKERS is:
    i. JAMES JOSEPH[10] KUNAVICH, JR., b. March 29, 1963, Chicago, Cook co., IL.

    Notes for JAMES JOSEPH KUNAVICH, JR.:
    Because his Mother divorced Kunavich and married Curtis, John Kunavich, Jr. assumed the surname 'Curtis' to carry the same name as his Mother, affidavit of 20 Aug. 1992, Fulton, IL in the Donald Hunt estate case.
    COUSIN 3 TIMES REMOVED FROM RONALD REAGAN

102. TERRY[9] SMITH *(ROBERT CLARE[8], HORACE VERNON[7], SARA JANE[6] WILSON, THOMAS[5], JANE[4] BLUE, CATHERINE[3] MCFARLANE, JOHN M.[2], WILLIAM[1])* was born November 20, 1946. He married (1) DONNA ANN RURY January 13, 1967. He married (2) MARIA MARTINEZ August 14, 1983. He married (3) MARGARITA MARISEAL August 17, 1996.

Notes for TERRY SMITH:
Divorced 1981, from Donna, divorced from Maria.
COUSIN TWICE REMOVED OF RONALD REAGAN

Notes for DONNA ANN RURY:
Divorced 1981

Children of TERRY SMITH and DONNA RURY are:
    i. CHRISTOPHER SCOTT[10] SMITH, b. January 29, 1968.

    Notes for CHRISTOPHER SCOTT SMITH:
    COUSIN 3 TIMES REMOVED FROM RONALD REAGAN

    ii. JAMIE SMITH, b. January 23, 1973.

    Notes for JAMIE SMITH:
    Twin of Corie
    COUSIN 3 TIMES REMOVED OF RONALD REAGAN

    iii. CORY SMITH, b. January 23, 1973.

    Notes for CORY SMITH:
    Twin of Jamie
    COUSIN 3 TIMES REMOVED OF RONALD REAGAN

    iv. JENIFER ERIN SMITH, b. January 24, 1978.

    Notes for JENIFER ERIN SMITH:
    COUSIN 3 TIMES REMOVED OF RONALD REAGAN

103. VICKI[9] SMITH *(ROBERT CLARE[8], HORACE VERNON[7], SARA JANE[6] WILSON, THOMAS[5], JANE[4] BLUE, CATHERINE[3] MCFARLANE, JOHN M.[2], WILLIAM[1])* was born March 01, 1952. She married (1) BRUCE UNGER August 07, 1971 in Morrison, IL. He died March 17, 1974. She married (2) RON WIEBENGA October 24, 1975.

Notes for VICKI SMITH:
COUSIN TWICE REMOVED OF RONALD REAGAN

Notes for BRUCE UNGER:
Deceased

More About BRUCE UNGER:
Burial: Grove Hill cemetery, Morrison

Child of VICKI SMITH and BRUCE UNGER is:
    i. BRUCE EDWIN[10] UNGER, JR., b. July 04, 1974; m. KAREN GEORGE, November 06, 1999, Peoria, IL.

        Notes for BRUCE EDWIN UNGER, JR.:
        COUSIN 3 TIMES REMOVED OF RONALD REAGAN

Child of VICKI SMITH and RON WIEBENGA is:
    ii. LESLEY DAWN[10] WIEBENGA, b. April 24, 1977, Morrison, IL; m. CHAD PAUL DEVER, June 06, 1998, Morrison, IL.

        Notes for LESLEY DAWN WIEBENGA:
        COUSIN 3 TIMES REMOVED OF RONALD REAGAN

104. DAVID[9] SMITH *(GENE MEAKIN[8], HORACE VERNON[7], SARA JANE[6] WILSON, THOMAS[5], JANE[4] BLUE, CATHERINE[3] MCFARLANE, JOHN M.[2], WILLIAM[1])* was born May 21, 1948. He married DEE ANN BILDSTEIN August 09, 1975.

Notes for DAVID SMITH:
Lives in Iowa, divorced.
COUSIN TWICE REMOVED OF RONALD REAGAN

Child of DAVID SMITH and DEE BILDSTEIN is:
    i. CHELSEY[10] SMITH, b. May 20, 1982.

105. THOMAS[9] SMITH *(GENE MEAKIN[8], HORACE VERNON[7], SARA JANE[6] WILSON, THOMAS[5], JANE[4] BLUE, CATHERINE[3] MCFARLANE, JOHN M.[2], WILLIAM[1])* was born February 25, 1952. He married (1) CHRISTINE PYRON July 07, 1973. He married (2) DAWN SCHRYVER March 31, 1978. He married (3) CINDY OSTEMA March 09, 1984.

Notes for THOMAS SMITH:
Divorced Feb. 1975 - Christine
Divorced - Dawn - Dec. 1979
COUSIN TWICE REMOVED OF RONALD REAGAN

Notes for CHRISTINE PYRON:
Divorced Feb. 1975

Child of THOMAS SMITH and DAWN SCHRYVER is:
    i. THOMAS S.[10] SMITH, m. CINDY.

Children of THOMAS SMITH and CINDY OSTEMA are:
- ii. MARSHALL[10] SMITH, b. August 22, 1984.
- iii. TAYLOR SMITH, b. December 17, 1996.

106. NANCY[9] SMITH *(GENE MEAKIN[8], HORACE VERNON[7], SARA JANE[6] WILSON, THOMAS[5], JANE[4] BLUE, CATHERINE[3] MCFARLANE, JOHN M.[2], WILLIAM[1])* was born October 12, 1955. She married (1) MITCHELL FOREMAN January 04, 1975. She married (2) STEVE MERRILL Aft. January 1980.

Notes for NANCY SMITH:
Divorced Steve Jan. 5, 1980
COUSIN TWICE REMOVED OF RONALD REAGAN

Child of NANCY SMITH and MITCHELL FOREMAN is:
- i. CAMERON RYAN[10] FOREMAN, b. July 14, 1978.

  Notes for CAMERON RYAN FOREMAN:
  COUSIN 3 TIMES REMOVED OF RONALD REAGAN

Child of NANCY SMITH and STEVE MERRILL is:
- ii. DUSTIN[10] MERRILL, b. May 05, 1982.

107. PAUL EDWARD[9] WALTERS *(HAROLD EDWARD[8], ELSEY MAE[7] PIERCE, SARA JANE[6] WILSON, THOMAS[5], JANE[4] BLUE, CATHERINE[3] MCFARLANE, JOHN M.[2], WILLIAM[1])* was born May 03, 1946 in Morrison, IL. He married (1) PATRICIA BARTZ February 26, 1965 in Morrison, IL. She was born May 11, 1949 in Morrison, IL. He married (2) SHARON TIESMAN March 19, 1970 in Lyndon, Whiteside co., IL. She was born April 27, 1945.

Notes for PAUL EDWARD WALTERS:
Divorce 1970

Notes for PATRICIA BARTZ:
Divorced 1970

Child of PAUL WALTERS and PATRICIA BARTZ is:
- i. WENDY LEE[10] WALTERS, b. August 21, 1965, Morrison, IL; m. WILLIAM CHARLES HUTCHINSON; b. September 08, 1964, Carroll co., IL.

  Notes for WILLIAM CHARLES HUTCHINSON:
  Divorced

Children of PAUL WALTERS and SHARON TIESMAN are:
- ii. BABY[10] WALTERS, b. March 19, 1973; d. March 19, 1973.

  Notes for BABY WALTERS:
  Stillborn

  More About BABY WALTERS:
  Burial: Fulton cemetery. Fulton, IL

- 127. iii. TORI CHERYL WALTERS, b. April 25, 1974, Morrison, IL.
- 128. iv. TROY J WALTERS, b. November 05, 1975, Morrison, IL.

108. HARLAN GENE[9] WALTERS *(HAROLD EDWARD[8], ELSEY MAE[7] PIERCE, SARA JANE[6] WILSON, THOMAS[5], JANE[4] BLUE, CATHERINE[3] MCFARLANE, JOHN M.[2], WILLIAM[1])* was born February 05, 1948 in Morrison, IL. He married (1) MARIE SHARER February 24, 1967 in Fulton, Whiteside co., IL. She was born

May 25, 1947. He married (2) BETH RICK August 31, 1974 in Morrison, IL. She was born January 27, 1945. He married (3) LINDA ROBINSON December 02, 1983 in TX.

Notes for HARLAN GENE WALTERS:
Divorced from Marie 1974
Divorced from Beth Rick
Divorced from Linda 2002

Notes for MARIE SHARER:
Divorce 1974

Notes for BETH RICK:
Divorced

Notes for LINDA ROBINSON:
She has two children, Carolyn and Rebecca. They are children of her previous marriage.

Children of HARLAN WALTERS and MARIE SHARER are:
    i. TERRY HARLAN[10] WALTERS, b. June 06, 1968, Morrison, IL.
    ii. MARK DOUGLAS WALTERS, b. June 16, 1969, Morrison, IL.
    iii. DAVID GENE WALTERS, b. August 26, 1971, Morrison, IL.

Children of HARLAN WALTERS and LINDA ROBINSON are:
    iv. CAROLYN[10].

        Notes for CAROLYN:
        Child of Mother's previous marriage.

    v. REBECCA.

        Notes for REBECCA:
        Child of Mother's previous marriage.

109. JANE KAYE[9] WALTERS (*HAROLD EDWARD*[8], *ELSEY MAE*[7] *PIERCE*, *SARA JANE*[6] *WILSON*, *THOMAS*[5], *JANE*[4] *BLUE*, *CATHERINE*[3] *McFARLANE*, *JOHN M.*[2], *WILLIAM*[1]) was born April 16, 1950 in Morrison, IL. She married (1) LEONARD PRITCHARD March 07, 1969 in Morrison, IL. He was born November 16, 1946. She married (2) FRANK MATCHIE October 07, 1972 in Morrison, IL. He was born June 07, 1947. She married (3) WALTER G. HEATH October 22, 1990 in Morrison, IL.

Notes for JANE KAYE WALTERS:
Divorced 3 Aug 1970 from Pritchard
Divorced from Matchie

Notes for LEONARD PRITCHARD:
Divorced from Jane Kaye 3 Aug. 1970

Notes for FRANK MATCHIE:
Divorced

Child of JANE WALTERS and LEONARD PRITCHARD is:
    i. TIMOTHY ALLEN[10] PRITCHARD, b. September 22, 1969, Morrison, IL; m. ANGELA KAY MACHIE, May 1987, Morrison, IL; b. December 22, 1974, Morrison, IL.

Child of JANE WALTERS and FRANK MATCHIE is:
129.   ii. ANGELA[10] MATCHIE, b. December 22, 1974.

110. DAWN GAIL⁹ WALTERS *(HAROLD EDWARD⁸, ELSEY MAE⁷ PIERCE, SARA JANE⁶ WILSON, THOMAS⁵, JANE⁴ BLUE, CATHERINE³ MCFARLANE, JOHN M.², WILLIAM¹)* was born March 19, 1962 in Morrison, IL. She married ROBERT JAMES BAUER May 02, 1981 in Morrison, IL. He was born August 06, 1960 in Morrison, IL.

Children of DAWN WALTERS and ROBERT BAUER are:
    i. AMANDA GAIL¹⁰ BAUER, b. July 31, 1991, Clinton, Clinton Co., IA.
    ii. LAYLA MARIE BAUER, b. August 27, 1994, Clinton, Clinton Co., IA.

111. PHILIP DALE⁹ WALTERS *(HAROLD EDWARD⁸, ELSEY MAE⁷ PIERCE, SARA JANE⁶ WILSON, THOMAS⁵, JANE⁴ BLUE, CATHERINE³ MCFARLANE, JOHN M.², WILLIAM¹)* was born July 15, 1968 in Morrison, IL. He married CHRISTINE KRAUSE May 30, 1989 in Dixon, Lee co., IL.

Notes for CHRISTINE KRAUSE:
Adopted by Baughman

Children of PHILIP WALTERS and CHRISTINE KRAUSE are:
    i. STEPHANIE ANNE¹⁰ WALTERS, b. February 11, 1988, Dixon, Lee co., IL.
    ii. TIFFANY MARIE WALTERS, b. May 22, 1990, Dallas, TX.
    iii. MATTHEW WALTERS, b. September 15, 1992.

112. KURT REINHARD⁹ JANVRIN *(MERNA JOY⁸ HABBEN, VERA MARIE⁷ PIERCE, SARA JANE⁶ WILSON, THOMAS⁵, JANE⁴ BLUE, CATHERINE³ MCFARLANE, JOHN M.², WILLIAM¹)* was born August 04, 1960 in Morrison, IL. He married YVONNE AMMON June 16, 1984 in Long Grove, Lake co., IL. She was born December 19, 1961 in Decatur, Macon co., IL.

Children of KURT JANVRIN and YVONNE AMMON are:
    i. REBECCA LINDSEY¹⁰ JANVRIN, b. May 23, 1988, Trenton, Mercer co., NJ.
    ii. HANNAH KATE JANVRIN, b. October 07, 1990, Trenton, Mercer co., NJ.
    iii. GENEVIEVE JANVRIN, b. 1993.
    iv. MABELINE JANVRIN, b. 1997.

113. BRUCE CLYDE⁹ JANVRIN *(MERNA JOY⁸ HABBEN, VERA MARIE⁷ PIERCE, SARA JANE⁶ WILSON, THOMAS⁵, JANE⁴ BLUE, CATHERINE³ MCFARLANE, JOHN M.², WILLIAM¹)* was born December 22, 1961 in Morrison, IL. He married DIANE MEHLHAUS August 11, 1990 in Dysart, Benton co., IA. She was born February 20, 1961 in Dysart, Benton co., Iowa.

Children of BRUCE JANVRIN and DIANE MEHLHAUS are:
    i. BRICE¹⁰ JANVRIN, b. 1993.
    ii. BRYLEIGH JANVRIN, b. 1998.

114. ARON KYLE⁹ JANVRIN *(MERNA JOY⁸ HABBEN, VERA MARIE⁷ PIERCE, SARA JANE⁶ WILSON, THOMAS⁵, JANE⁴ BLUE, CATHERINE³ MCFARLANE, JOHN M.², WILLIAM¹)* was born November 13, 1964 in Morrison, IL. He married CAROLYN BROWN June 28, 1998.

Child of ARON JANVRIN and CAROLYN BROWN is:
    i. TYLER¹⁰ JANVRIN, b. February 29, 2000.

115. RHONDA JANE⁹ HABBEN *(NORMAN WALTER⁸, VERA MARIE⁷ PIERCE, SARA JANE⁶ WILSON, THOMAS⁵, JANE⁴ BLUE, CATHERINE³ MCFARLANE, JOHN M.², WILLIAM¹)* was born June 24, 1957. She married (1) ALLEN GREELEY June 10, 1978 in Morrison, IL. He was born August 05, 1951 in Morrison, IL. She married (2) ALLEN RAY GREELEY June 10, 1978 in Morrison, IL. He was born August 05,

1951 in Morrison, IL.

Children of RHONDA HABBEN and ALLEN GREELEY are:
  i. MELLISSA JEAN[10] GREELEY, b. December 08, 1980, Morrison, IL.
  ii. WILLIAM NORMAN GREELEY, b. June 19, 1983, Morrison, IL.
  iii. MARLA JANE GREELEY, b. September 04, 1984, Morrison, IL.

116. GENE LEROY[9] HABBEN *(NORMAN WALTER[8], VERA MARIE[7] PIERCE, SARA JANE[6] WILSON, THOMAS[5], JANE[4] BLUE, CATHERINE[3] MCFARLANE, JOHN M.[2], WILLIAM[1])* was born July 07, 1960 in Morrison, IL. He married KAREN ROENIKE February 25, 1989 in Clinton, Iowa.

Children of GENE HABBEN and KAREN ROENIKE are:
  i. TRAVIS[10] HABBEN, b. 1993.
  ii. RYAN HABBEN, b. 1996.
  iii. KRISTIN, b. 1999.

117. SARA LEANNE[9] HABBEN *(NORMAN WALTER[8], VERA MARIE[7] PIERCE, SARA JANE[6] WILSON, THOMAS[5], JANE[4] BLUE, CATHERINE[3] MCFARLANE, JOHN M.[2], WILLIAM[1])* was born March 09, 1967 in Morrison, IL. She married (1) COONAN DICKMAN March 29, 1986 in Morrison, IL. He was born March 24, 1967. She married (2) RANDY FAUST September 1990 in Mo-.

Notes for SARA LEANNE HABBEN:
Divorced Dickman 1990, no children with him.

Notes for COONAN DICKMAN:
Divorced 1990, no children.

Children of SARA HABBEN and RANDY FAUST are:
  i. ADAM CHARLES[10] FAUST, b. March 23, 1991, Virginia Beach, VA.
  ii. ASHLEY FAUST, b. 1994.

118. DANIEL LEE[9] HABBEN *(RONALD LEE[8], VERA MARIE[7] PIERCE, SARA JANE[6] WILSON, THOMAS[5], JANE[4] BLUE, CATHERINE[3] MCFARLANE, JOHN M.[2], WILLIAM[1])* was born June 26, 1962 in Morrison, IL. He married BETH HACKER June 20, 1987 in Morrison, IL. She was born January 10, 1962.

Children of DANIEL HABBEN and BETH HACKER are:
  i. LOGAN DANIEL[10] HABBEN, b. May 14, 1989, Sterling, Whiteside co., IL.
  ii. ABBEY HABBEN, b. 1994.

119. DEBRA LOU[9] HABBEN *(RONALD LEE[8], VERA MARIE[7] PIERCE, SARA JANE[6] WILSON, THOMAS[5], JANE[4] BLUE, CATHERINE[3] MCFARLANE, JOHN M.[2], WILLIAM[1])* was born September 17, 1964 in Morrison, IL. She married JAMES LEE SNYDER June 11, 1983 in Morrison, IL. He was born October 30, 1963 in Morrison, IL.

Notes for DEBRA LOU HABBEN:
Divorced 1988

Notes for JAMES LEE SNYDER:
Divorced 1988

Children of DEBRA HABBEN and JAMES SNYDER are:
  i. BRANDON[10] SNYDER, b. October 31, 1985, Germany.
  ii. TIMOTHY SNYDER, b. February 12, 1987, Sterling, Whiteside co., IL.

120. CATHERINE JEAN[9] HABBEN *(MILFORD GENE[8], VERA MARIE[7] PIERCE, SARA JANE[6] WILSON, THOMAS[5], JANE[4] BLUE, CATHERINE[3] MCFARLANE, JOHN M.[2], WILLIAM[1])* was born May 08, 1966 in Morrison, IL. She married MARK BENNET June 27, 1987 in Dixon, Lee co., IL.

Notes for CATHERINE JEAN HABBEN:
Divorced

Children of CATHERINE HABBEN and MARK BENNET are:
     i. JENNIFER ANN[10] BENNET, b. October 06, 1990, Sterling, Whiteside co., IL.
     ii. AMANDA BENNET, b. 1994.

121. JEFFERY MICHAEL[9] NORTON *(VELMA JANE[8] HABBEN, VERA MARIE[7] PIERCE, SARA JANE[6] WILSON, THOMAS[5], JANE[4] BLUE, CATHERINE[3] MCFARLANE, JOHN M.[2], WILLIAM[1])* was born December 23, 1971 in Freport, Stephenson co., IL. He married ANGIE.

Child of JEFFERY NORTON and ANGIE is:
     i. GRACE[10] NORTON, b. 1999.

122. CALE RICHARD[9] ALBRECHT *(CAROL ANN[8] HABBEN, VERA MARIE[7] PIERCE, SARA JANE[6] WILSON, THOMAS[5], JANE[4] BLUE, CATHERINE[3] MCFARLANE, JOHN M.[2], WILLIAM[1])* was born June 06, 1973 in Freport, Stephenson co., IL. He married CHRIS.

Notes for CALE RICHARD ALBRECHT:
3rd Great-grandson of John Wilson.
Divorced, 2000

Child of CALE ALBRECHT and CHRIS is:
     i. CARRIE[10] ALBRECHT, b. 1995.

123. ROBERT MATHEW[9] ROWE *(JUDITH SUZANE[8] WILSON, DWIGHT ALVIN[7], PAUL FLETCHER[6], ALEXANDER B[5], JANE[4] BLUE, CATHERINE[3] MCFARLANE, JOHN M.[2], WILLIAM[1])* was born September 06, 1970. He married HEIDI ANN HULBERT October 10, 1992, daughter of STEPHEN HULBERT and DIANE. She was born March 22, 1969.

Children of ROBERT ROWE and HEIDI HULBERT are:
     i. AMANDA[10] ROWE, b. April 29, 1995.
     ii. LUCAS MATHEW ROWE, b. February 10, 1998.

124. KIMBERLY JANE[9] MORAN *(DEBORAH ANN[8] WILSON, ROBERT BRISTLE[7], PAUL FLETCHER[6], ALEXANDER B[5], JANE[4] BLUE, CATHERINE[3] MCFARLANE, JOHN M.[2], WILLIAM[1])* was born February 27, 1965. She married 'MALE' KIDWELL.

Children of KIMBERLY MORAN and 'MALE' KIDWELL are:
     i. TYLER[10] KIDWELL.
     ii. JACOB KIDWELL.
     iii. STEVEN KIDWELL.

125. JHODY JEAN[9] MEDEMA *(DONNA JEAN[8] WITT, LEPHA MAE[7] MILNES, MAUDE MAE[6] GSELL, MARGARET MAE[5] WILSON, JANE[4] BLUE, CATHERINE[3] MCFARLANE, JOHN M.[2], WILLIAM[1])* was born March 11, 1952. He married KATHY DITTMAR.

Child of JHODY MEDEMA and KATHY DITTMAR is:
     i. JACOB[10] MEDEMA.

126. JULIE MARIE[9] MEDEMA *(DONNA JEAN[8] WITT, LEPHA MAE[7] MILNES, MAUDE MAE[6] GSELL, MARGARET MAE[5] WILSON, JANE[4] BLUE, CATHERINE[3] MCFARLANE, JOHN M.[2], WILLIAM[1])* was born June 09, 1953. She married THOMAS SCHUMACHER.

Children of JULIE MEDEMA and THOMAS SCHUMACHER are:
    i. MATTHEW COLLIN[10] SCHUMACHER.
    ii. LUCAS SCHUMACHER.

Generation No. 10

127. TORI CHERYL[10] WALTERS *(PAUL EDWARD[9], HAROLD EDWARD[8], ELSEY MAE[7] PIERCE, SARA JANE[6] WILSON, THOMAS[5], JANE[4] BLUE, CATHERINE[3] MCFARLANE, JOHN M.[2], WILLIAM[1])* was born April 25, 1974 in Morrison, IL. She married JUSTIN EADS January 13, 1996.

Children of TORI WALTERS and JUSTIN EADS are:
    i. CHELSEA CHERYL[11] EADS, b. June 20, 1996, Sterling, IL.
    ii. JOSEPH JAMES EADS, b. December 29, 1998, Sterling, IL.
    iii. ZACHARY PHILIP EADS, b. March 07, 2003, Davenport, IA.

128. TROY J.[10] WALTERS *(PAUL EDWARD[9], HAROLD EDWARD[8], ELSEY MAE[7] PIERCE, SARA JANE[6] WILSON, THOMAS[5], JANE[4] BLUE, CATHERINE[3] MCFARLANE, JOHN M.[2], WILLIAM[1])* was born November 05, 1975 in Morrison, IL. He married CHRISTINA.

Notes for TROY J. WALTERS:
Divorced 2002

Notes for CHRISTINA:
Divorced 2002

Children of TROY WALTERS and CHRISTINA are:
    i. JULIA ANNA[11] WALTERS, b. September 26, 1999, Sterling, IL.
    ii. DREW PHILIP WALTERS, b. December 23, 2000, Sterling, IL.

129. ANGELA[10] MATCHIE *(JANE KAYE[9] WALTERS, HAROLD EDWARD[8], ELSEY MAE[7] PIERCE, SARA JANE[6] WILSON, THOMAS[5], JANE[4] BLUE, CATHERINE[3] MCFARLANE, JOHN M.[2], WILLIAM[1])* was born December 22, 1974. She married SHANE FERGUSON August 31, 1996.

Children of ANGELA MATCHIE and SHANE FERGUSON are:
    i. MIRISSA JANE[11], b. March 10, 1995.
    ii. HUNTER MICHAEL FERGUSON, b. January 03, 1997, Sterling, IL.

Kinship of William McFarlane

Name	Relationship with William McFarlane	Civil	Canon
<Unnamed>	Great-granddaughter	III	3
Ackerman, D. G.	Husband of the great-granddaughter		
Aitken, Mayme	Wife of the 3rd great-grandson		
Aldritt	Wife of the 2nd great-grandson		
Alex	3rd great-grandson	V	5
Alldritt, Emma A.	Wife of the 2nd great-grandson		
Allison, Elizabeth	Wife		
Ammon, Yvonne	Wife of the 6th great-grandson		
Anderson, Amy Adele	Wife of the 5th great-grandson		
Barrett, Maxine Joy	Wife of the 4th great-grandson		
Bartz, Patricia	Wife of the 6th great-grandson		
Bauer, Amanda Gail	7th great-granddaughter	IX	9
Bauer, Robert James	Husband of the 6th great-granddaughter		
Bayles, Rhonda Kay	Wife of the 6th great-grandson		
Bechtel, Albert	4th great-grandson	VI	6
Bechtel, Bonnie	6th great-granddaughter	VIII	8
Bechtel, Carol	6th great-granddaughter	VIII	8
Bechtel, E. M.	Wife of the great-grandson		
Bechtel, Ellen	6th great-granddaughter	VIII	8
Bechtel, Ellen W.	3rd great-granddaughter	V	5
Bechtel, Ephraim Myers	Husband of the 2nd great-granddaughter		
Bechtel, Everett	5th great-grandson	VII	7
Bechtel, Gary	6th great-grandson	VIII	8
Bechtel, Glenda	6th great-granddaughter	VIII	8
Bechtel, Glenn	5th great-grandson	VII	7
Bechtel, Helena	3rd great-granddaughter	V	5
Bechtel, Ivy May	4th great-granddaughter	VI	6
Bechtel, John Wilson	3rd great-grandson	V	5
Bechtel, Lucille Fern	5th great-granddaughter	VII	7
Bechtel, Rebecca Jane	3rd great-granddaughter	V	5
Bechtel, Scott	6th great-grandson	VIII	8
Bechtel, William Deter	4th great-grandson	VI	6
Belle	Wife of the 2nd great-grandson		
Benjamin, Helen May	Wife of the great-grandson		
Bennet, Amanda	7th great-granddaughter	IX	9
Bennet, Jennifer Ann	7th great-granddaughter	IX	9
Bennet, Mark	Husband of the 6th great-granddaughter		
Bessie	4th great-granddaughter	VI	6
Beswick, Mary	Wife of the great-grandson		
Bildstein, Dee Ann	Wife of the 6th great-grandson		
Birt, Ella	Wife of the great-grandson		
Blue, Alexander	Great-grandson	III	3
Blue, Catharine	Great-granddaughter	III	3
Blue, Charles	Great-grandson	III	3
Blue, Elizabeth	2nd great-granddaughter	IV	4
Blue, George	2nd great-grandson	IV	4
Blue, Girl	3rd great-grandson	V	5
Blue, I, John	Great-grandson	III	3
Blue, Isabell	Great-granddaughter	III	3
Blue, Jane	Great-granddaughter	III	3
Blue, John A.	2nd great-grandson	IV	4

Name	Relationship with William McFarlane	Civil	Canon
Blue, John, 2	Great-grandson	III	3
Blue, Jr., Donald Daniel	Great-grandson	III	3
Blue, Margaret	Great-granddaughter	III	3
Blue, Mary Elizabeth	3rd great-granddaughter	V	5
Blue, Richard Beswick	2nd great-grandson	IV	4
Blue, Samuel A	3rd great-grandson	V	5
Blue, Sr, Donald Daniel	Husband of the granddaughter		
Blue, Wilford T.	3rd great-grandson	V	5
Brett, Alexander	2nd great-grandson	IV	4
Brett, Charles	2nd great-grandson	IV	4
Brett, Donald	2nd great-grandson	IV	4
Brett, George	2nd great-grandson	IV	4
Brett, John	Husband of the great-granddaughter		
Brett, John W.	2nd great-grandson	IV	4
Brett, Kate	2nd great-granddaughter	IV	4
Brett, Thomas C.	2nd great-grandson	IV	4
Brickley, Dorothy	Wife of the 5th great-grandson		
Bristle, Etta May	Wife of the 3rd great-grandson		
Brooks, Pauline Catherine	Wife of the 4th great-grandson		
Brown, Carolyn	Wife of the 6th great-grandson		
Buikema, Mary	Wife of the 5th great-grandson		
Bush, Douglas	Husband of the 6th great-granddaughter		
Bush, Virginia Kay	Wife of the 5th great-grandson		
C., Henry	4th great-grandson	VI	6
Capone, James A	Husband of the 5th great-granddaughter		
Carolyn	7th great-granddaughter	IX	9
Carroll, Christine Lea	6th great-granddaughter	VIII	8
Carroll, David Ivan	5th great-grandson	VII	7
Carroll, Erick Paul	6th great-grandson	VIII	8
Carroll, Ivan Ralph	Husband of the 4th great-granddaughter		
Carroll, Karla Jean	6th great-granddaughter	VIII	8
Carroll, Lisa Pamela	6th great-granddaughter	VIII	8
Carroll, Lynn Andrea	6th great-granddaughter	VIII	8
Carroll, Matthew Thomas	6th great-grandson	VIII	8
Carroll, Terry Dee	5th great-grandson	VII	7
Carroll, Troy Andrew	6th great-grandson	VIII	8
Christina	Wife of the 7th great-grandson		
Cindy	Wife of the 7th great-grandson		
Conant	Husband of the 5th great-granddaughter		
Cook, Norma Jean	Wife of the 5th great-grandson		
Curtis, James J.	7th great-grandson	IX	9
Cutler, Francis Louise	Wife of the 3rd great-grandson		
Daniel	Husband of the granddaughter		
Daniel	Great-grandson	III	3
Davis, Nancy	Wife of the 4th great-grandson		
Debbie	Wife of the 2nd great-grandson		
Deter, Sarah E.	Wife of the 3rd great-grandson		
Deutermann, David	Husband of the 5th great-granddaughter		
Deutermann, David Whitford	6th great-grandson	VIII	8
Deutermann, Julia Ann	6th great-granddaughter	VIII	8
Dever, Chad Paul	Husband of the 7th great-granddaughter		
Dickman, Coonan	Husband of the 6th great-granddaughter		
Dillon, Jacklyn Ann	6th great-granddaughter	VIII	8

Name	Relationship with William McFarlane	Civil	Canon
Dillon, John Charles	5th great-grandson	VII	7
Dillon, Katherine Annabelle	5th great-granddaughter	VII	7
Dillon, Margaret Eliza	5th great-granddaughter	VII	7
Dillon, Raymond James	Husband of the 4th great-granddaughter		
Dillon, Raymond James	5th great-grandson	VII	7
Dingman, Theodore	Husband of the 5th great-granddaughter		
Dittmar, Kathy	Wife of the 6th great-grandson		
Dougherty, Brian	6th great-grandson	VIII	8
Dougherty, Dennie	6th great-grandson	VIII	8
Dougherty, Douglas	6th great-grandson	VIII	8
Dougherty, 'Male'	Husband of the 5th great-granddaughter		
Dougherty, Patrick	6th great-grandson	VIII	8
Dougherty, Timothy	6th great-grandson	VIII	8
Dutch	4th great-grandson	VI	6
Eads, Justin	Husband of the 7th great-granddaughter		
Ella	3rd great-granddaughter	V	5
Ella	3rd great-granddaughter	V	5
Elsey, Mary Ann	Wife of the 2nd great-grandson		
Enright, Shirley	Wife of the 6th great-grandson		
Fannie	3rd great-granddaughter	V	5
Faust, Adam Charles	7th great-grandson	IX	9
Faust, Ashley	7th great-granddaughter	IX	9
Faust, Randy	Husband of the 6th great-granddaughter		
Ferguson, Shane	Husband of the 7th great-granddaughter		
Fike, Ida	Wife of the 4th great-grandson		
Flack, Clarence	Husband of the 3rd great-granddaughter		
Flack, Kathryn	5th great-granddaughter	VII	7
Flack, Pamela	5th great-granddaughter	VII	7
Flack, Thomas Oliver	4th great-grandson	VI	6
Flack, Timothy Conrad	4th great-grandson	VI	6
Flack, William C.	5th great-grandson	VII	7
Fletcher, Deborah A.	Wife of the 2nd great-grandson		
Foreman, Cameron Ryan	7th great-grandson	IX	9
Foreman, Mitchell	Husband of the 6th great-granddaughter		
Forsyth, Cunningham	Daughter-in-law		
Foster, 'Male'	Husband of the 6th great-granddaughter		
Francis, Linda	Wife of the 5th great-grandson		
Fredrick, Lisa	Wife of the 6th great-grandson		
Fulks, Sara Jane	Wife of the 4th great-grandson		
Gallentine, Randy Gale	Husband of the 5th great-granddaughter		
George, Karen	Wife of the 7th great-grandson		
Gerdes, David Edmond	Husband of the 3rd great-granddaughter		
Gerdes, Ephraim Lawrence	4th great-grandson	VI	6
Gerdes, Galen Glenn	4th great-grandson	VI	6
Gerdes, Henry Ralph	4th great-grandson	VI	6
Gerdes, Lloyd	4th great-grandson	VI	6
Gerdes, Robert	5th great-grandson	VII	7
Gerdes, Ruth	5th great-granddaughter	VII	7
Gerdes, Virgil E.	4th great-grandson	VI	6
Gerdes, Wayne	5th great-grandson	VII	7
Gibson, Shirley	Wife of the 5th great-grandson		
Glispie, John Wesley	6th great-grandson	VIII	8
Glispie, Paul	Husband of the 5th great-granddaughter		

Name	Relationship with William McFarlane	Civil	Canon
Goff, Hulda Philena	Wife of the 4th great-grandson		
Goldsmith, Robin N.	Husband of the 5th great-granddaughter		
Gorzney, Donald	Husband of the 5th great-granddaughter		
Gorzney, Glen	6th great-grandson	VIII	8
Gorzney, James	6th great-grandson	VIII	8
Gorzney, John	6th great-grandson	VIII	8
Gorzney, Susan Jane	6th great-granddaughter	VIII	8
Greeley, Allen	Husband of the 6th great-granddaughter		
Greeley, Allen Ray	Husband of the 6th great-granddaughter		
Greeley, Marla Jane	7th great-granddaughter	IX	9
Greeley, Mellissa Jean	7th great-granddaughter	IX	9
Greeley, William Norman	7th great-grandson	IX	9
Green, Rhea	Wife of the 5th great-grandson		
Gsell, Blythe Ann	6th great-granddaughter	VIII	8
Gsell, Brian David	6th great-grandson	VIII	8
Gsell, Clair Le Roy	4th great-grandson	VI	6
Gsell, Clifford Leroy	3rd great-grandson	V	5
Gsell, David B.	Husband of the 2nd great-granddaughter		
Gsell, Dawn Elizabeth	6th great-granddaughter	VIII	8
Gsell, Earl Wilson	3rd great-grandson	V	5
Gsell, Estella Jane	3rd great-granddaughter	V	5
Gsell, Howard Wilson	4th great-grandson	VI	6
Gsell, Maude Mae	3rd great-granddaughter	V	5
Gsell, Richard Lee	5th great-grandson	VII	7
Gsell, Steven Allen	5th great-grandson	VII	7
Gsell, Sue Ellen	5th great-granddaughter	VII	7
Gsell, William B.	Husband of the 2nd great-granddaughter		
Habben, Catherine Jean	6th great-granddaughter	VIII	8
Habben, Donald Patrick	6th great-grandson	VIII	8
Habben, Gene LeRoy	6th great-grandson	VIII	8
Habben, Merna Joy	5th great-granddaughter	VII	7
Habben, Milford Gene	5th great-grandson	VII	7
Habben, Norman Walter	5th great-grandson	VII	7
Habben, Reinhard F.	Husband of the 4th great-granddaughter		
Habben, Rhonda Jane	6th great-granddaughter	VIII	8
Habben, Robert Allen	6th great-grandson	VIII	8
Habben, Ryan	7th great-grandson	IX	9
Habben, Sara Leanne	6th great-granddaughter	VIII	8
Habben, Travis	7th great-grandson	IX	9
Hammer, Edna Julia	Wife of the 3rd great-grandson		
Heath, Walter G.	Husband of the 6th great-granddaughter		
Helms, Mayme	Wife of the 3rd great-grandson		
Herrold, Edith	4th great-granddaughter	VI	6
Herrold, Lloyd	Husband of the 3rd great-granddaughter		
Herrold, Lloyd Wilson	4th great-grandson	VI	6
Hicks, Earl Clyde	5th great-grandson	VII	7
Hicks, Harriet	5th great-granddaughter	VII	7
Hicks, Harry John	Husband of the 4th great-granddaughter		
Hicks, Katherine Jane	5th great-granddaughter	VII	7
High, Bessie Luella Jane	3rd great-granddaughter	V	5
High, Joseph	Husband of the 6th great-granddaughter		
High, William G.	Husband of the 2nd great-granddaughter		
Hoffman, Ruth	Wife of the 4th great-grandson		

Name	Relationship with William McFarlane	Civil	Canon
Holly	Husband of the 3rd great-granddaughter		
Homerding, Margie	Wife of the 4th great-grandson		
Howard, Iona Mae	Wife of the 4th great-grandson		
Howell, William	Husband of the 3rd great-granddaughter		
Hulbert, Heidi Ann	Wife of the 6th great-grandson		
Hulda	Wife of the 4th great-grandson		
Hummel, Georgianne	Wife of the 5th great-grandson		
Hunt, Donald Wilson	4th great-grandson	VI	6
Hunt, Louis Herman	Husband of the 3rd great-granddaughter		
Hutchinson, William Charles	Husband of the 7th great-granddaughter		
J., Katie	2nd great-granddaughter	IV	4
Jack	Husband of the 3rd great-granddaughter		
Janke, Janet	Wife of the 5th great-grandson		
Janvrin, Aron Kyle	6th great-grandson	VIII	8
Janvrin, Brice	7th great-grandson	IX	9
Janvrin, Bruce Clyde	6th great-grandson	VIII	8
Janvrin, Bryleigh	7th great-granddaughter	IX	9
Janvrin, Clyde Elmer	Husband of the 5th great-granddaughter		
Janvrin, Eric Paul	6th great-grandson	VIII	8
Janvrin, Genevieve	7th great-granddaughter	IX	9
Janvrin, Hannah Kate	7th great-granddaughter	IX	9
Janvrin, Kurt Reinhard	6th great-grandson	VIII	8
Janvrin, Mabeline	7th great-granddaughter	IX	9
Janvrin, Rebecca Lindsey	7th great-granddaughter	IX	9
Janvrin, Tyler	7th great-grandson	IX	9
Jean	Wife of the 5th great-grandson		
Jellerichs, Gail A.	Husband of the 5th great-granddaughter		
Jennie	3rd great-granddaughter	V	5
Joe	6th great-grandson	VIII	8
Johnson, Donald LeRoy	Husband of the 5th great-granddaughter		
Jr.	4th great-grandson	VI	6
Jr.	5th great-grandson	VII	7
Katherine	Great-granddaughter	III	3
Keith, Thelma Lillian	Wife of the 3rd great-grandson		
	Wife of the 4th great-grandson		
Kennedy, Danny	Husband of the 6th great-granddaughter		
Kent, Ella A.	Wife of the 2nd great-grandson		
Kidwell, Jacob	7th great-grandson	IX	9
Kidwell, 'Male'	Husband of the 6th great-granddaughter		
Kidwell, Steven	7th great-grandson	IX	9
Kidwell, Tyler	7th great-grandson	IX	9
Kimberlin, Corinne	6th great-granddaughter	VIII	8
Kimberlin, John	Husband of the 5th great-granddaughter		
Klosterman, Nora	Wife of the 3rd great-grandson		
Krause, Christine	Wife of the 6th great-grandson		
Kristin	7th great-granddaughter	IX	9
Kunavich, Adolph G.	Husband of the 5th great-granddaughter		
Kunavich, James Joseph	6th great-grandson	VIII	8
Kunavich, James Joseph, Jr.	7th great-grandson	IX	9
Kunavich, Ronald George	6th great-grandson	VIII	8
Lane, Dorothy Ann	5th great-granddaughter	VII	7
Lane, Mildred	5th great-granddaughter	VII	7
Lane, William	Husband of the 4th great-granddaughter		

Name	Relationship with William McFarlane	Civil	Canon
Lane, William	5th great-grandson	VII	7
Layla Marie Bauer	7th great-granddaughter	IX	9
Lewis	Husband of the 3rd great-granddaughter		
Liggett, Isabelle Mary	Wife of the 2nd great-grandson		
Lizzie	2nd great-granddaughter	IV	4
Longanecker, Samuel L.	Husband of the 3rd great-granddaughter		
Machie, Angela Kay	Wife of the 7th great-grandson		
Maggie	2nd great-granddaughter	IV	4
Maggie	3rd great-granddaughter	V	5
Manning, Shirley	Wife of the 5th great-grandson		
Mariseal, Margarita	Wife of the 6th great-grandson		
Marr, Barbara	5th great-granddaughter	VII	7
Marr, George L.	Husband of the 4th great-granddaughter		
Marr, George Michael	5th great-grandson	VII	7
Martinez, Maria	Wife of the 6th great-grandson		
Mary	Wife of the 3rd great-grandson		
Matchie, Angela	7th great-granddaughter	IX	9
Matchie, Frank	Husband of the 6th great-granddaughter		
Mathew, Janice Lucille	Wife of the 4th great-grandson		
May, Denzie	Wife of the 4th great-grandson		
May, Iva	4th great-granddaughter	VI	6
Mayme	4th great-granddaughter	VI	6
McFarlain, Katharine	Granddaughter	II	2
McFarlane, Catherine	Granddaughter	II	2
McFarlane, John M.	Son	I	1
McFarlane, William	Self		0
McKay, Daniel	2nd great-grandson	IV	4
McKay, Robert	Husband of the great-granddaughter		
McKee, Carlene	Wife of the 5th great-grandson		
Meakins, Dossie May	Wife of the 4th great-grandson		
Medema, George	Husband of the 5th great-granddaughter		
Medema, Jacob	7th great-grandson	IX	9
Medema, James Greg	6th great-grandson	VIII	8
Medema, Janice Lyne	6th great-granddaughter	VIII	8
Medema, Jeanie Larie	6th great-granddaughter	VIII	8
Medema, Jerry Allen	6th great-grandson	VIII	8
Medema, Jhody Jean	6th great-grandson	VIII	8
Medema, Jon Craig	6th great-grandson	VIII	8
Medema, Julie Marie	6th great-granddaughter	VIII	8
Mehlhaus, Diane	Wife of the 6th great-grandson		
Meinsma, Jeff	Husband of the 7th great-granddaughter		
Merrill, Dustin	7th great-grandson	IX	9
Merrill, Steve	Husband of the 6th great-granddaughter		
Milnes, Bryan Thomas	6th great-grandson	VIII	8
Milnes, Diane Louise	5th great-granddaughter	VII	7
Milnes, Lepha Mae	4th great-granddaughter	VI	6
Milnes, Margaret Elizabeth	4th great-granddaughter	VI	6
Milnes, Scott T.	6th great-grandson	VIII	8
Milnes, Shaun Mathew	6th great-grandson	VIII	8
Milnes, Thomas Brent	5th great-grandson	VII	7
Milnes, Tina Elizabeth	6th great-granddaughter	VIII	8
Milnes, Walter	4th great-grandson	VI	6
Milnes, Walter Richard	Husband of the 3rd great-granddaughter		

Name	Relationship with William McFarlane	Civil	Canon
Milnes, Wanda Vey	5th great-granddaughter	VII	7
Milnes, Winnie	Wife of the 4th great-grandson		
Mitchell, Jane Whitford	5th great-granddaughter	VII	7
Mitchell, John Wilson	5th great-grandson	VII	7
Mitchell, Martha Ann	5th great-granddaughter	VII	7
Mitchell, Whitford	Husband of the 4th great-granddaughter		
Mitchell, Whitford Kimball	6th great-grandson	VIII	8
Moon	4th great-grandson	VI	6
Moran, Christine Elizabeth	6th great-granddaughter	VIII	8
Moran, Kimberly Jane	6th great-granddaughter	VIII	8
Moran, Michael	Husband of the 5th great-granddaughter		
Moran, Stephen Michael	6th great-grandson	VIII	8
Muschal, Robert Michael	Husband of the 5th great-granddaughter		
Naftzger, Beulah Vey	Wife of the 4th great-grandson		
Nellie, Helen	Wife of the great-grandson		
Nelson, Dorothy	Wife of the 3rd great-grandson		
Nelson, Helen Marie	Wife of the 4th great-grandson		
Nice, Elwin	6th great-grandson	VIII	8
Nice, Judy	7th great-granddaughter	IX	9
Nice, Linda	7th great-granddaughter	IX	9
Nice, Lyle	Husband of the 5th great-granddaughter		
Nice, Marjorie	6th great-granddaughter	VIII	8
Nice, Pam	7th great-granddaughter	IX	9
Nice, William	7th great-grandson	IX	9
Nicke, Darrel	Husband of the 6th great-granddaughter		
Onken, Sally Ann	Wife of the 5th great-grandson		
Ostema, Cindy	Wife of the 6th great-grandson		
Palmier, Doria	Wife of the 5th great-grandson		
Patrick, JoAnne	Wife of the 5th great-grandson		
Patti	5th great-granddaughter	VII	7
Pessman, Greg	Husband of the 6th great-granddaughter		
Petticord, Patricia	Wife of the 7th great-grandson		
Pierce, Elsey Mae	4th great-granddaughter	VI	6
Pierce, James H.	Husband of the 5th great-granddaughter		
Pierce, Vera Marie	4th great-granddaughter	VI	6
Pierce, Walter S.	Husband of the 3rd great-granddaughter		
Pritchard, Leonard	Husband of the 6th great-granddaughter		
Pritchard, Timothy Allen	7th great-grandson	IX	9
Pyron, Christine	Wife of the 6th great-grandson		
Rains, O. Darlene	Wife of the 5th great-grandson		
Reagan, Cameron Michael	6th great-grandson	VIII	8
Reagan, John Edward	Husband of the 3rd great-granddaughter		
Reagan, John Neil	4th great-grandson	VI	6
Reagan, Maureen Elizabeth	5th great-granddaughter	VII	7
Reagan, Michael	5th great-grandson	VII	7
Reagan, Patricia	5th great-granddaughter	VII	7
Reagan, Ronald Prescott	5th great-grandson	VII	7
Reagan, Ronald Wilson	4th great-grandson	VI	6
Rebecca	7th great-granddaughter	IX	9
Reinhardt	Husband of the 4th great-granddaughter		
Reiter, Glenda	Wife of the 5th great-grandson		
Rick, Beth	Wife of the 6th great-grandson		
Rick, Patricia	Wife of the 5th great-grandson		

Name	Relationship with William McFarlane	Civil	Canon
Robbins, Anne Frances	Wife of the 4th great-grandson		
Robinson, Linda	Wife of the 6th great-grandson		
Roenike, Karen	Wife of the 6th great-grandson		
Rowe, Amanda	7th great-granddaughter	IX	9
Rowe, David Keith	6th great-grandson	VIII	8
Rowe, James Keith	Husband of the 5th great-granddaughter		
Rowe, Lucas Mathew	7th great-grandson	IX	9
Rowe, Robert Mathew	6th great-grandson	VIII	8
Rury, Donna Ann	Wife of the 6th great-grandson		
Rush, Stephen A.	Husband of the 3rd great-granddaughter		
Ryan, Daniel Joseph	Husband of the 5th great-granddaughter		
Schneider, Marian D.	Wife of the 5th great-grandson		
Schryver, Dawn	Wife of the 6th great-grandson		
Schumacher, Lucas	7th great-grandson	IX	9
Schumacher, Matthew Collin	7th great-grandson	IX	9
Schumacher, Thomas	Husband of the 6th great-granddaughter		
Sharer, Marie	Wife of the 6th great-grandson		
Shrider, Mareta	Wife of the 4th great-grandson		
Silvis, Verlee Ann	Wife of the 5th great-grandson		
Smith, Barbara	6th great-granddaughter	VIII	8
Smith, Charles Alfred	4th great-grandson	VI	6
Smith, Chelsey	7th great-granddaughter	IX	9
Smith, Christopher Scott	7th great-grandson	IX	9
Smith, Cory	7th great-granddaughter	IX	9
Smith, Dale	6th great-grandson	VIII	8
Smith, David	6th great-grandson	VIII	8
Smith, Dean	6th great-grandson	VIII	8
Smith, Dennis	6th great-grandson	VIII	8
Smith, Gene Meakin	5th great-grandson	VII	7
Smith, Gordon M.	6th great-grandson	VIII	8
Smith, Harry Wilson	4th great-grandson	VI	6
Smith, Harry Wilson, Jr	5th great-grandson	VII	7
Smith, Horace C.	Husband of the 3rd great-granddaughter		
Smith, Horace Vernon	4th great-grandson	VI	6
Smith, Hudson B.	6th great-grandson	VIII	8
Smith, Jamie	7th great-grandson	IX	9
Smith, Jenie Alice	Wife of the 2nd great-grandson		
Smith, Jenifer Erin	7th great-granddaughter	IX	9
Smith, Karen	6th great-granddaughter	VIII	8
Smith, Marshall	7th great-grandson	IX	9
Smith, Mathew Lee	Husband of the 5th great-granddaughter		
Smith, Milford L.	5th great-grandson	VII	7
Smith, Nancy	6th great-granddaughter	VIII	8
Smith, Penny	Wife of the 5th great-grandson		
Smith, Raymond	5th great-grandson	VII	7
Smith, Robert Clare	5th great-grandson	VII	7
Smith, Sally	6th great-granddaughter	VIII	8
Smith, Taylor	7th great-grandson	IX	9
Smith, Terry	6th great-grandson	VIII	8
Smith, Thomas	6th great-grandson	VIII	8
Smith, Thomas S.	7th great-grandson	IX	9
Smith, Vicki	6th great-granddaughter	VIII	8
Sprague, Nancy Lee	Wife of the 6th great-grandson		

Name	Relationship with William McFarlane	Civil	Canon
Springman, David Robert	Husband of the 6th great-granddaughter		
Stapleton, Gladys Eloise	4th great-granddaughter	VI	6
Stapleton, Glen	4th great-grandson	VI	6
Stapleton, William	Husband of the 3rd great-granddaughter		
Starck, Catherine	Wife of the 3rd great-grandson		
Stark, Katie	Wife of the 3rd great-grandson		
Stearns, Colleen	Wife of the 5th great-grandson		
Stella	3rd great-granddaughter	V	5
Steven	Husband of the 3rd great-granddaughter		
Stevens, 'Male'	Husband of the 5th great-granddaughter		
Stuart, Ruth Jane	Wife of the 5th great-grandson		
Swanson, Charles	Husband of the 6th great-granddaughter		
Sweigert, Mabel May	Wife of the 4th great-grandson		
Thomas, Iona Jean	Wife of the 4th great-grandson		
Tiesman, Sharon	Wife of the 6th great-grandson		
Traum, David	7th great-grandson	IX	9
Traum, John	7th great-grandson	IX	9
Traum, Robert	Husband of the 6th great-granddaughter		
Traum, Susan	7th great-granddaughter	IX	9
Trimble, Carol	Wife of the 6th great-grandson		
Tucker, 'Male'	Husband of the 5th great-granddaughter		
Tug	3rd great-grandson	V	5
Ufken, Eugene	Husband of the 5th great-granddaughter		
Unger, Bruce	Husband of the 6th great-granddaughter		
Unger, Bruce Edwin, Jr.	7th great-grandson	IX	9
Van Horn, James Jerry	Husband of the 5th great-granddaughter		
Veihl, Darlene E.	Wife of the 5th great-grandson		
Vina	3rd great-granddaughter	V	5
Vos, Arlyn	5th great-grandson	VII	7
Vos, Arlyn Dale	6th great-grandson	VIII	8
Vos, Debra Jane	6th great-granddaughter	VIII	8
Vos, Ernest	Husband of the 4th great-granddaughter		
Vos, Kari Sue	6th great-granddaughter	VIII	8
Vos, Kathy Lynn	6th great-granddaughter	VIII	8
Vos, Larry	5th great-grandson	VII	7
Vos, Lauri Ann	5th great-granddaughter	VII	7
Vos, Marla Ann	6th great-granddaughter	VIII	8
Vos, Teri Ann	6th great-granddaughter	VIII	8
Walters, Baby	7th great-granddaughter	IX	9
Walters, Carl B.	Husband of the 4th great-granddaughter		
Walters, David Gene	7th great-grandson	IX	9
Walters, Dawn Gail	6th great-granddaughter	VIII	8
Walters, Harlan Gene	6th great-grandson	VIII	8
Walters, Harold Edward	5th great-grandson	VII	7
Walters, Jane Kaye	6th great-granddaughter	VIII	8
Walters, Mark Douglas	7th great-grandson	IX	9
Walters, Matthew	7th great-grandson	IX	9
Walters, Paul Edward	6th great-grandson	VIII	8
Walters, Philip Dale	6th great-grandson	VIII	8
Walters, Rhonda Ruth	6th great-granddaughter	VIII	8
Walters, Sandra	Wife of the 6th great-grandson		
Walters, Stephanie Anne	7th great-granddaughter	IX	9
Walters, Terry Harlan	7th great-grandson	IX	9

Name	Relationship with William McFarlane	Civil	Canon
Walters, Tiffany Marie	7th great-granddaughter	IX	9
Walters, Tori Cheryl	7th great-granddaughter	IX	9
Walters, Troy J.	7th great-grandson	IX	9
Walters, Wendy Lee	7th great-granddaughter	IX	9
Warner, Catherine	5th great-granddaughter	VII	7
Warner, James	Husband of the 3rd great-granddaughter		
Warner, James	5th great-grandson	VII	7
Warner, Robert Wilson	4th great-grandson	VI	6
Watson, Mary	Wife of the 4th great-grandson		
Webb, Jeanne	Wife of the 5th great-grandson		
Weyrauch, Madeline	Wife of the 5th great-grandson		
Whistler, Florence I.	4th great-granddaughter	VI	6
Whistler, Glenn Otto	Husband of the 3rd great-granddaughter		
Whistler, Lois W.	4th great-granddaughter	VI	6
Wiebenga, Lesley Dawn	7th great-granddaughter	IX	9
Wiebenga, Ron	Husband of the 6th great-granddaughter		
Wiersema, Patricia	Wife of the 6th great-grandson		
Wilkinson, Margaret	Wife of the 3rd great-grandson		
Willson	Husband of the great-granddaughter		
Wilson, Alexander B	2nd great-grandson	IV	4
Wilson, Alexander Thomas	3rd great-grandson	V	5
Wilson, Alice Jane	3rd great-granddaughter	V	5
Wilson, Catherine	2nd great-granddaughter	IV	4
Wilson, Charles Abram	3rd great-grandson	V	5
Wilson, Charles Desmond	2nd great-grandson	IV	4
Wilson, Charles LeRoy	4th great-grandson	VI	6
Wilson, Deborah Ann	5th great-granddaughter	VII	7
Wilson, Dwight Alvin	4th great-grandson	VI	6
Wilson, Earl Charles	5th great-grandson	VII	7
Wilson, Earl Clyde	4th great-grandson	VI	6
Wilson, Elizabeth Evelyn	2nd great-granddaughter	IV	4
Wilson, Elizabeth Mary	4th great-granddaughter	VI	6
Wilson, Emily G.	3rd great-granddaughter	V	5
Wilson, Frances Jane	3rd great-granddaughter	V	5
Wilson, George John	3rd great-grandson	V	5
Wilson, George Orville	3rd great-grandson	V	5
Wilson, Janet Mae	5th great-granddaughter	VII	7
Wilson, Jeanette	4th great-granddaughter	VI	6
Wilson, Jeannette Lynn	5th great-granddaughter	VII	7
Wilson, Jody Allen	5th great-grandson	VII	7
Wilson, John	Husband of the great-granddaughter		
Wilson, John	2nd great-grandson	IV	4
Wilson, John Charles	3rd great-grandson	V	5
Wilson, John Charles III	6th great-grandson	VIII	8
Wilson, John Charles, Jr	5th great-grandson	VII	7
Wilson, John James	4th great-grandson	VI	6
Wilson, Judith Suzane	5th great-granddaughter	VII	7
Wilson, Kathy Elizabeth	5th great-granddaughter	VII	7
Wilson, Kimberly Ann	5th great-granddaughter	VII	7
Wilson, Leo Vernon, Sr.	4th great-grandson	VI	6
Wilson, Linda Kay	5th great-granddaughter	VII	7
Wilson, Marc Lee	5th great-grandson	VII	7
Wilson, Margaret Mae	2nd great-granddaughter	IV	4

Name	Relationship with William McFarlane	Civil	Canon
Wilson, Margaret May	3rd great-granddaughter	V	5
Wilson, Marie	5th great-granddaughter	VII	7
Wilson, Marilyn Joan	5th great-granddaughter	VII	7
Wilson, Mary LaVina	3rd great-granddaughter	V	5
Wilson, Mary Margaret	4th great-granddaughter	VI	6
Wilson, Naomi Jean	5th great-granddaughter	VII	7
Wilson, Nellie Clyde	3rd great-granddaughter	V	5
Wilson, Paul Fletcher	3rd great-grandson	V	5
Wilson, Paul Mathew	6th great-grandson	VIII	8
Wilson, Phoebe Mae	3rd great-granddaughter	V	5
Wilson, Robert Bristle	4th great-grandson	VI	6
Wilson, Robert Thomas	5th great-grandson	VII	7
Wilson, Ronald Stanley	5th great-grandson	VII	7
Wilson, Sara	2nd great-granddaughter	IV	4
Wilson, Sara Jane	3rd great-granddaughter	V	5
Wilson, Thomas	2nd great-grandson	IV	4
Wilson, Thomas Robert	6th great-grandson	VIII	8
Wilson, Trudy Jean	5th great-granddaughter	VII	7
Wilson, Vaughn Fae	5th great-granddaughter	VII	7
Wilson, Winifred M.	3rd great-granddaughter	V	5
Witt, Andrew F.	Husband of the 4th great-granddaughter		
Witt, Donna Jean	5th great-granddaughter	VII	7
Witt, Harlan Andrew	5th great-grandson	VII	7
Witt, Jeffrey Andrew	6th great-grandson	VIII	8
Witt, Kimberly Lynn	6th great-granddaughter	VIII	8
Witt, Kristen Les	6th great-granddaughter	VIII	8
Witt, Sandra Mae	5th great-granddaughter	VII	7
Witz, 'Male'	Husband of the 5th great-granddaughter		
Yates, Naomi	Wife of the 5th great-grandson		
Yonkers, Alberta Lynn	Wife of the 6th great-grandson		

Descendants of Nathaniel Pierce

Generation No. 1

1. NATHANIEL[1] PIERCE was born August 19, 1840 in Leland, LaSalle co, IL, and died February 05, 1905 in Churdan, Greene co., IA. He married ESTHER HUGGETT February 01, 1863 in Ottawa, LaSalle co., IL, daughter of LUM HUGGETT and JUDITH RUMNEY. She was born April 28, 1844 in England, and died July 09, 1895 in Leland, LaSalle co, IL.

More About NATHANIEL PIERCE:
Burial: Leland cem.

More About ESTHER HUGGETT:
Burial: Leland cem.

Children of NATHANIEL PIERCE and ESTHER HUGGETT are:
- i. WILLIAM G.[2] PIERCE, b. January 03, 1865, Wateska, WI; d. March 23, 1928, Des Moines, Polk co., IA; m. ELIZA J. PEISHA, February 02, 1889, Rollo, DeKalb co., IL; b. December 1871, Leland, LaSalle co, IL; d. July 06, 1952.

    Notes for WILLIAM G. PIERCE:
    Twin of Walter
    Mrs. Janvrin Muschal obtained Pierce information from 'The Rumneys' by Cara Metcalf, 3654 Bausell St., Sacramento, CA 95821. He worked on the Pierce History. All the Pierce family not followed in this report of the Reagan family.

2.
- ii. WALTER S. PIERCE, b. January 03, 1865, Wateska, WI; d. January 04, 1932, Morrison, IL.
- iii. JAMES HENRY OLIVER PIERCE.
- iv. JUDITH M. PIERCE.
- v. SAMUEL LEVI PIERCE.
- vi. NATHAN PIERCE.
- vii. JESSE G. PIERCE.
- viii. CLARA PIERCE.
- ix. BERTHA A. PIERCE.
- x. PETER PIERCE.
- xi. NELLIE PIERCE.
- xii. MYRTLE PIERCE.

Generation No. 2

2. WALTER S.[2] PIERCE *(NATHANIEL[1])* was born January 03, 1865 in Wateska, WI, and died January 04, 1932 in Morrison, IL. He married SARA JANE WILSON January 20, 1904 in Morrison, Whiteside co., IL, daughter of THOMAS WILSON and MARY ELSEY. She was born June 16, 1871 in Clyde twp, Whiteside co., IL, and died March 08, 1920 in White Pigeon, Clyde twp, Whiteside Co., IL.

Notes for WALTER S. PIERCE:
1900 Clyde twp., Whiteside co., IL census: William Pierce, farmer, Jan. 1865 WI IL En, Eliza wife Dec 1871, md , IL Can VT, Walter S. Pierce, twin brother, farmer Jan 1865 WI
1910 Clyde twp., Whiteside co., IL census: Walter Pierce, retail grocer, 44 WI En En, Jennie wf 318 IL md 6yrs., 5 children living, IL EN, Elsey dau. 5 IL, Vera dau 2 NE

More About WALTER S. PIERCE:
Burial: West Genesee cem, Coleta, IL

Notes for SARA JANE WILSON:
Place of death not known, but buried in Fulton.
Divorced 31 May 1897. Death certificate says birthdate is June 16, 1871, age at death 48 yrs., 8 mos. 22 days. Cause of death: cerebral hemorrhage.
AUNT OF RONALD REAGAN

More About SARA JANE WILSON:
Burial: Fulton cemetery. Fulton, IL

Children of WALTER PIERCE and SARA WILSON are:
- 3. i. ELSEY MAE[3] PIERCE, b. September 17, 1904, White Pigeon, Whiteside co., IL; d. November 30, 1993, Whiteside co, Clyde twp., IL.
- 4. ii. VERA MARIE PIERCE, b. February 16, 1908, Tekamah, Burt, Nebraska; d. January 30, 1986, White Pigeon, Whiteside co., IL.
- iii. MARIE MUNDT, b. November 04, 1911; d. September 27, 1978; Foster child; m. GEORGE ERNST.

    Notes for MARIE MUNDT:
    Foster daughter

Generation No. 3

3. ELSEY MAE[3] PIERCE *(WALTER S.[2], NATHANIEL[1])* was born September 17, 1904 in White Pigeon, Whiteside co., IL, and died November 30, 1993 in Whiteside co, Clyde twp., IL. She married CARL B. WALTERS May 20, 1925 in Jordan, Whiteside co., IL. He was born October 22, 1901 in White Pigeon, Whiteside co., IL, and died August 07, 1987.

Notes for ELSEY MAE PIERCE:
Birth certificate says '4th child of this mother'. Vicky Wiebenga / Hunt material, 3 half brothers from Mother's Smith marriage.
She provided much of the information to the Heritage Quest author, Michael F. Pollock.

More About ELSEY MAE PIERCE:
Burial: West Genesee cem., Whiteside co.

More About CARL B. WALTERS:
Burial: West Genesee cem, Coleta, IL

Child of ELSEY PIERCE and CARL WALTERS is:
- 5. i. HAROLD EDWARD[4] WALTERS, b. December 02, 1925, White Pigeon, Whiteside co., IL; d. February 19, 1988, Morrison, IL.

4. VERA MARIE[3] PIERCE *(WALTER S.[2], NATHANIEL[1])* was born February 16, 1908 in Tekamah, Burt, Nebraska, and died January 30, 1986 in White Pigeon, Whiteside co., IL. She married REINHARD F. HABBEN April 03, 1933 in Somonauk, DeKalb co., IL, son of EILT HABBEN and MARIE HOLMRICK. He was born April 30, 1902 in Frisia, nr. Bremerhaven, Germany, and died March 22, 1980 in Morrison, IL.

Notes for VERA MARIE PIERCE:
Married at St. Johns Lutheran Church, Somonauk, IL.
COUSIN OF RONALD REAGAN

More About VERA MARIE PIERCE:
Burial: West Genesee cem, Coleta, IL

Notes for REINHARD F. HABBEN:
Became a US citizen 9 Oct. 1931, Chicago, IL.

More About REINHARD F. HABBEN:
Burial: West Genesee cem, Coleta, IL

Children of VERA PIERCE and REINHARD HABBEN are:
- 6.   i.   MERNA JOY[4] HABBEN, b. October 12, 1933, Coleta, Whiteside co., IL.
- 7.   ii.   NORMAN WALTER HABBEN, b. September 10, 1935, Coleta, Whiteside co., IL.
- 8.   iii.   RONALD LEE HABBEN, b. July 17, 1938, Coleta, Whiteside co., IL.
- 9.   iv.   MILFORD GENE HABBEN, b. July 04, 1940, Coleta, Whiteside co., IL.
- 10.   v.   VELMA JANE HABBEN, b. April 10, 1943, Morrison, IL.
- 11.   vi.   JUDITH MAY HABBEN, b. April 28, 1946, Morrison, IL.
- 12.   vii.   CAROL ANN HABBEN, b. June 04, 1948, Morrison, IL.
- 13.   viii.   BEVERLY JOAN HABBEN, b. July 10, 1952, Morrison, IL.
- 14.   ix.   DONNA ELAINE HABBEN, b. August 04, 1954, Morrison, IL.

Generation No. 4

5. HAROLD EDWARD[4] WALTERS *(ELSEY MAE[3] PIERCE, WALTER S.[2], NATHANIEL[1])* was born December 02, 1925 in White Pigeon, Whiteside co., IL, and died February 19, 1988 in Morrison, IL. He married RUTH JANE STUART October 22, 1945 in Morrison, IL. She was born July 07, 1924 in Morrison, IL.

More About HAROLD EDWARD WALTERS:
Burial: West Genesee cem., Whiteside co.

Children of HAROLD WALTERS and RUTH STUART are:
- 15.   i.   PAUL EDWARD[5] WALTERS, b. May 03, 1946, Morrison, IL.
- 16.   ii.   HARLAN GENE WALTERS, b. February 05, 1948, Morrison, IL.
- 17.   iii.   JANE KAYE WALTERS, b. April 16, 1950, Morrison, IL.
-    iv.   RHONDA RUTH WALTERS, b. September 15, 1952, Morrison, IL; m. DANNY KENNEDY, December 02, 1977, Morrison, IL; b. August 27, 1946.

    Notes for RHONDA RUTH WALTERS:
    Divorced Aug. 30, 1978

    Notes for DANNY KENNEDY:
    Divorced Aug. 30, 1978

- 18.   v.   DAWN GAIL WALTERS, b. March 19, 1962, Morrison, IL.
- 19.   vi.   PHILIP DALE WALTERS, b. July 15, 1968, Morrison, IL.

6. MERNA JOY[4] HABBEN *(VERA MARIE[3] PIERCE, WALTER S.[2], NATHANIEL[1])* was born October 12, 1933 in Coleta, Whiteside co., IL. She married (1) CLYDE ELMER JANVRIN September 02, 1956 in Sterling, Whiteside co., IL. He was born August 24, 1925 in Morrison, IL, and died May 20, 1970 in Morrison, IL. She married (2) ROBERT MICHAEL MUSCHAL Aft. 1971, son of NICHOLAS MUSCHAL and KATHERINE MARX. He was born June 20, 1940 in Chicago, IL.

Notes for MERNA JOY HABBEN:
Md. in St. Johns Lutheran Church, Sterling
Dairy farmer.
Mrs. Merna Habben-Muschal has been of tremendous help in furnishing material and in proofreading my pages. If there are errors, blame me. CJG
COUSIN ONCE REMOVED OF RONALD REAGAN

Notes for CLYDE ELMER JANVRIN:
Dairy farmer, served in the Army.

More About CLYDE ELMER JANVRIN:
Burial: South Clyde cemetery

Notes for ROBERT MICHAEL MUSCHAL:
Painter. Marriage to Merna was his second marriage, also her 2nd.
Auditor and Inspector. Married in United Methodist Church, Morrison, IL.

Children of MERNA HABBEN and CLYDE JANVRIN are:
- i. ERIC PAUL[5] JANVRIN, b. August 31, 1958, Morrison, IL; m. CAROL TRIMBLE, October 10, 1986, Fulton, Whiteside co., IL; b. November 06, 1956, Fulton, IL.
- 20. ii. KURT REINHARD JANVRIN, b. August 04, 1960, Morrison, IL.
- 21. iii. BRUCE CLYDE JANVRIN, b. December 22, 1961, Morrison, IL.
- 22. iv. ARON KYLE JANVRIN, b. November 13, 1964, Morrison, IL.

7. NORMAN WALTER[4] HABBEN (*VERA MARIE[3] PIERCE, WALTER S.[2], NATHANIEL[1]*) was born September 10, 1935 in Coleta, Whiteside co., IL. He married NORMA JEAN COOK June 02, 1956 in Rock Falls, Whiteside co., IL. She was born June 02, 1937 in Rock Falls, Whiteside co., IL.

Notes for NORMAN WALTER HABBEN:
COUSIN ONCE REMOVED OF RONALD REAGAN

Children of NORMAN HABBEN and NORMA COOK are:
- 23. i. RHONDA JANE[5] HABBEN, b. June 24, 1957.
- ii. ROBERT ALLEN HABBEN, b. August 02, 1958, Morrison, IL.
- 24. iii. GENE LEROY HABBEN, b. July 07, 1960, Morrison, IL.
- 25. iv. SARA LEANNE HABBEN, b. March 09, 1967, Morrison, IL.

8. RONALD LEE[4] HABBEN (*VERA MARIE[3] PIERCE, WALTER S.[2], NATHANIEL[1]*) was born July 17, 1938 in Coleta, Whiteside co., IL. He married NANCY JOAN BIELEMA September 02, 1961 in Fulton, Whiteside co., IL. She was born November 15, 1940 in Fulton, IL.

Notes for RONALD LEE HABBEN:
COUSIN ONCE REMOVED OF RONALD REAGAN

Children of RONALD HABBEN and NANCY BIELEMA are:
- 26. i. DANIEL LEE[5] HABBEN, b. June 26, 1962, Morrison, IL.
- 27. ii. DEBRA LOU HABBEN, b. September 17, 1964, Morrison, IL.
- iii. DAVID ALLEN HABBEN, b. November 08, 1978, Morrison, IL.

9. MILFORD GENE[4] HABBEN (*VERA MARIE[3] PIERCE, WALTER S.[2], NATHANIEL[1]*) was born July 04, 1940 in Coleta, Whiteside co., IL. He married JOANNE PATRICK July 06, 1964 in San Jose, Santa Clara co., CA. She was born May 23, 1943 in Santa Clara, CA.

Notes for MILFORD GENE HABBEN:
COUSIN ONCE REMOVED OF RONALD REAGAN

Children of MILFORD HABBEN and JOANNE PATRICK are:
- 28. i. CATHERINE JEAN[5] HABBEN, b. May 08, 1966, Morrison, IL.
- ii. DONALD PATRICK HABBEN, b. April 08, 1969, Morrison, IL; m. LISA FREDRICK, November 10, 1990, Dixon, Lee co., IL.

    Notes for DONALD PATRICK HABBEN:
    Divorced, no children.

10. VELMA JANE[4] HABBEN (*VERA MARIE[3] PIERCE, WALTER S.[2], NATHANIEL[1]*) was born April 10, 1943 in Morrison, IL. She married WILLIAM RICHARD NORTON, JR December 07, 1963 in Freeport, Stephenson co., IL, son of WILLIAM NORTON and EDNA LOTT. He was born October 20, 1938 in

Rockford, ILL.

Notes for VELMA JANE HABBEN:
COUSIN ONCE REMOVED OF RONALD REAGAN

Notes for WILLIAM RICHARD NORTON, JR:
Railroad telegrapher at time of marriage, later truck driver.

Children of VELMA HABBEN and WILLIAM NORTON are:
   i. JAMES RICHARD[5] NORTON, b. June 30, 1967, Freport, Stephenson co., IL.
29. ii. JEFFERY MICHAEL NORTON, b. December 23, 1971, Freport, Stephenson co., IL.

11. JUDITH MAY[4] HABBEN *(VERA MARIE[3] PIERCE, WALTER S.[2], NATHANIEL[1])* was born April 28, 1946 in Morrison, IL. She married DONALD RAY BURMEISTER August 28, 1976 in Dewitt, Clinton co., Iowa. He was born January 23, 1939 in Dewitt, Clinton co., IA.

Notes for JUDITH MAY HABBEN:
COUSIN ONCE REMOVED OF RONALD REAGAN

Notes for DONALD RAY BURMEISTER:
His second marriage.

Children of JUDITH HABBEN and DONALD BURMEISTER are:
   i. JOHN BRANDON[5] BURMEISTER, b. August 25, 1977, Dewitt, Clinton co., IA.
   ii. BRIAN DOUGLAS BURMEISTER, b. October 09, 1980, Dewitt, Clinton co., IA.

12. CAROL ANN[4] HABBEN *(VERA MARIE[3] PIERCE, WALTER S.[2], NATHANIEL[1])* was born June 04, 1948 in Morrison, IL. She met CHARLES ROBERT ALBRECHT March 01, 1969 in Belvidere, Boone co., IL, son of FRANK ALBRECHT and IRENE HOWE. He was born November 28, 1937.

Notes for CAROL ANN HABBEN:
Born at Morrison Community Hospital
COUSIN ONCE REMOVED OF RONALD REAGAN

Notes for CHARLES ROBERT ALBRECHT:
Married by Robert A. Blodgett, Magistrate, at Belvidere, Boone co., IL
He was an 'assembler' when married.
This was his second marriage. Data from marriage license/Wiebenga material

Children of CAROL HABBEN and CHARLES ALBRECHT are:
30. i. CALE RICHARD[5] ALBRECHT, b. June 06, 1973, Freport, Stephenson co., IL.
   ii. CALEB WILLAIM ALBRECHT, b. May 17, 1975, Freport, Stephenson co., IL.

    Notes for CALEB WILLAIM ALBRECHT:
    Married 1999, one child b. April 2000

13. BEVERLY JOAN[4] HABBEN *(VERA MARIE[3] PIERCE, WALTER S.[2], NATHANIEL[1])* was born July 10, 1952 in Morrison, IL. She married KENNETH ALDEN ETHRIDGE November 25, 1972 in Pearl City, Jo Davies co., IL. He was born 1939 in Freport, Stephenson co., IL.

Notes for BEVERLY JOAN HABBEN:
COUSIN ONCE REMOVED OF RONALD REAGAN

Children of BEVERLY HABBEN and KENNETH ETHRIDGE are:
   i. JEREMY M.[5] ETHRIDGE, b. July 08, 1978, Freport, Stephenson co., IL.
   ii. KEVIN MARSHALL ETHRIDGE, b. June 29, 1980, Freport, Stephenson co., IL.

iii. LAURA MARIE ETHRIDGE, b. May 29, 1983, Freport, Stephenson co., IL.

Notes for LAURA MARIE ETHRIDGE:

iv. BRADLEY ETHRIDGE, b. March 18, 1988, Freport, Stephenson co., IL.

14. DONNA ELAINE[4] HABBEN *(VERA MARIE[3] PIERCE, WALTER S.[2], NATHANIEL[1])* was born August 04, 1954 in Morrison, IL. She married THOMAS MICHAEL ARDWIN November 02, 1982 in North Glenn, Adams co., CO, son of DETER ARDWIN and ANNA GAFKA. He was born January 15, 1942 in Detroit, MI.

Notes for DONNA ELAINE HABBEN:
Divorced Jan. 29, 1971, per marriage application, Detroit, MI
COUSIN ONCE REMOVED OF RONALD REAGAN

Notes for THOMAS MICHAEL ARDWIN:
Divorced: Jan. 29, 1971, per marriage application, Detroit, MI

Children of DONNA HABBEN and THOMAS ARDWIN are:
    i. DONNA MARIE[5] ARDWIN, b. March 28, 1987, Denver, Adams co., CO.
    ii. MICHAEL THOMAS ARDWIN, b. January 19, 1989, Denver, Adams co., CO.
    iii. LISA ARDWIN.

Generation No. 5

15. PAUL EDWARD[5] WALTERS *(HAROLD EDWARD[4], ELSEY MAE[3] PIERCE, WALTER S.[2], NATHANIEL[1])* was born May 03, 1946 in Morrison, IL. He married (1) PATRICIA BARTZ February 26, 1965 in Morrison, IL. She was born May 11, 1949 in Morrison, IL. He married (2) SHARON TIESMAN March 19, 1970 in Lyndon, Whiteside co., IL. She was born April 27, 1945.

Notes for PAUL EDWARD WALTERS:
Divorce 1970

Notes for PATRICIA BARTZ:
Divorced 1970

Child of PAUL WALTERS and PATRICIA BARTZ is:
    i. WENDY LEE[6] WALTERS, b. August 21, 1965, Morrison, IL; m. WILLIAM CHARLES HUTCHINSON; b. September 08, 1964, Carroll co., IL.

    Notes for WILLIAM CHARLES HUTCHINSON:
    Divorced

Children of PAUL WALTERS and SHARON TIESMAN are:
    ii. BABY[6] WALTERS, b. March 19, 1973; d. March 19, 1973.

    Notes for BABY WALTERS:
    Stillborn

    More About BABY WALTERS:
    Burial: Fulton cemetery. Fulton, IL

31.   iii. TORI CHERYL WALTERS, b. April 25, 1974, Morrison, IL.
32.   iv. TROY J. WALTERS, b. November 05, 1975, Morrison, IL.

16. HARLAN GENE[5] WALTERS (*HAROLD EDWARD[4], ELSEY MAE[3] PIERCE, WALTER S.[2], NATHANIEL[1]*) was born February 05, 1948 in Morrison, IL. He married (1) MARIE SHARER February 24, 1967 in Fulton, Whiteside co., IL. She was born May 25, 1947. He married (2) BETH RICK August 31, 1974 in Morrison, IL. She was born January 27, 1945. He married (3) LINDA ROBINSON December 02, 1983 in TX.

Notes for HARLAN GENE WALTERS:
Divorced from Marie 1974
Divorced from Beth Rick
Divorced from Linda 2002

Notes for MARIE SHARER:
Divorce 1974

Notes for BETH RICK:
Divorced

Notes for LINDA ROBINSON:
She has two children, Carolyn and Rebecca. They are children of her previous marriage.

Children of HARLAN WALTERS and MARIE SHARER are:
    i. TERRY HARLAN[6] WALTERS, b. June 06, 1968, Morrison, IL.
    ii. MARK DOUGLAS WALTERS, b. June 16, 1969, Morrison, IL.
    iii. DAVID GENE WALTERS, b. August 26, 1971, Morrison, IL.

Children of HARLAN WALTERS and LINDA ROBINSON are:
    iv. CAROLYN[6].

        Notes for CAROLYN:
        Child of Mother's previous marriage.

    v. REBECCA.

        Notes for REBECCA:
        Child of Mother's previous marriage.

17. JANE KAYE[5] WALTERS (*HAROLD EDWARD[4], ELSEY MAE[3] PIERCE, WALTER S.[2], NATHANIEL[1]*) was born April 16, 1950 in Morrison, IL. She married (1) LEONARD PRITCHARD March 07, 1969 in Morrison, IL. He was born November 16, 1946. She married (2) FRANK MATCHIE October 07, 1972 in Morrison, IL. He was born June 07, 1947. She married (3) WALTER G. HEATH October 22, 1990 in Morrison, IL.

Notes for JANE KAYE WALTERS:
Divorced 3 Aug 1970 from Pritchard
Divorced from Matchie

Notes for LEONARD PRITCHARD:
Divorced from Jane Kaye 3 Aug. 1970

Notes for FRANK MATCHIE:
Divorced

Child of JANE WALTERS and LEONARD PRITCHARD is:
    i. TIMOTHY ALLEN[6] PRITCHARD, b. September 22, 1969, Morrison, IL; m. ANGELA KAY MACHIE, May 1987, Morrison, IL; b. December 22, 1974, Morrison, IL.

Child of JANE WALTERS and FRANK MATCHIE is:
33.   ii. ANGELA[6] MATCHIE, b. December 22, 1974.

18. DAWN GAIL[5] WALTERS *(HAROLD EDWARD[4], ELSEY MAE[3] PIERCE, WALTER S.[2], NATHANIEL[1])* was born March 19, 1962 in Morrison, IL. She married ROBERT JAMES BAUER May 02, 1981 in Morrison, IL. He was born August 06, 1960 in Morrison, IL.

Children of DAWN WALTERS and ROBERT BAUER are:
   i.   AMANDA GAIL[6] BAUER, b. July 31, 1991, Clinton, Clinton Co., IA.
   ii. LAYLA MARIE BAUER, b. August 27, 1994, Clinton, Clinton Co., IA.

19. PHILIP DALE[5] WALTERS *(HAROLD EDWARD[4], ELSEY MAE[3] PIERCE, WALTER S.[2], NATHANIEL[1])* was born July 15, 1968 in Morrison, IL. He married CHRISTINE KRAUSE May 30, 1989 in Dixon, Lee co., IL.

Notes for CHRISTINE KRAUSE:
Adopted by Baughman

Children of PHILIP WALTERS and CHRISTINE KRAUSE are:
   i.   STEPHANIE ANNE[6] WALTERS, b. February 11, 1988, Dixon, Lee co., IL.
   ii. TIFFANY MARIE WALTERS, b. May 22, 1990, Dallas, TX.
   iii. MATTHEW WALTERS, b. September 15, 1992.

20. KURT REINHARD[5] JANVRIN *(MERNA JOY[4] HABBEN, VERA MARIE[3] PIERCE, WALTER S.[2], NATHANIEL[1])* was born August 04, 1960 in Morrison, IL. He married YVONNE AMMON June 16, 1984 in Long Grove, Lake co., IL. She was born December 19, 1961 in Decatur, Macon co., IL.

Children of KURT JANVRIN and YVONNE AMMON are:
   i.   REBECCA LINDSEY[6] JANVRIN, b. May 23, 1988, Trenton, Mercer co., NJ.
   ii. HANNAH KATE JANVRIN, b. October 07, 1990, Trenton, Mercer co., NJ.
   iii. GENEVIEVE JANVRIN, b. 1993.
   iv. MABELINE JANVRIN, b. 1997.

21. BRUCE CLYDE[5] JANVRIN *(MERNA JOY[4] HABBEN, VERA MARIE[3] PIERCE, WALTER S.[2], NATHANIEL[1])* was born December 22, 1961 in Morrison, IL. He married DIANE MEHLHAUS August 11, 1990 in Dysart, Benton co., IA. She was born February 20, 1961 in Dysart, Benton co., Iowa.

Children of BRUCE JANVRIN and DIANE MEHLHAUS are:
   i.   BRICE[6] JANVRIN, b. 1993.
   ii. BRYLEIGH JANVRIN, b. 1998.

22. ARON KYLE[5] JANVRIN *(MERNA JOY[4] HABBEN, VERA MARIE[3] PIERCE, WALTER S.[2], NATHANIEL[1])* was born November 13, 1964 in Morrison, IL. He married CAROLYN BROWN June 28, 1998.

Child of ARON JANVRIN and CAROLYN BROWN is:
   i.   TYLER[6] JANVRIN, b. February 29, 2000.

23. RHONDA JANE[5] HABBEN *(NORMAN WALTER[4], VERA MARIE[3] PIERCE, WALTER S.[2], NATHANIEL[1])* was born June 24, 1957. She married (1) ALLEN GREELEY June 10, 1978 in Morrison, IL. He was born August 05, 1951 in Morrison, IL. She married (2) ALLEN RAY GREELEY June 10, 1978 in Morrison, IL. He was born August 05, 1951 in Morrison, IL.

Children of RHONDA HABBEN and ALLEN GREELEY are:
- i. MELLISSA JEAN[6] GREELEY, b. December 08, 1980, Morrison, IL.
- ii. WILLIAM NORMAN GREELEY, b. June 19, 1983, Morrison, IL.
- iii. MARLA JANE GREELEY, b. September 04, 1984, Morrison, IL.

24. GENE LEROY[5] HABBEN *(NORMAN WALTER[4], VERA MARIE[3] PIERCE, WALTER S.[2], NATHANIEL[1])* was born July 07, 1960 in Morrison, IL. He married KAREN ROENIKE February 25, 1989 in Clinton, Iowa.

Children of GENE HABBEN and KAREN ROENIKE are:
- i. TRAVIS[6] HABBEN, b. 1993.
- ii. RYAN HABBEN, b. 1996.
- iii. KRISTIN, b. 1999.

25. SARA LEANNE[5] HABBEN *(NORMAN WALTER[4], VERA MARIE[3] PIERCE, WALTER S.[2], NATHANIEL[1])* was born March 09, 1967 in Morrison, IL. She married (1) COONAN DICKMAN March 29, 1986 in Morrison, IL. He was born March 24, 1967. She married (2) RANDY FAUST September 1990 in Mo-.

Notes for SARA LEANNE HABBEN:
Divorced Dickman 1990, no children with him.

Notes for COONAN DICKMAN:
Divorced 1990, no children.

Children of SARA HABBEN and RANDY FAUST are:
- i. ADAM CHARLES[6] FAUST, b. March 23, 1991, Virginia Beach, VA.
- ii. ASHLEY FAUST, b. 1994.

26. DANIEL LEE[5] HABBEN *(RONALD LEE[4], VERA MARIE[3] PIERCE, WALTER S.[2], NATHANIEL[1])* was born June 26, 1962 in Morrison, IL. He married BETH HACKER June 20, 1987 in Morrison, IL. She was born January 10, 1962.

Children of DANIEL HABBEN and BETH HACKER are:
- i. LOGAN DANIEL[6] HABBEN, b. May 14, 1989, Sterling, Whiteside co., IL.
- ii. ABBEY HABBEN, b. 1994.

27. DEBRA LOU[5] HABBEN *(RONALD LEE[4], VERA MARIE[3] PIERCE, WALTER S.[2], NATHANIEL[1])* was born September 17, 1964 in Morrison, IL. She married JAMES LEE SNYDER June 11, 1983 in Morrison, IL. He was born October 30, 1963 in Morrison, IL.

Notes for DEBRA LOU HABBEN:
Divorced 1988

Notes for JAMES LEE SNYDER:
Divorced 1988

Children of DEBRA HABBEN and JAMES SNYDER are:
- i. BRANDON[6] SNYDER, b. October 31, 1985, Germany.
- ii. TIMOTHY SNYDER, b. February 12, 1987, Sterling, Whiteside co., IL.

28. CATHERINE JEAN[5] HABBEN *(MILFORD GENE[4], VERA MARIE[3] PIERCE, WALTER S.[2], NATHANIEL[1])* was born May 08, 1966 in Morrison, IL. She married MARK BENNET June 27, 1987 in Dixon, Lee co., IL.

Notes for CATHERINE JEAN HABBEN:
Divorced

Children of CATHERINE HABBEN and MARK BENNET are:
  i. JENNIFER ANN[6] BENNET, b. October 06, 1990, Sterling, Whiteside co., IL.
  ii. AMANDA BENNET, b. 1994.

29. JEFFERY MICHAEL[5] NORTON *(VELMA JANE[4] HABBEN, VERA MARIE[3] PIERCE, WALTER S.[2], NATHANIEL[1])* was born December 23, 1971 in Freport, Stephenson co., IL. He married ANGIE.

Child of JEFFERY NORTON and ANGIE is:
  i. GRACE[6] NORTON, b. 1999.

30. CALE RICHARD[5] ALBRECHT *(CAROL ANN[4] HABBEN, VERA MARIE[3] PIERCE, WALTER S.[2], NATHANIEL[1])* was born June 06, 1973 in Freport, Stephenson co., IL. He married CHRIS.

Notes for CALE RICHARD ALBRECHT:
3rd Great-grandson of John Wilson.
Divorced, 2000

Child of CALE ALBRECHT and CHRIS is:
  i. CARRIE[6] ALBRECHT, b. 1995.

Generation No. 6

31. TORI CHERYL[6] WALTERS *(PAUL EDWARD[5], HAROLD EDWARD[4], ELSEY MAE[3] PIERCE, WALTER S.[2], NATHANIEL[1])* was born April 25, 1974 in Morrison, IL. She married JUSTIN EADS January 13, 1996.

Children of TORI WALTERS and JUSTIN EADS are:
  i. CHELSEA CHERYL[7] EADS, b. June 20, 1996, Sterling, IL.
  ii. JOSEPH JAMES EADS, b. December 29, 1998, Sterling, IL.
  iii. ZACHARY PHILIP EADS, b. March 07, 2003, Davenport, IA.

32. TROY J.[6] WALTERS *(PAUL EDWARD[5], HAROLD EDWARD[4], ELSEY MAE[3] PIERCE, WALTER S.[2], NATHANIEL[1])* was born November 05, 1975 in Morrison, IL. He married CHRISTINA.

Notes for TROY J. WALTERS:
Divorced 2002

Notes for CHRISTINA:
Divorced 2002

Children of TROY WALTERS and CHRISTINA are:
  i. JULIA ANNA[7] WALTERS, b. September 26, 1999, Sterling, IL.
  ii. DREW PHILIP WALTERS, b. December 23, 2000, Sterling, IL.

33. ANGELA[6] MATCHIE *(JANE KAYE[5] WALTERS, HAROLD EDWARD[4], ELSEY MAE[3] PIERCE, WALTER S.[2], NATHANIEL[1])* was born December 22, 1974. She married SHANE FERGUSON August 31, 1996.

Children of ANGELA MATCHIE and SHANE FERGUSON are:
  i. MIRISSA JANE[7], b. March 10, 1995.
  ii. HUNTER MICHAEL FERGUSON, b. January 03, 1997, Sterling, IL.

Kinship of Nathaniel Pierce

Name	Relationship with Nathaniel Pierce	Civil	Canon
Ammon, Yvonne	Wife of the 2nd great-grandson		
Bartz, Patricia	Wife of the 2nd great-grandson		
Bauer, Amanda Gail	3rd great-granddaughter	V	5
Bauer, Robert James	Husband of the 2nd great-granddaughter		
Bennet, Amanda	3rd great-granddaughter	V	5
Bennet, Jennifer Ann	3rd great-granddaughter	V	5
Bennet, Mark	Husband of the 2nd great-granddaughter		
Brown, Carolyn	Wife of the 2nd great-grandson		
Carolyn	3rd great-granddaughter	V	5
Christina	Wife of the 3rd great-grandson		
Cook, Norma Jean	Wife of the great-grandson		
Dickman, Coonan	Husband of the 2nd great-granddaughter		
Eads, Justin	Husband of the 3rd great-granddaughter		
Faust, Adam Charles	3rd great-grandson	V	5
Faust, Ashley	3rd great-granddaughter	V	5
Faust, Randy	Husband of the 2nd great-granddaughter		
Ferguson, Shane	Husband of the 3rd great-granddaughter		
Fredrick, Lisa	Wife of the 2nd great-grandson		
Greeley, Allen	Husband of the 2nd great-granddaughter		
Greeley, Allen Ray	Husband of the 2nd great-granddaughter		
Greeley, Marla Jane	3rd great-granddaughter	V	5
Greeley, Mellissa Jean	3rd great-granddaughter	V	5
Greeley, William Norman	3rd great-grandson	V	5
Habben, Catherine Jean	2nd great-granddaughter	IV	4
Habben, Donald Patrick	2nd great-grandson	IV	4
Habben, Gene LeRoy	2nd great-grandson	IV	4
Habben, Merna Joy	Great-granddaughter	III	3
Habben, Milford Gene	Great-grandson	III	3
Habben, Norman Walter	Great-grandson	III	3
Habben, Reinhard F.	Husband of the granddaughter		
Habben, Rhonda Jane	2nd great-granddaughter	IV	4
Habben, Robert Allen	2nd great-grandson	IV	4
Habben, Ryan	3rd great-grandson	V	5
Habben, Sara Leanne	2nd great-granddaughter	IV	4
Habben, Travis	3rd great-grandson	V	5
Heath, Walter G.	Husband of the 2nd great-granddaughter		
Huggett, Esther	Wife		
Hutchinson, William Charles	Husband of the 3rd great-granddaughter		
Janvrin, Aron Kyle	2nd great-grandson	IV	4
Janvrin, Brice	3rd great-grandson	V	5
Janvrin, Bruce Clyde	2nd great-grandson	IV	4
Janvrin, Bryleigh	3rd great-granddaughter	V	5
Janvrin, Clyde Elmer	Husband of the great-granddaughter		
Janvrin, Eric Paul	2nd great-grandson	IV	4
Janvrin, Genevieve	3rd great-granddaughter	V	5
Janvrin, Hannah Kate	3rd great-granddaughter	V	5
Janvrin, Kurt Reinhard	2nd great-grandson	IV	4
Janvrin, Mabeline	3rd great-granddaughter	V	5
Janvrin, Rebecca Lindsey	3rd great-granddaughter	V	5
Janvrin, Tyler	3rd great-grandson	V	5
Jennie	Daughter-in-law		

Name	Relationship with Nathaniel Pierce	Civil	Canon
Kennedy, Danny	Husband of the 2nd great-granddaughter		
Krause, Christine	Wife of the 2nd great-grandson		
Kristin	3rd great-granddaughter	V	5
Layla Marie Bauer	3rd great-granddaughter	V	5
Machie, Angela Kay	Wife of the 3rd great-grandson		
Matchie, Angela	3rd great-granddaughter	V	5
Matchie, Frank	Husband of the 2nd great-granddaughter		
Mehlhaus, Diane	Wife of the 2nd great-grandson		
Muschal, Robert Michael	Husband of the great-granddaughter		
Patrick, JoAnne	Wife of the great-grandson		
Peisha, Eliza J.	Daughter-in-law		
Pierce, Bertha A.	Daughter	I	1
Pierce, Clara	Daughter	I	1
Pierce, Elsey Mae	Granddaughter	II	2
Pierce, James Henry Oliver	Son	I	1
Pierce, Jesse G.	Daughter	I	1
Pierce, Judith M.	Daughter	I	1
Pierce, Myrtle	Daughter	I	1
Pierce, Nathan	Son	I	1
Pierce, Nathaniel	Self		0
Pierce, Nellie	Daughter	I	1
Pierce, Peter	Son	I	1
Pierce, Samuel Levi	Son	I	1
Pierce, Vera Marie	Granddaughter	II	2
Pierce, Walter S.	Son	I	1
Pierce, William G.	Son	I	1
Pritchard, Leonard	Husband of the 2nd great-granddaughter		
Pritchard, Timothy Allen	3rd great-grandson	V	5
Rebecca	3rd great-granddaughter	V	5
Reinhardt	Husband of the granddaughter		
Rick, Beth	Wife of the 2nd great-grandson		
Robinson, Linda	Wife of the 2nd great-grandson		
Roenike, Karen	Wife of the 2nd great-grandson		
Sharer, Marie	Wife of the 2nd great-grandson		
Stuart, Ruth Jane	Wife of the great-grandson		
Tiesman, Sharon	Wife of the 2nd great-grandson		
Trimble, Carol	Wife of the 2nd great-grandson		
Walters, Baby	3rd great-granddaughter	V	5
Walters, Carl B.	Husband of the granddaughter		
Walters, David Gene	3rd great-grandson	V	5
Walters, Dawn Gail	2nd great-granddaughter	IV	4
Walters, Harlan Gene	2nd great-grandson	IV	4
Walters, Harold Edward	Great-grandson	III	3
Walters, Jane Kaye	2nd great-granddaughter	IV	4
Walters, Mark Douglas	3rd great-grandson	V	5
Walters, Matthew	3rd great-grandson	V	5
Walters, Paul Edward	2nd great-grandson	IV	4
Walters, Philip Dale	2nd great-grandson	IV	4
Walters, Rhonda Ruth	2nd great-granddaughter	IV	4
Walters, Stephanie Anne	3rd great-granddaughter	V	5
Walters, Terry Harlan	3rd great-grandson	V	5
Walters, Tiffany Marie	3rd great-granddaughter	V	5
Walters, Tori Cheryl	3rd great-granddaughter	V	5

Name	Relationship with Nathaniel Pierce	Civil	Canon
Walters, Troy J.	3rd great-grandson	V	5
Walters, Wendy Lee	3rd great-granddaughter	V	5
Wilson, Sara Jane	Daughter-in-law		

Descendants of Jacob Smith

Generation No. 1

1. JACOB[1] SMITH He married MARTHA SIMONDS.

Child of JACOB SMITH and MARTHA SIMONDS is:
2.   i.   HORACE C[2] SMITH, b. 1866, Maquoketa, Iowa.

Generation No. 2

2. HORACE C.[2] SMITH *(JACOB[1])* was born 1866 in Maquoketa, Iowa. He married SARA JANE WILSON October 30, 1889 in Fulton, Whiteside co., IL, daughter of THOMAS WILSON and MARY ELSEY. She was born June 16, 1871 in Clyde twp, Whiteside co., IL, and died March 08, 1920 in White Pigeon, Clyde twp, Whiteside Co., IL.

Notes for HORACE C SMITH:
Wside co IL marriage record #7748
Divorced May 31, 1897. Holley is used in all legal documents.
Teamster at time of marriage to Sarah Jane. Marriage license gives Maquoketa.
Perhaps 'Horace'?
UNCLE OF RONALD REAGAN

Notes for SARA JANE WILSON:
Place of death not known, but buried in Fulton.
Divorced 31 May 1897. Death certificate says birthdate is June 16, 1871, age at death 48 yrs., 8 mos. 22 days. Cause of death: cerebral hemorrhage.
AUNT OF RONALD REAGAN

More About SARA JANE WILSON:
Burial: Fulton cemetery. Fulton, IL

Children of HORACE SMITH and SARA WILSON are:
3.   i.   CHARLES ALFRED[3] SMITH, b. August 22, 1890, Fulton, Whiteside Co., IL; d. December 30, 1968, Sterling, Whiteside co., IL.
4.   ii.   HORACE VERNON SMITH, b. August 18, 1892, Fulton, Whiteside Co., IL; d. October 19, 1968, Walden, CO.
5.   iii.   HARRY WILSON SMITH, b. January 11, 1895, Fulton, Whiteside Co., IL; d. December 12, 1967, Morrison, IL.

Generation No. 3

3. CHARLES ALFRED[3] SMITH *(HORACE C.[2], JACOB[1])* was born August 22, 1890 in Fulton, Whiteside Co., IL, and died December 30, 1968 in Sterling, Whiteside co., IL. He married MABEL MAY SWEIGERT June 26, 1912 in Sterling, Whiteside co., IL, daughter of MILTON SWEIGERT and EVELYN REES. She was born September 18, 1888 in Elroy, Stephenson co., IL, and died February 17, 1972 in Rock Falls, Whiteside co., IL.

Notes for CHARLES ALFRED SMITH:
Retired in 1959 as Manager of Johnston Lumber co., Rock Falls after 50 years of service.
COUSIN OF RONALD REAGAN

More About CHARLES ALFRED SMITH:
Burial: January 02, 1969, Oak Knoll cemetery, Sterling, IL

Notes for MABEL MAY SWEIGERT:
WsidecoIL marriage record # 139760.0

More About MABEL MAY SWEIGERT:
Burial: Oak Knoll cemetery, Sterling, IL

Children of CHARLES SMITH and MABEL SWEIGERT are:
6.   i.   MILFORD L.⁴ SMITH, b. February 21, 1916, Rock Falls, Whiteside co., IL; d. October 29, 1980, Sterling, Whiteside co., IL.
7.   ii.   RAYMOND SMITH, b. February 07, 1918, Sterling, Whiteside co., IL; d. March 07, 1997.

4. HORACE VERNON³ SMITH *(HORACE C.², JACOB¹)* was born August 18, 1892 in Fulton, Whiteside Co., IL, and died October 19, 1968 in Walden, CO. He married DOSSIE MAY MEAKINS February 20, 1915 in Morrison, IL. She was born July 17, 1890 in Coleta, Whiteside co., IL, and died December 03, 1972.

Notes for HORACE VERNON SMITH:
WsidecoIL birth record #7,422,   Supt. of Public Aid Department, Whiteside co..
COUSIN OF RONALD REAGAN

More About HORACE VERNON SMITH:
Burial: Grove Hill cemetery, Morrison

Notes for DOSSIE MAY MEAKINS:
School teacher

More About DOSSIE MAY MEAKINS:
Burial: Grove Hill cemetery, Morrison

Children of HORACE SMITH and DOSSIE MEAKINS are:
8.   i.   ROBERT CLARE⁴ SMITH, b. November 05, 1917, Sterling, Whiteside co., IL.
9.   ii.   GENE MEAKIN SMITH, b. March 27, 1922, Sterling, Whiteside co., IL; d. July 09, 1995.

5. HARRY WILSON³ SMITH *(HORACE C.², JACOB¹)* was born January 11, 1895 in Fulton, Whiteside Co., IL, and died December 12, 1967 in Morrison, IL. He married HULDA PHILENA GOFF January 26, 1916 in Fulton, Whiteside co., IL, daughter of LYMAN GOFF and DELLA BULL. She was born April 20, 1893, and died December 14, 1974.

Notes for HARRY WILSON SMITH:
Owned auto body and paint shop
At time of marriage, lived at Ashton, IL, railroad employee. In 1922 he lived at Elmhurst, II and was a signal maintainer, C&NW Ry..
COUSIN OF RONALD REAGAN

More About HARRY WILSON SMITH:
Burial: Grove Hill cemetery, Morrison

More About HULDA PHILENA GOFF:
Burial: Grove Hill cemetery, Morrison

Child of HARRY SMITH and HULDA GOFF is:
10.   i.   HARRY WILSON⁴ SMITH, JR, b. January 20, 1922, Oak Park, Cook co., IL.

Generation No. 4

6. MILFORD L.⁴ SMITH *(CHARLES ALFRED³, HORACE C.², JACOB¹)* was born February 21, 1916 in Rock Falls, Whiteside co., IL, and died October 29, 1980 in Sterling, Whiteside co., IL. He married MARIAN D SCHNEIDER June 01, 1938 in Sterling, Whiteside co., IL, daughter of JOSEPH SCHNEIDER and DELLA MACQUAY. She was born 1916 in Coleta, Whiteside co., IL.

Notes for MILFORD L. SMITH:
Served in the military WW II. Cashier, International Harvester.
COUSIN ONCE REMOVED OF RONALD REAGAN

More About MILFORD L. SMITH:
Burial: Oak Knoll cemetery, Sterling, IL

More About MARIAN D. SCHNEIDER:
Burial: Oak Knoll cemetery, Sterling, IL

Children of MILFORD SMITH and MARIAN SCHNEIDER are:
- i. GORDON M.⁵ SMITH, b. October 31, 1940, Rock Falls, Whiteside co., IL; d. September 10, 1971, Rock Falls, Whiteside co., IL.

    Notes for GORDON M. SMITH:
    Not married
    COUSIN TWICE REMOVED OF RONALD REAGAN

    More About GORDON M. SMITH:
    Burial: Oak Knoll cemetery, Sterling, IL

- ii. DENNIS SMITH, b. September 14, 1943, Rock Falls, Whiteside co., IL; d. January 28, 1983, Morrison, Whiteside co., IL.

    Notes for DENNIS SMITH:
    Not married
    COUSIN TWICE REMOVED OF RONALD REAGAN

    More About DENNIS SMITH:
    Burial: Oak Knoll cem.

7. RAYMOND⁴ SMITH *(CHARLES ALFRED³, HORACE C.², JACOB¹)* was born February 07, 1918 in Sterling, Whiteside co., IL, and died March 07, 1997. He married MADELINE WEYRAUCH August 27, 1942.

Notes for RAYMOND SMITH:
FIRST COUSIN ONCE REMOVED OF RONALD REAGAN

More About RAYMOND SMITH:
Burial: Oak Knoll cemetery, Sterling, IL

Children of RAYMOND SMITH and MADELINE WEYRAUCH are:
- i. HUDSON B.⁵ SMITH, b. March 12, 1944.

    Notes for HUDSON B. SMITH:
    COUSIN TWICE REMOVED OF RONALD REAGAN

- ii. KAREN SMITH, b. April 1947.

    Notes for KAREN SMITH:
    COUSIN TWICE REMOVED OF RONALD REAGAN

- iii. SALLY SMITH, b. May 1950.

Notes for SALLY SMITH:
COUSIN TWICE REMOVED OF RONALD REAGAN

8. ROBERT CLARE[4] SMITH *(HORACE VERNON[3], HORACE C.[2], JACOB[1])* was born November 05, 1917 in Sterling, Whiteside co., IL. He married (1) DOROTHY BRICKLEY. She was born June 20, 1920, and died May 17, 1984. He married (2) JEANNE WEBB January 11, 1935.

Notes for ROBERT CLARE SMITH:
COUSIN ONCE REMOVED OF RONALD REAGAN

Children of ROBERT SMITH and DOROTHY BRICKLEY are:
11.   i.   TERRY[5] SMITH, b. November 20, 1946.
12.   ii.   VICKI SMITH, b. March 01, 1952.

9. GENE MEAKIN[4] SMITH *(HORACE VERNON[3], HORACE C.[2], JACOB[1])* was born March 27, 1922 in Sterling, Whiteside co., IL, and died July 09, 1995. He married JANET JANKE February 09, 1946 in Morrison, IL, daughter of HERBERT JANKE and EMMA KLEIST. She was born September 20, 1919 in Weyauwega, WI, and died October 24, 1989 in Sterling, Whiteside co., IL.

Notes for GENE MEAKIN SMITH:
COUSIN ONCE REMOVED OF RONALD REAGAN

Children of GENE SMITH and JANET JANKE are:
13.   i.   DAVID[5] SMITH, b. May 21, 1948.
14.   ii.   THOMAS SMITH, b. February 25, 1952.
15.   iii.   NANCY SMITH, b. October 12, 1955.

10. HARRY WILSON[4] SMITH, JR *(HARRY WILSON[3], HORACE C.[2], JACOB[1])* was born January 20, 1922 in Oak Park, Cook co., IL. He married JEAN.

Notes for HARRY WILSON SMITH, JR:
Living in TN, 2000.
COUSIN ONCE REMOVED OF RONALD REAGAN

Children of HARRY SMITH and JEAN are:
      i.   DALE[5] SMITH, m. NANCY LEE SPRAGUE, July 02, 1960.

           Notes for DALE SMITH:
           COUSIN TWICE REMOVED OF RONALD REAGAN

      ii.   BARBARA SMITH.

           Notes for BARBARA SMITH:
           COUSIN TWICE REMOVED OF RONALD REAGAN

      iii.   DEAN SMITH.

           Notes for DEAN SMITH:
           COUSIN TWICE REMOVED OF RONALD REAGAN

Generation No. 5

11. TERRY[5] SMITH *(ROBERT CLARE[4], HORACE VERNON[3], HORACE C.[2], JACOB[1])* was born November 20, 1946. He married (1) DONNA ANN RURY January 13, 1967. He married (2) MARIA MARTINEZ August 14, 1983. He married (3) MARGARITA MARISEAL August 17, 1996.

Notes for TERRY SMITH:
Divorced 1981, from Donna, divorced from Maria.
COUSIN TWICE REMOVED OF RONALD REAGAN

Notes for DONNA ANN RURY:
Divorced 1981

Children of TERRY SMITH and DONNA RURY are:
  i. CHRISTOPHER SCOTT[6] SMITH, b. January 29, 1968.

     Notes for CHRISTOPHER SCOTT SMITH:
     COUSIN 3 TIMES REMOVED FROM RONALD REAGAN

  ii. JAMIE SMITH, b. January 23, 1973.

     Notes for JAMIE SMITH:
     Twin of Corie
     COUSIN 3 TIMES REMOVED OF RONALD REAGAN

  iii. CORY SMITH, b. January 23, 1973.

     Notes for CORY SMITH:
     Twin of Jamie
     COUSIN 3 TIMES REMOVED OF RONALD REAGAN

  iv. JENIFER ERIN SMITH, b. January 24, 1978.

     Notes for JENIFER ERIN SMITH:
     COUSIN 3 TIMES REMOVED OF RONALD REAGAN

12. VICKI[5] SMITH *(ROBERT CLARE[4], HORACE VERNON[3], HORACE C.[2], JACOB[1])* was born March 01, 1952. She married (1) BRUCE UNGER August 07, 1971 in Morrison, IL. He died March 17, 1974. She married (2) RON WIEBENGA October 24, 1975.

Notes for VICKI SMITH:
COUSIN TWICE REMOVED OF RONALD REAGAN

Notes for BRUCE UNGER:
Deceased

More About BRUCE UNGER:
Burial: Grove Hill cemetery, Morrison

Child of VICKI SMITH and BRUCE UNGER is:
  i. BRUCE EDWIN[6] UNGER, JR., b. July 04, 1974; m. KAREN GEORGE, November 06, 1999, Peoria, IL.

     Notes for BRUCE EDWIN UNGER, JR.:
     COUSIN 3 TIMES REMOVED OF RONALD REAGAN

Child of VICKI SMITH and RON WIEBENGA is:
  ii. LESLEY DAWN[6] WIEBENGA, b. April 24, 1977, Morrison, IL; m. CHAD PAUL DEVER, June 06, 1998, Morrison, IL.

     Notes for LESLEY DAWN WIEBENGA:
     COUSIN 3 TIMES REMOVED OF RONALD REAGAN

13. DAVID[5] SMITH *(GENE MEAKIN[4], HORACE VERNON[3], HORACE C.[2], JACOB[1])* was born May 21, 1948.

He married DEE ANN BILDSTEIN August 09, 1975.

Notes for DAVID SMITH:
Lives in Iowa, divorced.
COUSIN TWICE REMOVED OF RONALD REAGAN

Child of DAVID SMITH and DEE BILDSTEIN is:
    i. CHELSEY[6] SMITH, b. May 20, 1982.

14. THOMAS[5] SMITH *(GENE MEAKIN[4], HORACE VERNON[3], HORACE C.[2], JACOB[1])* was born February 25, 1952. He married (1) CHRISTINE PYRON July 07, 1973. He married (2) DAWN SCHRYVER March 31, 1978. He married (3) CINDY OSTEMA March 09, 1984.

Notes for THOMAS SMITH:
Divorced Feb. 1975 · Christine
Divorced · Dawn · Dec. 1979
COUSIN TWICE REMOVED OF RONALD REAGAN

Notes for CHRISTINE PYRON:
Divorced Feb. 1975

Child of THOMAS SMITH and DAWN SCHRYVER is:
    i. THOMAS S.[6] SMITH, m. CINDY.

Children of THOMAS SMITH and CINDY OSTEMA are:
    ii. MARSHALL[6] SMITH, b. August 22, 1984.
    iii. TAYLOR SMITH, b. December 17, 1996.

15. NANCY[5] SMITH *(GENE MEAKIN[4], HORACE VERNON[3], HORACE C.[2], JACOB[1])* was born October 12, 1955. She married (1) MITCHELL FOREMAN January 04, 1975. She married (2) STEVE MERRILL Aft. January 1980.

Notes for NANCY SMITH:
Divorced Steve Jan. 5, 1980
COUSIN TWICE REMOVED OF RONALD REAGAN

Child of NANCY SMITH and MITCHELL FOREMAN is:
    i. CAMERON RYAN[6] FOREMAN, b. July 14, 1978.

    Notes for CAMERON RYAN FOREMAN:
    COUSIN 3 TIMES REMOVED OF RONALD REAGAN

Child of NANCY SMITH and STEVE MERRILL is:
    ii. DUSTIN[6] MERRILL, b. May 05, 1982.

Kinship of Jacob Smith

Name	Relationship with Jacob Smith	Civil	Canon
Bildstein, Dee Ann	Wife of the 2nd great-grandson		
Brickley, Dorothy	Wife of the great-grandson		
Cindy	Wife of the 3rd great-grandson		
Dever, Chad Paul	Husband of the 3rd great-granddaughter		
Foreman, Cameron Ryan	3rd great-grandson	V	5
Foreman, Mitchell	Husband of the 2nd great-granddaughter		
George, Karen	Wife of the 3rd great-grandson		
Goff, Hulda Philena	Wife of the grandson		
Holly	Son	I	1
Hulda	Wife of the grandson		
Janke, Janet	Wife of the great-grandson		
Jean	Wife of the great-grandson		
Jennie	Daughter-in-law		
Jr.	Great-grandson	III	3
Mariseal, Margarita	Wife of the 2nd great-grandson		
Martinez, Maria	Wife of the 2nd great-grandson		
May, Denzie	Wife of the grandson		
Meakins, Dossie May	Wife of the grandson		
Merrill, Dustin	3rd great-grandson	V	5
Merrill, Steve	Husband of the 2nd great-granddaughter		
Ostema, Cindy	Wife of the 2nd great-grandson		
Pyron, Christine	Wife of the 2nd great-grandson		
Rury, Donna Ann	Wife of the 2nd great-grandson		
Schneider, Marian D.	Wife of the great-grandson		
Schryver, Dawn	Wife of the 2nd great-grandson		
Simonds, Martha	Wife		
Smith, Barbara	2nd great-granddaughter	IV	4
Smith, Charles Alfred	Grandson	II	2
Smith, Chelsey	3rd great-granddaughter	V	5
Smith, Christopher Scott	3rd great-grandson	V	5
Smith, Cory	3rd great-granddaughter	V	5
Smith, Dale	2nd great-grandson	IV	4
Smith, David	2nd great-grandson	IV	4
Smith, Dean	2nd great-grandson	IV	4
Smith, Dennis	2nd great-grandson	IV	4
Smith, Gene Meakin	Great-grandson	III	3
Smith, Gordon M.	2nd great-grandson	IV	4
Smith, Harry Wilson	Grandson	II	2
Smith, Harry Wilson, Jr	Great-grandson	III	3
Smith, Horace C.	Son	I	1
Smith, Horace Vernon	Grandson	II	2
Smith, Hudson B.	2nd great-grandson	IV	4
Smith, Jacob	Self		0
Smith, Jamie	3rd great-grandson	V	5
Smith, Jenifer Erin	3rd great-granddaughter	V	5
Smith, Karen	2nd great-granddaughter	IV	4
Smith, Marshall	3rd great-grandson	V	5
Smith, Milford L.	Great-grandson	III	3
Smith, Nancy	2nd great-granddaughter	IV	4
Smith, Raymond	Great-grandson	III	3
Smith, Robert Clare	Great-grandson	III	3

Name	Relationship with Jacob Smith	Civil	Canon
Smith, Sally	2nd great-granddaughter	IV	4
Smith, Taylor	3rd great-grandson	V	5
Smith, Terry	2nd great-grandson	IV	4
Smith, Thomas	2nd great-grandson	IV	4
Smith, Thomas S.	3rd great-grandson	V	5
Smith, Vicki	2nd great-granddaughter	IV	4
Sprague, Nancy Lee	Wife of the 2nd great-grandson		
Sweigert, Mabel May	Wife of the grandson		
Unger, Bruce	Husband of the 2nd great-granddaughter		
Unger, Bruce Edwin, Jr.	3rd great-grandson	V	5
Webb, Jeanne	Wife of the great-grandson		
Weyrauch, Madeline	Wife of the great-grandson		
Wiebenga, Lesley Dawn	3rd great-granddaughter	V	5
Wiebenga, Ron	Husband of the 2nd great-granddaughter		
Wilson, Sara Jane	Daughter-in-law		

Descendants of Andrew Wilson

Generation No. 1

1. ANDREW[1] WILSON He married AMEILIA GLASGOW.

Notes for ANDREW WILSON:
Andrew Wilson from Ronald V. Jackson, 'Reagan/Davis Ancestry'.
ASSUMPTION;   The obituary of Claudio says he was one of triplets. He came to Massachusetts then to Mexico for some years. Then he came to Clyde twp.. I presume because of relatives. Perhaps he is a brother of Andrew. If this is so he is a great great uncle of Reagan.
GREAT GREAT GRANDFATHER OF RONALD REAGAN

Notes for AMEILIA GLASGOW:
This parentage from Ronald V. Jackson, 'Reagan/Davis Ancestry'.

Child of ANDREW WILSON and AMEILIA GLASGOW is:
2.   i.   JOHN[2] WILSON, b. February 09, 1812, Paisley, Renfrewshire, Scotland; d. March 09, 1883, Wside co., Clydetwp., IL.

Generation No. 2

2. JOHN[2] WILSON *(ANDREW[1])* was born February 09, 1812 in Paisley, Renfrewshire, Scotland, and died March 09, 1883 in Wside co., Clydetwp., IL. He married JANE BLUE November 23, 1841 in Whiteside co., IL, daughter of DONALD BLUE, SR and CATHERINE MCFARLANE. She was born April 01, 1821 in Nova Scotia, Canada, and died June 01, 1894 in Morrison, IL.

Notes for JOHN WILSON:
To Nova Scotia in 1832.   Probably met his wife in Canada. He took part in the "Patriot War". He came to Clyde twp in 1839. Married in Whiteside co. Nov. 23, 1841 per marriage record # 54, not the 28th per Heritage Quest article.
Willson in marriage record Whiteside co., IL #54.
1860 Whitesideco37thDistIL census 4854/484, age 40, farmer, Scotland
1860 WsidecoIL Clyde twp census 476/464. Age 50, Scotland, Farmer, $8,000,$1,000, Jane 34 F Nova Scotia, Sarah 16 F IL, Thos. 14 M IL, John 12 M IL, Wilson, Alexander 10 M IL, Margrer 3 M? IL Catherine 7mo. F IL
1870 WsidecoClytwpIL census 168/168, $16,000, age 58, nat citizen, Scotland, Farmer
WsidecoIL death record #930
Original land grants:
6-24-1845. FD   NWSW S9 22N 5E. 40 acres. $1.25 $50.00. V. 714, p. 131
014622.
7-19-1848. NWSW S17, 22N, 5E 40 acres, S$50.00 014623
12-30- 1853. 40 acres, $50.00. 091044
FD NWNE S23 22N 4E 40 acres. $50.00 091045
12-30-1853. FD NWNE S23 22N 4E 40 acres, $50.00. 091045
Ronald V. Jackson, 'Reagan/Davis Ancestry', gives father as Andrew Wilson, mother as Ameila Glassgow. He also gives deathdate as 6 February 1879. This does not agree with County records.
  Per Eliz. Carroll: Four men emigrated to Canada together. Donald Blue, Richard Beswick, John Wilson and William Wilson. William went to CA, possibly a brother of John?
ASSUMPTION: Claudio, b. 1786 as one of triplets, came to Clyde after emigration to MA and Mexico for some years.

Funeral at Clyde ME church
GREAT GRANDFATHER OF RONALD WILSON

More About JOHN WILSON:
Burial: North Clyde Cemetery

Notes for JANE BLUE:
Bd. Center Clyde cem. age 71 years. (Born 1823?)
1850 Wsideco37th D IL census 484, Nova Scotia, age 25.
1860 WsidecoClytwpIL census476/464.   Jane 34, John 50, Sarah 16, Thos. 14, John 12.
1870 WsidecoClytwpIL cen 168, age 44, Parent foreign born, born New Brunswick.
Ronald V. Jackson, 'Reagan/Davis Ancestry', gives birth date as abt. 1824 at Queens, New Brunswick, Canada, marriage as Nov. 28, 1841, death as abt. 1880.
Birth also given as 1823
2 children died in infancy.   Chapman Whiteside co. History, p. 63 'of Scotch parentage.
Donald E. Farr email of 19 Oct. 2002 gives her birth place as Queens, New Brunswick, Canada, and death date as June 3, 1894.
GREAT GRANDMOTHER OF RONALD REAGAN

More About JANE BLUE:
Burial: North Clyde cemetery

Children of JOHN WILSON and JANE BLUE are:
- 3. i. SARA³ WILSON, b. March 29, 1841, Wside co., Clydetwp, IL; d. November 17, 1920, Wside co., Clydetwp, IL.
- 4. ii. THOMAS WILSON, b. April 28, 1844, Wside co., Clydetwp, IL; d. December 10, 1909, WSide co., Clydetwp, IL.
- 5. iii. JOHN WILSON, b. July 11, 1846, Whiteside co., Clydetwp, IL; d. February 15, 1909, Morrison, IL.
- 6. iv. ALEXANDER B WILSON, b. February 21, 1848, WSide co., Clydetwp, IL; d. May 25, 1932.
- 7. v. MARGARET MAE WILSON, b. April 28, 1857, Whiteside co., Clydetwp, IL; d. March 12, 1944, Whiteside co., Clydetwp, IL.
- 8. vi. CATHERINE WILSON, b. November 09, 1859, Wside co., Clydetwp, IL; d. July 13, 1932, Highland Park, IL.
- 9. vii. ELIZABETH EVELYN WILSON, b. December 10, 1861, Whiteside co., Clyde twp., IL; d. November 19, 1945.
- 10. viii. REV. CHARLES DESMOND WILSON, b. November 10, 1865; d. 1937.

Generation No. 3

3. SARA³ WILSON *(JOHN², ANDREW¹)* was born March 29, 1841 in Wside co., Clydetwp, IL, and died November 17, 1920 in Wside co., Clydetwp, IL. She married EPHRAIM MYERS BECHTEL February 22, 1861 in Whiteside co., IL, son of BENJAMIN BECHTEL and REBECCA MYERS. He was born March 23, 1833 in Columbiana Co., OH, and died January 16, 1928 in Wside co., Clydetwp, IL.

Notes for SARA WILSON:
1850 WsidecoIL census484, age 8, IL
1870 WsidecoIL census95, age 36, I
1910 WsideClytwpIL census, age 68, IL Sc Sc
1920 WsideClytwpcoIL census with David E Gerdes, age 78, with husband Ephraim Bechtel, 86
Bd. Malvern cemetery next to husband
Married by Rev. J. W. White, in Ustick twp., in her parent's home., Wside Sentinel 26 Feb1861
GREAT AUNT OF RONALD WILSON

More About SARA WILSON:
Burial: Malvern cemetery

Notes for EPHRAIM MYERS BECHTEL:
He came to Clyde Twp. at 19 with his parents.
1870 WsideUsttwpIL census 95/95, age 32, farmer, OH, Sarah 36 F IL, John 8 M IL, Rebecca 6 F IL, Ella 4 F IL. [Only Bechtel in census]

1880 WsideClydetwpIL census 119/121 with son in law David E. Gerdes, dau. Ella (Ellen)
1910 WsideClytwpIL census 56/58, age77, own income, IL Gr PA, Sarah F 68 wf IL Sc Sc
Whiteside marriage record #563. Ephraim N. on marriage record.
Bd. Malvern cemetery.
He died at the home of his daughter, Mrs. David (Ellen) Gerdes. He had been blind for a number of years. He was the last of 11 children to die.
COUSIN OF RONALD REAGAN

More About EPHRAIM MYERS BECHTEL:
Burial: Malvern cemetery

Children of SARA WILSON and EPHRAIM BECHTEL are:

11.   i.   JOHN WILSON[4] BECHTEL, b. February 17, 1862, Wside co., Clydetwp, IL; d. February 22, 1933, Wside co., Clydetwp, IL.
        ii.   REBECCA JANE BECHTEL, b. 1864; d. March 11, 1878, WSide co., Clydetwp, IL.

             Notes for REBECCA JANE BECHTEL:
             Bd. Malvern cemetery with parents, died at 14 years. 'Buried from the Franklin School House' from the Sentinel of May 11, 1878. Whiteside co. death certificate #88.
             1870 WsidecoIL cen95, age 6, IL
             COUSIN ONCE REMOVED OF RONALD REAGAN

12.   iii.   ELLEN W. BECHTEL, b. July 01, 1866, Wside co., Clydetwp, IL.
        iv.   HELENA BECHTEL, b. November 01, 1876, ILL.; d. June 24, 1953, Washington; m. SAMUEL L. LONGANECKER, May 16, 1903, Whiteside co., IL; b. December 24, 1875; d. December 22, 1946, Orville, WA.

             Notes for HELENA BECHTEL:
             COUSIN ONCE REMOVED OF RONALD REAGAN

             Notes for SAMUEL L. LONGANECKER:
             Wside co. marriage record #11,484, she is listed as Helen

4. THOMAS[3] WILSON (JOHN[2], ANDREW[1]) was born April 28, 1844 in Wside co., Clydetwp, IL, and died December 10, 1909 in WSide co., Clydetwp, IL. He married MARY ANN ELSEY January 25, 1866 in Whiteside co., IL, daughter of ROBERT ELSEY and MARY BAKER. She was born December 28, 1843 in Epsom, County Surrey, England, and died October 06, 1900 in Fulton, Whiteside Co., IL.

Notes for THOMAS WILSON:
Thomas was a prosperous farmer in Whiteside County.
Bd. N. Clyde cem., Wside co.. Place of death uncertain.
WsidecoIL mar rcd #1454
1850 WsidecoIL census484, age 6.
1880 Clyde twp. Whiteside co., IL census: Thomas Wilson 36 farmer IL En En, Mary A. 36 En En En, Emily dau 13 IL, John son 10 IL Jennie dau 8 IL, Alexande 7 IL, George son 4 IL, Mary dau 2 IL.
Not in 1900 census. Absent from home for periods of time, perhaps at this time.
Farmed near White Pigeon, Whiteside co., IL
GRANDFATHER OF RONALD REAGAN

More About THOMAS WILSON:
Burial: North Clyde cemetery

Notes for MARY ANN ELSEY:
Bd. Fulton Cem.
Married by Rev. George T. Crissman, per Sentinel 1Feb1860, Whiteside co. marriage record #1454.

1900 Fulton twp., Whiteside co., IL census: Mary Wilson, Dec 1843, En En En, Alexander son Mar 1874, IL, factory worker, Vina dau Apr 18ll80 IL, Nellie dau 16 July 1883 IL
GRANDMOTHER OF RONALD REAGAN

More About MARY ANN ELSEY:
Burial: Fulton Catholic cemetery

Children of THOMAS WILSON and MARY ELSEY are:

  i. EMILY G.^{4} WILSON, b. November 12, 1867, Fulton, Whiteside Co., IL; d. February 21, 1947, O'Fallon, St. Clair, IL; m. STEPHEN A. RUSH, June 03, 1884, Morrison, Whiteside co., IL; b. April 1865, Fulton, Whiteside Co., IL; d. April 05, 1936, O'Fallon, IL.

  Notes for EMILY G. WILSON:
  1900 Wsideco Fulton ILL cen 165, age 31 IL IL En
  They had no children.
  AUNT OF RONALD REAGAN

  More About EMILY G. WILSON:
  Burial: February 25, 1947, Shilo cemetery

  Notes for STEPHEN A. RUSH:
  They had no children.
  Wside co IL marriage record #6376
  1900 Wsideco., Fulton, IL census 165/165, age 35, IL PA PA, boarding house, next door is a long listing of of occupants, probably his boarding house. Also lists: Pannell, Lawra F 20 S IL IL IL servant, domestic.
  1870 WsidecoAlbanyIL census 92/92. Stephen is 8, IL, in family of Henry W. Rush, age. 40, PA wife Marybea, age 37, NY, 8 children.
  Tavern owner, death date from wife's obituary.

13. ii. JOHN CHARLES WILSON, b. October 09, 1870, Wsideco, Clyde twp, IL; d. June 21, 1942, Clinton, IA.
14. iii. SARA JANE WILSON, b. June 16, 1871, Clyde twp, Whiteside co., IL; d. March 08, 1920, White Pigeon, Clyde twp, Whiteside Co., IL.
  iv. ALEXANDER THOMAS WILSON, b. March 30, 1874, Whiteside Co., Clyde twp., IL; d. April 26, 1962, Quincy, Adams co., IL; m. (1) MAYME AITKEN; m. (2) MAYME HELMS, June 12, 1912.

  Notes for ALEXANDER THOMAS WILSON:
  They had no children. Obituary in (unnamed) newspaper gives birth as March 30, 1876. Employed 44 years at Monroe Chemical Co., foreman of the mill rooom. Member First Christian Church and Quincy Lodge of Masons.
  UNCLE OF RONALD REAGAN

  More About ALEXANDER THOMAS WILSON:
  Burial: Greenmount cemetery, Quincy, IL

15. v. GEORGE ORVILLE WILSON, b. March 02, 1876, Cordova, Whiteside co., IL; d. April 03, 1951, Clinton, IA.
16. vi. MARY LAVINA WILSON, b. April 06, 1879, Wside co., Clydetwp, IL; d. September 06, 1951, Minneapolis, Hennepin co., MN.
17. vii. NELLIE CLYDE WILSON, b. July 24, 1883, Fulton, Whiteside co., IL; d. July 25, 1962, Santa Monica, Los Angeles co., CA.

5. JOHN^3 WILSON (JOHN^2, ANDREW^1) was born July 11, 1846 in Whiteside co., Clydetwp, IL, and died February 15, 1909 in Morrison, IL. He married ISABELLE MARY LIGGETT March 14, 1872. She was born October 1850 in OH.

Notes for JOHN WILSON:
1850 Wsideco37thDisIL census 484, age 4, IL
Citizenship paper, Whiteside co., IL, circuit court, 7 Dec. 1877, renounces Victoria, Queen of England.
Bd. Grove Hill cem., Morrison, Lot 7M, age 65 years.
1870 WsidecoClytwpIL cen73, age 23, IL

1880 Whiteside co., Ustick twp., IL cen110/112: Wilson, John M 34 md. Farmer IL Sc Sc, Isabell F 29 wf md OH OH OH, Fannie J. F 7 S IL IL OH.
1920 Whitesideco
John R. Wilson, land grant:
793,372. 12-30-1871. RR SESE S34 21N 7E 40 acres @$15. $600.00
GREAT UNCLE OF RONALD REAGAN

More About JOHN WILSON:
Burial: Grove Hill cemetery, Morrison

Notes for ISABELLE MARY LIGGETT:
1910 WsidecoMorrisonIL census 11/11, age 54, widow, OH OH OH, has `own income'. Fannie dau 36 S IL IL OH, and Alexander 66 widowed,, her `brother in law', IL Sc Sc 'own income'.

Children of JOHN WILSON and ISABELLE LIGGETT are:
    i.   FRANCES JANE[4] WILSON, b. January 1873, Whiteside co., IL; d. November 07, 1968, Morrison, IL.

        Notes for FRANCES JANE WILSON:
        Birth date from Heritage Quest
        1910 Wsideco Morrison, IL census 11/11, age 36, single, IL IL OH
        School teacher.
        Died: 95 years, 7 months

        More About FRANCES JANE WILSON:
        Burial: Grove Hill cemetery, Morrison

18.   ii.   MARGARET MAY WILSON, b. June 10, 1883, Whiteside co., IL.

6. ALEXANDER B[3] WILSON (*JOHN*[2], *ANDREW*[1]) was born February 21, 1848 in WSide co., Clydetwp, IL, and died May 25, 1932. He married DEBORAH A. FLETCHER June 14, 1876 in Whiteside co., IL, daughter of ISAAC FLETCHER and ELIZABETH SMITH. She was born March 08, 1853 in Chautauqua Co., NY, and died 1899.

Notes for ALEXANDER B WILSON:
WsidecoUGtwpIL cen 186 gives age 65, widowed, father of Paul, IL SC SC
1850 WsidcoIL cen 484, age 1
1860 WsidcoClytwpIL cen464 with John, Margaret 3, Catharine 7mo.
1870 WsidecoClytwpIL census 73, age 21, IL
1880 Whitesid co., Ustick twp., IL cen111/113: Wilson, Alexander M 28 md. IL Sc Sc, Debbie A. F 26 wf md. NY Eng Eng, Green, Lewis md in yr. M 24 md. Farmer IL OH NJ, Clara md in yr. F 19 wf md CA VA OH, Probuscaj, Gracie F 12 sister S CA VA OH
1910 Wsideco Morrison, ILL census 11/11 with Isabel, as brother in law, age 66, widowed, has `own income', IL Sc Sc
Also on the 1910 census with Paul Wilson as Alex, father, age 67, NY NY NY.
Birth date also given as 21 Feb. 1849, Mrs. Dwight Wilson
Lot 109B, cemetery

More About ALEXANDER B WILSON:
Burial: Grove Hill, Morrison, IL

Notes for DEBORAH A. FLETCHER:
Chapman, History of Whiteside County, ILL, p. 437: 'Debbie A. Fletcher b. March 8, 1853 md. Alexander Wilson June 15, 1876, resides Ustick. She was a teacher for many years. Daughter of Isaac Fletcher, Eng., April 23, 1826 and Betsy Smith'   Whiteside co., IL marriage record #4191 gives June 14, 1876, Alexander R. Wilson md. Debbie A. Fletcher.

Child of ALEXANDER WILSON and DEBORAH FLETCHER is:
19. i. PAUL FLETCHER⁴ WILSON, b. January 1883, Whiteside co., IL; d. 1964.

7. MARGARET MAE³ WILSON *(JOHN², ANDREW¹)* was born April 28, 1857 in Whiteside co., Clydetwp, IL, and died March 12, 1944 in Whiteside co., Clydetwp, IL. She married DAVID B. GSELL February 25, 1879 in Mt. Carroll, Carroll Co., IL, son of WILLIAM GSELL and MARIA BARKHART. He was born December 15, 1852 in Letterkenny twp, Franklin co., PA, and died January 01, 1907 in Whiteside co., Clydetwp, IL.

Notes for MARGARET MAE WILSON:
Bd. N. Clyde Cem.
1870 WsidecoClyTwpIL cen73, age 13, IL
Married by Rev. J. P. Phillips, per Sentinel 27Feb1879
Death date from Mrs. D. Wilson.   Member Methodist Episcopal church.

More About MARGARET MAE WILSON:
Burial: North Clyde Cemetery

Notes for DAVID B. GSELL:
Bd. N. Clyde cem.
Came west in 1864, per Carroll. Lived Section 7, Clyde Twp.. He was a Republican. See p. 389 of Chapman, Portrait and Biographical Album of Whiteside County, IL.

More About DAVID B. GSELL:
Burial: North Clyde Cemetery

Children of MARGARET WILSON and DAVID GSELL are:
20. i. CLIFFORD LEROY⁴ GSELL, b. November 17, 1880, Whiteside co, Clyde twp., IL; d. August 11, 1951, Clinton, Iowa.
21. ii. MAUDE MAE GSELL, b. November 18, 1884, WsidClytwpIL; d. August 26, 1966, Fulton, IL.
22. iii. ESTELLA JANE GSELL, b. May 27, 1894, Whiteside co, Clyde twp., IL.

8. CATHERINE³ WILSON *(JOHN², ANDREW¹)* was born November 09, 1859 in Wside co., Clydetwp, IL, and died July 13, 1932 in Highland Park, IL. She married WILLIAM B. GSELL October 07, 1879 in Sterling, Whiteside co., IL, son of WILLIAM GSELL and MARIA BARKHART. He was born February 15, 1854 in Letterkenny twp, Franklin co., PA, and died April 02, 1921 in Highland Park, IL.

Notes for CATHERINE WILSON:
WsidecoIL marriage record #5104, Katie Wilson
1860 WsidecoClytwpIL cen464 7mo., census taken 15 June 1860.
1870 WsidecoClytwpIL census73, age 10, IL
Married at Sterling, IL, at the residence of Rev. J. T. Mason.
Buried Lot 31R; 72 yrs, 10 m, 1 d.. Chapman gives her birth as Nov. 9, 1861.

More About CATHERINE WILSON:
Burial: Grove Hill cemetery, Morrison

Notes for WILLIAM B. GSELL:
Died at 67 yrs., 1 mo., 17 d.. Lot 31R. Lived Section 30, Clyde Twp.. Came there in 1864. See p. 463 of Chapman, Port. & Biog. Album of Whiteside County, IL.

More About WILLIAM B. GSELL:
Burial: Grove Hill cemetery, Morrison

Child of CATHERINE WILSON and WILLIAM GSELL is:
    i. EARL WILSON[4] GSELL, b. August 18, 1882, WsidecoUsttwpIL; d. January 25, 1960, Highland Park, IL; m. FRANCIS LOUISE CUTLER; b. 1888; d. 1961.

    Notes for EARL WILSON GSELL:
    WsidecoIL birth record #2,733
    Death date from Grove Hill records
    Died at 77 yrs, bd. Lot 31R

    More About EARL WILSON GSELL:
    Burial: Grove Hill cemetery, Morrison

9. ELIZABETH EVELYN[3] WILSON *(JOHN[2], ANDREW[1])* was born December 10, 1861 in Whiteside co., Clyde twp., IL, and died November 19, 1945. She married WILLIAM G. HIGH December 19, 1882 in Whiteside Co., IL.

Notes for ELIZABETH EVELYN WILSON:
1919 WsideRockFalls ILL census 38, age 46 IL NY NY
1870 WsidecoClytwpIL cen73, age 7, `Lizzie', IL
1900 WsideColtwpIL census 487, age 35, IL VA IL
WsidcoIL marriage record # 5945, as Lizzie E..
Whiteside co., IL birth record #84,728.
Mother died at her home in Morrison, leaving her home in Chicago about April 1, ill. Jane Wilson obituary

Child of ELIZABETH WILSON and WILLIAM HIGH is:
    i. BESSIE LUELLA JANE[4] HIGH, b. October 15, 1887, Wside co., IL; m. WILLIAM HOWELL, 1945; d. Boston, MA.

    Notes for BESSIE LUELLA JANE HIGH:
    WsidecoIL birth record #84728

10. REV. CHARLES DESMOND[3] WILSON *(JOHN[2], ANDREW[1])* was born November 10, 1865, and died 1937. He married JENIE ALICE SMITH June 26, 1896. She was born March 24, 1873, and died 1927.

Notes for REV. CHARLES DESMOND WILSON:
1870 WsidecoClytwpIL cen 73, age 4, IL
Methodist minister.

Children of CHARLES WILSON and JENIE SMITH are:
23.   i. ALICE JANE[4] WILSON, b. April 15, 1897; d. July 05, 1952.
24.   ii. PHOEBE MAE WILSON, b. May 10, 1899; d. May 10, 1960.
25.   iii. WINIFRED M. WILSON, b. September 15, 1901.
    iv. CHARLES ABRAM WILSON, b. December 29, 1903; d. 1928.
    v. GEORGE JOHN WILSON, b. September 08, 1903; d. 1979; m. (1) MARGARET WILKINSON; m. (2) DOROTHY NELSON.

Generation No. 4

11. JOHN WILSON[4] BECHTEL *(SARA[3] WILSON, JOHN[2], ANDREW[1])* was born February 17, 1862 in Wside co., Clydetwp, IL, and died February 22, 1933 in Wside co., Clydetwp, IL. He married SARAH E. DETER 1886 in Whiteside co., IL. She was born August 28, 1858 in PA, and died March 28, 1908 in Wside co., Clydetwp, IL.

Notes for JOHN WILSON BECHTEL:

1870 WsideUstcen 95, age 8, IL
1910 WsidecoUsttwpIL census 47/49, age 48, widowed, IL OH IL
1920 WsidecoMorrisonIL census 152/156, age57, widowed IL OH IL, farm laborer
Bd. Malvern cemetery in plot with parents and wife, Sara E.
COUSIN ONCE REMOVED OF RONALD REAGAN

Notes for SARAH E. DETER:
Bd. Malvern cemetery

Children of JOHN BECHTEL and SARAH DETER are:
    i. ALBERT[5] BECHTEL, b. August 12, 1887, Whiteside co., IL.

    Notes for ALBERT BECHTEL:
    Whiteside co., IL marriage record: #5385 & & 104,677
    1880 Wsideco, 103 Genesee Ave., Morrison, IL age 32, IL IL PA
    1910 Wsideco cen 49, age 22, single, IL IL PA, as `Bert D.'. Farmer
    Never married
    SECOND COUSIN OF RONALD REAGAN

26.   ii. WILLIAM DETER BECHTEL, b. March 11, 1891, Wside co., Clydetwp, IL.
    iii. GEORGE DETER BECHTEL 2, b. March 29, 1892, Wside co., Clydetwp, IL; m. ELOISE; b. 1906, ILL..

    Notes for GEORGE DETER BECHTEL 2:
    WsidecoIL birth record #93,973.
    1910 Wsideco UsticktwpIL cen 49, age 18, farm laborer.
    1920 WsidecoUsttwpIL cen150/154 with wife Eloise
    SECOND COUSIN OF RONALD REAGAN

    Notes for ELOISE:
    1920 WsidecoUsttwpIL census 150/54 , age 24 IL IL IL, wife

27.   iv. IVY MAY BECHTEL, b. May 1898.

12. ELLEN W.[4] BECHTEL (SARA[3] WILSON, JOHN[2], ANDREW[1]) was born July 01, 1866 in Wside co., Clydetwp, IL. She married DAVID EDMOND GERDES January 08, 1888 in Whiteside co., IL, son of HENRY GERDES and REBECCA KALLENOR. He was born December 1864 in Whiteside co., IL, and died January 13, 1934 in Whiteside co., IL.

Notes for ELLEN W. BECHTEL:
1870 WsidecoIL cen95, age 4, IL
1910 Wside census 163 age 43, IL OH IL
COUSIN ONCE REMOVED OF RONALD REAGAN

Notes for DAVID EDMOND GERDES:
WsidcoIL marriage record #7289. Minister of the Dunkard Church, Clyde & Rock Creek, ILL.
1910 WsidecoUsttwpIL census 61/63. David 45, farmer, IL Gr PA
1920 WsidecoClytwpIL. census119/121m age 55, farmer, IL Gr PA
1920 census has Ephraim Bechtel, 86, f in law, OH PA PA and Sarah (Wilson), his wife, 78, IL Sc Sc with David's family
The Clyde Twp. farm was in the family since 1863.

Children of ELLEN BECHTEL and DAVID GERDES are:
28.   i. EPHRAIM LAWRENCE[5] GERDES, b. October 11, 1888, Wside co., Clydetwp, IL.
    ii. REBECCA H GERDES, b. December 05, 1889, WSide co., Clydetwp, IL; d. April 28, 1981, Whiteside co., IL.

    Notes for REBECCA H GERDES:
    WsidecoIL birth record #6,315.
    1910 Wside census 163, age 20, single, servant
    Did not marry.

1920 Wside Clyde census, with father, 30, servant, IL IL IL
She lived on the family farm all her life, never married, kept house for her brothers.

More About REBECCA H GERDES:
Burial: Malvern cemetery

   iii. EDMUND WAYNE GERDES, b. March 02, 1892, Wside co., Clydetwp, IL; d. July 10, 1969, WHiteside co., IL.

Notes for EDMUND WAYNE GERDES:
WsidecoIL birth rcd #7,402
1910 WsideIL census 163, age 17, farm laborer, 'Wayne'
Living at RFD 2, Dixon, IL Feb. 1981, minister
WsidecoIL death records

29.   iv. GALEN GLENN GERDES, b. January 1894, Wside co., Clydetwp, IL; d. September 01, 1976, N. Manchester, IN.
    v. HENRY RALPH GERDES, b. November 03, 1899, Wside co., Clydetwp, IL; d. February 07, 1981, Morrison, IL.

Notes for HENRY RALPH GERDES:
1910 WsidecoIL, cen 163, age 10
1920 WsidecoIL, cen 121, age 20, laborer
Never married, lived on family farm all his life.

More About HENRY RALPH GERDES:
Burial: Malvern cemetery

  vi. LLOYD GERDES, b. August 02, 1903, Wside co., Clydetwp, IL.

Notes for LLOYD GERDES:
WsidecoIL birth record #10,211 as 'boy'. 1920 census lists him as 16.
1910 WsidecoIL census age 6
1920 WsidecoIL cen 121, age 16
Died in truck accident, not married.

  vii. VIRGIL E. GERDES, b. August 25, 1905, Wside co., Clydetwp, IL; d. April 23, 1987, Whiteside co., IL.

Notes for VIRGIL E. GERDES:
WsidecoIL birth record #12,024
1910 WsidecoIL cen163 age 4
1920 WsidecoIL cen 121, age 14
WsidecoIL death records
The author has a taped conversation with Virgil in which he remenisces about playing with Ronald Reagan as a child.
Lived on the family farm all his life, enjoyed antique farm machinery, never married.

More About VIRGIL E. GERDES:
Burial: Malvern cemetery

13. JOHN CHARLES[4] WILSON (THOMAS[3], JOHN[2], ANDREW[1]) was born October 09, 1870 in Wsideco, Clyde twp, IL, and died June 21, 1942 in Clinton, IA. He married (1) THELMA LILLIAN KEITH, daughter of HERBERT KEITH and JULIA KRAMER. She was born 1911 in Freeport, Stephenson co., IL. He married (2) CATHERINE STARCK January 16, 1893 in Fulton, Whiteside co., IL, daughter of MATHEW STARCK and ELIZABETH BONZLET. She was born November 1873 in Fulton, Whiteside Co., IL.

Notes for JOHN CHARLES WILSON:
WsidecoIL mar records #8634 for middle name, Katie Stark
Mrs. D Wilson gives death date as 21 June 1942
Death certificate, Hunt/Wiebenga material, night watchman, Mfg. plant

UNCLE OF RONALD REAGAN

Notes for CATHERINE STARCK:
Katie on marriage record, Katherine and Kate on birth records
4 sons, 5 girls, lived in Clinton, Iowa

Children of JOHN WILSON and CATHERINE STARCK are:
    i. CHARLES LEROY[5] WILSON, b. August 10, 1894, Whiteside co., IL.

    Notes for CHARLES LEROY WILSON:
    WsidecoIL birth rcd #8,050
    COUSIN OF RONALD REAGAN

30.   ii. ELIZABETH MARY WILSON, b. December 15, 1895, Fulton, Whiteside co., IL; d. August 18, 1984, Estes Park, Larimer co., CO.
31.   iii. MARY MARGARET WILSON, b. December 19, 1897, Whiteside co., IL; d. February 17, 1985, Clinton, Iowa.
32.   iv. EARL CLYDE WILSON, b. November 16, 1902, Muscatine, IA; d. December 20, 1971, Rockford, Winnebago co., IL.
33.   v. LEO VERNON WILSON, SR., b. September 16, 1908, Chadwick, Whiteside co., IL; d. February 16, 1975, Key West, FL.
34.   vi. JOHN JAMES WILSON, b. May 25, 1905, Iowa; d. March 30, 1970, Freeport, Stephenson co., IL.
    vii. JEANETTE WILSON, b. April 22, 1910, Chadwick, Whiteside co., IL; d. August 20, 1925, Sterling, Whiteside co., IL.

    Notes for JEANETTE WILSON:
    'Explosion started fire with kerosene. Accidently burned to death. Home not destroyed' on death certificate.
    COUSIN OF RONALD REAGAN

14. SARA JANE[4] WILSON (*THOMAS[3], JOHN[2], ANDREW[1]*) was born June 16, 1871 in Clyde twp, Whiteside co., IL, and died March 08, 1920 in White Pigeon, Clyde twp, Whiteside Co., IL. She married (1) HORACE C. SMITH October 30, 1889 in Fulton, Whiteside co., IL, son of JACOB SMITH and MARTHA SIMONDS. He was born 1866 in Maquoketa, Iowa. She married (2) WALTER S. PIERCE January 20, 1904 in Morrison, Whiteside co., IL, son of NATHANIEL PIERCE and ESTHER HUGGETT. He was born January 03, 1865 in Wateska, WI, and died January 04, 1932 in Morrison, IL.

Notes for SARA JANE WILSON:
Place of death not known, but buried in Fulton.
Divorced 31 May 1897. Death certificate says birthdate is June 16, 1871, age at death 48 yrs., 8 mos. 22 days. Cause of death: cerebral hemorrhage.
AUNT OF RONALD REAGAN

More About SARA JANE WILSON:
Burial: Fulton cemetery. Fulton, IL

Notes for HORACE C. SMITH:
Wside co IL marriage record #7748
Divorced May 31, 1897. Holley is used in all legal documents.
Teamster at time of marriage to Sarah Jane. Marriage license gives Maquoketa.
Perhaps 'Horace'?
UNCLE OF RONALD REAGAN

Notes for WALTER S. PIERCE:
1900 Clyde twp., Whiteside co., IL census: William Pierce, farmer, Jan. 1865 WI IL En, Eliza wife Dec 1871, md , IL Can VT, Walter S. Pierce, twin brother, farmer Jan 1865 WI
1910 Clyde twp., Whiteside co., IL census: Walter Pierce, retail grocer, 44 WI En En, Jennie wf 3l8 IL md 6yrs., 5 children living, IL EN, Elsey dau. 5 IL, Vera dau 2 NE

More About WALTER S. PIERCE:
Burial: West Genesee cem, Coleta, IL

Children of SARA WILSON and HORACE SMITH are:
35. i. CHARLES ALFRED[5] SMITH, b. August 22, 1890, Fulton, Whiteside Co., IL; d. December 30, 1968, Sterling, Whiteside co., IL.
36. ii. HORACE VERNON SMITH, b. August 18, 1892, Fulton, Whiteside Co., IL; d. October 19, 1968, Walden, CO.
37. iii. HARRY WILSON SMITH, b. January 11, 1895, Fulton, Whiteside Co., IL; d. December 12, 1967, Morrison, IL.

Children of SARA WILSON and WALTER PIERCE are:
38. iv. ELSEY MAE[5] PIERCE, b. September 17, 1904, White Pigeon, Whiteside co., IL; d. November 30, 1993, Whiteside co, Clyde twp., IL.
39. v. VERA MARIE PIERCE, b. February 16, 1908, Tekamah, Burt, Nebraska; d. January 30, 1986, White Pigeon, Whiteside co., IL.
vi. MARIE MUNDT, b. November 04, 1911; d. September 27, 1978; Foster child; m. GEORGE ERNST.

Notes for MARIE MUNDT:
Foster daughter

15. GEORGE ORVILLE[4] WILSON (*THOMAS[3], JOHN[2], ANDREW[1]*) was born March 02, 1876 in Cordova, Whiteside co., IL, and died April 03, 1951 in Clinton, IA. He married NORA KLOSTERMAN August 03, 1904 in Lyons, Clinton co., IA. She was born 1882.

Notes for GEORGE ORVILLE WILSON:
UNCLE OF RONALD REAGAN

Notes for NORA KLOSTERMAN:
Age 22 at marriage, per certificate

Child of GEORGE WILSON and NORA KLOSTERMAN is:
i. GERTRUDE[5] WILSON, Adopted child; m. FRANCIS BURMEISTER, Clinton, Iowa.

Notes for GERTRUDE WILSON:
Adopted
COUSIN OF RONALD REAGAN

16. MARY LAVINA[4] WILSON (*THOMAS[3], JOHN[2], ANDREW[1]*) was born April 06, 1879 in Wside co., Clydetwp, IL, and died September 06, 1951 in Minneapolis, Hennepin co., MN. She married LOUIS HERMAN HUNT September 23, 1903 in Fulton, Whiteside co., IL, son of HERMAN HUNT and MINNIE SCHAUB. He was born October 1879 in Aurora, Adams co., IL.

Notes for MARY LAVINA WILSON:
WsidecoIL marriage record #11586 as Mary Lavina. Also on Social Security application of Donald.
AUNT OF RONALD REAGAN

More About MARY LAVINA WILSON:
Burial: Fulton, IL

Notes for LOUIS HERMAN HUNT:
Wside co., IL marriage record #11588
Name from Social Security application of Donald
1880 census shows him 8/12, taken June 1880
AUNT OF RONALD REAGAN

Child of MARY WILSON and LOUIS HUNT is:

      i.   DONALD WILSON[5] HUNT, b. March 30, 1909, Quincy, Adams co., IL; d. April 15, 1991, Los Angeles, CA; m. PAULINE CATHERINE BROOKS, June 18, 1944, Los Angeles, CA; b. 1911, New York, NY.

Notes for DONALD WILSON HUNT:
Final decree of divorce July 30, 1946.
He died intestate, widower, no children so the court ordered a genealogical search for heirs. The result:
A lengthy document to the Superior Court of the State of California, undated in this file, details the relationships of Donald Hunt and the shares to be alloted to the relatives. A genealogy chart is also appended. From this and related material I have entered the various people listed, supplementing genealogy previously shared with me by members of the families and research by me in various county records. Curt J. Gronner, DDS
Birth certificate, Adams co., IL. Ronald Reagan witnessed the wedding.
COUSIN OF RONALD REAGAN

More About DONALD WILSON HUNT:
Burial: Rosedale cemetery, Los Angeles, CA

Notes for PAULINE CATHERINE BROOKS:
Decree of divorce granted her 25 July 1945.

17. NELLIE CLYDE[4] WILSON *(THOMAS[3], JOHN[2], ANDREW[1])* was born July 24, 1883 in Fulton, Whiteside co., IL, and died July 25, 1962 in Santa Monica, Los Angeles co., CA. She married JOHN EDWARD REAGAN November 18, 1904 in Fulton, Whiteside Co., IL, son of JOHN REAGAN and JENNIE CUSICK. He was born July 13, 1883 in Fulton, Whiteside Co., IL, and died 1941.

Notes for NELLIE CLYDE WILSON:
Marriage date from WsidecoIL marriage rcd #11878

More About NELLIE CLYDE WILSON:
Burial: Calvary cemetery, Santa Monica, CA

Notes for JOHN EDWARD REAGAN:
    Lived with his aunt Margaret Reagan Baldwin after her marriage in 1895 at Buchanan, Iowa. Later Marguerite Chapman also came there after the death of her parents.
    Married in St. Emanuel's Catholic Church, Fulton. Marriage application says 'Jack', marriage certificate says 'John'.
    1910 Tampico twp., Whiteside co., IL census: John E. Reagan 26 IL En IL clerk in store, Nellie C. sife 26 IL IL En md 5 yrs. 1 ch living, Neal son 1 IL.

Children of NELLIE WILSON and JOHN REAGAN are:
      i.   JOHN NEIL[5] REAGAN, b. September 16, 1908, Tampico, Wside Co., IL; d. California; m. RUTH HOFFMAN, August 31, 1935, Adel, Dallas Co., IA; b. February 23, 1908, Des Moines, Polk Co., Iowa.

Notes for JOHN NEIL REAGAN:
They have no children.

40.   ii.   RONALD WILSON REAGAN, b. February 06, 1911, Tampico, Wside Co., IL.

18. MARGARET MAY[4] WILSON *(JOHN[3], JOHN[2], ANDREW[1])* was born June 10, 1883 in Whiteside co., IL. She married GLENN OTTO WHISTLER October 06, 1908 in WHiteside co., IL. He died June 15, 1962 in Sterling, Whiteside co., IL.

Notes for MARGARET MAY WILSON:
Wside co., IL birth record #4,043, as Maggie May.

Notes for GLENN OTTO WHISTLER:
WsidecoIL marriage record #12,899.
Bd. Lot 7M

More About GLENN OTTO WHISTLER:
Burial: Grove Hill, Morrison, IL

Children of MARGARET WILSON and GLENN WHISTLER are:
41.   i. LOIS W.[5] WHISTLER.
42.   ii. FLORENCE I. WHISTLER, b. 1912; d. Peoria, IL.

19. PAUL FLETCHER[4] WILSON *(ALEXANDER B[3], JOHN[2], ANDREW[1])* was born January 1883 in Whiteside co., IL, and died 1964. He married ETTA MAY BRISTLE October 11, 1905 in Whiteside co., IL, daughter of JOHN BRISTLE and ADDIE BODY. She was born November 27, 1883, and died May 14, 1956 in Morrison, IL.

Notes for PAUL FLETCHER WILSON:
Heritage Quest gives his connection. 1920 WsidecoUGrovetwpIL cen186/186 gives age 36, IL IL NY, farmer. His father, Alexander is with them, age 65, IL Sc Sc
1910 WsidecoUGrtwpIL census 60/63, Age 27, IL NY NY, wife May 26 IL IL IL, father Alex 67 Widower NY NY NY 'own income'.
Xerox of Sentinel, Oct. 12, 1905.

Notes for ETTA MAY BRISTLE:
1900 WsidecoIL census277, age 16, as Mary, IL IL IL
1910 WsidecoUGrIL census 60/63, age 26, IL IL IL
WsidecoIL birth certificate #4,020, mother as Addie F. Boda
Whiteside co., IL marriage record #2117.0.

More About ETTA MAY BRISTLE:
Burial: Grove Hill cemetery, Morrison

Children of PAUL WILSON and ETTA BRISTLE are:
43.   i. DWIGHT ALVIN[5] WILSON, b. January 24, 1914; d. December 05, 1993, Sterling, Whiteside co., IL.
44.   ii. ROBERT BRISTLE WILSON, b. September 12, 1917; d. May 07, 1942.

20. CLIFFORD LEROY[4] GSELL *(MARGARET MAE[3] WILSON, JOHN[2], ANDREW[1])* was born November 17, 1880 in Whiteside co, Clyde twp., IL, and died August 11, 1951 in Clinton, Iowa. He married EDNA JULIA HAMMER. She was born 1890, and died 1981.

Notes for CLIFFORD LEROY GSELL:
WsidecoIL birth record #1,859, as 'boy'.
Buried lot 31HE

More About CLIFFORD LEROY GSELL:
Burial: Grove Hill cemetery, Morrison

Children of CLIFFORD GSELL and EDNA HAMMER are:
45.   i. CLAIR LE ROY[5] GSELL, b. December 30, 1918.
      ii. HOWARD WILSON GSELL, b. June 23, 1920.

21. MAUDE MAE[4] GSELL *(MARGARET MAE[3] WILSON, JOHN[2], ANDREW[1])* was born November 18, 1884 in WsidClytwpIL, and died August 26, 1966 in Fulton, IL. She married WALTER RICHARD MILNES January 16, 1902 in Whiteside co., IL. He was born July 29, 1877, and died March 05, 1953.

Notes for MAUDE MAE GSELL:
WsidecoIL birth record #3,547 as Maude Mae. Whiteside co., IL marriage record #11,091. Died at Harbor Crest, Fulton. Buried Lot 22W.

More About MAUDE MAE GSELL:
Burial: Grove Hill cemetery, Morrison

Children of MAUDE GSELL and WALTER MILNES are:
46. i. LEPHA MAE⁵ MILNES, b. April 22, 1903; d. November 30, 1963.
47. ii. MARGARET ELIZABETH MILNES, b. June 07, 1913.
48. iii. WALTER MILNES, b. June 17, 1919.

22. ESTELLA JANE⁴ GSELL *(MARGARET MAE³ WILSON, JOHN², ANDREW¹)* was born May 27, 1894 in Whiteside co, Clyde twp., IL. She married WILLIAM STAPLETON.

Notes for ESTELLA JANE GSELL:
WsidecoIL birth record #8,060 as Estella Jane.
Day of birth from Carroll

Children of ESTELLA GSELL and WILLIAM STAPLETON are:
49. i. GLADYS ELOISE⁵ STAPLETON.
     ii. GLEN STAPLETON.

>   Notes for GLEN STAPLETON:
>   Died at birth

23. ALICE JANE⁴ WILSON *(CHARLES DESMOND³, JOHN², ANDREW¹)* was born April 15, 1897, and died July 05, 1952. She married JAMES WARNER.

Child of ALICE WILSON and JAMES WARNER is:
50. i. ROBERT WILSON⁵ WARNER.

24. PHOEBE MAE⁴ WILSON *(CHARLES DESMOND³, JOHN², ANDREW¹)* was born May 10, 1899, and died May 10, 1960. She married LLOYD HERROLD.

Notes for LLOYD HERROLD:
Probably another son, also

Children of PHOEBE WILSON and LLOYD HERROLD are:
  i. EDITH⁵ HERROLD.
  ii. LLOYD WILSON HERROLD.

25. WINIFRED M.⁴ WILSON *(CHARLES DESMOND³, JOHN², ANDREW¹)* was born September 15, 1901. She married CLARENCE FLACK.

Children of WINIFRED WILSON and CLARENCE FLACK are:
51. i. THOMAS OLIVER⁵ FLACK, d. 1981.
52. ii. TIMOTHY CONRAD FLACK.

Generation No. 5

26. WILLIAM DETER⁵ BECHTEL *(JOHN WILSON⁴, SARA³ WILSON, JOHN², ANDREW¹)* was born March 11, 1891 in Wside co., Clydetwp, IL. He married WINNIE MILNES, daughter of FRANK MILNES and MINNIE PAPE. She was born 1894 in ILL..

Notes for WILLIAM DETER BECHTEL:
WsidecoIL birth record #6,845.
1910 WsidecoIL cen 49, age 19, IL IL PA. Farm laborer

1920 WsidecoUsttwpIL census 152/156, age 29 farmer, IL IL PA, Winnie F 26 md wife IL IL IL, Lucille f 5 S cau IL IL IL, Everett M 1 S son IL IL IL.   [This does not agree with earlier records, perhaps Everett (1) died, another new son was named Everett)
SECOND COUSIN OF RONALD REAGAN

Notes for WINNIE MILNES:
1920 WsideUsttwpcoIL cen156, age 24, wife, IL IL IL

Children of WILLIAM BECHTEL and WINNIE MILNES are:
53.   i.   EVERETT[6] BECHTEL, b. 1905, ILL..
54.   ii.   LUCILLE FERN BECHTEL, b. March 09, 1914, Whiteside co., IL.
55.   iii.   GLENN BECHTEL.

27. IVY MAY[5] BECHTEL *(JOHN WILSON[4], SARA[3] WILSON, JOHN[2], ANDREW[1])* was born May 1898. She married WILLIAM LANE.

Notes for IVY MAY BECHTEL:
1910 WsidecoIL cen 49, age 12, farm laborer
SECOND COUSIN OF RONALD REAGAN

Children of IVY BECHTEL and WILLIAM LANE are:
    i.   MILDRED[6] LANE.
    ii.   DOROTHY ANN LANE.
    iii.   WILLIAM LANE.

28. EPHRAIM LAWRENCE[5] GERDES *(ELLEN W.[4] BECHTEL, SARA[3] WILSON, JOHN[2], ANDREW[1])* was born October 11, 1888 in Wside co., Clydetwp, IL.

Notes for EPHRAIM LAWRENCE GERDES:
WsidecoIL birth #5,888.   Married, 2 boys, lived near Dixon.

Child of EPHRAIM LAWRENCE GERDES is:
    i.   WAYNE[6] GERDES, b. 1904.

    Notes for WAYNE GERDES:
    Living in Dixon in 1998 at 94, not married

29. GALEN GLENN[5] GERDES *(ELLEN W.[4] BECHTEL, SARA[3] WILSON, JOHN[2], ANDREW[1])* was born January 1894 in Wside co., Clydetwp, IL, and died September 01, 1976 in N. Manchester, IN. He married (1) IDA FIKE September 02, 1923. She died September 12, 1923. He married (2) MARETA SHRIDER August 05, 1951.

Notes for GALEN GLENN GERDES:
Children per obituary
Minister, retired.

More About GALEN GLENN GERDES:
Burial: Yellow Creek Cemetery, Pearl City

Children of GALEN GERDES and MARETA SHRIDER are:
    i.   ROBERT[6] GERDES.
    ii.   RUTH GERDES.

30. ELIZABETH MARY[5] WILSON *(JOHN CHARLES[4], THOMAS[3], JOHN[2], ANDREW[1])* was born December 15, 1895 in Fulton, Whiteside co., IL, and died August 18, 1984 in Estes Park, Larimer co., CO.

She married RAYMOND JAMES DILLON August 24, 1918 in Chicago, Cook co., ILL. He was born 1898 in Iowa, and died in Chicago, Cook co., IL.

Notes for ELIZABETH MARY WILSON:
Whiteside co., IL birth certificate #101765, #8,416
Death certificate, Hunt material, Wiebenga
COUSIN OF RONALD REAGAN

Notes for RAYMOND JAMES DILLON:
Birth date from birth certificate of child, Katherine
Brakeman , birth cert. 2nd child.
Raymond W. on marriage certificate
COUSIN OF RONALD REAGAN

Children of ELIZABETH WILSON and RAYMOND DILLON are:

    i. MARGARET ELIZA[6] DILLON, b. December 28, 1918, Chicago, Cook co., IL; m. CONANT.

        Notes for MARGARET ELIZA DILLON:
        Twin of Raymond
        COUSIN ONCE REMOVED OF RONALD REAGAN

    ii. RAYMOND JAMES DILLON, b. December 26, 1918, Chicago, Cook co., IL; d. May 15, 1942, Denmark.

        Notes for RAYMOND JAMES DILLON:
        Twin of Margaret, killed in action18 May 1942 while serving on overseas air operations with 408 (RCAF) Squadron. Buried in Vaerlose Churchyard,, Vaerlose, Denmark. From Wiebenga material, Hunt descendants.
        COUSIN ONCE REMOVED OF RONALD REAGAN

        More About RAYMOND JAMES DILLON:
        Burial: Vearlose Churchyard, Vearlose, Denmark

    iii. KATHERINE ANNABELLE DILLON, b. July 03, 1924, Chicago, Cook co., IL.

        Notes for KATHERINE ANNABELLE DILLON:
        COUSIN ONCE REMOVED OF RONALD REAGAN

56.   iv. JOHN CHARLES DILLON, b. October 14, 1921, Clinton, ILL; d. December 21, 1963, Rockford, Winnebago co., IL.

31. MARY MARGARET[5] WILSON *(JOHN CHARLES[4], THOMAS[3], JOHN[2], ANDREW[1])* was born December 19, 1897 in Whiteside co., IL, and died February 17, 1985 in Clinton, Iowa. She married HARRY JOHN HICKS. He was born 1892 in Morrison, IL, and died Bef. 1985.

Notes for MARY MARGARET WILSON:
WsidecoIL birth rcd #8,769
Death certificate, Clinton co., Iowa, bk 3-7-85, p. 3.
Widowed at time of death
COUSIN OF RONALD REAGAN

More About MARY MARGARET WILSON:
Burial: Grove Hill cemetery, Morrison

Notes for HARRY JOHN HICKS:
Birth certificate shows him as salesman

Children of MARY WILSON and HARRY HICKS are:
    i. EARL CLYDE[6] HICKS, b. September 15, 1929, Freeport, Stephenson co., IL.

        Notes for EARL CLYDE HICKS:

COUSIN, ONCE REMOVED, OF RONALD REAGAN

57. ii. KATHERINE JANE HICKS, b. January 09, 1917, Garden Plain Twp., Whiteside co., IL; d. November 05, 1986, Garden Plain Twp., Whiteside co., IL.
  iii. HARRIET HICKS.

Notes for HARRIET HICKS:
COUSIN ONCE REMOVED OF REAGAN REAGAN

32. EARL CLYDE[5] WILSON *(JOHN CHARLES[4], THOMAS[3], JOHN[2], ANDREW[1])* was born November 16, 1902 in Muscatine, IA, and died December 20, 1971 in Rockford, Winnebago co., IL. He married HELEN MARIE NELSON November 03, 1923 in Crown Point, Lake co., IN, daughter of ELMER NELSON and EDITH JOHANNSEN. She was born December 26, 1904 in Clinton, Clinton co., IA.

Notes for EARL CLYDE WILSON:
Birth certificate gives birth 1902, marriage certificate gives 1901.
Widowed
COUSIN OF RONALD REAGAN

More About EARL CLYDE WILSON:
Burial: Dakota cemetery, Dakota, IL

Children of EARL WILSON and HELEN NELSON are:
 i. EARL CHARLES[6] WILSON, b. February 10, 1925, Chicago, Cook co., IL.

  Notes for EARL CHARLES WILSON:
  COUSIN ONCE REMOVED OF RONALD REAGAN

 ii. JANET MAE WILSON, b. September 29, 1931, Chicago, Cook co., IL; m. (1) 'MALE' WITZ, Bef. 1969; m. (2) DONALD LEROY JOHNSON, July 25, 1970, Rockford, Winnebago co., IL; b. 1937.

  Notes for JANET MAE WILSON:
  Name correction of birth certificate dated 21 April 1976 by Janet.
  Janet md. previous to Johnson marriage, a Witz.
  COUSIN ONCE REMOVED OF RONALD REAGAN

 iii. VAUGHN FAE WILSON, b. November 24, 1936, Freeport, Stephenson co., IL; m. EUGENE UFKEN, November 19, 1955, Dubuque, Dubuque co., IA; b. August 05, 1921, Huron, SD.

  Notes for VAUGHN FAE WILSON:
  COUSIN ONCE REMOVED OF RONALD REAGAN

 iv. RONALD STANLEY WILSON, b. March 30, 1942, Freeport, Stephenson co., IL.

  Notes for RONALD STANLEY WILSON:
  COUSIN ONCE REMOVED OF RONALD REAGAN

33. LEO VERNON[5] WILSON, SR. *(JOHN CHARLES[4], THOMAS[3], JOHN[2], ANDREW[1])* was born September 16, 1908 in Chadwick, Whiteside co., IL, and died February 16, 1975 in Key West, FL. He married (1) THELMA LILLIAN KEITH, daughter of HERBERT KEITH and JULIA KRAMER. She was born 1911 in Freeport, Stephenson co., IL. He married (2) IONA MAE HOWARD. She was born 1916 in Sheldon Grove, IL. He married (3) IONA JEAN THOMAS February 08, 1957 in Quincy, Adams co., ILL, daughter of CHARLES THOMAS and EMMA MELVIN. She was born 1934 in Kellysville, WV.

Notes for LEO VERNON WILSON, SR.:
His first marriage to Iona Howard??
Business man, Sterling, ILL at time of marriage to Norma jean, age 49, his 3rd marriage. He

owned 'Recreation Vehicles Agency' at time of death.
Owned 'Lunch Room' Sterling when Marc was born.
At the time of Marilyn's birth, 1931, he lived at Marion, OH, Thelma at Freeport.
1930 lived at Freeport, ILL
Chadwick birth place from Linda Kay birth certificate
COUSIN OF RONALD REAGAN

More About LEO VERNON WILSON, SR.:
Burial: Oak Knoll cemetery, Sterling, IL

Notes for IONA JEAN THOMAS:
Marriage to Wilson, her first

Children of LEO WILSON and THELMA KEITH are:
    i. JAMES KEITH[6] WILSON, b. January 30, 1938, Galesburg, ILL.

        Notes for JAMES KEITH WILSON:
        Birth certificate #29769, V. 1938, Knox co., IL

    ii. MARILYN JOAN WILSON, b. September 24, 1941, Freeport, Stephenson co., IL; d. December 17, 1951, Beloit, Rock co., IL.

        Notes for MARILYN JOAN WILSON:
        Died in an auto accident

    iii. NAOMI JEAN WILSON, b. February 12, 1930, Freeport, Stephenson co., IL; m. JAMES A CAPONE, September 19, 1954, Freeport, Stephenson co., IL; b. 1921.

Children of LEO WILSON and IONA HOWARD are:
    iv. JEANNETTE LYNN[6] WILSON, b. August 03, 1938, Galesburg, Knox co., ILL; m. JAMES H. PIERCE, October 05, 1956, Rock Falls, Whiteside co., IL; b. 1935, Sterling, Whiteside co., IL.

        Notes for JEANNETTE LYNN WILSON:
        Age 19 at marriage to James Pierce
        Birth certificate, Knox co., IL #40686, V. 1944

        Notes for JAMES H. PIERCE:
        Laborer, Prince Castle Manufactury

    v. TRUDY JEAN WILSON, b. May 18, 1945, Sterling, Whiteside co., IL; m. (1) RANDY GALE GALLENTINE; b. September 06, 1947, Morrison, IL; m. (2) 'MALE' STEVENS.
    vi. LINDA KAY WILSON, b. June 20, 1947, Sterling, Whiteside co., IL; m. (1) 'MALE' TUCKER; m. (2) JAMES JERRY VAN HORN, October 04, 1974, Sterling, Whiteside co., IL; b. 1946, Sterling, Whiteside co., IL; m. (3) DANIEL JOSEPH RYAN, December 18, 1982, Sterling, Whiteside co., IL; b. 1944.

        Notes for LINDA KAY WILSON:
        COUSIN ONCE REMOVED OF RONALD REAGAN

        Notes for DANIEL JOSEPH RYAN:
        Lived at Erie , IL at time of marriage to Linda Kay

    vii. KATHY ELIZABETH WILSON, b. February 24, 1949, Sterling, Whiteside co., IL; m. GAIL A. JELLERICHS, March 28, 1970, Sterling, Whiteside co., IL; b. February 18, 1949, Sterling, Whiteside co., IL.

        Notes for KATHY ELIZABETH WILSON:
        COUSIN ONCE REMOVED OF RONALD REAGAN

        Notes for GAIL A. JELLERICHS:
        In military service when married to Kathy

viii. GLENDA JOYCE WILSON, b. September 23, 1957, Sterling, Whiteside co., IL; m. MICHAEL GRANT GIBSON, August 28, 1978, Sterling, Whiteside co., IL; b. September 17, 1957, Sterling, Whiteside co., IL.

    Notes for GLENDA JOYCE WILSON:
    Married at First Christian Church, Sterling, IL
    COUSIN ONCE REMOVED OF RONALD REAGAN

Children of LEO WILSON and IONA THOMAS are:
ix. MARC LEE[6] WILSON, b. October 12, 1940, Sterling, Whiteside co., IL.

    Notes for MARC LEE WILSON:
    COUSIN ONCE REMOVED OF RONALD REAGAN

x. KIMBERLY ANN WILSON, b. April 05, 1960, Sterling, Whiteside co., IL; m. MATHEW LEE SMITH, August 04, 1979, Rock Falls, Whiteside co., IL; b. February 03, 1960, ILL.

xi. JODY ALLEN WILSON, b. January 24, 1967, Sterling, Whiteside co., IL.

34. JOHN JAMES[5] WILSON (*JOHN CHARLES[4], THOMAS[3], JOHN[2], ANDREW[1]*) was born May 25, 1905 in Iowa, and died March 30, 1970 in Freeport, Stephenson co., IL. He married MARGIE HOMERDING February 04, 1928 in Chicago, Cook co., ILL.

Notes for JOHN JAMES WILSON:
COUSIN OF RONALD REAGAN

More About JOHN JAMES WILSON:
Burial: Calvary cemetery, Freeport, IL

Children of JOHN WILSON and MARGIE HOMERDING are:
i. MARIE[6] WILSON.

    Notes for MARIE WILSON:
    Signed Father's death certificate, more of signature is unreadable.
    COUSIN ONCE REMOVED OF RONALD REAGAN

58. ii. JOHN CHARLES WILSON, JR, b. December 14, 1928, IL; d. October 30, 1983, Mesa, Maricopa co., AZ.

35. CHARLES ALFRED[5] SMITH (*SARA JANE[4] WILSON, THOMAS[3], JOHN[2], ANDREW[1]*) was born August 22, 1890 in Fulton, Whiteside Co., IL, and died December 30, 1968 in Sterling, Whiteside co., IL. He married MABEL MAY SWEIGERT June 26, 1912 in Sterling, Whiteside co., IL, daughter of MILTON SWEIGERT and EVELYN REES. She was born September 18, 1888 in Elroy, Stephenson co., IL, and died February 17, 1972 in Rock Falls, Whiteside co., IL.

Notes for CHARLES ALFRED SMITH:
Retired in 1959 as Manager of Johnston Lumber co., Rock Falls after 50 years of service.
COUSIN OF RONALD REAGAN

More About CHARLES ALFRED SMITH:
Burial: January 02, 1969, Oak Knoll cemetery, Sterling, IL

Notes for MABEL MAY SWEIGERT:
WsidecoIL marriage record # 139760.0

More About MABEL MAY SWEIGERT:
Burial: Oak Knoll cemetery, Sterling, IL

Children of CHARLES SMITH and MABEL SWEIGERT are:

59.	i.	MILFORD L.⁶ SMITH, b. February 21, 1916, Rock Falls, Whiteside co., IL; d. October 29, 1980, Sterling, Whiteside co., IL.
60.	ii.	RAYMOND SMITH, b. February 07, 1918, Sterling, Whiteside co., IL; d. March 07, 1997.

36. HORACE VERNON⁵ SMITH *(SARA JANE⁴ WILSON, THOMAS³, JOHN², ANDREW¹)* was born August 18, 1892 in Fulton, Whiteside Co., IL, and died October 19, 1968 in Walden, CO. He married DOSSIE MAY MEAKINS February 20, 1915 in Morrison, IL. She was born July 17, 1890 in Coleta, Whiteside co., IL, and died December 03, 1972.

Notes for HORACE VERNON SMITH:
WsidecolL birth record #7,422,   Supt. of Public Aid Department, Whiteside co..
COUSIN OF RONALD REAGAN

More About HORACE VERNON SMITH:
Burial: Grove Hill cemetery, Morrison

Notes for DOSSIE MAY MEAKINS:
School teacher

More About DOSSIE MAY MEAKINS:
Burial: Grove Hill cemetery, Morrison

Children of HORACE SMITH and DOSSIE MEAKINS are:

61.	i.	ROBERT CLARE⁶ SMITH, b. November 05, 1917, Sterling, Whiteside co., IL.
62.	ii.	GENE MEAKIN SMITH, b. March 27, 1922, Sterling, Whiteside co., IL; d. July 09, 1995.

37. HARRY WILSON⁵ SMITH *(SARA JANE⁴ WILSON, THOMAS³, JOHN², ANDREW¹)* was born January 11, 1895 in Fulton, Whiteside Co., IL, and died December 12, 1967 in Morrison, IL. He married HULDA PHILENA GOFF January 26, 1916 in Fulton, Whiteside co., IL, daughter of LYMAN GOFF and DELLA BULL. She was born April 20, 1893, and died December 14, 1974.

Notes for HARRY WILSON SMITH:
Owned auto body and paint shop
At time of marriage, lived at Ashton, IL, railroad employee. In 1922 he lived at Elmhurst, II and was a signal maintainer, C&NW Ry..
COUSIN OF RONALD REAGAN

More About HARRY WILSON SMITH:
Burial: Grove Hill cemetery, Morrison

More About HULDA PHILENA GOFF:
Burial: Grove Hill cemetery, Morrison

Child of HARRY SMITH and HULDA GOFF is:

63.	i.	HARRY WILSON⁶ SMITH, JR, b. January 20, 1922, Oak Park, Cook co., IL.

38. ELSEY MAE⁵ PIERCE *(SARA JANE⁴ WILSON, THOMAS³, JOHN², ANDREW¹)* was born September 17, 1904 in White Pigeon, Whiteside co., IL, and died November 30, 1993 in Whiteside co, Clyde twp., IL. She married CARL B. WALTERS May 20, 1925 in Jordan, Whiteside co., IL. He was born October 22, 1901 in White Pigeon, Whiteside co., IL, and died August 07, 1987.

Notes for ELSEY MAE PIERCE:
Birth certificate says '4th child of this mother'. Vicky Wiebenga / Hunt material, 3 half brothers from Mother's Smith marriage.
She provided much of the information to the Heritage Quest author, Michael F. Pollock.

More About ELSEY MAE PIERCE:
Burial: West Genesee cem., Whiteside co.

More About CARL B. WALTERS:
Burial: West Genesee cem, Coleta, IL

Child of ELSEY PIERCE and CARL WALTERS is:
64.   i.   HAROLD EDWARD[6] WALTERS, b. December 02, 1925, White Pigeon, Whiteside co., IL; d. February 19, 1988, Morrison, IL.

39. VERA MARIE[5] PIERCE *(SARA JANE[4] WILSON, THOMAS[3], JOHN[2], ANDREW[1])* was born February 16, 1908 in Tekamah, Burt, Nebraska, and died January 30, 1986 in White Pigeon, Whiteside co., IL. She married REINHARD F. HABBEN April 03, 1933 in Somonauk, DeKalb co., IL, son of EILT HABBEN and MARIE HOLMRICK. He was born April 30, 1902 in Frisia, nr. Bremerhaven, Germany, and died March 22, 1980 in Morrison, IL.

Notes for VERA MARIE PIERCE:
Married at St. Johns Lutheran Church, Somonauk, IL.
COUSIN OF RONALD REAGAN

More About VERA MARIE PIERCE:
Burial: West Genesee cem, Coleta, IL

Notes for REINHARD F. HABBEN:
Became a US citizen 9 Oct. 1931, Chicago, IL.

More About REINHARD F. HABBEN:
Burial: West Genesee cem, Coleta, IL

Children of VERA PIERCE and REINHARD HABBEN are:
65.   i.   MERNA JOY[6] HABBEN, b. October 12, 1933, Coleta, Whiteside co., IL.
66.   ii.   NORMAN WALTER HABBEN, b. September 10, 1935, Coleta, Whiteside co., IL.
67.   iii.   RONALD LEE HABBEN, b. July 17, 1938, Coleta, Whiteside co., IL.
68.   iv.   MILFORD GENE HABBEN, b. July 04, 1940, Coleta, Whiteside co., IL.
69.   v.   VELMA JANE HABBEN, b. April 10, 1943, Morrison, IL.
70.   vi.   JUDITH MAY HABBEN, b. April 28, 1946, Morrison, IL.
71.   vii.   CAROL ANN HABBEN, b. June 04, 1948, Morrison, IL.
72.   viii.   BEVERLY JOAN HABBEN, b. July 10, 1952, Morrison, IL.
73.   ix.   DONNA ELAINE HABBEN, b. August 04, 1954, Morrison, IL.

40. RONALD WILSON[5] REAGAN *(NELLIE CLYDE[4] WILSON, THOMAS[3], JOHN[2], ANDREW[1])* was born February 06, 1911 in Tampico, Wside Co., IL. He married (1) SARA JANE FULKS January 16, 1940 in Glendale, CA. She was born January 04, 1914 in St. Joseph, MO. He married (2) ANNE FRANCES ROBBINS March 04, 1952 in North Hollywood, CA, daughter of KENNETH ROBBINS and EDITH LUCKETT. She was born July 06, 1923 in New York, NY.

Notes for RONALD WILSON REAGAN:
    They were divorced June 28, 1948. Michael was adopted. A daughter died in infancy.
    During his 1981 visit to Scotland, Reagan became an Honorary Keeper of the Keepers of the Quaich, a society of connoisseurs of Scotch whiskey. He was unaware of his relationship to Johnnie Blue, the last moonshine distiller on the Scottish peninsula of Kintyre. From the Chicago Tribune of Oct 21, 1981. This article also gives Claudio Wilson, a weaver [whom see] and Peggy Downey [Downie] whom he married in 1807 as the parents of John Wilson, grandparents of Thomas. Claudio married a second time. [see Claudio 1787]

Notes for SARA JANE FULKS:
Also known as Jane Durrell and Jane Wyman

Notes for ANNE FRANCES ROBBINS:
Her legal name was 'Nancy Davis' through adoption.

Children of RONALD REAGAN and SARA FULKS are:
       i. MAUREEN ELIZABETH[6] REAGAN, b. January 04, 1941, Los Angeles, CA.
74.   ii. MICHAEL REAGAN, b. March 18, 1945.

Children of RONALD REAGAN and ANNE ROBBINS are:
       iii. PATRICIA[6] REAGAN, b. October 21, 1952.
       iv. RONALD PRESCOTT REAGAN, b. May 20, 1958; m. DORIA PALMIER, November 24, 1980.

41. LOIS W.[5] WHISTLER *(MARGARET MAY[4] WILSON, JOHN[3], JOHN[2], ANDREW[1])* She married WHITFORD MITCHELL.

Children of LOIS WHISTLER and WHITFORD MITCHELL are:
75.   i. MARTHA ANN[6] MITCHELL.
76.   ii. JOHN WILSON MITCHELL.
77.   iii. JANE WHITFORD MITCHELL.

42. FLORENCE I.[5] WHISTLER *(MARGARET MAY[4] WILSON, JOHN[3], JOHN[2], ANDREW[1])* was born 1912, and died in Peoria, IL. She married GEORGE L. MARR. He died in Peoria, IL.

Children of FLORENCE WHISTLER and GEORGE MARR are:
78.   i. BARBARA[6] MARR.
       ii. GEORGE MICHAEL MARR.

43. DWIGHT ALVIN[5] WILSON *(PAUL FLETCHER[4], ALEXANDER B[3], JOHN[2], ANDREW[1])* was born January 24, 1914, and died December 05, 1993 in Sterling, Whiteside co., IL. He married JANICE LUCILLE MATHEW December 25, 1937 in Sterling, Whiteside co., IL. She was born November 30, 1917.

Notes for DWIGHT ALVIN WILSON:
WsidecoUGtwpIL census 186
WsidecoIL birth record #17,965
Retired from 1st National Bank, Sterling, Jan. 1, 1978.

More About DWIGHT ALVIN WILSON:
Burial: Grove Hill cemetery, Morrison

Children of DWIGHT WILSON and JANICE MATHEW are:
79.   i. JUDITH SUZANE[6] WILSON, b. November 21, 1942.
80.   ii. ROBERT THOMAS WILSON, b. June 29, 1944.

44. ROBERT BRISTLE[5] WILSON *(PAUL FLETCHER[4], ALEXANDER B[3], JOHN[2], ANDREW[1])* was born September 12, 1917, and died May 07, 1942. He married MAXINE JOY BARRETT March 22, 1940, daughter of HARVEY BARRETT and EDNA LAWTON. She was born August 01, 1920, and died April 11, 1997 in Cedar Rapids, Iowa.

More About ROBERT BRISTLE WILSON:
Burial: Grove Hill cemetery, Morrison

Child of ROBERT WILSON and MAXINE BARRETT is:
81.   i. DEBORAH ANN[6] WILSON, b. February 09, 1941.

45. CLAIR LE ROY[5] GSELL *(CLIFFORD LEROY[4], MARGARET MAE[3] WILSON, JOHN[2], ANDREW[1])* was born December 30, 1918. He married MARY WATSON.

Children of CLAIR GSELL and MARY WATSON are:
- 82.   i.   STEVEN ALLEN[6] GSELL, b. April 24, 1939.
-       ii. RICHARD LEE GSELL, b. December 17, 1945; m. SHIRLEY MANNING.
- 83.   iii. SUE ELLEN GSELL, b. September 25, 1955.

46. LEPHA MAE[5] MILNES *(MAUDE MAE[4] GSELL, MARGARET MAE[3] WILSON, JOHN[2], ANDREW[1])* was born April 22, 1903, and died November 30, 1963. She married ANDREW F. WITT. He was born December 16, 1898.

Children of LEPHA MILNES and ANDREW WITT are:
- 84.   i.   DONNA JEAN[6] WITT, b. April 09, 1933.
-       ii. MAJOR SANDRA MAE WITT, b. April 13, 1938.

  Notes for MAJOR SANDRA MAE WITT:
  Major

- 85.   iii. DR. HARLAN ANDREW WITT, b. April 27, 1946.

47. MARGARET ELIZABETH[5] MILNES *(MAUDE MAE[4] GSELL, MARGARET MAE[3] WILSON, JOHN[2], ANDREW[1])* was born June 07, 1913. She married IVAN RALPH CARROLL. He was born October 12, 1907, and died June 25, 1950.

Children of MARGARET MILNES and IVAN CARROLL are:
- 86.   i.   DAVID IVAN[6] CARROLL, b. January 02, 1938.
- 87.   ii. TERRY DEE CARROLL, b. January 03, 1946.

48. WALTER[5] MILNES *(MAUDE MAE[4] GSELL, MARGARET MAE[3] WILSON, JOHN[2], ANDREW[1])* was born June 17, 1919. He married BEULAH VEY NAFTZGER. She was born July 03, 1918.

Children of WALTER MILNES and BEULAH NAFTZGER are:
-       i.   WANDA VEY[6] MILNES, b. December 29, 1943.

  Notes for WANDA VEY MILNES:
  Never married.

- 88.   ii. DIANE LOUISE MILNES, b. September 04, 1945.
- 89.   iii. THOMAS BRENT MILNES, b. September 01, 1950.

49. GLADYS ELOISE[5] STAPLETON *(ESTELLA JANE[4] GSELL, MARGARET MAE[3] WILSON, JOHN[2], ANDREW[1])* She married ERNEST VOS.

Children of GLADYS STAPLETON and ERNEST VOS are:
- 90.   i.   ARLYN[6] VOS, b. May 03, 1940.
- 91.   ii. LARRY VOS.
-       iii. LAURI ANN VOS, m. ROBIN N. GOLDSMITH.

50. ROBERT WILSON[5] WARNER *(ALICE JANE[4] WILSON, CHARLES DESMOND[3], JOHN[2], ANDREW[1])*

Children of ROBERT WILSON WARNER are:
-       i.   JAMES[6] WARNER.
-       ii. CATHERINE WARNER.

51. THOMAS OLIVER[5] FLACK *(WINIFRED M.[4] WILSON, CHARLES DESMOND[3], JOHN[2], ANDREW[1])* died 1981.

Child of THOMAS OLIVER FLACK is:
  i. PAMELA[6] FLACK.

52. TIMOTHY CONRAD[5] FLACK *(WINIFRED M.[4] WILSON, CHARLES DESMOND[3], JOHN[2], ANDREW[1])*

Children of TIMOTHY CONRAD FLACK are:
  i. KATHRYN[6] FLACK.
  ii. WILLIAM C. FLACK.

Generation No. 6

53. EVERETT[6] BECHTEL *(WILLIAM DETER[5], JOHN WILSON[4], SARA[3] WILSON, JOHN[2], ANDREW[1])* was born 1905 in ILL.. He married CARLENE MCKEE.

Notes for EVERETT BECHTEL:
1920 WsidecolL cen 156 Ustick

Children of EVERETT BECHTEL and CARLENE MCKEE are:
  i. GARY[7] BECHTEL, m. PATRICIA WIERSEMA.
  ii. BONNIE BECHTEL, m. DOUGLAS BUSH.

54. LUCILLE FERN[6] BECHTEL *(WILLIAM DETER[5], JOHN WILSON[4], SARA[3] WILSON, JOHN[2], ANDREW[1])* was born March 09, 1914 in Whiteside co., IL. She married LYLE NICE.

Notes for LUCILLE FERN BECHTEL:
WsidecolL birth record # 17,783.
SECOND COUSIN ONCE REMOVED OF RONALD REAGAN

Children of LUCILLE BECHTEL and LYLE NICE are:
92.   i. ELWIN[7] NICE.
93.   ii. MARJORIE NICE.

55. GLENN[6] BECHTEL *(WILLIAM DETER[5], JOHN WILSON[4], SARA[3] WILSON, JOHN[2], ANDREW[1])* He married RHEA GREEN.

Children of GLENN BECHTEL and RHEA GREEN are:
  i. GLENDA[7] BECHTEL, m. DARREL NICKE.
  ii. ELLEN BECHTEL, m. GREG PESSMAN.
  iii. SCOTT BECHTEL, m. SANDRA WALTERS.
  iv. CAROL BECHTEL, m. JOSEPH HIGH, July 17, 1876, Whiteside co., IL.

   Notes for CAROL BECHTEL:
   Whiteside co., IL marriage record #4216.

56. JOHN CHARLES[6] DILLON *(ELIZABETH MARY[5] WILSON, JOHN CHARLES[4], THOMAS[3], JOHN[2], ANDREW[1])* was born October 14, 1921 in Clinton, ILL, and died December 21, 1963 in Rockford, Winnebago co., IL. He married AMY ADELE ANDERSON July 11, 1942 in Peoria, Peoria co., ILL, daughter of ALEX ANDERSON and EDNA CLARK. She was born 1924 in Freeport, Stephenson co., IL.

Notes for JOHN CHARLES DILLON:
Died in Highway accident.
COUSIN ONCE REMOVED OF RONALD REAGAN

Child of JOHN DILLON and AMY ANDERSON is:
- i. JACKLYN ANN[7] DILLON, b. August 27, 1943, Freeport, Stephenson co., IL; m. DAVID ROBERT SPRINGMAN, October 13, 1978, Freeport, Stephenson co., IL; b. June 20, 1944, Freeport, Stephenson co., IL.

   Notes for JACKLYN ANN DILLON:
   COUSIN, ONCE REMOVED, OF RONALD REAGAN

57. KATHERINE JANE[6] HICKS *(MARY MARGARET[5] WILSON, JOHN CHARLES[4], THOMAS[3], JOHN[2], ANDREW[1])* was born January 09, 1917 in Garden Plain Twp., Whiteside co., IL, and died November 05, 1986 in Garden Plain Twp., Whiteside co., IL. She married (1) ADOLPH G. KUNAVICH. She married (2) THEODORE DINGMAN Aft. 1946.

Notes for KATHERINE JANE HICKS:
Divorced from Kunavich 1946.
Divorced from Dingman 1960 and resumed her maiden name, Kay J. Hicks, per Ronald G. Kunavich affidavit.
COUSIN, ONCE REMOVED, OF RONALD REAGAN

Notes for ADOLPH G. KUNAVICH:
Divorce 1946 per affidavit of Ronald G. Kunavich

Children of KATHERINE HICKS and ADOLPH KUNAVICH are:
- i. RONALD GEORGE[7] KUNAVICH, b. April 25, 1942, Clinton, Clinton co., IA.

   Notes for RONALD GEORGE KUNAVICH:
   Was 'DPCM Ronald G. Kunavich CM/C' aboard the USS O'Brien DD-975' in Oct. 1987.
   COUSIN TWICE REMOVED FROM RONALD REAGAN

94.   - ii. JAMES JOSEPH KUNAVICH, b. October 22, 1943, Clinton, Clinton co., IA; d. April 24, 1971, Oaklawn, Cook co., IL.

58. JOHN CHARLES[6] WILSON, JR *(JOHN JAMES[5], JOHN CHARLES[4], THOMAS[3], JOHN[2], ANDREW[1])* was born December 14, 1928 in IL, and died October 30, 1983 in Mesa, Maricopa co., AZ. He married (1) O. DARLENE RAINS. He married (2) SHIRLEY GIBSON February 21, 1948 in Freeport, Stephenson co., IL. She was born 1930 in Freeport, Stephenson co., IL. He married (3) GLENDA REITER January 20, 1958 in Alcorn co, MS, daughter of RODNEY REITER and ZELDA. She was born 1937.

Notes for JOHN CHARLES WILSON, JR:
Cremated.
COUSIN ONCE REMOVED OF RONALD REAGAN

Notes for O. DARLENE RAINS:
She gave the information on the death certificate of John, Jr.

Notes for GLENDA REITER:
Noeske marriage assumed from marriage application with John Wilson. Marriage certificate, Alcorn co., MS.

Child of JOHN WILSON and O. RAINS is:
- i. JOHN CHARLES[7] WILSON III, b. June 09, 1948, Freeport, Stephenson co., IL.

   Notes for JOHN CHARLES WILSON III:

Listed as 'Jr.' on his birth certificate.
COUSIN TWICE REMOVED OF RONALD REAGAN

59. MILFORD L.^{6} SMITH (*CHARLES ALFRED^5, SARA JANE^4 WILSON, THOMAS^3, JOHN^2, ANDREW^1*) was born February 21, 1916 in Rock Falls, Whiteside co., IL, and died October 29, 1980 in Sterling, Whiteside co., IL. He married MARIAN D. SCHNEIDER June 01, 1938 in Sterling, Whiteside co., IL, daughter of JOSEPH SCHNEIDER and DELLA MACQUAY. She was born 1916 in Coleta, Whiteside co., IL.

Notes for MILFORD L. SMITH:
Served in the military WW II. Cashier, International Harvester.
COUSIN ONCE REMOVED OF RONALD REAGAN

More About MILFORD L. SMITH:
Burial: Oak Knoll cemetery, Sterling, IL

More About MARIAN D. SCHNEIDER:
Burial: Oak Knoll cemetery, Sterling, IL

Children of MILFORD SMITH and MARIAN SCHNEIDER are:
    i. GORDON M.^{7} SMITH, b. October 31, 1940, Rock Falls, Whiteside co., IL; d. September 10, 1971, Rock Falls, Whiteside co., IL.

    Notes for GORDON M. SMITH:
    Not married
    COUSIN TWICE REMOVED OF RONALD REAGAN

    More About GORDON M SMITH:
    Burial: Oak Knoll cemetery, Sterling, IL

    ii. DENNIS SMITH, b. September 14, 1943, Rock Falls, Whiteside co., IL; d. January 28, 1983, Morrison, Whiteside co., IL.

    Notes for DENNIS SMITH:
    Not married
    COUSIN TWICE REMOVED OF RONALD REAGAN

    More About DENNIS SMITH:
    Burial: Oak Knoll cem.

60. RAYMOND^6 SMITH (*CHARLES ALFRED^5, SARA JANE^4 WILSON, THOMAS^3, JOHN^2, ANDREW^1*) was born February 07, 1918 in Sterling, Whiteside co., IL, and died March 07, 1997. He married MADELINE WEYRAUCH August 27, 1942.

Notes for RAYMOND SMITH:
FIRST COUSIN ONCE REMOVED OF RONALD REAGAN

More About RAYMOND SMITH:
Burial: Oak Knoll cemetery, Sterling, IL

Children of RAYMOND SMITH and MADELINE WEYRAUCH are:
    i. HUDSON B^7 SMITH, b. March 12, 1944.

    Notes for HUDSON B. SMITH:
    COUSIN TWICE REMOVED OF RONALD REAGAN

    ii. KAREN SMITH, b. April 1947.

Notes for KAREN SMITH:
COUSIN TWICE REMOVED OF RONALD REAGAN

   iii. SALLY SMITH, b. May 1950.

Notes for SALLY SMITH:
COUSIN TWICE REMOVED OF RONALD REAGAN

61. ROBERT CLARE[6] SMITH (*HORACE VERNON[5], SARA JANE[4] WILSON, THOMAS[3], JOHN[2], ANDREW[1]*) was born November 05, 1917 in Sterling, Whiteside co., IL. He married (1) DOROTHY BRICKLEY. She was born June 20, 1920, and died May 17, 1984. He married (2) JEANNE WEBB January 11, 1935.

Notes for ROBERT CLARE SMITH:
COUSIN ONCE REMOVED OF RONALD REAGAN

Children of ROBERT SMITH and DOROTHY BRICKLEY are:
95.   i. TERRY[7] SMITH, b. November 20, 1946.
96.   ii. VICKI SMITH, b. March 01, 1952.

62. GENE MEAKIN[6] SMITH (*HORACE VERNON[5], SARA JANE[4] WILSON, THOMAS[3], JOHN[2], ANDREW[1]*) was born March 27, 1922 in Sterling, Whiteside co., IL, and died July 09, 1995. He married JANET JANKE February 09, 1946 in Morrison, IL, daughter of HERBERT JANKE and EMMA KLEIST. She was born September 20, 1919 in Weyauwega, WI, and died October 24, 1989 in Sterling, Whiteside co., IL.

Notes for GENE MEAKIN SMITH:
COUSIN ONCE REMOVED OF RONALD REAGAN

Children of GENE SMITH and JANET JANKE are:
97.   i. DAVID[7] SMITH, b. May 21, 1948.
98.   ii. THOMAS SMITH, b. February 25, 1952.
99.   iii. NANCY SMITH, b. October 12, 1955.

63. HARRY WILSON[6] SMITH, JR (*HARRY WILSON[5], SARA JANE[4] WILSON, THOMAS[3], JOHN[2], ANDREW[1]*) was born January 20, 1922 in Oak Park, Cook co., IL. He married JEAN.

Notes for HARRY WILSON SMITH, JR:
Living in TN, 2000.
COUSIN ONCE REMOVED OF RONALD REAGAN

Children of HARRY SMITH and JEAN are:
   i. DALE[7] SMITH, m. NANCY LEE SPRAGUE, July 02, 1960.

Notes for DALE SMITH:
COUSIN TWICE REMOVED OF RONALD REAGAN

   ii. BARBARA SMITH.

Notes for BARBARA SMITH:
COUSIN TWICE REMOVED OF RONALD REAGAN

   iii. DEAN SMITH.

Notes for DEAN SMITH:
COUSIN TWICE REMOVED OF RONALD REAGAN

64. HAROLD EDWARD[6] WALTERS *(ELSEY MAE[5] PIERCE, SARA JANE[4] WILSON, THOMAS[3], JOHN[2], ANDREW[1])* was born December 02, 1925 in White Pigeon, Whiteside co., IL, and died February 19, 1988 in Morrison, IL. He married RUTH JANE STUART October 22, 1945 in Morrison, IL. She was born July 07, 1924 in Morrison, IL.

More About HAROLD EDWARD WALTERS:
Burial: West Genesee cem., Whiteside co.

Children of HAROLD WALTERS and RUTH STUART are:
- 100.   i.   PAUL EDWARD[7] WALTERS, b. May 03, 1946, Morrison, IL.
- 101.   ii.   HARLAN GENE WALTERS, b. February 05, 1948, Morrison, IL.
- 102.   iii.   JANE KAYE WALTERS, b. April 16, 1950, Morrison, IL.
-      iv.   RHONDA RUTH WALTERS, b. September 15, 1952, Morrison, IL; m. DANNY KENNEDY, December 02, 1977, Morrison, IL; b. August 27, 1946.

    Notes for RHONDA RUTH WALTERS:
    Divorced Aug. 30, 1978

    Notes for DANNY KENNEDY:
    Divorced Aug. 30, 1978

- 103.   v.   DAWN GAIL WALTERS, b. March 19, 1962, Morrison, IL.
- 104.   vi.   PHILIP DALE WALTERS, b. July 15, 1968, Morrison, IL.

65. MERNA JOY[6] HABBEN *(VERA MARIE[5] PIERCE, SARA JANE[4] WILSON, THOMAS[3], JOHN[2], ANDREW[1])* was born October 12, 1933 in Coleta, Whiteside co., IL. She married (1) CLYDE ELMER JANVRIN September 02, 1956 in Sterling, Whiteside co., IL. He was born August 24, 1925 in Morrison, IL, and died May 20, 1970 in Morrison, IL. She married (2) ROBERT MICHAEL MUSCHAL Aft. 1971, son of NICHOLAS MUSCHAL and KATHERINE MARX. He was born June 20, 1940 in Chicago, IL.

Notes for MERNA JOY HABBEN:
Md. in St. Johns Lutheran Church, Sterling
Dairy farmer.
Mrs. Merna Habben-Muschal has been of tremendous help in furnishing material and in proofreading my pages. If there are errors, blame me. CJG
COUSIN ONCE REMOVED OF RONALD REAGAN

Notes for CLYDE ELMER JANVRIN:
Dairy farmer, served in the Army.

More About CLYDE ELMER JANVRIN:
Burial: South Clyde cemetery

Notes for ROBERT MICHAEL MUSCHAL:
Painter. Marriage to Merna was his second marriage, also her 2nd.
Auditor and Inspector. Married in United Methodist Church, Morrison, IL.

Children of MERNA HABBEN and CLYDE JANVRIN are:
-      i.   ERIC PAUL[7] JANVRIN, b. August 31, 1958, Morrison, IL; m. CAROL TRIMBLE, October 10, 1986, Fulton, Whiteside co., IL; b. November 06, 1956, Fulton, IL.
- 105.   ii.   KURT REINHARD JANVRIN, b. August 04, 1960, Morrison, IL.
- 106.   iii.   BRUCE CLYDE JANVRIN, b. December 22, 1961, Morrison, IL.
- 107.   iv.   ARON KYLE JANVRIN, b. November 13, 1964, Morrison, IL.

66. NORMAN WALTER[6] HABBEN *(VERA MARIE[5] PIERCE, SARA JANE[4] WILSON, THOMAS[3], JOHN[2], ANDREW[1])* was born September 10, 1935 in Coleta, Whiteside co., IL. He married NORMA JEAN COOK June 02, 1956 in Rock Falls, Whiteside co., IL. She was born June 02, 1937 in Rock Falls, Whiteside co., IL.

Notes for NORMAN WALTER HABBEN:
COUSIN ONCE REMOVED OF RONALD REAGAN

Children of NORMAN HABBEN and NORMA COOK are:
108.   i. RHONDA JANE[7] HABBEN, b. June 24, 1957.
      ii. ROBERT ALLEN HABBEN, b. August 02, 1958, Morrison, IL.
109.   iii. GENE LEROY HABBEN, b. July 07, 1960, Morrison, IL.
110.   iv. SARA LEANNE HABBEN, b. March 09, 1967, Morrison, IL.

67. RONALD LEE[6] HABBEN (*VERA MARIE[5] PIERCE, SARA JANE[4] WILSON, THOMAS[3], JOHN[2], ANDREW[1]*) was born July 17, 1938 in Coleta, Whiteside co., IL. He married NANCY JOAN BIELEMA September 02, 1961 in Fulton, Whiteside co., IL. She was born November 15, 1940 in Fulton, IL.

Notes for RONALD LEE HABBEN:
COUSIN ONCE REMOVED OF RONALD REAGAN

Children of RONALD HABBEN and NANCY BIELEMA are:
111.   i. DANIEL LEE[7] HABBEN, b. June 26, 1962, Morrison, IL.
112.   ii. DEBRA LOU HABBEN, b. September 17, 1964, Morrison, IL.
      iii. DAVID ALLEN HABBEN, b. November 08, 1978, Morrison, IL.

68. MILFORD GENE[6] HABBEN (*VERA MARIE[5] PIERCE, SARA JANE[4] WILSON, THOMAS[3], JOHN[2], ANDREW[1]*) was born July 04, 1940 in Coleta, Whiteside co., IL. He married JOANNE PATRICK July 06, 1964 in San Jose, Santa Clara co., CA. She was born May 23, 1943 in Santa Clara, CA.

Notes for MILFORD GENE HABBEN:
COUSIN ONCE REMOVED OF RONALD REAGAN

Children of MILFORD HABBEN and JOANNE PATRICK are:
113.   i. CATHERINE JEAN[7] HABBEN, b. May 08, 1966, Morrison, IL.
      ii. DONALD PATRICK HABBEN, b. April 08, 1969, Morrison, IL; m. LISA FREDRICK, November 10, 1990, Dixon, Lee co., IL.

      Notes for DONALD PATRICK HABBEN:
      Divorced, no children.

69. VELMA JANE[6] HABBEN (*VERA MARIE[5] PIERCE, SARA JANE[4] WILSON, THOMAS[3], JOHN[2], ANDREW[1]*) was born April 10, 1943 in Morrison, IL. She married WILLIAM RICHARD NORTON, JR December 07, 1963 in Freeport, Stephenson co., IL, son of WILLIAM NORTON and EDNA LOTT. He was born October 20, 1938 in Rockford, ILL.

Notes for VELMA JANE HABBEN:
COUSIN ONCE REMOVED OF RONALD REAGAN

Notes for WILLIAM RICHARD NORTON, JR:
Railroad telegrapher at time of marriage, later truck driver.

Children of VELMA HABBEN and WILLIAM NORTON are:
      i. JAMES RICHARD[7] NORTON, b. June 30, 1967, Freport, Stephenson co., IL.
114.   ii. JEFFERY MICHAEL NORTON, b. December 23, 1971, Freport, Stephenson co., IL.

70. JUDITH MAY[6] HABBEN *(VERA MARIE[5] PIERCE, SARA JANE[4] WILSON, THOMAS[3], JOHN[2], ANDREW[1])* was born April 28, 1946 in Morrison, IL. She married DONALD RAY BURMEISTER August 28, 1976 in Dewitt,Clinton co., Iowa. He was born January 23, 1939 in Dewitt, Clinton co., IA.

Notes for JUDITH MAY HABBEN:
COUSIN ONCE REMOVED OF RONALD REAGAN

Notes for DONALD RAY BURMEISTER:
His second marriage.

Children of JUDITH HABBEN and DONALD BURMEISTER are:
    i. JOHN BRANDON[7] BURMEISTER, b. August 25, 1977, Dewitt, Clinton co., IA.
    ii. BRIAN DOUGLAS BURMEISTER, b. October 09, 1980, Dewitt, Clinton co., IA.

71. CAROL ANN[6] HABBEN *(VERA MARIE[5] PIERCE, SARA JANE[4] WILSON, THOMAS[3], JOHN[2], ANDREW[1])* was born June 04, 1948 in Morrison, IL. She met CHARLES ROBERT ALBRECHT March 01, 1969 in Belvidere, Boone co., IL, son of FRANK ALBRECHT and IRENE HOWE. He was born November 28, 1937.

Notes for CAROL ANN HABBEN:
Born at Morrison Community Hospital
COUSIN ONCE REMOVED OF RONALD REAGAN

Notes for CHARLES ROBERT ALBRECHT:
Married by Robert A. Blodgett, Magistrate, at Belvidere, Boone co., IL
He was an 'assembler' when married.
This was his second marriage. Data from marriage license/Wiebenga material

Children of CAROL HABBEN and CHARLES ALBRECHT are:
115.   i. CALE RICHARD[7] ALBRECHT, b. June 06, 1973, Freport, Stephenson co., IL.
    ii. CALEB WILLAIM ALBRECHT, b. May 17, 1975, Freport, Stephenson co., IL.

    Notes for CALEB WILLAIM ALBRECHT:
    Married 1999, one child b. April 2000

72. BEVERLY JOAN[6] HABBEN *(VERA MARIE[5] PIERCE, SARA JANE[4] WILSON, THOMAS[3], JOHN[2], ANDREW[1])* was born July 10, 1952 in Morrison, IL. She married KENNETH ALDEN ETHRIDGE November 25, 1972 in Pearl City, Jo Davies co., IL. He was born 1939 in Freport, Stephenson co., IL.

Notes for BEVERLY JOAN HABBEN:
COUSIN ONCE REMOVED OF RONALD REAGAN

Children of BEVERLY HABBEN and KENNETH ETHRIDGE are:
    i. JEREMY M.[7] ETHRIDGE, b. July 08, 1978, Freport, Stephenson co., IL.
    ii. KEVIN MARSHALL ETHRIDGE, b. June 29, 1980, Freport, Stephenson co., IL.
    iii. LAURA MARIE ETHRIDGE, b. May 29, 1983, Freport, Stephenson co., IL.

    Notes for LAURA MARIE ETHRIDGE:

    iv. BRADLEY ETHRIDGE, b. March 18, 1988, Freport, Stephenson co., IL.

73. DONNA ELAINE[6] HABBEN *(VERA MARIE[5] PIERCE, SARA JANE[4] WILSON, THOMAS[3], JOHN[2], ANDREW[1])* was born August 04, 1954 in Morrison, IL. She married THOMAS MICHAEL ARDWIN November 02, 1982 in North Glenn, Adams co., CO, son of DETER ARDWIN and ANNA GAFKA. He was born January 15, 1942 in Detroit, MI.

Notes for DONNA ELAINE HABBEN:
Divorced Jan. 29, 1971, per marriage application, Detroit, MI
COUSIN ONCE REMOVED OF RONALD REAGAN

Notes for THOMAS MICHAEL ARDWIN:
Divorced: Jan. 29, 1971, per marriage application, Detroit, MI

Children of DONNA HABBEN and THOMAS ARDWIN are:
    i. DONNA MARIE[7] ARDWIN, b. March 28, 1987, Denver, Adams co., CO.
    ii. MICHAEL THOMAS ARDWIN, b. January 19, 1989, Denver, Adams co., CO.
    iii. LISA ARDWIN.

74. MICHAEL[6] REAGAN *(RONALD WILSON[5], NELLIE CLYDE[4] WILSON, THOMAS[3], JOHN[2], ANDREW[1])* was born March 18, 1945. He married COLLEEN STEARNS.

Notes for COLLEEN STEARNS:
Information from Mrs. Vickie Wiebenga

Child of MICHAEL REAGAN and COLLEEN STEARNS is:
    i. CAMERON MICHAEL[7] REAGAN, b. May 30, 1978.

75. MARTHA ANN[6] MITCHELL *(LOIS W.[5] WHISTLER, MARGARET MAY[4] WILSON, JOHN[3], JOHN[2], ANDREW[1])* She married DAVID DEUTERMANN.

Children of MARTHA MITCHELL and DAVID DEUTERMANN are:
    i. DAVID WHITFORD[7] DEUTERMANN.
    ii. JULIA ANN DEUTERMANN.

76. JOHN WILSON[6] MITCHELL *(LOIS W.[5] WHISTLER, MARGARET MAY[4] WILSON, JOHN[3], JOHN[2], ANDREW[1])* He married NAOMI YATES.

Child of JOHN MITCHELL and NAOMI YATES is:
    i. WHITFORD KIMBALL[7] MITCHELL.

77. JANE WHITFORD[6] MITCHELL *(LOIS W.[5] WHISTLER, MARGARET MAY[4] WILSON, JOHN[3], JOHN[2], ANDREW[1])* She married DONALD GORZNEY.

Children of JANE MITCHELL and DONALD GORZNEY are:
    i. JOHN[7] GORZNEY.
    ii. JAMES GORZNEY.
    iii. SUSAN JANE GORZNEY.
    iv. GLEN GORZNEY.

78. BARBARA[6] MARR *(FLORENCE I.[5] WHISTLER, MARGARET MAY[4] WILSON, JOHN[3], JOHN[2], ANDREW[1])* She married 'MALE' DOUGHERTY.

Children of BARBARA MARR and 'MALE' DOUGHERTY are:
    i. DENNIE[7] DOUGHERTY.
    ii. TIMOTHY DOUGHERTY.
    iii. DOUGLAS DOUGHERTY.
    iv. BRIAN DOUGHERTY.
    v. PATRICK DOUGHERTY.

79. JUDITH SUZANE[6] WILSON *(DWIGHT ALVIN[5], PAUL FLETCHER[4], ALEXANDER B[3], JOHN[2], ANDREW[1])* was born November 21, 1942. She married JAMES KEITH ROWE June 13, 1964, son of V. ROWE and MARY. He was born November 25, 1941.

Notes for JUDITH SUZANE WILSON:
Teacher

Notes for JAMES KEITH ROWE:
Teacher
Divorced August, 1994

Children of JUDITH WILSON and JAMES ROWE are:
      i. DAVID KEITH[7] ROWE, b. March 17, 1968; m. RHONDA KAY BAYLES, November 23, 1996; b. April 14, 1967.
116. ii. ROBERT MATHEW ROWE, b. September 06, 1970.

80. ROBERT THOMAS[6] WILSON *(DWIGHT ALVIN[5], PAUL FLETCHER[4], ALEXANDER B[3], JOHN[2], ANDREW[1])* was born June 29, 1944. He married GEORGIANNE HUMMEL March 21, 1972. She was born August 10, 1949.

Notes for GEORGIANNE HUMMEL:
Legal secretary

Children of ROBERT WILSON and GEORGIANNE HUMMEL are:
      i. THOMAS ROBERT[7] WILSON, b. August 24, 1984, Danville, IL.
      ii. PAUL MATHEW WILSON, b. October 27, 1985, Danville, IL.

81. DEBORAH ANN[6] WILSON *(ROBERT BRISTLE[5], PAUL FLETCHER[4], ALEXANDER B[3], JOHN[2], ANDREW[1])* was born February 09, 1941. She married MICHAEL MORAN September 02, 1961, son of DON MORAN and LIENNE VITE. He was born January 26, 1941.

Children of DEBORAH WILSON and MICHAEL MORAN are:
      i. CHRISTINE ELIZABETH[7] MORAN, b. April 18, 1963; m. 'MALE' FOSTER.
117. ii. KIMBERLY JANE MORAN, b. February 27, 1965.
      iii. STEPHEN MICHAEL MORAN, b. December 08, 1968.

82. STEVEN ALLEN[6] GSELL *(CLAIR LE ROY[5], CLIFFORD LEROY[4], MARGARET MAE[3] WILSON, JOHN[2], ANDREW[1])* was born April 24, 1939. He married DARLENE E. VEIHL.

Children of STEVEN GSELL and DARLENE VEIHL are:
      i. BRIAN DAVID[7] GSELL.

        Notes for BRIAN DAVID GSELL:
        Twin of Dawn

      ii. DAWN ELIZABETH GSELL.

        Notes for DAWN ELIZABETH GSELL:
        Twin of Brian

      iii. BLYTHE ANN GSELL.

83. SUE ELLEN[6] GSELL *(CLAIR LE ROY[5], CLIFFORD LEROY[4], MARGARET MAE[3] WILSON, JOHN[2], ANDREW[1])* was born September 25, 1955. She married JOHN KIMBERLIN.

Notes for JOHN KIMBERLIN:
2 other children

Child of SUE GSELL and JOHN KIMBERLIN is:
    i. CORINNE^7 KIMBERLIN.

84. DONNA JEAN^6 WITT *(LEPHA MAE^5 MILNES, MAUDE MAE^4 GSELL, MARGARET MAE^3 WILSON, JOHN^2, ANDREW^1)* was born April 09, 1933. She married GEORGE MEDEMA. He was born July 17, 1933.

Children of DONNA WITT and GEORGE MEDEMA are:
118.   i. JHODY JEAN^7 MEDEMA, b. March 11, 1952.
119.   ii. JULIE MARIE MEDEMA, b. June 09, 1953.
    iii. JEANIE LARIE MEDEMA, b. May 31, 1954.
    iv. JANICE LYNE MEDEMA, b. November 27, 1956; m. CHARLES SWANSON.
    v. JERRY ALLEN MEDEMA, b. August 27, 1963.
    vi. JON CRAIG MEDEMA, b. November 29, 1966.
    vii. JAMES GREG MEDEMA, b. December 03, 1969.

85. DR. HARLAN ANDREW^6 WITT *(LEPHA MAE^5 MILNES, MAUDE MAE^4 GSELL, MARGARET MAE^3 WILSON, JOHN^2, ANDREW^1)* was born April 27, 1946. He married VERLEE ANN SILVIS.

Children of HARLAN WITT and VERLEE SILVIS are:
    i. JEFFREY ANDREW^7 WITT, b. October 19, 1967.
    ii. KIMBERLY LYNN WITT.

        Notes for KIMBERLY LYNN WITT:
        Twin of Kristen

    iii. KRISTEN LES WITT.

        Notes for KRISTEN LES WITT:
        Twin of Kimberly

86. DAVID IVAN^6 CARROLL *(MARGARET ELIZABETH^5 MILNES, MAUDE MAE^4 GSELL, MARGARET MAE^3 WILSON, JOHN^2, ANDREW^1)* was born January 02, 1938. He married SALLY ANN ONKEN. She was born December 12, 1938.

Children of DAVID CARROLL and SALLY ONKEN are:
    i. TROY ANDREW^7 CARROLL, b. April 13, 1965.
    ii. ERICK PAUL CARROLL, b. May 20, 1967.
    iii. LYNN ANDREA CARROLL, b. July 01, 1971.
    iv. LISA PAMELA CARROLL, b. December 27, 1973.

87. TERRY DEE^6 CARROLL *(MARGARET ELIZABETH^5 MILNES, MAUDE MAE^4 GSELL, MARGARET MAE^3 WILSON, JOHN^2, ANDREW^1)* was born January 03, 1946. He married VIRGINIA KAY BUSH. She was born April 15, 1947.

Children of TERRY CARROLL and VIRGINIA BUSH are:
    i. CHRISTINE LEA^7 CARROLL, b. December 17, 1968.
    ii. KARLA JEAN CARROLL, b. October 13, 1975.
    iii. MATTHEW THOMAS CARROLL, b. July 04, 1980.

88. DIANE LOUISE^6 MILNES *(WALTER^5, MAUDE MAE^4 GSELL, MARGARET MAE^3 WILSON, JOHN^2, ANDREW^1)* was born September 04, 1945. She married PAUL GLISPIE.

Child of DIANE MILNES and PAUL GLISPIE is:
    i. JOHN WESLEY[7] GLISPIE.

    Notes for JOHN WESLEY GLISPIE:
    Married 1999

89. THOMAS BRENT[6] MILNES *(WALTER[5], MAUDE MAE[4] GSELL, MARGARET MAE[3] WILSON, JOHN[2], ANDREW[1])* was born September 01, 1950. He married (1) PATRICIA RICK 1976. He married (2) PENNY SMITH 1980.

Notes for THOMAS BRENT MILNES:
Divorced from Patricia.
Dairy farmer

Child of THOMAS MILNES and PATRICIA RICK is:
    i. TINA ELIZABETH[7] MILNES, b. March 02, 1977.

    Notes for TINA ELIZABETH MILNES:
    School teacher, no children, not married (2000)

Children of THOMAS MILNES and PENNY SMITH are:
    ii. SCOTT T.[7] MILNES, b. October 31, 1981.
    iii. BRYAN THOMAS MILNES, b. January 22, 1985.
    iv. SHAUN MATHEW MILNES, b. April 13, 1986.

90. ARLYN[6] VOS *(GLADYS ELOISE[5] STAPLETON, ESTELLA JANE[4] GSELL, MARGARET MAE[3] WILSON, JOHN[2], ANDREW[1])* was born May 03, 1940. He married MARY BUIKEMA. She was born November 20, 1939.

Children of ARLYN VOS and MARY BUIKEMA are:
    i. KATHY LYNN[7] VOS.
    ii. ARLYN DALE VOS.
    iii. DEBRA JANE VOS.
    iv. MARLA ANN VOS.

91. LARRY[6] VOS *(GLADYS ELOISE[5] STAPLETON, ESTELLA JANE[4] GSELL, MARGARET MAE[3] WILSON, JOHN[2], ANDREW[1])* He married LINDA FRANCIS.

Children of LARRY VOS and LINDA FRANCIS are:
    i. KARI SUE[7] VOS.
    ii. TERI ANN VOS.

Generation No. 7

92. ELWIN[7] NICE *(LUCILLE FERN[6] BECHTEL, WILLIAM DETER[5], JOHN WILSON[4], SARA[3] WILSON, JOHN[2], ANDREW[1])* He married SHIRLEY ENRIGHT.

Notes for ELWIN NICE:
SECOND COUSIN TWICE REMOVED OF RONALD REAGAN

Children of ELWIN NICE and SHIRLEY ENRIGHT are:
    i. WILLIAM[8] NICE, m. PATRICIA PETTICORD.
    ii. LINDA NICE.
    iii. PAM NICE.
    iv. JUDY NICE, m. JEFF MEINSMA.

93. MARJORIE[7] NICE *(LUCILLE FERN[6] BECHTEL, WILLIAM DETER[5], JOHN WILSON[4], SARA[3] WILSON, JOHN[2], ANDREW[1])* She married ROBERT TRAUM.

Children of MARJORIE NICE and ROBERT TRAUM are:
    i. SUSAN[8] TRAUM.
    ii. JOHN TRAUM.
    iii. DAVID TRAUM.

94. JAMES JOSEPH[7] KUNAVICH *(KATHERINE JANE[6] HICKS, MARY MARGARET[5] WILSON, JOHN CHARLES[4], THOMAS[3], JOHN[2], ANDREW[1])* was born October 22, 1943 in Clinton, Clinton co., IA, and died April 24, 1971 in Oaklawn, Cook co., IL. He married ALBERTA LYNN YONKERS January 10, 1963 in Chicago, Cook co., ILL. She was born 1945 in Chicago, Cook co., IL.

Notes for JAMES JOSEPH KUNAVICH:
Divorced before death. Accidental injury, car, Palos Hill, Cook co, IL.
COUSIN TWICE REMOVED OF RONALD REAGAN

More About JAMES JOSEPH KUNAVICH:
Burial: Grove Hill, Morrison, IL

Notes for ALBERTA LYNN YONKERS:
Divorce from Kunavich September, 1969. Married Curtis

Child of JAMES KUNAVICH and ALBERTA YONKERS is:
    i. JAMES JOSEPH[8] KUNAVICH, JR., b. March 29, 1963, Chicago, Cook co., IL.

        Notes for JAMES JOSEPH KUNAVICH, JR.:
        Because his Mother divorced Kunavich and married Curtis, John Kunavich, Jr. assumed the surname 'Curtis' to carry the same name as his Mother, affidavit of 20 Aug. 1992, Fulton, IL in the Donald Hunt estate case.
        COUSIN 3 TIMES REMOVED FROM RONALD REAGAN

95. TERRY[7] SMITH *(ROBERT CLARE[6], HORACE VERNON[5], SARA JANE[4] WILSON, THOMAS[3], JOHN[2], ANDREW[1])* was born November 20, 1946. He married (1) DONNA ANN RURY January 13, 1967. He married (2) MARIA MARTINEZ August 14, 1983. He married (3) MARGARITA MARISEAL August 17, 1996.

Notes for TERRY SMITH:
Divorced 1981, from Donna, divorced from Maria.
COUSIN TWICE REMOVED OF RONALD REAGAN

Notes for DONNA ANN RURY:
Divorced 1981

Children of TERRY SMITH and DONNA RURY are:
    i. CHRISTOPHER SCOTT[8] SMITH, b. January 29, 1968.

        Notes for CHRISTOPHER SCOTT SMITH:
        COUSIN 3 TIMES REMOVED FROM RONALD REAGAN

    ii. JAMIE SMITH, b. January 23, 1973.

        Notes for JAMIE SMITH:
        Twin of Corie
        COUSIN 3 TIMES REMOVED OF RONALD REAGAN

  iii. CORY SMITH, b. January 23, 1973.

    Notes for CORY SMITH:
    Twin of Jamie
    COUSIN 3 TIMES REMOVED OF RONALD REAGAN

  iv. JENIFER ERIN SMITH, b. January 24, 1978.

    Notes for JENIFER ERIN SMITH:
    COUSIN 3 TIMES REMOVED OF RONALD REAGAN

96. VICKI[7] SMITH (*ROBERT CLARE[6], HORACE VERNON[5], SARA JANE[4] WILSON, THOMAS[3], JOHN[2], ANDREW[1]*) was born March 01, 1952. She married (1) BRUCE UNGER August 07, 1971 in Morrison, IL. He died March 17, 1974. She married (2) RON WIEBENGA October 24, 1975.

Notes for VICKI SMITH:
COUSIN TWICE REMOVED OF RONALD REAGAN

Notes for BRUCE UNGER:
Deceased

More About BRUCE UNGER:
Burial: Grove Hill cemetery, Morrison

Child of VICKI SMITH and BRUCE UNGER is:
  i. BRUCE EDWIN[8] UNGER, JR., b. July 04, 1974; m. KAREN GEORGE, November 06, 1999, Peoria, IL.

    Notes for BRUCE EDWIN UNGER, JR.:
    COUSIN 3 TIMES REMOVED OF RONALD REAGAN

Child of VICKI SMITH and RON WIEBENGA is:
  ii. LESLEY DAWN[8] WIEBENGA, b. April 24, 1977, Morrison, IL; m. CHAD PAUL DEVER, June 06, 1998, Morrison, IL.

    Notes for LESLEY DAWN WIEBENGA:
    COUSIN 3 TIMES REMOVED OF RONALD REAGAN

97. DAVID[7] SMITH (*GENE MEAKIN[6], HORACE VERNON[5], SARA JANE[4] WILSON, THOMAS[3], JOHN[2], ANDREW[1]*) was born May 21, 1948. He married DEE ANN BILDSTEIN August 09, 1975.

Notes for DAVID SMITH:
Lives in Iowa, divorced.
COUSIN TWICE REMOVED OF RONALD REAGAN

Child of DAVID SMITH and DEE BILDSTEIN is:
  i. CHELSEY[8] SMITH, b. May 20, 1982.

98. THOMAS[7] SMITH (*GENE MEAKIN[6], HORACE VERNON[5], SARA JANE[4] WILSON, THOMAS[3], JOHN[2], ANDREW[1]*) was born February 25, 1952. He married (1) CHRISTINE PYRON July 07, 1973. He married (2) DAWN SCHRYVER March 31, 1978. He married (3) CINDY OSTEMA March 09, 1984.

Notes for THOMAS SMITH:
Divorced Feb. 1975 - Christine
Divorced - Dawn - Dec. 1979
COUSIN TWICE REMOVED OF RONALD REAGAN

Notes for CHRISTINE PYRON:
Divorced Feb. 1975

Child of THOMAS SMITH and DAWN SCHRYVER is:
    i. THOMAS S^8 SMITH, m. CINDY.

Children of THOMAS SMITH and CINDY OSTEMA are:
    ii. MARSHALL^8 SMITH, b. August 22, 1984.
    iii. TAYLOR SMITH, b. December 17, 1996.

99. NANCY^7 SMITH *(GENE MEAKIN^6, HORACE VERNON^5, SARA JANE^4 WILSON, THOMAS^3, JOHN^2, ANDREW^1)* was born October 12, 1955. She married (1) MITCHELL FOREMAN January 04, 1975. She married (2) STEVE MERRILL Aft. January 1980.

Notes for NANCY SMITH:
Divorced Steve Jan. 5, 1980
COUSIN TWICE REMOVED OF RONALD REAGAN

Child of NANCY SMITH and MITCHELL FOREMAN is:
    i. CAMERON RYAN^8 FOREMAN, b. July 14, 1978.

    Notes for CAMERON RYAN FOREMAN:
    COUSIN 3 TIMES REMOVED OF RONALD REAGAN

Child of NANCY SMITH and STEVE MERRILL is:
    ii. DUSTIN^8 MERRILL, b. May 05, 1982.

100. PAUL EDWARD^7 WALTERS *(HAROLD EDWARD^6, ELSEY MAE^5 PIERCE, SARA JANE^4 WILSON, THOMAS^3, JOHN^2, ANDREW^1)* was born May 03, 1946 in Morrison, IL. He married (1) PATRICIA BARTZ February 26, 1965 in Morrison, IL. She was born May 11, 1949 in Morrison, IL. He married (2) SHARON TIESMAN March 19, 1970 in Lyndon, Whiteside co., IL. She was born April 27, 1945.

Notes for PAUL EDWARD WALTERS:
Divorce 1970

Notes for PATRICIA BARTZ:
Divorced 1970

Child of PAUL WALTERS and PATRICIA BARTZ is:
    i. WENDY LEE^8 WALTERS, b. August 21, 1965, Morrison, IL; m. WILLIAM CHARLES HUTCHINSON; b. September 08, 1964, Carroll co., IL.

    Notes for WILLIAM CHARLES HUTCHINSON:
    Divorced

Children of PAUL WALTERS and SHARON TIESMAN are:
    ii. BABY^8 WALTERS, b. March 19, 1973; d. March 19, 1973.

    Notes for BABY WALTERS:
    Stillborn

    More About BABY WALTERS:
    Burial: Fulton cemetery. Fulton, IL

  iii. TORI CHERYL WALTERS, b. April 25, 1974, Morrison, IL; m. JUSTIN EADS, January 13, 1996.
  iv. TROY J. WALTERS, b. November 05, 1975, Morrison, IL; m. CHRISTINA.

   Notes for TROY J. WALTERS:
   Divorced 2002

   Notes for CHRISTINA:
   Divorced 2002

101. HARLAN GENE[7] WALTERS *(HAROLD EDWARD[6], ELSEY MAE[5] PIERCE, SARA JANE[4] WILSON, THOMAS[3], JOHN[2], ANDREW[1])* was born February 05, 1948 in Morrison, IL. He married (1) MARIE SHARER February 24, 1967 in Fulton, Whiteside co., IL. She was born May 25, 1947. He married (2) BETH RICK August 31, 1974 in Morrison, IL. She was born January 27, 1945. He married (3) LINDA ROBINSON December 02, 1983 in TX.

Notes for HARLAN GENE WALTERS:
Divorced from Marie 1974
Divorced from Beth Rick
Divorced from Linda 2002

Notes for MARIE SHARER:
Divorce 1974

Notes for BETH RICK:
Divorced

Notes for LINDA ROBINSON:
She has two children, Carolyn and Rebecca. They are children of her previous marriage.

Children of HARLAN WALTERS and MARIE SHARER are:
  i. TERRY HARLAN[8] WALTERS, b. June 06, 1968, Morrison, IL.
  ii. MARK DOUGLAS WALTERS, b. June 16, 1969, Morrison, IL.
  iii. DAVID GENE WALTERS, b. August 26, 1971, Morrison, IL.

Children of HARLAN WALTERS and LINDA ROBINSON are:
  iv. CAROLYN[8].

   Notes for CAROLYN:
   Child of Mother's previous marriage.

  v. REBECCA.

   Notes for REBECCA:
   Child of Mother's previous marriage.

102. JANE KAYE[7] WALTERS *(HAROLD EDWARD[6], ELSEY MAE[5] PIERCE, SARA JANE[4] WILSON, THOMAS[3], JOHN[2], ANDREW[1])* was born April 16, 1950 in Morrison, IL. She married (1) LEONARD PRITCHARD March 07, 1969 in Morrison, IL. He was born November 16, 1946. She married (2) FRANK MATCHIE October 07, 1972 in Morrison, IL. He was born June 07, 1947. She married (3) WALTER G. HEATH October 22, 1990 in Morrison, IL.

Notes for JANE KAYE WALTERS:
Divorced 3 Aug 1970 from Pritchard
Divorced from Matchie

Notes for LEONARD PRITCHARD:
Divorced from Jane Kaye 3 Aug. 1970

Notes for FRANK MATCHIE:
Divorced

Child of JANE WALTERS and LEONARD PRITCHARD is:
    i. TIMOTHY ALLEN[8] PRITCHARD, b. September 22, 1969, Morrison, IL; m. ANGELA KAY MACHIE, May 1987, Morrison, IL; b. December 22, 1974, Morrison, IL.

Child of JANE WALTERS and FRANK MATCHIE is:
    ii. ANGELA[8] MATCHIE, b. December 22, 1974; m. SHANE FERGUSON, August 31, 1996.

103. DAWN GAIL[7] WALTERS *(HAROLD EDWARD[6], ELSEY MAE[5] PIERCE, SARA JANE[4] WILSON, THOMAS[3], JOHN[2], ANDREW[1])* was born March 19, 1962 in Morrison, IL. She married ROBERT JAMES BAUER May 02, 1981 in Morrison, IL. He was born August 06, 1960 in Morrison, IL.

Children of DAWN WALTERS and ROBERT BAUER are:
    i. AMANDA GAIL[8] BAUER, b. July 31, 1991, Clinton, Clinton Co., IA.
    ii. LAYLA MARIE BAUER, b. August 27, 1994, Clinton, Clinton Co., IA.

104. PHILIP DALE[7] WALTERS *(HAROLD EDWARD[6], ELSEY MAE[5] PIERCE, SARA JANE[4] WILSON, THOMAS[3], JOHN[2], ANDREW[1])* was born July 15, 1968 in Morrison, IL. He married CHRISTINE KRAUSE May 30, 1989 in Dixon, Lee co., IL.

Notes for CHRISTINE KRAUSE:
Adopted by Baughman

Children of PHILIP WALTERS and CHRISTINE KRAUSE are:
    i. STEPHANIE ANNE[8] WALTERS, b. February 11, 1988, Dixon, Lee co., IL.
    ii. TIFFANY MARIE WALTERS, b. May 22, 1990, Dallas, TX.
    iii. MATTHEW WALTERS, b. September 15, 1992.

105. KURT REINHARD[7] JANVRIN *(MERNA JOY[6] HABBEN, VERA MARIE[5] PIERCE, SARA JANE[4] WILSON, THOMAS[3], JOHN[2], ANDREW[1])* was born August 04, 1960 in Morrison, IL. He married YVONNE AMMON June 16, 1984 in Long Grove, Lake co., IL. She was born December 19, 1961 in Decatur, Macon co., IL.

Children of KURT JANVRIN and YVONNE AMMON are:
    i. REBECCA LINDSEY[8] JANVRIN, b. May 23, 1988, Trenton, Mercer co., NJ.
    ii. HANNAH KATE JANVRIN, b. October 07, 1990, Trenton, Mercer co., NJ.
    iii. GENEVIEVE JANVRIN, b. 1993.
    iv. MABELINE JANVRIN, b. 1997.

106. BRUCE CLYDE[7] JANVRIN *(MERNA JOY[6] HABBEN, VERA MARIE[5] PIERCE, SARA JANE[4] WILSON, THOMAS[3], JOHN[2], ANDREW[1])* was born December 22, 1961 in Morrison, IL. He married DIANE MEHLHAUS August 11, 1990 in Dysart, Benton co., IA. She was born February 20, 1961 in Dysart, Benton co., Iowa.

Children of BRUCE JANVRIN and DIANE MEHLHAUS are:
    i. BRICE[8] JANVRIN, b. 1993.
    ii. BRYLEIGH JANVRIN, b. 1998.

107. ARON KYLE[7] JANVRIN *(MERNA JOY[6] HABBEN, VERA MARIE[5] PIERCE, SARA JANE[4] WILSON, THOMAS[3], JOHN[2], ANDREW[1])* was born November 13, 1964 in Morrison, IL. He married CAROLYN BROWN June 28, 1998.

Child of ARON JANVRIN and CAROLYN BROWN is:
  i. TYLER[8] JANVRIN, b. February 29, 2000.

108. RHONDA JANE[7] HABBEN *(NORMAN WALTER[6], VERA MARIE[5] PIERCE, SARA JANE[4] WILSON, THOMAS[3], JOHN[2], ANDREW[1])* was born June 24, 1957. She married (1) ALLEN GREELEY June 10, 1978 in Morrison, IL. He was born August 05, 1951 in Morrison, IL. She married (2) ALLEN RAY GREELEY June 10, 1978 in Morrison, IL. He was born August 05, 1951 in Morrison, IL.

Children of RHONDA HABBEN and ALLEN GREELEY are:
  i. MELLISSA JEAN[8] GREELEY, b. December 08, 1980, Morrison, IL.
  ii. WILLIAM NORMAN GREELEY, b. June 19, 1983, Morrison, IL.
  iii. MARLA JANE GREELEY, b. September 04, 1984, Morrison, IL.

109. GENE LEROY[7] HABBEN *(NORMAN WALTER[6], VERA MARIE[5] PIERCE, SARA JANE[4] WILSON, THOMAS[3], JOHN[2], ANDREW[1])* was born July 07, 1960 in Morrison, IL. He married KAREN ROENIKE February 25, 1989 in Clinton, Iowa.

Children of GENE HABBEN and KAREN ROENIKE are:
  i. TRAVIS[8] HABBEN, b. 1993.
  ii. RYAN HABBEN, b. 1996.
  iii. KRISTIN, b. 1999.

110. SARA LEANNE[7] HABBEN *(NORMAN WALTER[6], VERA MARIE[5] PIERCE, SARA JANE[4] WILSON, THOMAS[3], JOHN[2], ANDREW[1])* was born March 09, 1967 in Morrison, IL. She married (1) COONAN DICKMAN March 29, 1986 in Morrison, IL. He was born March 24, 1967. She married (2) RANDY FAUST September 1990 in Mo-.

Notes for SARA LEANNE HABBEN:
Divorced Dickman 1990, no children with him.

Notes for COONAN DICKMAN:
Divorced 1990, no children.

Children of SARA HABBEN and RANDY FAUST are:
  i. ADAM CHARLES[8] FAUST, b. March 23, 1991, Virginia Beach, VA.
  ii. ASHLEY FAUST, b. 1994.

111. DANIEL LEE[7] HABBEN *(RONALD LEE[6], VERA MARIE[5] PIERCE, SARA JANE[4] WILSON, THOMAS[3], JOHN[2], ANDREW[1])* was born June 26, 1962 in Morrison, IL. He married BETH HACKER June 20, 1987 in Morrison, IL. She was born January 10, 1962.

Children of DANIEL HABBEN and BETH HACKER are:
  i. LOGAN DANIEL[8] HABBEN, b. May 14, 1989, Sterling, Whiteside co., IL.
  ii. ABBEY HABBEN, b. 1994.

112. DEBRA LOU[7] HABBEN *(RONALD LEE[6], VERA MARIE[5] PIERCE, SARA JANE[4] WILSON, THOMAS[3], JOHN[2], ANDREW[1])* was born September 17, 1964 in Morrison, IL. She married JAMES LEE SNYDER June 11, 1983 in Morrison, IL. He was born October 30, 1963 in Morrison, IL.

Notes for DEBRA LOU HABBEN:

Divorced 1988

Notes for JAMES LEE SNYDER:
Divorced 1988

Children of DEBRA HABBEN and JAMES SNYDER are:
  i. BRANDON[8] SNYDER, b. October 31, 1985, Germany.
  ii. TIMOTHY SNYDER, b. February 12, 1987, Sterling, Whiteside co., IL.

113. CATHERINE JEAN[7] HABBEN *(MILFORD GENE[6], VERA MARIE[5] PIERCE, SARA JANE[4] WILSON, THOMAS[3], JOHN[2], ANDREW[1])* was born May 08, 1966 in Morrison, IL. She married MARK BENNET June 27, 1987 in Dixon, Lee co., IL.

Notes for CATHERINE JEAN HABBEN:
Divorced

Children of CATHERINE HABBEN and MARK BENNET are:
  i. JENNIFER ANN[8] BENNET, b. October 06, 1990, Sterling, Whiteside co., IL.
  ii. AMANDA BENNET, b. 1994.

114. JEFFERY MICHAEL[7] NORTON *(VELMA JANE[6] HABBEN, VERA MARIE[5] PIERCE, SARA JANE[4] WILSON, THOMAS[3], JOHN[2], ANDREW[1])* was born December 23, 1971 in Freport, Stephenson co., IL. He married ANGIE.

Child of JEFFERY NORTON and ANGIE is:
  i. GRACE[8] NORTON, b. 1999.

115. CALE RICHARD[7] ALBRECHT *(CAROL ANN[6] HABBEN, VERA MARIE[5] PIERCE, SARA JANE[4] WILSON, THOMAS[3], JOHN[2], ANDREW[1])* was born June 06, 1973 in Freport, Stephenson co., IL. He married CHRIS.

Notes for CALE RICHARD ALBRECHT:
3rd Great-grandson of John Wilson.
Divorced, 2000

Child of CALE ALBRECHT and CHRIS is:
  i. CARRIE[8] ALBRECHT, b. 1995.

116. ROBERT MATHEW[7] ROWE *(JUDITH SUZANE[6] WILSON, DWIGHT ALVIN[5], PAUL FLETCHER[4], ALEXANDER B[3], JOHN[2], ANDREW[1])* was born September 06, 1970. He married HEIDI ANN HULBERT October 10, 1992, daughter of STEPHEN HULBERT and DIANE. She was born March 22, 1969.

Children of ROBERT ROWE and HEIDI HULBERT are:
  i. AMANDA[8] ROWE, b. April 29, 1995.
  ii. LUCAS MATHEW ROWE, b. February 10, 1998.

117. KIMBERLY JANE[7] MORAN *(DEBORAH ANN[6] WILSON, ROBERT BRISTLE[5], PAUL FLETCHER[4], ALEXANDER B[3], JOHN[2], ANDREW[1])* was born February 27, 1965. She married 'MALE' KIDWELL.

Children of KIMBERLY MORAN and 'MALE' KIDWELL are:
  i. TYLER[8] KIDWELL.
  ii. JACOB KIDWELL.
  iii. STEVEN KIDWELL.

118. JHODY JEAN[7] MEDEMA *(DONNA JEAN[6] WITT, LEPHA MAE[5] MILNES, MAUDE MAE[4] GSELL, MARGARET MAE[3] WILSON, JOHN[2], ANDREW[1])* was born March 11, 1952. He married KATHY DITTMAR.

Child of JHODY MEDEMA and KATHY DITTMAR is:
    i. JACOB[8] MEDEMA.

119. JULIE MARIE[7] MEDEMA *(DONNA JEAN[6] WITT, LEPHA MAE[5] MILNES, MAUDE MAE[4] GSELL, MARGARET MAE[3] WILSON, JOHN[2], ANDREW[1])* was born June 09, 1953. She married THOMAS SCHUMACHER.

Children of JULIE MEDEMA and THOMAS SCHUMACHER are:
    i. MATTHEW COLLIN[8] SCHUMACHER.
    ii. LUCAS SCHUMACHER.

Kinship of Andrew Wilson

Name	Relationship with Andrew Wilson	Civil	Canon
Aitken, Mayme	Wife of the great-grandson		
Alex	Great-grandson	III	3
Ammon, Yvonne	Wife of the 4th great-grandson		
Anderson, Amy Adele	Wife of the 3rd great-grandson		
Barrett, Maxine Joy	Wife of the 2nd great-grandson		
Bartz, Patricia	Wife of the 4th great-grandson		
Bauer, Amanda Gail	5th great-granddaughter	VII	7
Bauer, Robert James	Husband of the 4th great-granddaughter		
Bayles, Rhonda Kay	Wife of the 4th great-grandson		
Bechtel, Albert	2nd great-grandson	IV	4
Bechtel, Bonnie	4th great-granddaughter	VI	6
Bechtel, Carol	4th great-granddaughter	VI	6
Bechtel, Ellen	4th great-granddaughter	VI	6
Bechtel, Ellen W.	Great-granddaughter	III	3
Bechtel, Ephraim Myers	Husband of the granddaughter		
Bechtel, Everett	3rd great-grandson	V	5
Bechtel, Gary	4th great-grandson	VI	6
Bechtel, Glenda	4th great-granddaughter	VI	6
Bechtel, Glenn	3rd great-grandson	V	5
Bechtel, Helena	Great-granddaughter	III	3
Bechtel, Ivy May	2nd great-granddaughter	IV	4
Bechtel, John Wilson	Great-grandson	III	3
Bechtel, Lucille Fern	3rd great-granddaughter	V	5
Bechtel, Rebecca Jane	Great-granddaughter	III	3
Bechtel, Scott	4th great-grandson	VI	6
Bechtel, William Deter	2nd great-grandson	IV	4
Belle	Wife of the grandson		
Bennet, Amanda	5th great-granddaughter	VII	7
Bennet, Jennifer Ann	5th great-granddaughter	VII	7
Bennet, Mark	Husband of the 4th great-granddaughter		
Bessie	2nd great-granddaughter	IV	4
Bildstein, Dee Ann	Wife of the 4th great-grandson		
Blue, Jane	Daughter-in-law		
Brickley, Dorothy	Wife of the 3rd great-grandson		
Bristle, Etta May	Wife of the great-grandson		
Brooks, Pauline Catherine	Wife of the 2nd great-grandson		
Brown, Carolyn	Wife of the 4th great-grandson		
Buikema, Mary	Wife of the 3rd great-grandson		
Bush, Douglas	Husband of the 4th great-granddaughter		
Bush, Virginia Kay	Wife of the 3rd great-grandson		
C., Henry	2nd great-grandson	IV	4
Capone, James A	Husband of the 3rd great-granddaughter		
Carolyn	5th great-granddaughter	VII	7
Carroll, Christine Lea	4th great-granddaughter	VI	6
Carroll, David Ivan	3rd great-grandson	V	5
Carroll, Erick Paul	4th great-grandson	VI	6
Carroll, Ivan Ralph	Husband of the 2nd great-granddaughter		
Carroll, Karla Jean	4th great-granddaughter	VI	6
Carroll, Lisa Pamela	4th great-granddaughter	VI	6
Carroll, Lynn Andrea	4th great-granddaughter	VI	6
Carroll, Matthew Thomas	4th great-grandson	VI	6

Name	Relationship with Andrew Wilson	Civil	Canon
Carroll, Terry Dee	3rd great-grandson	V	5
Carroll, Troy Andrew	4th great-grandson	VI	6
Christina	Wife of the 5th great-grandson		
Cindy	Wife of the 5th great-grandson		
Conant	Husband of the 3rd great-granddaughter		
Cook, Norma Jean	Wife of the 3rd great-grandson		
Curtis, James J.	5th great-grandson	VII	7
Cutler, Francis Louise	Wife of the great-grandson		
Davis, Nancy	Wife of the 2nd great-grandson		
Debbie	Wife of the grandson		
Deter, Sarah E.	Wife of the great-grandson		
Deutermann, David	Husband of the 3rd great-granddaughter		
Deutermann, David Whitford	4th great-grandson	VI	6
Deutermann, Julia Ann	4th great-granddaughter	VI	6
Dever, Chad Paul	Husband of the 5th great-granddaughter		
Dickman, Coonan	Husband of the 4th great-granddaughter		
Dillon, Jacklyn Ann	4th great-granddaughter	VI	6
Dillon, John Charles	3rd great-grandson	V	5
Dillon, Katherine Annabelle	3rd great-granddaughter	V	5
Dillon, Margaret Eliza	3rd great-granddaughter	V	5
Dillon, Raymond James	Husband of the 2nd great-granddaughter		
Dillon, Raymond James	3rd great-grandson	V	5
Dingman, Theodore	Husband of the 3rd great-granddaughter		
Dittmar, Kathy	Wife of the 4th great-grandson		
Dougherty, Brian	4th great-grandson	VI	6
Dougherty, Dennie	4th great-grandson	VI	6
Dougherty, Douglas	4th great-grandson	VI	6
Dougherty, 'Male'	Husband of the 3rd great-granddaughter		
Dougherty, Patrick	4th great-grandson	VI	6
Dougherty, Timothy	4th great-grandson	VI	6
Dutch	2nd great-grandson	IV	4
Eads, Chelsea Cheryl	6th great-granddaughter	VIII	8
Eads, Joseph James	6th great-grandson	VIII	8
Eads, Justin	Husband of the 5th great-granddaughter		
Eads, Zachary Philip	6th great-grandson	VIII	8
Ella	Great-granddaughter	III	3
Elsey, Mary Ann	Wife of the grandson		
Enright, Shirley	Wife of the 4th great-grandson		
Fannie	Great-granddaughter	III	3
Faust, Adam Charles	5th great-grandson	VII	7
Faust, Ashley	5th great-granddaughter	VII	7
Faust, Randy	Husband of the 4th great-granddaughter		
Ferguson, Hunter Michael	6th great-grandson	VIII	8
Ferguson, Shane	Husband of the 5th great-granddaughter		
Fike, Ida	Wife of the 2nd great-grandson		
Flack, Clarence	Husband of the great-granddaughter		
Flack, Kathryn	3rd great-granddaughter	V	5
Flack, Pamela	3rd great-granddaughter	V	5
Flack, Thomas Oliver	2nd great-grandson	IV	4
Flack, Timothy Conrad	2nd great-grandson	IV	4
Flack, William C.	3rd great-grandson	V	5
Fletcher, Deborah A.	Wife of the grandson		
Foreman, Cameron Ryan	5th great-grandson	VII	7

Name	Relationship with Andrew Wilson	Civil	Canon
Foreman, Mitchell	Husband of the 4th great-granddaughter		
Foster, 'Male'	Husband of the 4th great-granddaughter		
Francis, Linda	Wife of the 3rd great-grandson		
Fredrick, Lisa	Wife of the 4th great-grandson		
Fulks, Sara Jane	Wife of the 2nd great-grandson		
Gallentine, Randy Gale	Husband of the 3rd great-granddaughter		
George, Karen	Wife of the 5th great-grandson		
Gerdes, David Edmond	Husband of the great-granddaughter		
Gerdes, Ephraim Lawrence	2nd great-grandson	IV	4
Gerdes, Galen Glenn	2nd great-grandson	IV	4
Gerdes, Henry Ralph	2nd great-grandson	IV	4
Gerdes, Lloyd	2nd great-grandson	IV	4
Gerdes, Robert	3rd great-grandson	V	5
Gerdes, Ruth	3rd great-granddaughter	V	5
Gerdes, Virgil E.	2nd great-grandson	IV	4
Gerdes, Wayne	3rd great-grandson	V	5
Gibson, Shirley	Wife of the 3rd great-grandson		
Glasgow, Ameilia	Wife		
Glispie, John Wesley	4th great-grandson	VI	6
Glispie, Paul	Husband of the 3rd great-granddaughter		
Goff, Hulda Philena	Wife of the 2nd great-grandson		
Goldsmith, Robin N.	Husband of the 3rd great-granddaughter		
Gorzney, Donald	Husband of the 3rd great-granddaughter		
Gorzney, Glen	4th great-grandson	VI	6
Gorzney, James	4th great-grandson	VI	6
Gorzney, John	4th great-grandson	VI	6
Gorzney, Susan Jane	4th great-granddaughter	VI	6
Greeley, Allen	Husband of the 4th great-granddaughter		
Greeley, Allen Ray	Husband of the 4th great-granddaughter		
Greeley, Marla Jane	5th great-granddaughter	VII	7
Greeley, Mellissa Jean	5th great-granddaughter	VII	7
Greeley, William Norman	5th great-grandson	VII	7
Green, Rhea	Wife of the 3rd great-grandson		
Gsell, Blythe Ann	4th great-granddaughter	VI	6
Gsell, Brian David	4th great-grandson	VI	6
Gsell, Clair Le Roy	2nd great-grandson	IV	4
Gsell, Clifford Leroy	Great-grandson	III	3
Gsell, David B.	Husband of the granddaughter		
Gsell, Dawn Elizabeth	4th great-granddaughter	VI	6
Gsell, Earl Wilson	Great-grandson	III	3
Gsell, Estella Jane	Great-granddaughter	III	3
Gsell, Howard Wilson	2nd great-grandson	IV	4
Gsell, Maude Mae	Great-granddaughter	III	3
Gsell, Richard Lee	3rd great-grandson	V	5
Gsell, Steven Allen	3rd great-grandson	V	5
Gsell, Sue Ellen	3rd great-granddaughter	V	5
Gsell, William B.	Husband of the granddaughter		
Habben, Catherine Jean	4th great-granddaughter	VI	6
Habben, Donald Patrick	4th great-grandson	VI	6
Habben, Gene LeRoy	4th great-grandson	VI	6
Habben, Merna Joy	3rd great-granddaughter	V	5
Habben, Milford Gene	3rd great-grandson	V	5
Habben, Norman Walter	3rd great-grandson	V	5

Name	Relationship with Andrew Wilson	Civil	Canon
Habben, Reinhard F.	Husband of the 2nd great-granddaughter		
Habben, Rhonda Jane	4th great-granddaughter	VI	6
Habben, Robert Allen	4th great-grandson	VI	6
Habben, Ryan	5th great-grandson	VII	7
Habben, Sara Leanne	4th great-granddaughter	VI	6
Habben, Travis	5th great-grandson	VII	7
Hammer, Edna Julia	Wife of the great-grandson		
Heath, Walter G.	Husband of the 4th great-granddaughter		
Helms, Mayme	Wife of the great-grandson		
Herrold, Edith	2nd great-granddaughter	IV	4
Herrold, Lloyd	Husband of the great-granddaughter		
Herrold, Lloyd Wilson	2nd great-grandson	IV	4
Hicks, Earl Clyde	3rd great-grandson	V	5
Hicks, Harriet	3rd great-granddaughter	V	5
Hicks, Harry John	Husband of the 2nd great-granddaughter		
Hicks, Katherine Jane	3rd great-granddaughter	V	5
High, Bessie Luella Jane	Great-granddaughter	III	3
High, Joseph	Husband of the 4th great-granddaughter		
High, William G.	Husband of the granddaughter		
Hoffman, Ruth	Wife of the 2nd great-grandson		
Holly	Husband of the great-granddaughter		
Homerding, Margie	Wife of the 2nd great-grandson		
Howard, Iona Mae	Wife of the 2nd great-grandson		
Howell, William	Husband of the great-granddaughter		
Hulbert, Heidi Ann	Wife of the 4th great-grandson		
Hulda	Wife of the 2nd great-grandson		
Hummel, Georgianne	Wife of the 3rd great-grandson		
Hunt, Donald Wilson	2nd great-grandson	IV	4
Hunt, Louis Herman	Husband of the great-granddaughter		
Hutchinson, William Charles	Husband of the 5th great-granddaughter		
J., Katie	Granddaughter	II	2
Jack	Husband of the great-granddaughter		
Janke, Janet	Wife of the 3rd great-grandson		
Janvrin, Aron Kyle	4th great-grandson	VI	6
Janvrin, Brice	5th great-grandson	VII	7
Janvrin, Bruce Clyde	4th great-grandson	VI	6
Janvrin, Bryleigh	5th great-granddaughter	VII	7
Janvrin, Clyde Elmer	Husband of the 3rd great-granddaughter		
Janvrin, Eric Paul	4th great-grandson	VI	6
Janvrin, Genevieve	5th great-granddaughter	VII	7
Janvrin, Hannah Kate	5th great-granddaughter	VII	7
Janvrin, Kurt Reinhard	4th great-grandson	VI	6
Janvrin, Mabeline	5th great-granddaughter	VII	7
Janvrin, Rebecca Lindsey	5th great-granddaughter	VII	7
Janvrin, Tyler	5th great-grandson	VII	7
Jean	Wife of the 3rd great-grandson		
Jellerichs, Gail A.	Husband of the 3rd great-granddaughter		
Jennie	Great-granddaughter	III	3
Joe	4th great-grandson	VI	6
Johnson, Donald LeRoy	Husband of the 3rd great-granddaughter		
Jr.	2nd great-grandson	IV	4
Jr.	3rd great-grandson	V	5
Keith, Thelma Lillian	Wife of the great-grandson		

Name	Relationship with Andrew Wilson	Civil	Canon
	Wife of the 2nd great-grandson		
Kennedy, Danny	Husband of the 4th great-granddaughter		
Kidwell, Jacob	5th great-grandson	VII	7
Kidwell, 'Male'	Husband of the 4th great-granddaughter		
Kidwell, Steven	5th great-grandson	VII	7
Kidwell, Tyler	5th great-grandson	VII	7
Kimberlin, Corinne	4th great-granddaughter	VI	6
Kimberlin, John	Husband of the 3rd great-granddaughter		
Klosterman, Nora	Wife of the great-grandson		
Krause, Christine	Wife of the 4th great-grandson		
Kristin	5th great-granddaughter	VII	7
Kunavich, Adolph G.	Husband of the 3rd great-granddaughter		
Kunavich, James Joseph	4th great-grandson	VI	6
Kunavich, James Joseph, Jr.	5th great-grandson	VII	7
Kunavich, Ronald George	4th great-grandson	VI	6
Lane, Dorothy Ann	3rd great-granddaughter	V	5
Lane, Mildred	3rd great-granddaughter	V	5
Lane, William	Husband of the 2nd great-granddaughter		
Lane, William	3rd great-grandson	V	5
Layla Marie Bauer	5th great-granddaughter	VII	7
Lewis	Husband of the great-granddaughter		
Liggett, Isabelle Mary	Wife of the grandson		
Lizzie	Granddaughter	II	2
Longanecker, Samuel L.	Husband of the great-granddaughter		
Machie, Angela Kay	Wife of the 5th great-grandson		
Maggie	Granddaughter	II	2
Maggie	Great-granddaughter	III	3
Manning, Shirley	Wife of the 3rd great-grandson		
Mariseal, Margarita	Wife of the 4th great-grandson		
Marr, Barbara	3rd great-granddaughter	V	5
Marr, George L.	Husband of the 2nd great-granddaughter		
Marr, George Michael	3rd great-grandson	V	5
Martinez, Maria	Wife of the 4th great-grandson		
Mary	Wife of the great-grandson		
Matchie, Angela	5th great-granddaughter	VII	7
Matchie, Frank	Husband of the 4th great-granddaughter		
Mathew, Janice Lucille	Wife of the 2nd great-grandson		
May, Denzie	Wife of the 2nd great-grandson		
May, Iva	2nd great-granddaughter	IV	4
Mayme	2nd great-granddaughter	IV	4
McKee, Carlene	Wife of the 3rd great-grandson		
Meakins, Dossie May	Wife of the 2nd great-grandson		
Medema, George	Husband of the 3rd great-granddaughter		
Medema, Jacob	5th great-grandson	VII	7
Medema, James Greg	4th great-grandson	VI	6
Medema, Janice Lyne	4th great-granddaughter	VI	6
Medema, Jeanie Larie	4th great-granddaughter	VI	6
Medema, Jerry Allen	4th great-grandson	VI	6
Medema, Jhody Jean	4th great-grandson	VI	6
Medema, Jon Craig	4th great-grandson	VI	6
Medema, Julie Marie	4th great-granddaughter	VI	6
Mehlhaus, Diane	Wife of the 4th great-grandson		
Meinsma, Jeff	Husband of the 5th great-granddaughter		

Name	Relationship with Andrew Wilson	Civil	Canon
Merrill, Dustin	5th great-grandson	VII	7
Merrill, Steve	Husband of the 4th great-granddaughter		
Milnes, Bryan Thomas	4th great-grandson	VI	6
Milnes, Diane Louise	3rd great-granddaughter	V	5
Milnes, Lepha Mae	2nd great-granddaughter	IV	4
Milnes, Margaret Elizabeth	2nd great-granddaughter	IV	4
Milnes, Scott T.	4th great-grandson	VI	6
Milnes, Shaun Mathew	4th great-grandson	VI	6
Milnes, Thomas Brent	3rd great-grandson	V	5
Milnes, Tina Elizabeth	4th great-granddaughter	VI	6
Milnes, Walter	2nd great-grandson	IV	4
Milnes, Walter Richard	Husband of the great-granddaughter		
Milnes, Wanda Vey	3rd great-granddaughter	V	5
Milnes, Winnie	Wife of the 2nd great-grandson		
Mirissa Jane	6th great-granddaughter	VIII	8
Mitchell, Jane Whitford	3rd great-granddaughter	V	5
Mitchell, John Wilson	3rd great-grandson	V	5
Mitchell, Martha Ann	3rd great-granddaughter	V	5
Mitchell, Whitford	Husband of the 2nd great-granddaughter		
Mitchell, Whitford Kimball	4th great-grandson	VI	6
Moon	2nd great-grandson	IV	4
Moran, Christine Elizabeth	4th great-granddaughter	VI	6
Moran, Kimberly Jane	4th great-granddaughter	VI	6
Moran, Michael	Husband of the 3rd great-granddaughter		
Moran, Stephen Michael	4th great-grandson	VI	6
Muschal, Robert Michael	Husband of the 3rd great-granddaughter		
Naftzger, Beulah Vey	Wife of the 2nd great-grandson		
Nelson, Dorothy	Wife of the great-grandson		
Nelson, Helen Marie	Wife of the 2nd great-grandson		
Nice, Elwin	4th great-grandson	VI	6
Nice, Judy	5th great-granddaughter	VII	7
Nice, Linda	5th great-granddaughter	VII	7
Nice, Lyle	Husband of the 3rd great-granddaughter		
Nice, Marjorie	4th great-granddaughter	VI	6
Nice, Pam	5th great-granddaughter	VII	7
Nice, William	5th great-grandson	VII	7
Nicke, Darrel	Husband of the 4th great-granddaughter		
Onken, Sally Ann	Wife of the 3rd great-grandson		
Ostema, Cindy	Wife of the 4th great-grandson		
Palmier, Doria	Wife of the 3rd great-grandson		
Patrick, JoAnne	Wife of the 3rd great-grandson		
Patti	3rd great-granddaughter	V	5
Pessman, Greg	Husband of the 4th great-granddaughter		
Petticord, Patricia	Wife of the 5th great-grandson		
Pierce, Elsey Mae	2nd great-granddaughter	IV	4
Pierce, James H.	Husband of the 3rd great-granddaughter		
Pierce, Vera Marie	2nd great-granddaughter	IV	4
Pierce, Walter S.	Husband of the great-granddaughter		
Pritchard, Leonard	Husband of the 4th great-granddaughter		
Pritchard, Timothy Allen	5th great-grandson	VII	7
Pyron, Christine	Wife of the 4th great-grandson		
Rains, O. Darlene	Wife of the 3rd great-grandson		
Reagan, Cameron Michael	4th great-grandson	VI	6

Name	Relationship with Andrew Wilson	Civil	Canon
Reagan, John Edward	Husband of the great-granddaughter		
Reagan, John Neil	2nd great-grandson	IV	4
Reagan, Maureen Elizabeth	3rd great-granddaughter	V	5
Reagan, Michael	3rd great-grandson	V	5
Reagan, Patricia	3rd great-granddaughter	V	5
Reagan, Ronald Prescott	3rd great-grandson	V	5
Reagan, Ronald Wilson	2nd great-grandson	IV	4
Rebecca	5th great-granddaughter	VII	7
Reinhardt	Husband of the 2nd great-granddaughter		
Reiter, Glenda	Wife of the 3rd great-grandson		
Rick, Beth	Wife of the 4th great-grandson		
Rick, Patricia	Wife of the 3rd great-grandson		
Robbins, Anne Frances	Wife of the 2nd great-grandson		
Robinson, Linda	Wife of the 4th great-grandson		
Roenike, Karen	Wife of the 4th great-grandson		
Rowe, Amanda	5th great-granddaughter	VII	7
Rowe, David Keith	4th great-grandson	VI	6
Rowe, James Keith	Husband of the 3rd great-granddaughter		
Rowe, Lucas Mathew	5th great-grandson	VII	7
Rowe, Robert Mathew	4th great-grandson	VI	6
Rury, Donna Ann	Wife of the 4th great-grandson		
Rush, Stephen A.	Husband of the great-granddaughter		
Ryan, Daniel Joseph	Husband of the 3rd great-granddaughter		
Schneider, Marian D.	Wife of the 3rd great-grandson		
Schryver, Dawn	Wife of the 4th great-grandson		
Schumacher, Lucas	5th great-grandson	VII	7
Schumacher, Matthew Collin	5th great-grandson	VII	7
Schumacher, Thomas	Husband of the 4th great-granddaughter		
Sharer, Marie	Wife of the 4th great-grandson		
Shrider, Mareta	Wife of the 2nd great-grandson		
Silvis, Verlee Ann	Wife of the 3rd great-grandson		
Smith, Barbara	4th great-granddaughter	VI	6
Smith, Charles Alfred	2nd great-grandson	IV	4
Smith, Chelsey	5th great-granddaughter	VII	7
Smith, Christopher Scott	5th great-grandson	VII	7
Smith, Cory	5th great-granddaughter	VII	7
Smith, Dale	4th great-grandson	VI	6
Smith, David	4th great-grandson	VI	6
Smith, Dean	4th great-grandson	VI	6
Smith, Dennis	4th great-grandson	VI	6
Smith, Gene Meakin	3rd great-grandson	V	5
Smith, Gordon M.	4th great-grandson	VI	6
Smith, Harry Wilson	2nd great-grandson	IV	4
Smith, Harry Wilson, Jr	3rd great-grandson	V	5
Smith, Horace C.	Husband of the great-granddaughter		
Smith, Horace Vernon	2nd great-grandson	IV	4
Smith, Hudson B.	4th great-grandson	VI	6
Smith, Jamie	5th great-grandson	VII	7
Smith, Jenie Alice	Wife of the grandson		
Smith, Jenifer Erin	5th great-granddaughter	VII	7
Smith, Karen	4th great-granddaughter	VI	6
Smith, Marshall	5th great-grandson	VII	7
Smith, Mathew Lee	Husband of the 3rd great-granddaughter		

Name	Relationship with Andrew Wilson	Civil	Canon
Smith, Milford L.	3rd great-grandson	V	5
Smith, Nancy	4th great-granddaughter	VI	6
Smith, Penny	Wife of the 3rd great-grandson		
Smith, Raymond	3rd great-grandson	V	5
Smith, Robert Clare	3rd great-grandson	V	5
Smith, Sally	4th great-granddaughter	VI	6
Smith, Taylor	5th great-grandson	VII	7
Smith, Terry	4th great-grandson	VI	6
Smith, Thomas	4th great-grandson	VI	6
Smith, Thomas S.	5th great-grandson	VII	7
Smith, Vicki	4th great-granddaughter	VI	6
Sprague, Nancy Lee	Wife of the 4th great-grandson		
Springman, David Robert	Husband of the 4th great-granddaughter		
Stapleton, Gladys Eloise	2nd great-granddaughter	IV	4
Stapleton, Glen	2nd great-grandson	IV	4
Stapleton, William	Husband of the great-granddaughter		
Starck, Catherine	Wife of the great-grandson		
Stark, Katie	Wife of the great-grandson		
Stearns, Colleen	Wife of the 3rd great-grandson		
Stella	Great-granddaughter	III	3
Steven	Husband of the great-granddaughter		
Stevens, 'Male'	Husband of the 3rd great-granddaughter		
Stuart, Ruth Jane	Wife of the 3rd great-grandson		
Swanson, Charles	Husband of the 4th great-granddaughter		
Sweigert, Mabel May	Wife of the 2nd great-grandson		
Thomas, Iona Jean	Wife of the 2nd great-grandson		
Tiesman, Sharon	Wife of the 4th great-grandson		
Traum, David	5th great-grandson	VII	7
Traum, John	5th great-grandson	VII	7
Traum, Robert	Husband of the 4th great-granddaughter		
Traum, Susan	5th great-granddaughter	VII	7
Trimble, Carol	Wife of the 4th great-grandson		
Tucker, 'Male'	Husband of the 3rd great-granddaughter		
Tug	Great-grandson	III	3
Ufken, Eugene	Husband of the 3rd great-granddaughter		
Unger, Bruce	Husband of the 4th great-granddaughter		
Unger, Bruce Edwin, Jr.	5th great-grandson	VII	7
Van Horn, James Jerry	Husband of the 3rd great-granddaughter		
Veihl, Darlene E.	Wife of the 3rd great-grandson		
Vina	Great-granddaughter	III	3
Vos, Arlyn	3rd great-grandson	V	5
Vos, Arlyn Dale	4th great-grandson	VI	6
Vos, Debra Jane	4th great-granddaughter	VI	6
Vos, Ernest	Husband of the 2nd great-granddaughter		
Vos, Kari Sue	4th great-granddaughter	VI	6
Vos, Kathy Lynn	4th great-granddaughter	VI	6
Vos, Larry	3rd great-grandson	V	5
Vos, Lauri Ann	3rd great-granddaughter	V	5
Vos, Marla Ann	4th great-granddaughter	VI	6
Vos, Teri Ann	4th great-granddaughter	VI	6
Walters, Baby	5th great-granddaughter	VII	7
Walters, Carl B.	Husband of the 2nd great-granddaughter		
Walters, David Gene	5th great-grandson	VII	7

Name	Relationship with Andrew Wilson	Civil	Canon
Walters, Dawn Gail	4th great-granddaughter	VI	6
Walters, Drew Philip	6th great-grandson	VIII	8
Walters, Harlan Gene	4th great-grandson	VI	6
Walters, Harold Edward	3rd great-grandson	V	5
Walters, Jane Kaye	4th great-granddaughter	VI	6
Walters, Julia Anna	6th great-granddaughter	VIII	8
Walters, Mark Douglas	5th great-grandson	VII	7
Walters, Matthew	5th great-grandson	VII	7
Walters, Paul Edward	4th great-grandson	VI	6
Walters, Philip Dale	4th great-grandson	VI	6
Walters, Rhonda Ruth	4th great-granddaughter	VI	6
Walters, Sandra	Wife of the 4th great-grandson		
Walters, Stephanie Anne	5th great-granddaughter	VII	7
Walters, Terry Harlan	5th great-grandson	VII	7
Walters, Tiffany Marie	5th great-granddaughter	VII	7
Walters, Tori Cheryl	5th great-granddaughter	VII	7
Walters, Troy J.	5th great-grandson	VII	7
Walters, Wendy Lee	5th great-granddaughter	VII	7
Warner, Catherine	3rd great-granddaughter	V	5
Warner, James	Husband of the great-granddaughter		
Warner, James	3rd great-grandson	V	5
Warner, Robert Wilson	2nd great-grandson	IV	4
Watson, Mary	Wife of the 2nd great-grandson		
Webb, Jeanne	Wife of the 3rd great-grandson		
Weyrauch, Madeline	Wife of the 3rd great-grandson		
Whistler, Florence I.	2nd great-granddaughter	IV	4
Whistler, Glenn Otto	Husband of the great-granddaughter		
Whistler, Lois W.	2nd great-granddaughter	IV	4
Wiebenga, Lesley Dawn	5th great-granddaughter	VII	7
Wiebenga, Ron	Husband of the 4th great-granddaughter		
Wiersema, Patricia	Wife of the 4th great-grandson		
Wilkinson, Margaret	Wife of the great-grandson		
Willson	Son	I	1
Wilson, Alexander B	Grandson	II	2
Wilson, Alexander Thomas	Great-grandson	III	3
Wilson, Alice Jane	Great-granddaughter	III	3
Wilson, Andrew	Self		0
Wilson, Catherine	Granddaughter	II	2
Wilson, Charles Abram	Great-grandson	III	3
Wilson, Charles Desmond	Grandson	II	2
Wilson, Charles LeRoy	2nd great-grandson	IV	4
Wilson, Deborah Ann	3rd great-granddaughter	V	5
Wilson, Dwight Alvin	2nd great-grandson	IV	4
Wilson, Earl Charles	3rd great-grandson	V	5
Wilson, Earl Clyde	2nd great-grandson	IV	4
Wilson, Elizabeth Evelyn	Granddaughter	II	2
Wilson, Elizabeth Mary	2nd great-granddaughter	IV	4
Wilson, Emily G.	Great-granddaughter	III	3
Wilson, Frances Jane	Great-granddaughter	III	3
Wilson, George John	Great-grandson	III	3
Wilson, George Orville	Great-grandson	III	3
Wilson, Janet Mae	3rd great-granddaughter	V	5
Wilson, Jeanette	2nd great-granddaughter	IV	4

Name	Relationship with Andrew Wilson	Civil	Canon
Wilson, Jeannette Lynn	3rd great-granddaughter	V	5
Wilson, Jody Allen	3rd great-grandson	V	5
Wilson, John	Son	I	1
Wilson, John	Grandson	II	2
Wilson, John Charles	Great-grandson	III	3
Wilson, John Charles III	4th great-grandson	VI	6
Wilson, John Charles, Jr	3rd great-grandson	V	5
Wilson, John James	2nd great-grandson	IV	4
Wilson, Judith Suzane	3rd great-granddaughter	V	5
Wilson, Kathy Elizabeth	3rd great-granddaughter	V	5
Wilson, Kimberly Ann	3rd great-granddaughter	V	5
Wilson, Leo Vernon, Sr.	2nd great-grandson	IV	4
Wilson, Linda Kay	3rd great-granddaughter	V	5
Wilson, Marc Lee	3rd great-grandson	V	5
Wilson, Margaret Mae	Granddaughter	II	2
Wilson, Margaret May	Great-granddaughter	III	3
Wilson, Marie	3rd great-granddaughter	V	5
Wilson, Marilyn Joan	3rd great-granddaughter	V	5
Wilson, Mary LaVina	Great-granddaughter	III	3
Wilson, Mary Margaret	2nd great-granddaughter	IV	4
Wilson, Naomi Jean	3rd great-granddaughter	V	5
Wilson, Nellie Clyde	Great-granddaughter	III	3
Wilson, Paul Fletcher	Great-grandson	III	3
Wilson, Paul Mathew	4th great-grandson	VI	6
Wilson, Phoebe Mae	Great-granddaughter	III	3
Wilson, Robert Bristle	2nd great-grandson	IV	4
Wilson, Robert Thomas	3rd great-grandson	V	5
Wilson, Ronald Stanley	3rd great-grandson	V	5
Wilson, Sara	Granddaughter	II	2
Wilson, Sara Jane	Great-granddaughter	III	3
Wilson, Thomas	Grandson	II	2
Wilson, Thomas Robert	4th great-grandson	VI	6
Wilson, Trudy Jean	3rd great-granddaughter	V	5
Wilson, Vaughn Fae	3rd great-granddaughter	V	5
Wilson, Winifred M.	Great-granddaughter	III	3
Witt, Andrew F.	Husband of the 2nd great-granddaughter		
Witt, Donna Jean	3rd great-granddaughter	V	5
Witt, Harlan Andrew	3rd great-grandson	V	5
Witt, Jeffrey Andrew	4th great-grandson	VI	6
Witt, Kimberly Lynn	4th great-granddaughter	VI	6
Witt, Kristen Les	4th great-granddaughter	VI	6
Witt, Sandra Mae	3rd great-granddaughter	V	5
Witz, 'Male'	Husband of the 3rd great-granddaughter		
Yates, Naomi	Wife of the 3rd great-grandson		
Yonkers, Alberta Lynn	Wife of the 4th great-grandson		

Descendants of Claudio Wilson

Generation No. 1 (See Addendum on p. 283 for added information)

1. CLAUDIO[1] WILSON was born May 22, 1787 in Paisley, Renfrewshire, Scotland, and died November 25, 1870 in Whiteside co., Clydetwp, IL. He married (1) PEGGY DOWNIE May 23, 1807 in Castlehead Church, Paisley co., Scotland. She was born in Paisley, Renfrewshire, Scotland. He married (2) MARGARET REDFIELD August 03, 1867 in Whiteside Co., IL.

Notes for CLAUDIO WILSON:
Marriage date from 'Old Parish register of Paisley "Claud Wilson and Margaret Downie both in this parish married by Rev. McDairmid 23rd May 1807" [573;1/2 FR460] Reported by Ian Chad 3 Aug 2002, email <imchad@freeola.com>

1860 Whiteside Co., Clyde twp., IL census 485/474 of Wilson, Wm. Wilson, 45 M Farmer $2500/$600 Scotland, Sarah 36 F KY, John 17 M Farm laborer, IL, Mary E. 15 F IL, Claudio 11 M IL, Margaret D. 10 F IL, Bilderback, Nancy 13 F IL, Taylor, John A. 4 M IL, Wilson, Claudio 73 M Scotland, Marg. D. 77 F Scotland. [I don't know who the Bilderback, Taylor children are.]

1860 WsidecoClytwpIL cen474 with son William, 73 Scot., wife Marg. D. 73 Scot.

1870 Whiteside co., Clyde twp., IL census 83/83, p. 160: Wilson, Claudio 83 M Farmer Scot., xx, Margaret 58 F Scot xx

Whiteside co., IL marriage record #1866.0: Claudio Wilson to Margaret Goudielock.

Obituary, Whiteside Sentinel, Dec. 1, 1870: emigrated to Lowell, MA in 1823. Employed there by carpet corporations for 'a number of years, a number of years in Mexico' came west and settled in Clyde twp. 18 years ago (1852?). He was one of triplets. 'Leaves a widow - his second wife - a son and daughter in MA, and a son in CA. Peace to his ashes.'

Obituary: Gazette (Sweiger); Wilson, Claudio, 84 years, d. 25 Nov. 1870, Clyde twp. Born Paisley, Scotland, to Lowell, MA, 1823; in Mexico a few years; came to Clyde 18 years ago. One of triplets, leaves widow, 2nd wife, 1 son, 1 daughter, MA, 1 son CA. Edition of 5 Jan. 1867.   Information as above verified by Mrs. Verna Janvrin/Muschal as appearing in the newspapers during Pres. Reagan's visit to Scotland.

1860 WsidecoClytwpIL cen474 with son William, 73 Scot., wife Marg. D. 73 Scot.

He left a will appointing Richard Aldritt executor. He declined the position. The court then appointed James Dinsmore executor.

ASSUMPTION: He is a GREAT GREAT UNCLE OF RONALD REAGAN.

Notes for MARGARET REDFIELD:
WsidcoIL Marriage record #1886.
Burley marriage from courthouse computer record.

Children of CLAUDIO WILSON and PEGGY DOWNIE are:
2.   i. JANET[2] WILSON, b. July 04, 1812.
3.   ii. WILLIAM WILSON, b. August 15, 1814, Scotland; d. California.
       iii. THOMAS WILSON, b. June 15, 1822, Scotland; m. (1) MARY A. ELSEY, March 14, 1844, Whiteside co., IL; m. (2) MARGARET AGNES LAMB, March 14, 1844, Whiteside co., IL; b. 1818, Pennsylvania; d. Abt. 1849, Whiteside co., IL.

Notes for THOMAS WILSON:
Birth date from Still Bible records, 'Births'. No connection established.
The Still Bible also gives the death date of 'Cousin Thomas Wilson/November 17th 1843' following the Still children entries.

Information below probably does not fit this Thomas Wilson.
1850 13th district, Whiteside co., IL census: 1597/1597 or p. 432. Thomas 38, M farmer $1250 Scotland, Margaret 32 F PA, Alexander 12 M IL attended school, Walter 11 M IL atd sch., Agnes 10 F IL atd sch., Hannah 8 F IL atd sch., John 6 M IL atd sch., Thomas R. 2 M IL. This Thomas is 10 years older than the Still Thomas, one of whom is born June 15, 1822, the other born Nov. 22, 1839.
1860 Garden Plain twp., Whiteside co., IL 77/77 or p. 310: Wilson, Thomas 59 M Farmer Scotland, md. in year, citizen, Mary J. 48 F OH, Walter 31 M farm laborer, IL, Thomas R. 21 M student IL,, Ellen 18 F teacher IL, Mary 15 F domestic IL, Ann 13 F IL, Albert 10 M IL
Whiteside co., IL marriage record: #110 March 14, 1844, Margaret Agnes Lamb
Whiteside co., IL marriage record: #1454 January 25, 1866 Mary A. Elsey

Notes for MARY A. ELSEY:
Whiteside co., IL marriage record # 1454.

Notes for MARGARET AGNES LAMB:
Whitside co., IL marriage record #110

Generation No. 2

2. JANET² WILSON *(CLAUDIO¹)* was born July 04, 1812. She married JOHN WRIGHT December 05, 1831.

Children of JANET WILSON and JOHN WRIGHT are:
    i. AUGUST³ WRIGHT, b. 1835.

    Notes for AUGUST WRIGHT:
    Dates for these 5 children are derived from the 1850 Lowell Twp., Middlesex Co., MA census.

    ii. JANETTE WRIGHT, b. 1837.
    iii. JOHN WRIGT, b. 1842.
    iv. THOMAS WRIGHT, b. 1846.
    v. CLAUDIO WRIGHT, b. 1848.

3. WILLIAM² WILSON *(CLAUDIO¹)* was born August 15, 1814 in Scotland, and died in California. He married (1) MARY ANN WRESSELL October 18, 1837 in Prob. Whiteside Co., IL, daughter of SAMUEL WRESSELL and MARY S.. She was born January 29, 1821 in Canada, and died February 27, 1859 in Whiteside Co., Clyde Twp., IL. He married (2) SARAH E TAYLOR February 18, 1860 in WSide co., IL. She was born 1824 in KY.

Notes for WILLIAM WILSON:
Per Bent-Wilson, p. 145: Born in Scotland, to Canada, involved in 'Patriot War', was taken prisoner. Settled in Clyde twp, Whiteside co., in 1839. Married in Canada, wife died 'some time back'. To California.
This listing is just above that of John Wilson, b. 1812. Am assuming they are the brothers listed in the Claudio Wilson obituary.
1840 census WsidecoIL Clyde twp. arrived 1839, 2 people, 1 militia
1850 Wsideco37thdistIL cen488/488, Willson. Robert Wallace, 45 Scotland, is listed with them

1860 WsidecoClytwpIL cen485/474 Farmer, $2500/$600, Scotland, with new wife Sarah. Children: John 17, IL, Mary E. 15 IL, Claudio, 11 IL, Margaret D, 10 IL were with first wife. Also listed in 1860 with them is Bilderback, Nancy 13 IL and John A. Taylor., 4 IL perhaps siblings of Sarah, also William's parent, Claudio, 73 M Sc and his second wife Marg. D. 77 F Sc.
The Wilson, Blue, Wesley, Gerdes & Elsey families were all close neighbors.

Notes for MARY ANN WRESSELL:
Marriage date from 'Still Bible'. The Bible also gives the death of Mary Ann Wilson Feb. 27, 1859 at 7 oclock evening. Aged 38 years & 29 days. [This is an exact fit.]
The Wressel lived nearby in Clyde twp., Whiteside co., IL. see Bent 'History of Whiteside co., IL' p. 145. Samuel Wressel was a native of Lincolnshire, England. He first settled in Canada. Located in Clyde, S. 14, in 1838, later bought from Z. Dent. Wressel died at 80, his wife several years before him.

Notes for SARAH E. TAYLOR:
1860 WsidecoClytwpIL cen474 36 KY

Children of WILLIAM WILSON and MARY WRESSELL are:
    i. JOHN^3 WILSON, b. March 03, 1843, IL.

    Notes for JOHN WILSON:
    1850 Wsideco37thdistIL cen488/488, 7 IL. Birth date from 'Still Bible'. The Bible also gives the death of 'John Wilson, Jan. 17th 1863' immediately following the death of Mary Ann [Wressell] Wilson.

4.   ii. MARY E WILSON, b. October 03, 1844, Fulton, Whiteside co., IL; d. May 23, 1881, Whiteside co., IL.
    iii. CLAUDIO WILSON, b. March 06, 1849, IL; m. MARGARET GOUDIELOCK, August 03, 1867, WSide co., IL.

    Notes for CLAUDIO WILSON:
    Birth date from "Still Bible". Census, in this case, more probably correct. Should be 1850. Listed in Bible as Glaud Wilson, March 6th, 1849.
    1850 Wsideco37thdistIL cen488. Listed as Cloud. Age listed as 1month.
    1860 WsidecoClytwpIL cen474 as Claudio 10 IL
    The family moved to California per Grandfather's obituary

    Notes for MARGARET GOUDIELOCK:
    WsidecoIL marriage records

Generation No. 3

4. MARY E.^{3} WILSON *(WILLIAM^2, CLAUDIO^1)* was born October 03, 1844 in Fulton, Whiteside co., IL, and died May 23, 1881 in Whiteside co., IL. She married ISAAC CLARK STILL July 04, 1861 in Fulton, Whiteside co., IL. He was born October 04, 1836 in Dayton, Montgomery Co., OH, and died November 19, 1940 in Whiteside co.,., IL.

Notes for MARY E. WILSON:
1850 Wsideco37thdistIL cen488, 6 IL
Wside co., IL marriage records, Mary E. in record. #614 July 4, 1861 Mary Wilson to Isaac Still.
Birth date from 'Still Bible'. Also death date, and from printout of Leland Still.

Notes for ISAAC CLARK STILL:
Isaac Still on Whiteside Co., IL marriage record #614, July 4, 1861. Birth dates, of this pair, from 'Still Bible records'. This certainly helps give validity to the Still Bible dates.
Still information is Isaac died November 19, 1909, born July 28, 1835(6?).

Children of MARY WILSON and ISAAC STILL are:
    i. JOHN^4 STILL, b. March 21, 1862, Whiteside co, Clyde twp., IL; d. February 09, 1863, Whiteside co, Clyde

twp., IL.

Notes for JOHN STILL:
The Still Bible gives 'John Still February 9th 1863' following John Wilson death entry. Also on another page John, Katy, Mary, Willie death dates are given again.

  ii. HATY A. STILL, b. May 08, 1864, Whiteside co, Clyde twp., IL; d. April 27, 1865, Whiteside co, Clyde twp., IL.

Notes for HATY A. STILL:
The Still Bible gives the death of 'Katy Still April 1, 1863' following the death entry of John Still.

  iii. WILLIAM H. STILL, b. June 29, 1867, Whiteside co, Clyde twp., IL; d. May 23, 1887, Whiteside co, Clyde twp., IL.

Notes for WILLIAM H. STILL:
The Still Bible gives the death date 'William H. Still/May 23, 1887' following the entry for Mary Still.

5. iv. ALEXANDER STILL, b. December 18, 1869, Whiteside co., IL; d. August 01, 1940, Clinton, Clinton Co., IA.
  v. EVA MAY STILL, b. April 05, 1873.
  vi. FREDRIC STILL, b. January 31, 1876.
  vii. MARY STILL, b. October 09, 1880, Whiteside co, Clyde twp., IL; d. August 15, 1881, Whiteside co, Clyde twp., IL.

Notes for MARY STILL:
The Still Bible gives the death date of Mary 'Mary Still Aug. 15, 1881' following the entry for Katy Still.

Generation No. 4

5. ALEXANDER[4] STILL *(MARY E.[3] WILSON, WILLIAM[2], CLAUDIO[1])* was born December 18, 1869 in Whiteside co., IL, and died August 01, 1940 in Clinton, Clinton Co., IA. He married MARGARET FELDT July 16, 1888 in Lyons, Clinton co., IA. She was born December 27, 1870 in Fulton, Whiteside Co., IL, and died March 14, 1943 in Clinton, Clinton Co., IA.

Notes for ALEXANDER STILL:
1920 Whteside co., Morrison, IL census p. 178, ED165, Image217 West Wall St.: Alexander Still Hd. R M W 50 M yes yes IL MO IL Laborer Refrigerator Factory, Margaret F. wife F W 49 MD IL HOL[dutch] HOL, Harry W. son 15 S IL IL IL Lab Refrig, Leland son M W 12 IL IL IL , Helen E. dau 8 S IL IL IL, Stanley, Joe son in law M W 25 M KY KY KY, Marie D. dau F W 22 M IL IL IL, Ruth D. gdau F W 2 S IL KY IL, Russell gson M W 10/12 S IL KY IL.

The Illinois Refrigerator Company was a locally owned business which operated for many years on West Wall St. in Morrison.

Children of ALEXANDER STILL and MARGARET FELDT are:
  i. MARY NAUTE[5] STILL, b. April 07, 1889.
  ii. ARTHUR STILL, b. January 1891.
  iii. JOSEPH C. STILL, b. May 06, 1893.
  iv. GEORGE STILL, b. July 29, 1895.
  v. MARIE DOROTHY STILL, b. March 13, 1898.
  vi. HARRY W. STILL, b. March 16, 1906.
6. vii. LELAND STILL, b. May 25, 1907, Fulton, Whiteside Co., IL; d. December 05, 1981, Galesburg, IL.
  viii. HELEN STILL, b. February 08, 1911.

Generation No. 5

6. LELAND[5] STILL *(ALEXANDER[4], MARY E.[3] WILSON, WILLIAM[2], CLAUDIO[1])* was born May 25, 1907 in Fulton, Whiteside Co., IL, and died December 05, 1981 in Galesburg, IL. He married ETHEL

CARRIE ROGERS March 03, 1926, daughter of CHARLES ROGERS and MARY EVERHART. She was born in Davenport Co., IA.

Notes for LELAND STILL:
1930 Carroll co., York twp., IL, Dist. 28, p.15, census 179/179: Still, Leland hd. 24 IL IL IL farmer, general farmer, citizen, veteran WW; Ethel wife 23 Iowa IO IO; Carol dau. 3 S Iowa IL IO; Roger son 2 S IO IL IO; Lauren ? S IO IL IO.

Children of LELAND STILL and ETHEL ROGERS are:
    i. CAROL[6] STILL, b. December 05, 1926.
    ii. ROGER LELAND STILL, b. January 31, 1928, Clinton, Clinton Co., IA; d. November 15, 1981, Galesburg, IL; m. (1) MARY JOE BLAIR, December 20, 1947, Yuma, AZ; m. (2) DELORIES ANN ROAN, November 05, 1966, Las Vegas, Clark Co., NV.
    iii. LAUREN STILL, b. January 07, 1930; m. LUCILLE ALLEN, June 26, 1949; b. November 03, 1931.
    iv. JOAN STILL, b. June 25, 1933.
    v. MARY STILL, b. November 13, 1934.

Kinship of Claudio Wilson

Name	Relationship with Claudio Wilson	Civil	Canon
Allen, Lucille	Wife of the 3rd great-grandson		
August Wright	Grandson	II	2
Blair, Mary Joe	Wife of the 3rd great-grandson		
Downie, Peggy	Wife		
Elsey, Mary A.	Daughter-in-law		
Feldt, Margaret	Wife of the great-grandson		
Goudielock, Margaret	Wife of the grandson		
Hattie	Great-granddaughter	III	3
III	Grandson	II	2
Lamb, Margaret Agnes	Daughter-in-law		
Redfield, Margaret	Wife		
Roan, Delories Ann	Wife of the 3rd great-grandson		
Rogers, Ethel Carrie	Wife of the 2nd great-grandson		
Still, Alexander	Great-grandson	III	3
Still, Arthur	2nd great-granddaughter	IV	4
Still, Carol	3rd great-granddaughter	V	5
Still, Eva May	Great-granddaughter	III	3
Still, Fredric	Great-grandson	III	3
Still, George	2nd great-grandson	IV	4
Still, Harry W.	2nd great-grandson	IV	4
Still, Haty A.	Great-granddaughter	III	3
Still, Helen	2nd great-granddaughter	IV	4
Still, Isaac Clark	Husband of the granddaughter		
Still, Joan	3rd great-granddaughter	V	5
Still, John	Great-grandson	III	3
Still, Joseph C.	2nd great-grandson	IV	4
Still, Lauren	3rd great-grandson	V	5
Still, Leland	2nd great-grandson	IV	4
Still, Marie Dorothy	2nd great-granddaughter	IV	4
Still, Mary	Great-granddaughter	III	3
Still, Mary	3rd great-granddaughter	V	5
Still, Mary Naute	2nd great-granddaughter	IV	4
Still, Roger Leland	3rd great-grandson	V	5
Still, William H.	Great-grandson	III	3
Taylor, Sarah E.	Daughter-in-law		
Willie	Great-grandson	III	3
Willson	Son	I	1
Wilson, Claudio	Self		0
Wilson, Claudio	Grandson	II	2
Wilson, Janet	Daughter	I	1
Wilson, John	Grandson	II	2
Wilson, Mary E.	Granddaughter	II	2
Wilson, Thomas	Son	I	1
Wilson, William	Son	I	1
Wressell, Mary Ann	Daughter-in-law		
Wright, Claudio	Grandson	II	2
Wright, Janette	Granddaughter	II	2
Wright, John	Son-in-law		
Wright, Thomas	Grandson	II	2
Wrigt, John	Grandson	II	2

Index of Individuals

Unnamed: 54, 100, 133, 179
— -
Unnamed: 5-8, 10
2 -
George Deter Bechtel: 46, 64, 142, 220
Ackerman -
D. G.: 57, 100, 135, 179
Garret: 57, 135
Aitken -
Mayme: 13, 38, 59, 100, 137, 179, 216, 255
Albrecht -
Cale Richard: 29, 36, 86, 97, 98, 121, 124, 165, 176, 195, 200, 242, 253
Caleb Willaim: 29, 86, 121, 165, 195, 242
Carrie: 37, 98, 124, 176, 200, 253
Charles Robert: 29, 86, 121, 164, 165, 195, 242
Frank: 29, 86, 121, 164, 195, 242
Aldritt -
(name: Emma A. Alldritt): 63, 100, 141, 179
Alex -
(name: Alexander Thomas Wilson): 13, 14, 38, 42, 59, 100, 109, 137, 138, 179, 188, 216, 255, 263
Alldritt -
Emma A. (aka: Aldritt): 63, 100, 141, 179
Thomas: 63, 141
Allen -
Lucille: 269, 270
Allison -
Elizabeth: 131, 179
Ammon -
Yvonne: 34, 35, 38, 96, 100, 122, 125, 174, 179, 198, 201, 251, 255
Anderson -
Alex: 23, 81, 159, 236
Amy Adele: 23, 24, 38, 81, 100, 159, 179, 236, 237, 255
Angie -
Unnamed: 36, 97, 124, 176, 200, 253
Ann -
Unnamed: 11, 38
Anne -
Unnamed: 128
Ardwin -
Deter: 30, 87, 122, 165, 196, 242
Donna Marie: 30, 87, 122, 165, 196, 243
Lisa: 30, 87, 122, 165, 196, 243
Michael Thomas: 30, 87, 122, 165, 196, 243
Thomas Michael: 30, 87, 122, 165, 196, 242, 243
-
August Wright: 266, 270
Baker -
Jessie: 11, 38
John: 11-36, 38
Mary: 11-36, 38, 58, 136, 215
Baldwin -
Orson G.: 6, 10
Barkhart -
Maria: 61, 139, 218
Barrett -
Harvey: 78, 112, 157, 234

Maxine Joy: 78, 79, 100, 112, 114, 157, 179, 234, 255
Bartz -
Patricia: 32, 33, 38, 93, 94, 100, 172, 179, 196, 201, 249, 255
Bauer -
Amanda Gail: 34, 38, 95, 100, 174, 179, 198, 201, 251, 255
Robert James: 34, 38, 95, 100, 174, 179, 198, 201, 251, 255
Bayles -
Rhonda Kay: 88, 100, 113, 114, 166, 179, 244, 255
Beach -
Frank: 12, 38
Bechtel -
Albert: 46, 51, 64, 100, 142, 179, 220, 255
Benjamin R: 45, 46, 48-51, 57, 136, 214
Bonnie: 49, 51, 80, 100, 159, 179, 236, 255
Carol: 49, 51, 80, 81, 100, 159, 179, 236, 255
E. M.: 54, 100, 133, 179
Ellen: 49, 51, 80, 100, 159, 179, 236, 255
Ellen W. (aka: Ella): 46-49, 51, 58, 64, 71, 100, 102, 115, 118, 136, 142, 143, 149, 150, 179, 181, 215, 220, 227, 255, 256
Ephraim Myers: 45, 46, 48-51, 57, 58, 100, 115, 136, 179, 214, 215, 255
Everett: 48, 49, 51, 71, 80, 100, 149, 158, 179, 227, 236, 255
Gary: 49, 51, 80, 100, 159, 179, 236, 255
Glenda: 49, 51, 80, 100, 159, 179, 236, 255
Glenn: 48, 49, 51, 71, 80, 100, 149, 159, 179, 227, 236, 255
Helena: 46, 51, 58, 100, 136, 179, 215, 255
Ivy May (aka: Iva May): 46, 48, 51, 64, 71, 100, 105, 142, 149, 179, 184, 220, 227, 255, 259
John Wilson: 45, 46, 48-51, 58, 63, 64, 70, 71, 80, 91, 100, 136, 142, 149, 158, 159, 169, 179, 215, 219, 220, 226, 227, 236, 246, 247, 255
Lucille Fern: 48-51, 71, 80, 91, 100, 149, 159, 169, 179, 227, 236, 246, 247, 255
Rebecca Jane: 45, 51, 58, 100, 136, 179, 215, 255
Scott: 49, 51, 80, 100, 159, 179, 236, 255
William Deter: 46, 48-51, 64, 70, 71, 80, 91, 100, 142, 149, 158, 159, 169, 179, 220, 226, 227, 236, 246, 247, 255
Belle -
(name: Isabelle Mary Liggett): 59, 60, 100, 105, 138, 179, 184, 216, 217, 255, 259
Benjamin -
Helen May: 54, 100, 132, 133, 179
Bennet -
Amanda: 36, 38, 97, 100, 124, 125, 176, 179, 200, 201, 253, 255
Jennifer Ann: 36, 38, 97, 100, 124, 125, 176, 179, 200, 201, 253, 255
Mark: 36, 38, 97, 100, 124, 125, 176, 179, 199-201, 253, 255
Bessie -
(name: Elizabeth Mary Wilson): 14, 17, 23, 38, 43, 66, 71, 72, 81, 100, 109, 144, 150, 159, 179, 188, 222, 227, 228, 236, 255, 263

Beswick -
   Mary: 56, 100, 134, 179
Bielema -
   Nancy Joan: 28, 85, 120, 163, 164, 194, 241
Bildstein -
   Dee Ann: 32, 38, 93, 100, 171, 179, 210, 211, 248, 255
Birt -
   Ella (aka: Helen Nellie): 54, 100, 106, 132, 179, 185
Blair -
   Mary Joe: 269, 270
Blue -
   Alexander: 54, 56, 62, 63, 100, 132, 134, 141, 179
   Catharine (aka: Katherine): 54, 57, 100, 104, 133, 135, 179, 183
   Charles: 54, 100, 133, 179
   Elizabeth: 56, 100, 134, 179
   George: 56, 100, 134, 179
   Girl: 63, 100, 142, 179
Blue, I -
   John: 54, 100, 132, 179
Blue -
   Isabell: 54, 56, 100, 133, 135, 179
   Jane: 13, 45, 54, 55, 57-73, 75-100, 132-136, 138-140, 142, 144-177, 179, 213, 214, 255
   John A.: 56, 62, 100, 134, 141, 179
   John , 2: 54, 100, 133, 180
   Johnnie: 53, 54, 56-73, 75-99, 101, 131
Blue, Jr. -
   Donald Daniel (aka: Daniel): 54, 101, 132, 180
Blue -
   Margaret: 54, 101, 132, 180
   Mary Elizabeth (aka: Ella): 63, 101, 102, 141, 180, 181
   Richard Beswick: 56, 63, 101, 134, 141, 180
   Samuel A: 63, 101, 142, 180
Blue, Sr -
   Donald Daniel (aka: Daniel): 53, 54, 56-73, 75-99, 101, 131, 132, 180, 213
Blue -
   Wilford T.: 63, 101, 141, 180
Body -
   Addie F. Boda/Ada F (name: Addie Frances Body): 69, 111, 114, 147, 225
   Addie Frances (aka: Addie F. Boda/Ada F Body): 69, 111, 114, 147, 225
   Isaac: 111
Bonzlet -
   Elizabeth: 14, 65, 144, 221
Booth -
   'Male': 14, 38
Brett -
   Alexander: 56, 101, 135, 180
   Charles: 56, 101, 135, 180
   Donald: 56, 101, 135, 180
   George: 56, 101, 135, 180
   John: 56, 101, 135, 180
   John W.: 57, 101, 135, 180
   Kate: 56, 101, 135, 180
   Thomas C.: 57, 101, 135, 180
Brickley -
   Dorothy: 26, 38, 83, 101, 161, 180, 208, 211, 239, 255
Bridget -
   Unnamed: 6, 10
Bristle -
   Etta May (aka: Mary): 69, 101, 105, 111-114, 147, 180, 184, 225, 255, 259
   George: 111-114
   George Earl: 111, 114
   John J.: 69, 111-114, 147, 225
Brooks -
   Pauline Catherine: 16, 38, 67, 68, 101, 146, 180, 224, 255
Brown -
   Carolyn: 35, 38, 96, 101, 123, 125, 174, 180, 198, 201, 252, 255
Buikema -
   Mary: 90, 101, 169, 180, 246, 255
Bull -
   Della Betsy: 22, 76, 154, 206, 232
Burmeister -
   Brian Douglas: 29, 86, 121, 164, 195, 242
   Donald Ray: 29, 86, 121, 164, 195, 242
   Francis: 16, 67, 145, 223
   John Brandon: 29, 86, 121, 164, 195, 242
Bush -
   Douglas: 49, 51, 80, 101, 159, 180, 236, 255
   Virginia Kay: 90, 101, 168, 180, 245, 255
C. -
   Henry (name: Henry Ralph Gerdes): 47, 51, 65, 101, 102, 116, 118, 143, 180, 181, 221, 255, 257
Capone -
   James A: 20, 38, 74, 101, 152, 180, 230, 255
Carolyn -
   Unnamed: 33, 34, 38, 94, 95, 101, 173, 180, 197, 201, 250, 255
Carroll -
   Christine Lea: 90, 101, 168, 180, 245, 255
   David Ivan: 79, 89, 101, 158, 168, 180, 235, 245, 255
   Erick Paul: 90, 101, 168, 180, 245, 255
   Ivan Ralph: 79, 101, 157, 180, 235, 255
   Karla Jean: 90, 101, 168, 180, 245, 255
   Lisa Pamela: 90, 101, 168, 180, 245, 255
   Lynn Andrea: 90, 101, 168, 180, 245, 255
   Matthew Thomas: 90, 101, 168, 180, 245, 255
   Terry Dee: 79, 90, 101, 158, 168, 180, 235, 245, 256
   Troy Andrew: 90, 101, 168, 180, 245, 256
Chapman -
   Edward D: 7, 10
   Marguerite: 7, 10
   William: 7, 10
Chris -
   Unnamed: 36, 97, 98, 124, 176, 200, 253
Christina -
   Unnamed: 33, 38, 98, 99, 101, 177, 180, 200, 201, 250, 256
Cindy -
   Unnamed: 32, 38, 93, 101, 171, 180, 210, 211, 249, 256
Clark -
   Edna: 23, 81, 159, 236
Cohenauer -
   (name: Rebecca Kallenor): 46, 64, 115, 118, 142, 220
Conant -
   Unnamed: 17, 38, 72, 101, 150, 180, 228, 256
Cook -
   Norma Jean: 28, 38, 85, 101, 120, 125, 163, 180, 194,

201, 241, 256
Curtis -
    James J. (name: James Joseph Kunavich, Jr.): 30, 38, 40, 91, 101, 104, 170, 180, 183, 247, 256, 259
Cusick -
    Jennie (aka: Jane): 6, 10, 17, 68, 146, 224
    Patrick: 6
Cutler -
    Francis Louise: 61, 101, 140, 180, 219, 256
Daniel -
    (name: Donald DanielBlue, Sr): 53, 54, 56-73, 75-99, 101, 131, 132, 180, 213
    (name: Donald DanielBlue, Jr.): 54, 101, 132, 180
Date -
    Frances: 127
Davis -
    Dr. Loyal Edward: 128, 129
    Nancy (name: Anne Frances Robbins): 8, 10, 23, 38, 41, 77, 78, 101, 107, 128, 129, 156, 180, 186, 233, 234, 256, 261
Debbie -
    (name: Deborah A. Fletcher): 60, 101, 102, 111, 138, 139, 180, 181, 217, 218, 256
Dee -
    Ede or Dee (name: Edith Luckett): 8, 23, 77, 128, 129, 156, 233
Deter -
    Sarah E.: 46, 51, 63, 64, 101, 142, 180, 219, 220, 256
Deutermann -
    David: 87, 101, 166, 180, 243, 256
    David Whitford: 87, 101, 166, 180, 243, 256
    Julia Ann: 87, 101, 166, 180, 243, 256
Dever -
    Chad Paul: 31, 38, 92, 101, 171, 180, 209, 211, 248, 256
Diane -
    Unnamed: 98, 113, 176, 253
Dickman -
    Coonan: 35, 38, 96, 101, 123, 125, 175, 180, 199, 201, 252, 256
Dillon -
    Jacklyn Ann: 24, 38, 81, 101, 159, 180, 237, 256
    John Charles: 18, 23, 24, 38, 72, 81, 102, 150, 159, 181, 228, 236, 237, 256
    Katherine Annabelle: 18, 38, 72, 102, 150, 181, 228, 256
    Margaret Eliza: 17, 38, 72, 102, 150, 181, 228, 256
    Raymond James: 17, 38, 71, 72, 102, 150, 181, 228, 256
    Raymond James: 17, 18, 38, 72, 102, 150, 181, 228, 256
Dingman -
    Theodore: 24, 38, 81, 102, 159, 181, 237, 256
Dittmar -
    Kathy: 98, 102, 176, 181, 254, 256
Dorotha -
    Unnamed: 111, 114
Dougherty -
    Brian: 88, 102, 166, 181, 243, 256
    Dennie: 88, 102, 166, 181, 243, 256
    Douglas: 88, 102, 166, 181, 243, 256
    'Male': 88, 102, 166, 181, 243, 256
    Patrick: 88, 102, 166, 181, 243, 256
    Timothy: 88, 102, 166, 181, 243, 256
Downie -
    Peggy: 265, 270
Duffy -
    Ben: 14, 38
Dutch -
    (name: Ronald Wilson Reagan): 8, 10, 17, 23, 30, 38, 41, 68, 77, 78, 87, 102, 106, 128, 129, 147, 156, 165, 181, 185, 224, 233, 234, 243, 256, 261
Dyson -
    Cyrena: 111
Eads -
    Chelsea Cheryl: 38, 98, 102, 177, 200, 256
    Joseph James: 38, 98, 102, 177, 200, 256
    Justin: 33, 38, 98, 102, 177, 181, 200, 201, 250, 256
    Zachary Philip: 38, 98, 102, 177, 200, 256
Elizabeth -
    Unnamed: 128
Ella -
    (name: Ellen W. Bechtel): 46-49, 51, 58, 64, 71, 100, 102, 115, 118, 136, 142, 143, 149, 150, 179, 181, 215, 220, 227, 255, 256
    (name: Mary Elizabeth Blue): 63, 101, 102, 141, 180, 181
Eloise -
    Unnamed: 46, 64, 142, 220
Elsey -
    Allen: 14, 38
    Daughter: 14, 38
    Emily: 12, 38
    Frankie: 12
    George: 11, 12, 38
    Gertrude: 12, 38
    Harry: 12, 38
    Henry: 12, 14, 38
    Henry: 11
    Mary A.: 265, 266, 270
    Mary Ann: 7, 12-36, 39, 58, 59, 102, 136, 137, 181, 191, 205, 215, 216, 256
    Nellie: 12, 39
    Peter: 11, 39
    Phila: 14, 39
    Robert: 11, 39, 58, 136, 215
    Sarah: 12, 39
Enright -
    Shirley: 49-51, 91, 102, 169, 181, 246, 256
Ernst -
    George: 15, 67, 145, 192, 223
Ethridge -
    Bradley: 29, 87, 122, 165, 196, 242
    Jeremy M.: 29, 87, 122, 165, 195, 242
    Kenneth Alden: 29, 86, 87, 122, 165, 195, 242
    Kevin Marshall: 29, 87, 122, 165, 195, 242
    Laura Marie: 29, 87, 122, 165, 196, 242
Everhart -
    Mary: 269
Fannie -
    (name: Frances Jane Wilson): 60, 102, 109, 138, 181, 188, 217, 256, 263
Faust -
    Adam Charles: 36, 39, 97, 102, 123, 125, 175, 181, 199, 201, 252, 256
    Ashley: 36, 39, 97, 102, 123, 125, 175, 181, 199, 201, 252, 256
    Randy: 35, 36, 39, 96, 97, 102, 123, 125, 175, 181, 199, 201, 252, 256
Feldt -

Margaret: 268, 270
Ferguson -
  Hunter Michael: 39, 99, 102, 177, 200, 256
  Shane: 34, 39, 99, 102, 177, 181, 200, 201, 251, 256
Fike -
  Ida: 49, 51, 71, 102, 116, 118, 150, 181, 227, 256
Flack -
  Clarence: 70, 102, 149, 181, 226, 256
  Kathryn: 80, 102, 158, 181, 236, 256
  Pamela: 80, 102, 158, 181, 236, 256
  Thomas Oliver: 70, 80, 102, 149, 158, 181, 226, 236, 256
  Timothy Conrad: 70, 80, 102, 149, 158, 181, 226, 236, 256
  William C.: 80, 102, 158, 181, 236, 256
Fletcher -
  Deborah A. (aka: Debbie): 60, 101, 102, 111, 138, 139, 180, 181, 217, 218, 256
  Isaac: 60, 138, 217
Foreman -
  Cameron Ryan: 32, 39, 93, 102, 172, 181, 210, 211, 249, 256
  Mitchell: 32, 39, 93, 102, 172, 181, 210, 211, 249, 257
Forsyth -
  Cunningham: 53, 131, 181
Foster -
  'Male': 88, 102, 113, 114, 167, 181, 244, 257
Francis -
  Linda: 91, 102, 169, 181, 246, 257
Fredrick -
  Lisa: 28, 39, 85, 102, 121, 125, 164, 181, 194, 201, 241, 257
Fulks -
  Sara Jane: 8, 10, 23, 39, 77, 78, 102, 156, 181, 233, 234, 257
Gafka -
  Anna: 30, 87, 122, 165, 196, 242
Gallentine -
  Randy Gale: 20, 39, 74, 102, 153, 181, 230, 257
George -
  Karen: 31, 39, 92, 102, 171, 181, 209, 211, 248, 257
Gerdes -
  David Edmond: 46, 47, 51, 64, 102, 115, 116, 118, 142, 143, 181, 220, 257
  Edmund Wayne: 47, 65, 115, 116, 143, 221
  Ephraim Lawrence: 47, 48, 51, 64, 71, 102, 115, 116, 118, 143, 149, 181, 220, 227, 257
  Galen Glenn: 47, 49, 51, 65, 71, 102, 116-118, 143, 150, 181, 221, 227, 257
  Henry E.: 46, 64, 115, 116, 118, 142, 220
  Henry Ralph (aka: Henry C.): 47, 51, 65, 101, 102, 116, 118, 143, 180, 181, 221, 255, 257
  Lloyd: 47, 51, 65, 102, 116, 118, 143, 181, 221, 257
  Rebecca H: 47, 64, 115, 143, 220, 221
  Robert: 49, 51, 71, 102, 117, 118, 150, 181, 227, 257
  Ruth: 49, 51, 71, 102, 117, 118, 150, 181, 227, 257
  Virgil E.: 47, 48, 51, 65, 102, 116, 118, 143, 144, 181, 221, 257
  Wayne: 48, 51, 71, 102, 116, 118, 149, 150, 181, 227, 257
Gibson -
  Michael Grant: 20, 75, 153, 231
  Shirley: 24, 39, 81, 103, 160, 181, 237, 257

Glasgow -
  Ameilia: 55, 133, 213, 257
Glispie -
  John Wesley: 90, 103, 168, 181, 246, 257
  Paul: 90, 103, 168, 181, 245, 246, 257
Goff -
  Hulda Philena (aka: Hulda): 22, 39, 76, 103, 104, 154, 155, 182, 183, 206, 211, 232, 257, 258
  Lyman: 22, 76, 154, 206, 232
Goldsmith -
  Robin N.: 79, 103, 158, 182, 235, 257
Gorzney -
  Donald: 87, 103, 166, 182, 243, 257
  Glen: 88, 103, 166, 182, 243, 257
  James: 88, 103, 166, 182, 243, 257
  John: 88, 103, 166, 182, 243, 257
  Susan Jane: 88, 103, 166, 182, 243, 257
Goudielock -
  Margaret: 267, 270
Greeley -
  Allen: 35, 39, 96, 103, 123, 125, 174, 175, 182, 198, 199, 201, 252, 257
  Allen Ray: 35, 39, 96, 103, 123, 125, 174, 182, 198, 201, 252, 257
  Marla Jane: 35, 39, 96, 103, 123, 125, 175, 182, 199, 201, 252, 257
  Mellissa Jean: 35, 39, 96, 103, 123, 125, 175, 182, 199, 201, 252, 257
  William Norman: 35, 39, 96, 103, 123, 125, 175, 182, 199, 201, 252, 257
Green -
  Rhea: 49, 51, 80, 103, 159, 182, 236, 257
Gsell -
  Blythe Ann: 89, 103, 167, 182, 244, 257
  Brian David: 89, 103, 167, 182, 244, 257
  Clair Le Roy: 69, 79, 88, 89, 103, 148, 157, 167, 182, 225, 235, 244, 257
  Clifford Leroy: 61, 69, 79, 88, 89, 103, 139, 147, 148, 157, 167, 182, 218, 225, 235, 244, 257
  David B.: 61, 103, 139, 182, 218, 257
  Dawn Elizabeth: 89, 103, 167, 182, 244, 257
  Earl Wilson: 61, 62, 103, 140, 182, 219, 257
  Estella Jane (aka: Stella): 61, 70, 79, 90, 103, 108, 139, 148, 158, 169, 182, 187, 218, 226, 235, 246, 257, 262
  Howard Wilson: 69, 103, 148, 182, 225, 257
  Maude Mae: 61, 69, 70, 79, 89, 90, 98, 103, 139, 148, 157, 158, 167, 168, 176, 177, 182, 218, 225, 226, 235, 245, 246, 254, 257
  Richard Lee: 79, 103, 157, 182, 235, 257
  Steven Allen: 79, 88, 89, 103, 157, 167, 182, 235, 244, 257
  Sue Ellen: 79, 89, 103, 157, 167, 182, 235, 244, 245, 257
  William: 61, 139, 218
  William B.: 61, 103, 139, 140, 182, 218, 219, 257
Habben -
  Abbey: 36, 97, 123, 175, 199, 252
  Beverly Joan: 23, 29, 77, 86, 87, 119, 122, 156, 165, 193, 195, 233, 242
  Carol Ann: 23, 29, 36, 77, 86, 97, 119, 121, 124, 156, 164, 165, 176, 193, 195, 200, 233, 242, 253
  Catherine Jean: 28, 36, 39, 85, 97, 103, 121, 124, 125, 164, 176, 182, 194, 199-201, 241, 253, 257

Daniel Lee: 28, 36, 85, 97, 120, 123, 164, 175, 194, 199, 241, 252
David Allen: 28, 85, 120, 164, 194, 241
Debra Lou: 28, 36, 85, 97, 120, 123, 124, 164, 175, 194, 199, 241, 252, 253
Donald Patrick: 28, 39, 85, 103, 121, 125, 164, 182, 194, 201, 241, 257
Donna Elaine: 23, 30, 77, 87, 119, 122, 156, 165, 193, 196, 233, 242, 243
Eilt: 22, 77, 119-125, 155, 192, 233
Gene LeRoy: 28, 35, 39, 85, 96, 103, 120, 123, 125, 163, 175, 182, 194, 199, 201, 241, 252, 257
Judith May: 23, 29, 77, 86, 119, 121, 156, 164, 193, 195, 233, 242
Logan Daniel: 36, 97, 123, 175, 199, 252
Merna Joy: 23, 27, 34, 35, 39, 77, 84, 85, 95, 96, 103, 119, 120, 122, 125, 156, 163, 174, 182, 193, 194, 198, 201, 233, 240, 251, 252, 257
Milford Gene: 23, 28, 36, 39, 77, 85, 97, 103, 119-121, 124, 125, 156, 164, 176, 182, 193, 194, 199, 201, 233, 241, 253, 257
Norman Walter: 23, 28, 35, 39, 77, 85, 96, 103, 119, 120, 123, 125, 156, 163, 174, 175, 182, 193, 194, 198, 199, 201, 233, 240, 241, 252, 257
Reinhard F. (aka: Reinhardt): 22, 23, 39, 41, 77, 103, 106, 119-125, 155, 182, 185, 192, 193, 201, 202, 233, 258, 261
Rhonda Jane: 28, 35, 39, 85, 96, 103, 120, 123, 125, 163, 174, 175, 182, 194, 198, 199, 201, 241, 252, 258
Robert Allen: 28, 39, 85, 103, 120, 125, 163, 182, 194, 201, 241, 258
Ronald Lee: 23, 28, 36, 77, 85, 97, 119, 120, 123, 156, 163, 164, 175, 193, 194, 199, 233, 241, 252
Ryan: 35, 39, 96, 103, 123, 125, 175, 182, 199, 201, 252, 258
Sara Leanne: 28, 35, 36, 39, 85, 96, 97, 103, 120, 123, 125, 163, 175, 182, 194, 199, 201, 241, 252, 258
Travis: 35, 39, 96, 103, 123, 125, 175, 182, 199, 201, 252, 258
Velma Jane: 23, 28, 36, 77, 85, 86, 97, 119, 121, 124, 156, 164, 176, 193-195, 200, 233, 241, 253

Hacker -
  Beth: 36, 97, 123, 175, 199, 252
Hammer -
  Edna Julia: 69, 103, 147, 148, 182, 225, 258
Hattie -
  (name: Haty A. Still): 268, 270
Heacock -
  (name: Lavina T. Heacox): 63, 141
  Maria S. (aka: Mona): 12, 39, 40
Heacox -
  Lavina T. (aka: Heacock): 63, 141
Heath -
  Walter G.: 34, 39, 95, 103, 173, 182, 197, 201, 250, 258
Helms -
  Mayme: 13, 39, 59, 103, 137, 182, 216, 258
Herrold -
  Edith: 70, 103, 149, 182, 226, 258
  Lloyd: 70, 103, 148, 149, 182, 226, 258
  Lloyd Wilson (aka: Jr.): 70, 103, 104, 149, 182, 183, 226, 258
Hicks -
  Earl Clyde: 18, 39, 72, 103, 151, 182, 228, 258
  Harriet: 18, 39, 73, 103, 151, 182, 229, 258
  Harry John: 18, 39, 72, 103, 151, 182, 228, 258
  Katherine Jane: 18, 24, 30, 39, 73, 81, 91, 103, 151, 159, 160, 170, 182, 229, 237, 247, 258
Higgins -
  Sarah: 6
High -
  Bessie Luella Jane: 62, 103, 140, 182, 219, 258
  Joseph: 49, 51, 80, 104, 159, 182, 236, 258
  William G.: 62, 104, 140, 182, 219, 258
Hobbs -
  Susan Evaline: 127, 129
Hoffman -
  Ruth: 8, 10, 17, 39, 68, 104, 147, 182, 224, 258
Holly -
  (name: Horace C. Smith): 15, 39, 41, 66, 104, 107, 144, 145, 183, 186, 205-211, 222, 223, 258, 261
Holmrick -
  Marie: 22, 77, 119, 125, 155, 192, 233
Homerding -
  Margie: 20, 21, 39, 75, 104, 153, 183, 231, 258
Howard -
  Iona Mae: 19, 20, 39, 73, 74, 104, 152, 183, 229, 230, 258
Howe -
  Irene: 29, 86, 121, 164, 195, 242
Howell -
  William: 62, 104, 140, 183, 219, 258
Huggett -
  Esther: 15, 66, 144, 191, 201, 222
  Lum H.: 191
Hulbert -
  Heidi Ann: 98, 104, 113, 114, 176, 183, 253, 258
  Stephen: 98, 113, 176, 253
Hulda -
  (name: Hulda Philena Goff): 22, 39, 76, 103, 104, 154, 155, 182, 183, 206, 211, 232, 257, 258
Hummel -
  Georgianne: 88, 104, 113, 114, 167, 183, 244, 258
Hunt -
  Donald Wilson: 16, 39, 67, 68, 104, 146, 183, 224, 258
  Herman: 16, 67, 146, 223
  Louis Herman (aka: Lewis): 16, 39, 40, 67, 104, 105, 146, 183, 184, 223, 258, 259
Hussey -
  Elizabeth: 127, 129
Hutchinson -
  William Charles: 33, 39, 94, 104, 172, 183, 196, 201, 249, 258
III -
  (name: Claudio Wright): 266, 270
J. -
  Katie (name: Catherine Wilson): 56, 61, 104, 109, 134, 139, 140, 183, 188, 214, 218, 219, 258, 263
Jack -
  (name: John Edward Reagan): 7, 8, 10, 17, 39, 41, 68, 104, 106, 146, 147, 183, 185, 224, 258, 261
Jane -
  (name: Jennie Cusick): 6, 10, 17, 68, 146, 224
Janke -
  Herbert: 26, 83, 162, 208, 239
  Janet: 26, 39, 83, 104, 162, 183, 208, 211, 239, 258

Janvrin -
- Aron Kyle: 27, 35, 40, 85, 96, 104, 120, 122, 123, 125, 163, 174, 183, 194, 198, 201, 240, 252, 258
- Brice: 35, 40, 96, 104, 122, 125, 174, 183, 198, 201, 251, 258
- Bruce Clyde: 27, 35, 40, 85, 96, 104, 120, 122, 125, 163, 174, 183, 194, 198, 201, 240, 251, 258
- Bryleigh: 35, 40, 96, 104, 122, 125, 174, 183, 198, 201, 251, 258
- Clyde Elmer: 27, 40, 84, 85, 104, 119, 120, 125, 163, 183, 193, 194, 201, 240, 258
- Eric Paul: 27, 40, 85, 104, 120, 125, 163, 183, 194, 201, 240, 258
- Genevieve: 35, 40, 96, 104, 122, 125, 174, 183, 198, 201, 251, 258
- Hannah Kate: 35, 40, 96, 104, 122, 125, 174, 183, 198, 201, 251, 258
- Kurt Reinhard: 27, 34, 35, 40, 85, 95, 96, 104, 120, 122, 125, 163, 174, 183, 194, 198, 201, 240, 251, 258
- Mabeline: 35, 40, 96, 104, 122, 125, 174, 183, 198, 201, 251, 258
- Rebecca Lindsey: 35, 40, 96, 104, 122, 125, 174, 183, 198, 201, 251, 258
- Tyler: 35, 40, 96, 104, 123, 125, 174, 183, 198, 201, 252, 258

Jean -
- Unnamed: 26, 40, 83, 104, 162, 183, 208, 211, 239, 258

Jellerichs -
- Gail A.: 20, 40, 74, 104, 153, 183, 230, 258

Jennie -
- (name: Sara Jane Wilson): 13, 15, 21, 22, 25-36, 40, 43, 59, 66, 67, 75-77, 82-87, 91-99, 104, 110, 119, 137, 144, 145, 154, 155, 160-165, 170-177, 183, 189, 191, 192, 201, 203, 205, 211, 212, 216, 222, 223, 231-233, 238-242, 247-253, 258, 264

Joe -
- (name: Jhody Jean Medema): 89, 98, 104, 105, 167, 176, 183, 184, 245, 254, 258, 259

Johannsen -
- Edith M.: 18, 73, 151, 229

Johnson -
- Donald LeRoy: 19, 40, 73, 104, 151, 183, 229, 258

Jr. -
- (name: Lloyd Wilson Herrold): 70, 103, 104, 149, 182, 183, 226, 258
- (name: Harry Wilson Smith, Jr): 22, 26, 40, 41, 76, 83, 104, 107, 155, 162, 183, 186, 206, 208, 211, 232, 239, 258, 261

Kallenor -
- Rebecca (aka: Cohenauer): 46, 64, 115, 118, 142, 220

Katherine -
- (name: Catharine Blue): 54, 57, 100, 104, 133, 135, 179, 183

Keith -
- Herbert James: 14, 19, 65, 73, 144, 152, 221, 229
- Thelma Lillian: 14, 19, 40, 65, 73, 74, 104, 144, 152, 183, 221, 229, 230, 258, 259

Kennedy -
- Danny: 27, 40, 84, 104, 162, 183, 193, 202, 240, 259

Kent -
- Ella A.: 62, 104, 141, 183

Kidwell -
- Jacob: 98, 104, 113, 114, 176, 183, 253, 259
- 'Male': 98, 104, 113, 114, 176, 183, 253, 259
- Steven: 98, 104, 113, 114, 176, 183, 253, 259
- Tyler: 98, 104, 113, 114, 176, 183, 253, 259

Kimberlin -
- Corinne: 89, 104, 167, 183, 245, 259
- John: 89, 104, 167, 183, 244, 245, 259

Kleist -
- Emma: 26, 83, 162, 208, 239

Klosterman -
- Nora: 16, 40, 67, 104, 145, 183, 223, 259

Kramer -
- Julia: 14, 19, 65, 73, 144, 152, 221, 229

Krause -
- Christine: 34, 40, 95, 104, 174, 183, 198, 202, 251, 259

Kristin -
- Unnamed: 35, 40, 96, 104, 123, 125, 175, 183, 199, 202, 252, 259

Kunavich -
- Adolph G.: 24, 40, 81, 104, 159, 160, 183, 237, 259
- James Joseph: 24, 30, 40, 81, 91, 104, 160, 170, 183, 237, 247, 259
- James Joseph, Jr. (aka: James J. Curtis): 30, 38, 40, 91, 101, 104, 170, 180, 183, 247, 256, 259
- Ronald George: 24, 40, 81, 104, 160, 183, 237, 259

Lamb -
- Margaret Agnes: 265, 266, 270

Lane -
- Dorothy Ann: 48, 51, 71, 105, 149, 183, 227, 259
- Mildred: 48, 51, 71, 105, 149, 183, 227, 259
- William: 48, 51, 71, 105, 149, 183, 227, 259
- William: 48, 51, 71, 105, 149, 184, 227, 259

Lawton -
- Edna Joy: 78, 112, 157, 234

-
- Layla Marie Bauer: 34, 40, 95, 105, 174, 184, 198, 202, 251, 259

Levin -
- (name: Levi Luckett): 127-129

Lewis -
- (name: Louis Herman Hunt): 16, 39, 40, 67, 104, 105, 146, 183, 184, 223, 258, 259

Liggett -
- Isabelle Mary (aka: Belle): 59, 60, 100, 105, 138, 179, 184, 216, 217, 255, 259

Lizzie -
- (name: Elizabeth Evelyn Wilson): 56, 62, 105, 109, 134, 140, 184, 188, 214, 219, 259, 263

Longanecker -
- Samuel L.: 46, 51, 58, 105, 136, 184, 215, 259

Lott -
- Edna: 28, 86, 121, 164, 194, 241

Luckett -
- Alfred Paxton: 127-129
- Charles Edward: 128, 129
- Edith (aka: Ede or Dee Dee): 8, 23, 77, 128, 129, 156, 233
- Dr. Edward Hobbs: 127-129
- Levi (aka: Levin): 127-129
- Samuel (aka: Sr.): 127-129
- Samuel: 127-129
- William: 127-129

Machie -
- Angela Kay: 34, 40, 95, 105, 173, 184, 197, 202, 251,

Macquay -
   Della: 25, 82, 160, 207, 238
Maggie -
   (name: Margaret Mae Wilson): 56, 61, 69, 70, 79, 88-90, 98, 105, 110, 134, 139, 147, 148, 157, 158, 167-169, 176, 177, 184, 188, 214, 218, 225, 226, 235, 244-246, 254, 259, 264
   (name: Margaret May Wilson): 60, 68, 69, 78, 87, 88, 105, 110, 138, 147, 156, 166, 184, 189, 217, 224, 225, 234, 243, 259, 264
Manning -
   Shirley: 79, 105, 157, 184, 235, 259
Mariseal -
   Margarita: 30, 40, 92, 105, 170, 184, 208, 211, 247, 259
Marr -
   Barbara: 78, 88, 105, 156, 166, 184, 234, 243, 259
   George L.: 78, 105, 156, 184, 234, 259
   George Michael: 78, 105, 156, 184, 234, 259
Martinez -
   Maria: 30, 40, 91, 105, 170, 184, 208, 211, 247, 259
Marx -
   Katherine: 27, 84, 119, 163, 193, 240
Mary -
   Unnamed: 88, 112, 166, 244
   (name: Etta May Bristle): 69, 101, 105, 111-114, 147, 180, 184, 225, 255, 259
Matchie -
   Angela: 34, 40, 95, 99, 105, 173, 177, 184, 198, 200, 202, 251, 259
   Frank: 34, 40, 95, 105, 173, 184, 197, 198, 202, 250, 251, 259
Mathew -
   Janice Lucille: 78, 105, 112, 114, 157, 184, 234, 259
May -
   Denzie (name: Dossie May Meakins): 21, 22, 40, 76, 105, 154, 184, 206, 211, 232, 259
   Iva (name: Ivy May Bechtel): 46, 48, 51, 64, 71, 100, 105, 142, 149, 179, 184, 220, 227, 255, 259
Mayme -
   (name: Mary Margaret Wilson): 14, 18, 24, 30, 40, 43, 66, 72, 81, 91, 105, 110, 144, 151, 159, 170, 184, 189, 222, 228, 237, 247, 259, 264
McFarlain -
   Katharine (name: Catherine McFarlane): 53, 54, 105, 131-136, 138-142, 144-177, 184, 213
McFarlane -
   Catherine (aka: Katharine McFarlain): 53, 54, 105, 131-136, 138-142, 144-177, 184, 213
   John M.: 53, 131, 133-136, 138-142, 144-177, 184
   William: 131, 133-136, 138-142, 144-177, 184
McKay -
   Daniel: 57, 105, 135, 184
   Robert: 57, 105, 135, 184
McKee -
   Carlene: 49, 51, 80, 105, 158, 184, 236, 259
Meakins -
   Dossie May (aka: Denzie May): 21, 22, 40, 76, 105, 154, 184, 206, 211, 232, 259
Medema -
   George: 89, 105, 167, 184, 245, 259
   Jacob: 98, 105, 176, 184, 254, 259
   James Greg: 89, 105, 168, 184, 245, 259
   Janice Lyne: 89, 105, 168, 184, 245, 259
   Jeanie Larie: 89, 105, 167, 184, 245, 259
   Jerry Allen: 89, 105, 168, 184, 245, 259
   Jhody Jean (aka: Joe): 89, 98, 104, 105, 167, 176, 183, 184, 245, 254, 258, 259
   Jon Craig: 89, 105, 168, 184, 245, 259
   Julie Marie: 89, 98, 105, 167, 177, 184, 245, 254, 259
Mehlhaus -
   Diane: 35, 40, 96, 105, 122, 125, 174, 184, 198, 202, 251, 259
Meinsma -
   Jeff: 50, 51, 91, 105, 169, 184, 246, 259
Melvin -
   Emma Mae: 19, 73, 152, 229
Merrill -
   Dustin: 32, 40, 93, 105, 172, 184, 210, 211, 249, 260
   Steve: 32, 40, 93, 105, 172, 184, 210, 211, 249, 260
Middleton -
   Charity: 127, 129
   John: 127
Milnes -
   Bryan Thomas: 90, 105, 169, 184, 246, 260
   Diane Louise: 79, 90, 105, 158, 168, 184, 235, 245, 246, 260
   Frank J.: 48, 70, 149, 226
   Lepha Mae: 70, 79, 89, 98, 105, 148, 157, 167, 168, 176, 177, 184, 226, 235, 245, 254, 260
   Margaret Elizabeth: 70, 79, 89, 90, 105, 148, 157, 168, 184, 226, 235, 245, 260
   Scott T.: 90, 105, 169, 184, 246, 260
   Shaun Mathew: 90, 105, 169, 184, 246, 260
   Thomas Brent: 79, 90, 105, 158, 168, 169, 184, 235, 246, 260
   Tina Elizabeth: 90, 105, 169, 184, 246, 260
   Walter: 70, 79, 90, 105, 148, 158, 168, 184, 226, 235, 245, 246, 260
   Walter Richard: 69, 70, 106, 148, 184, 225, 226, 260
   Wanda Vey: 79, 106, 158, 185, 235, 260
   Winnie: 48, 51, 70, 71, 106, 149, 185, 226, 227, 260

   Mirissa Jane: 40, 99, 106, 177, 200, 260
Mitchell -
   Jane Whitford: 78, 87, 106, 156, 166, 185, 234, 243, 260
   John Wilson: 78, 87, 106, 156, 166, 185, 234, 243, 260
   Martha Ann: 78, 87, 106, 156, 166, 185, 234, 243, 260
   Whitford: 78, 106, 156, 185, 234, 260
   Whitford Kimball: 87, 106, 166, 185, 243, 260
Mona -
   (name: Maria S. Heacock): 12, 39, 40
Moon -
   (name: John Neil Reagan): 8, 10, 17, 40, 41, 68, 106, 147, 185, 224, 260, 261
Moran -
   Christine Elizabeth: 88, 106, 113, 114, 167, 185, 244, 260
   Don Edward: 88, 113, 167, 244
   Kimberly Jane: 88, 98, 106, 113, 114, 167, 176, 185, 244, 253, 260
   Michael: 88, 106, 113, 114, 167, 185, 244, 260
   Stephen Michael: 88, 106, 113, 114, 167, 185, 244, 260
Mulcahy -
   Catherine: 5, 6, 10
   Patrick: 5

Mundt -
   Marie: 15, 67, 145, 192, 223
Murry -
   Ann Hartley: 128, 129
Muschal -
   Nicholas: 27, 84, 119, 163, 193, 240
   Robert Michael: 27, 40, 84, 106, 119, 120, 125, 163, 185, 193, 194, 202, 240, 260
Myers -
   Rebecca: 45, 51, 57, 136, 214
Naftzger -
   Beulah Vey: 79, 106, 158, 185, 235, 260
Nellie -
   Helen (name: Ella Birt): 54, 100, 106, 132, 179, 185
Nelson -
   Dorothy: 62, 106, 141, 185, 219, 260
   Elmer: 18, 73, 151, 229
   Helen Marie: 18, 40, 73, 106, 151, 185, 229, 260
Nice -
   Elwin: 49-51, 80, 91, 106, 159, 169, 185, 236, 246, 260
   Judy: 50, 51, 91, 106, 169, 185, 246, 260
   Linda: 50, 51, 91, 106, 169, 185, 246, 260
   Lyle: 49, 51, 80, 106, 159, 185, 236, 260
   Marjorie: 49-51, 80, 91, 106, 159, 169, 185, 236, 247, 260
   Pam: 50, 51, 91, 106, 169, 185, 246, 260
   William: 50, 52, 91, 106, 169, 185, 246, 260
Nicke -
   Darrel: 49, 52, 80, 106, 159, 185, 236, 260
Norton -
   Grace: 36, 97, 124, 176, 200, 253
   James Richard: 28, 86, 121, 164, 195, 241
   Jeffery Michael: 29, 36, 86, 97, 121, 124, 164, 176, 195, 200, 241, 253
   William: 28, 86, 121, 164, 194, 241
   William Richard, Jr.: 28, 85, 86, 121, 164, 194, 195, 241
Onken -
   Sally Ann: 89, 106, 168, 185, 245, 260
O'Regan -
   (name: Michael Reagan): 5-8, 10
Ostema -
   Cindy: 32, 40, 93, 106, 171, 172, 185, 210, 211, 248, 249, 260
Palmier -
   Doria: 8, 10, 23, 40, 78, 106, 129, 156, 185, 234, 260
Pape -
   Minnie: 48, 70, 149, 226
Patrick -
   JoAnne: 28, 40, 85, 106, 120, 121, 125, 164, 185, 194, 202, 241, 260
Patti -
   (name: Patricia Reagan): 8, 10, 23, 40, 41, 78, 106, 129, 156, 185, 234, 260, 261
Payton -
   Francis: 127
   Letitia: 127, 129
Peisha -
   Eliza J.: 191, 202
Pessman -
   Greg: 49, 52, 80, 106, 159, 185, 236, 260
Petticord -
   Patricia: 50, 52, 91, 106, 169, 185, 246, 260

Pierce -
   Bertha A.: 191, 202
   Clara: 191, 202
   Elsey Mae: 15, 22, 27, 32-34, 40, 67, 76, 77, 84, 93-95, 98, 99, 106, 145, 155, 162, 172-174, 177, 185, 192, 193, 196-198, 200, 202, 223, 232, 233, 240, 249-251, 260
   James H.: 20, 40, 74, 106, 152, 153, 185, 230, 260
   James Henry Oliver: 191, 202
   Jesse G.: 191, 202
   Judith M.: 191, 202
   Myrtle: 191, 202
   Nathan: 191, 202
   Nathaniel: 15, 66, 144, 191-200, 202, 222
   Nellie: 191, 202
   Peter: 191, 202
   Samuel Levi: 191, 202
   Vera Marie: 15, 22, 23, 27-30, 34-36, 40, 67, 77, 84-87, 95-97, 106, 119, 125, 145, 155, 163-165, 174-176, 185, 192-196, 198-200, 202, 223, 233, 240-242, 251-253, 260
   Walter S.: 15, 40, 66, 67, 106, 119, 144, 145, 185, 191-200, 202, 222, 223, 260
   William G.: 191, 202
Pritchard -
   Leonard: 34, 41, 95, 106, 173, 185, 197, 202, 250, 251, 260
   Timothy Allen: 34, 41, 95, 106, 173, 185, 197, 202, 251, 260
Pyron -
   Christine: 32, 41, 93, 106, 171, 185, 210, 211, 248, 249, 260
Rains -
   O. Darlene: 24, 41, 81, 82, 106, 160, 185, 237, 260
Reagan -
   Anna: 7, 10
   Cameron Michael: 9, 10, 30, 41, 87, 106, 166, 185, 243, 260
   Catherine: 6, 10
   John Edward (aka: Jack): 7, 8, 10, 17, 39, 41, 68, 104, 106, 146, 147, 183, 185, 224, 258, 261
   John Michael: 6-8, 10, 17, 68, 146, 224
   John Neil (aka: Moon): 8, 10, 17, 40, 41, 68, 106, 147, 185, 224, 260, 261
   Margaret: 6, 10
   Mary: 6, 7, 10
   Maureen Elizabeth: 8, 10, 23, 41, 78, 106, 156, 185, 234, 261
   Michael (aka: O'Regan): 5-8, 10
   Michael: 8-10, 23, 30, 41, 78, 87, 106, 156, 165, 166, 185, 234, 243, 261
   Patricia (aka: Patti): 8, 10, 23, 40, 41, 78, 106, 129, 156, 185, 234, 260, 261
   Ronald Prescott: 8, 10, 23, 41, 78, 106, 129, 156, 185, 234, 261
   Ronald Wilson (aka: Dutch): 8, 10, 17, 23, 30, 38, 41, 68, 77, 78, 87, 102, 106, 128, 129, 147, 156, 165, 181, 185, 224, 233, 234, 243, 256, 261
   Thomas: 6, 10
   William: 6, 10
   William: 7, 10
Rebecca -
   Unnamed: 34, 41, 95, 106, 173, 185, 197, 202, 250, 261
Redfield -

Margaret: 265, 270
Rees -
  Evelyn: 21, 75, 154, 205, 231
Reinhardt -
  (name: Reinhard F. Habben): 22, 23, 39, 41, 77, 103, 106, 119-125, 155, 182, 185, 192, 193, 201, 202, 233, 258, 261
Reiter -
  Glenda: 24, 41, 81, 82, 106, 160, 185, 237, 261
  Rodney: 24, 81, 160, 237
Rick -
  Beth: 33, 41, 94, 107, 173, 185, 197, 202, 250, 261
  Patricia: 90, 107, 168, 169, 185, 246, 261
Roan -
  Delories Ann: 269, 270
Robbins -
  Anne Frances (aka: Nancy Davis): 8, 10, 23, 38, 41, 77, 78, 101, 107, 128, 129, 156, 180, 186, 233, 234, 256, 261
  George: 128
  Kenneth: 8, 23, 77, 128, 129, 156, 233
Robinson -
  Linda: 33, 41, 94, 107, 173, 186, 197, 202, 250, 261
Roenike -
  Karen: 35, 41, 96, 107, 123, 125, 175, 186, 199, 202, 252, 261
Rogers -
  Charles: 269
  Ethel Carrie: 268-270
Rowe -
  Amanda: 98, 107, 113, 114, 176, 186, 253, 261
  David Keith: 88, 107, 113, 114, 166, 186, 244, 261
  James Keith: 88, 107, 112-114, 166, 186, 244, 261
  Lucas Mathew: 98, 107, 113, 114, 176, 186, 253, 261
  Robert Mathew: 88, 98, 107, 113, 114, 166, 176, 186, 244, 253, 261
  V. K.: 88, 112, 166, 244
Rumney -
  Judith: 191
Rury -
  Donna Ann: 30, 31, 41, 91, 92, 107, 170, 186, 208, 209, 211, 247, 261
Rush -
  Stephen A. (aka: Steven): 13, 41, 42, 59, 107, 108, 137, 186, 187, 216, 261, 262
Ryan -
  Daniel Joseph: 20, 41, 74, 107, 153, 186, 230, 261
S. -
  Mary: 266
Schaub -
  Minnie: 16, 67, 146, 223
Schneider -
  Joseph: 25, 82, 160, 207, 238
  Marian D.: 25, 41, 82, 107, 160, 186, 207, 211, 238, 261
Schryver -
  Dawn: 32, 41, 93, 107, 171, 186, 210, 211, 248, 249, 261
Schumacher -
  Lucas: 98, 107, 177, 186, 254, 261
  Matthew Collin: 98, 107, 177, 186, 254, 261
  Thomas: 98, 107, 177, 186, 254, 261
Sharer -
  Marie: 33, 41, 94, 107, 172, 173, 186, 197, 202, 250, 261
Shrider -
  Mareta: 49, 52, 71, 107, 116-118, 150, 186, 227, 261
Silvis -
  Verlee Ann: 89, 107, 168, 186, 245, 261
Simonds -
  Martha: 15, 66, 144, 205, 211, 222
Smith -
  Barbara: 26, 41, 84, 107, 162, 186, 208, 211, 239, 261
  Charles Alfred: 15, 21, 25, 41, 66, 75, 76, 82, 107, 145, 154, 160, 161, 186, 205-207, 211, 223, 231, 238, 261
  Chelsey: 32, 41, 93, 107, 171, 186, 210, 211, 248, 261
  Christopher Scott: 31, 41, 92, 107, 170, 186, 209, 211, 247, 261
  Cory: 31, 41, 92, 107, 170, 186, 209, 211, 248, 261
  Dale: 26, 41, 83, 84, 107, 162, 186, 208, 211, 239, 261
  David: 26, 31, 32, 41, 83, 93, 107, 162, 171, 186, 208-211, 239, 248, 261
  Dean: 26, 41, 84, 107, 162, 186, 208, 211, 239, 261
  Dennis: 25, 41, 82, 107, 161, 186, 207, 211, 238, 261
  Elizabeth: 60, 138, 217
  Gene Meakin: 22, 26, 31, 32, 41, 76, 83, 93, 107, 154, 161, 162, 171, 172, 186, 206, 208-211, 232, 239, 248, 249, 261
  Gordon M.: 25, 41, 82, 107, 160, 161, 186, 207, 211, 238, 261
  Harry Wilson: 15, 22, 26, 41, 67, 76, 83, 107, 145, 154, 155, 162, 186, 205, 206, 208, 211, 223, 232, 239, 261
  Harry Wilson , Jr (aka: Jr.): 22, 26, 40, 41, 76, 83, 104, 107, 155, 162, 183, 186, 206, 208, 211, 232, 239, 258, 261
  Horace C. (aka: Holly): 15, 39, 41, 66, 104, 107, 144, 145, 183, 186, 205-211, 222, 223, 258, 261
  Horace Vernon: 15, 21, 22, 26, 30-32, 41, 67, 76, 83, 91-93, 107, 145, 154, 161, 170-172, 186, 205, 206, 208-211, 223, 232, 239, 247-249, 261
  Hudson B.: 25, 41, 83, 107, 161, 186, 207, 211, 238, 261
  Jacob: 15, 66, 144, 205-211, 222
  Jamie: 31, 41, 92, 107, 170, 186, 209, 211, 247, 261
  Jenie Alice: 62, 107, 140, 141, 186, 219, 261
  Jenifer Erin: 31, 41, 92, 107, 170, 186, 209, 211, 248, 261
  Karen: 25, 26, 41, 83, 107, 161, 186, 207, 211, 238, 239, 261
  Marshall: 32, 41, 93, 107, 172, 186, 210, 211, 249, 261
  Mathew Lee: 20, 41, 75, 107, 153, 186, 231, 261
  Milford L.: 21, 25, 41, 76, 82, 107, 154, 160, 186, 206, 207, 211, 232, 238, 262
  Nancy: 26, 32, 41, 83, 93, 107, 162, 172, 186, 208, 210, 211, 239, 249, 262
  Penny: 90, 107, 168, 169, 186, 246, 262
  Raymond: 21, 25, 41, 76, 82, 83, 107, 154, 161, 186, 206, 207, 211, 232, 238, 262
  Robert Clare: 22, 26, 30, 31, 41, 76, 83, 91, 92, 107, 154, 161, 170, 171, 186, 206, 208, 209, 211, 232, 239, 247, 248, 262
  Sally: 26, 41, 83, 107, 161, 186, 207, 208, 212, 239, 262
  Taylor: 32, 41, 93, 107, 172, 186, 210, 212, 249, 262
  Terry: 26, 30, 31, 41, 83, 91, 92, 107, 161, 170, 186, 208, 209, 212, 239, 247, 262
  Thomas: 26, 32, 42, 83, 93, 107, 162, 171, 172, 186,

208, 210, 212, 239, 248, 249, 262
  Thomas S.: 32, 42, 93, 107, 171, 186, 210, 212, 249, 262
  Vicki: 26, 31, 42, 83, 92, 108, 161, 171, 186, 208, 209, 212, 239, 248, 262

Smoot -
  Ann: 127, 129

Snyder -
  Brandon: 36, 97, 124, 175, 199, 253
  James Lee: 36, 97, 123, 124, 175, 199, 252, 253
  Timothy: 36, 97, 124, 175, 199, 253

Spencer -
  Clarinda: 14, 42

Sprague -
  Nancy Lee: 26, 42, 83, 108, 162, 186, 208, 212, 239, 262

Springman -
  David Robert: 24, 42, 81, 108, 159, 187, 237, 262

Sr. -
  (name: Samuel Luckett): 127-129

Stapleton -
  Gladys Eloise: 70, 79, 90, 108, 148, 158, 169, 187, 226, 235, 246, 262
  Glen: 70, 108, 148, 187, 226, 262
  William: 70, 108, 148, 187, 226, 262

Starck -
  Catherine (aka: Katie Stark): 14, 42, 65, 66, 108, 144, 187, 221, 222, 262
  Mathew: 14, 65, 144, 221

Stark -
  Katie (name: Catherine Starck): 14, 42, 65, 66, 108, 144, 187, 221, 222, 262

Stearns -
  Colleen: 8-10, 30, 42, 87, 108, 165, 166, 187, 243, 262

Stella -
  (name: Estella Jane Gsell): 61, 70, 79, 90, 103, 108, 139, 148, 158, 169, 182, 187, 218, 226, 235, 246, 257, 262

Steven -
  (name: Stephen A. Rush): 13, 41, 42, 59, 107, 108, 137, 186, 187, 216, 261, 262

Stevens -
  'Male': 20, 42, 74, 108, 153, 187, 230, 262

Still -
  Alexander: 268, 270
  Arthur: 268, 270
  Carol: 269, 270
  Eva May: 268, 270
  Fredric: 268, 270
  George: 268, 270
  Harry W.: 268, 270
  Haty A. (aka: Hattie): 268, 270
  Helen: 268, 270
  Isaac Clark: 267, 270
  Joan: 269, 270
  John: 267, 268, 270
  Joseph C.: 268, 270
  Lauren: 269, 270
  Leland: 268-270
  Marie Dorothy: 268, 270
  Mary: 268, 270
  Mary: 269, 270
  Mary Naute: 268, 270
  Roger Leland: 269, 270
  William H. (aka: Willie): 268, 270

Stuart -
  Ruth Jane: 27, 42, 84, 108, 162, 187, 193, 202, 240, 262

Susannah -
  Unnamed: 11

Swanson -
  Charles: 89, 108, 168, 187, 245, 262

Sweigert -
  Mabel May: 21, 42, 75, 76, 108, 154, 187, 205, 206, 212, 231, 262
  Milton E.: 21, 75, 154, 205, 231

Taylor -
  Sarah E.: 266, 267, 270

Thomas -
  Charles B.: 19, 73, 152, 229
  Iona Jean: 19, 20, 42, 73-75, 108, 152, 153, 187, 229-231, 262

Tiesman -
  Sharon: 32, 33, 42, 93, 94, 108, 172, 187, 196, 202, 249, 262

Traum -
  David: 50, 52, 91, 108, 169, 187, 247, 262
  John: 50, 52, 91, 108, 169, 187, 247, 262
  Robert: 50, 52, 91, 108, 169, 187, 247, 262
  Susan: 50, 52, 91, 108, 169, 187, 247, 262

Trimble -
  Carol: 27, 42, 85, 108, 120, 125, 163, 187, 194, 202, 240, 262

Tucker -
  'Male': 20, 42, 74, 108, 153, 187, 230, 262

Tug -
  (name: George Orville Wilson): 14, 16, 42, 43, 59, 67, 108, 109, 138, 145, 187, 188, 216, 223, 262, 263

Ufken -
  Eugene: 19, 42, 73, 108, 152, 187, 229, 262

Unger -
  Bruce: 31, 42, 92, 108, 171, 187, 209, 212, 248, 262
  Bruce Edwin , Jr.: 31, 42, 92, 108, 171, 187, 209, 212, 248, 262

Van Horn -
  James Jerry: 20, 42, 74, 108, 153, 187, 230, 262

Veihl -
  Darlene E.: 88, 89, 108, 167, 187, 244, 262

Vina -
  (name: Mary LaVina Wilson): 14, 16, 42, 43, 59, 67, 108, 110, 138, 145, 146, 187, 189, 216, 223, 262, 264

Vite -
  Lienne: 88, 113, 167, 244

Vos -
  Arlyn: 79, 90, 108, 158, 169, 187, 235, 246, 262
  Arlyn Dale: 90, 108, 169, 187, 246, 262
  Debra Jane: 90, 108, 169, 187, 246, 262
  Ernest: 79, 108, 158, 187, 235, 262
  Kari Sue: 91, 108, 169, 187, 246, 262
  Kathy Lynn: 90, 108, 169, 187, 246, 262
  Larry: 79, 90, 91, 108, 158, 169, 187, 235, 246, 262
  Lauri Ann: 79, 108, 158, 187, 235, 262
  Marla Ann: 90, 108, 169, 187, 246, 262
  Teri Ann: 91, 108, 169, 187, 246, 262

Walters -
  Baby: 33, 42, 94, 108, 172, 187, 196, 202, 249, 262

Carl B.: 22, 42, 76, 77, 108, 155, 187, 192, 202, 232, 233, 262
David Gene: 33, 42, 94, 108, 173, 187, 197, 202, 250, 262
Dawn Gail: 27, 34, 42, 84, 95, 108, 163, 174, 187, 193, 198, 202, 240, 251, 263
Drew Philip: 42, 99, 108, 177, 200, 263
Harlan Gene: 27, 33, 42, 84, 94, 108, 162, 172, 173, 187, 193, 197, 202, 240, 250, 263
Harold Edward: 22, 27, 32-34, 42, 77, 84, 93-95, 98, 99, 108, 155, 162, 172-174, 177, 187, 192, 193, 196-198, 200, 202, 233, 240, 249-251, 263
Jane Kaye: 27, 34, 42, 84, 95, 99, 108, 162, 173, 177, 187, 193, 197, 198, 200, 202, 240, 250, 251, 263
Julia Anna: 42, 99, 108, 177, 200, 263
Mark Douglas: 33, 42, 94, 108, 173, 187, 197, 202, 250, 263
Matthew: 34, 42, 95, 108, 174, 187, 198, 202, 251, 263
Paul Edward: 27, 32, 33, 42, 84, 93, 94, 98, 108, 162, 172, 177, 187, 193, 196, 200, 202, 240, 249, 263
Philip Dale: 27, 34, 42, 84, 95, 108, 163, 174, 187, 193, 198, 202, 240, 251, 263
Rhonda Ruth: 27, 42, 84, 109, 162, 187, 193, 202, 240, 263
Sandra: 49, 52, 80, 109, 159, 187, 236, 263
Stephanie Anne: 34, 42, 95, 109, 174, 187, 198, 202, 251, 263
Terry Harlan: 33, 42, 94, 109, 173, 187, 197, 202, 250, 263
Tiffany Marie: 34, 42, 95, 109, 174, 188, 198, 202, 251, 263
Tori Cheryl: 33, 42, 94, 98, 109, 172, 177, 188, 196, 200, 202, 250, 263
Troy J.: 33, 42, 94, 98, 99, 109, 172, 177, 188, 196, 200, 203, 250, 263
Wendy Lee: 33, 42, 94, 109, 172, 188, 196, 203, 249, 263

Warner -
Catherine: 80, 109, 158, 188, 235, 263
James: 70, 109, 148, 188, 226, 263
James: 80, 109, 158, 188, 235, 263
Robert Wilson: 70, 80, 109, 148, 158, 188, 226, 235, 263

Watson -
Elizabeth: 57, 135
Mary: 79, 109, 157, 188, 235, 263

Webb -
Jeanne: 26, 42, 83, 109, 161, 188, 208, 212, 239, 263

Wesley -
Charles: 12, 42
Ellen: 12, 42

Weyrauch -
Madeline: 25, 42, 82, 83, 109, 161, 188, 207, 212, 238, 263

Wheeler -
Mary: 127

Whistler -
Florence I.: 69, 78, 88, 109, 147, 156, 166, 188, 225, 234, 243, 263
Glenn Otto: 68, 69, 109, 147, 188, 224, 225, 263
Lois W.: 69, 78, 87, 109, 147, 156, 166, 188, 225, 234, 243, 263

Whitlock -
Benjamin: 128

Sarah Francis: 128, 129

Wiebenga -
Lesley Dawn: 31, 42, 92, 109, 171, 188, 209, 212, 248, 263
Ron: 31, 42, 92, 109, 171, 188, 209, 212, 248, 263

Wiersema -
Patricia: 49, 52, 80, 109, 159, 188, 236, 263

Wilkinson -
Margaret: 62, 109, 141, 188, 219, 263

Willie -
(name: William H. Still): 268, 270

Willson -
(name: John Wilson): 13, 45, 55, 109, 133, 134, 188, 213-229, 231-254, 263, 264
(name: William Wilson): 265-268, 270

Wilson -
Alexander B: 55, 60, 69, 78, 88, 98, 109, 111, 134, 138, 139, 147, 157, 166, 167, 176, 188, 214, 217, 218, 225, 234, 244, 253, 263
Alexander Thomas (aka: Alex): 13, 14, 38, 42, 59, 100, 109, 137, 138, 179, 188, 216, 255, 263
Alice Jane: 62, 70, 80, 109, 141, 148, 158, 188, 219, 226, 235, 263
Andrew: 55, 133, 213-229, 231-254, 263
Catherine (aka: Katie J.): 56, 61, 104, 109, 134, 139, 140, 183, 188, 214, 218, 219, 258, 263
Charles Abram: 62, 109, 141, 188, 219, 263
Rev. Charles Desmond: 56, 62, 70, 80, 109, 134, 140, 141, 148, 149, 158, 188, 214, 219, 226, 235, 236, 263
Charles LeRoy: 14, 42, 66, 109, 144, 188, 222, 263
Claudio: 265-268, 270
Claudio: 267, 270
Deborah Ann: 79, 88, 98, 109, 112-114, 157, 167, 176, 188, 234, 244, 253, 263
Dwight Alvin: 69, 78, 88, 98, 109, 112-114, 147, 157, 166, 167, 176, 188, 225, 234, 244, 253, 263
Earl Charles: 19, 42, 73, 109, 151, 188, 229, 263
Earl Clyde: 14, 18, 42, 66, 73, 109, 144, 151, 188, 222, 229, 263
Elizabeth Evelyn (aka: Lizzie): 56, 62, 105, 109, 134, 140, 184, 188, 214, 219, 259, 263
Elizabeth Mary (aka: Bessie): 14, 17, 23, 38, 43, 66, 71, 72, 81, 100, 109, 144, 150, 159, 179, 188, 222, 227, 228, 236, 255, 263
Emily G.: 13, 43, 59, 109, 137, 188, 216, 263
Frances Jane (aka: Fannie): 60, 102, 109, 138, 181, 188, 217, 256, 263
George John: 62, 109, 141, 188, 219, 263
George Orville (aka: Tug): 14, 16, 42, 43, 59, 67, 108, 109, 138, 145, 187, 188, 216, 223, 262, 263
Gertrude: 16, 67, 145, 223
Glenda Joyce: 20, 75, 153, 231
James Keith: 19, 74, 152, 230
Janet: 265, 266, 270
Janet Mae: 19, 43, 73, 109, 151, 188, 229, 263
Jeanette: 15, 43, 66, 109, 144, 188, 222, 263
Jeannette Lynn: 20, 43, 74, 109, 152, 188, 230, 264
Jody Allen: 20, 43, 75, 109, 153, 188, 231, 264
John (aka: Willson): 13, 45, 55, 109, 133, 134, 188, 213-229, 231-254, 263, 264
John: 267, 270
John: 55, 59, 60, 68, 78, 87, 88, 109, 134, 138, 147, 156, 166, 188, 214, 216, 217, 224, 234, 243, 264

281

John Charles: 13, 14, 17-20, 23, 24, 30, 43, 59, 65, 66, 71-73, 75, 81, 91, 109, 137, 144, 150-153, 159, 160, 170, 188, 216, 221, 222, 227-229, 231, 236, 237, 247, 264
John Charles III: 24, 25, 43, 82, 109, 160, 188, 237, 264
John Charles, Jr: 21, 24, 43, 75, 81, 82, 109, 154, 160, 188, 231, 237, 264
John James: 15, 20, 21, 24, 43, 66, 75, 81, 109, 144, 153, 160, 188, 222, 231, 237, 264
Judith Suzane: 78, 88, 98, 109, 112-114, 157, 166, 176, 188, 234, 244, 253, 264
Kathy Elizabeth: 20, 43, 74, 109, 153, 188, 230, 264
Kimberly Ann: 20, 43, 75, 109, 153, 188, 231, 264
Leo Vernon, Sr.: 14, 19, 20, 43, 66, 73-75, 110, 144, 152, 153, 188, 222, 229-231, 264
Linda Kay: 20, 43, 74, 110, 153, 188, 230, 264
Marc Lee: 20, 43, 75, 110, 153, 188, 231, 264
Margaret Mae (aka: Maggie): 56, 61, 69, 70, 79, 88-90, 98, 105, 110, 134, 139, 147, 148, 157, 158, 167-169, 176, 177, 184, 188, 214, 218, 225, 226, 235, 244-246, 254, 259, 264
Margaret May (aka: Maggie): 60, 68, 69, 78, 87, 88, 105, 110, 138, 147, 156, 166, 184, 189, 217, 224, 225, 234, 243, 259, 264
Marie: 21, 43, 75, 110, 153, 189, 231, 264
Marilyn Joan: 19, 43, 74, 110, 152, 189, 230, 264
Mary E.: 267, 268, 270
Mary LaVina (aka: Vina): 14, 16, 42, 43, 59, 67, 108, 110, 138, 145, 146, 187, 189, 216, 223, 262, 264
Mary Margaret (aka: Mayme): 14, 18, 24, 30, 40, 43, 66, 72, 81, 91, 105, 110, 144, 151, 159, 170, 184, 189, 222, 228, 237, 247, 259, 264
Naomi Jean: 20, 43, 74, 110, 152, 189, 230, 264
Nellie Clyde: 7, 8, 10, 14, 17, 23, 30, 43, 59, 68, 77, 87, 110, 138, 146, 147, 156, 165, 189, 216, 224, 233, 243, 264
Paul Fletcher: 60, 69, 78, 88, 98, 110-112, 114, 139, 147, 157, 166, 167, 176, 189, 218, 225, 234, 244, 253, 264
Paul Mathew: 88, 110, 113, 114, 167, 189, 244, 264
Phoebe Mae: 62, 70, 110, 141, 148, 149, 189, 219, 226, 264
Robert Bristle: 69, 78, 79, 88, 98, 110, 112-114, 147, 157, 167, 176, 189, 225, 234, 244, 253, 264
Robert Thomas: 78, 88, 110, 112-114, 157, 167, 189, 234, 244, 264
Ronald Stanley: 19, 43, 73, 110, 152, 189, 229, 264
Sara: 45, 52, 55, 57, 58, 63, 64, 70, 71, 80, 91, 110, 115, 134-136, 142, 149, 150, 158, 159, 169, 189, 214, 215, 219, 220, 226, 227, 236, 246, 247, 264
Sara Jane (aka: Jennie): 13, 15, 21, 22, 25-36, 40, 43, 59, 66, 67, 75-77, 82-87, 91-99, 104, 110, 119, 137, 144, 145, 154, 155, 160-165, 170-177, 183, 189, 191, 192, 201, 203, 205, 211, 212, 216, 222, 223, 231-233, 238-242, 247-253, 258, 264
Thomas: 265, 266, 270
Thomas: 7, 13, 43, 55, 58, 59, 65-68, 71-73, 75-77, 81-87, 91-99, 110, 134, 136, 137, 144-146, 150-156, 159-165, 170-177, 189, 191, 205, 214-216, 221-224, 227-229, 231-233, 236-243, 247-253, 264
Thomas Robert: 88, 110, 113, 114, 167, 189, 244, 264
Trudy Jean: 20, 43, 74, 110, 153, 189, 230, 264
Vaughn Fae: 19, 43, 73, 110, 152, 189, 229, 264
William (aka: Willson): 265-268, 270
Winifred M.: 62, 70, 80, 110, 141, 149, 158, 189, 219, 226, 236, 264

Witt -
Andrew F.: 79, 110, 157, 189, 235, 264
Donna Jean: 79, 89, 98, 110, 157, 167, 176, 177, 189, 235, 245, 254, 264
Dr. Harlan Andrew: 79, 89, 110, 157, 168, 189, 235, 245, 264
Jeffrey Andrew: 89, 110, 168, 189, 245, 264
Kimberly Lynn: 89, 110, 168, 189, 245, 264
Kristen Les: 89, 110, 168, 189, 245, 264
Major Sandra Mae: 79, 110, 157, 189, 235, 264

Witz -
'Male': 19, 43, 73, 110, 151, 189, 229, 264

Wressell -
Mary Ann: 266, 267, 270
Samuel: 266

Wright -
Claudio (aka: III): 266, 270
Janette: 266, 270
John: 266, 270
Thomas: 266, 270

Wrigt -
John: 266, 270

Yates -
Naomi: 87, 110, 166, 189, 243, 264

Yonkers -
Alberta Lynn: 30, 43, 91, 110, 170, 189, 247, 264

Zelda -
Unnamed: 24, 81, 160, 237

Addendum

Grove Hill Cemetery [Morrison, IL] Section B, Lot 28- 1 stone- west side- Claudio Wilson born in Paisley, Scotland May 22, 1787 died in Clyde, IL Nov 25, 1870. south side- Margaret Downie wife of Claudio Wilson born in Paisley, Scotland Feb 13, 1783 died in Clyde, IL Feb 6, 1867.

Source: This information was provided by Mrs. Dawn Everling to Mrs. Delories Still and then to the author.

www.ingramcontent.com/pod-product-compliance
Lightning Source LLC
Chambersburg PA
CBHW080409300426
44113CB00015B/2446